JOURNAL FOR THE STUDY OF THE NEW TESTAMENT
SUPPLEMENT SERIES

83

Executive Editor
Stanley E. Porter

STUDIES IN SCRIPTURE IN EARLY JUDAISM
AND CHRISTIANITY

1

Series Editors
Craig A. Evans
James A. Sanders

JSOT Press
Sheffield

Paul and the
Scriptures of Israel

edited by
Craig A. Evans
and
James A. Sanders

Journal for the Study of the New Testament
Supplement Series 83

Studies in Scripture in Early Judaism and Christianity 1

Copyright © 1993 Sheffield Academic Press

Published by JSOT Press
JSOT Press is an imprint of
Sheffield Academic Press Ltd
343 Fulwood Road
Sheffield S10 3BP
England

Typeset by Sheffield Academic Press
and
Printed on acid-free paper in Great Britain
by Biddles Limited
Guildford

British Library Cataloguing in Publication Data

Paul and the Scriptures of Israel.—
(JSNT Supplement Series, ISSN 0143-5108;
No. 83)
I. Evans, Craig A. II. Sanders, James A.
III. Series
227

ISBN 1-85075-412-8

CONTENTS

PREFACE

In the first two years of the Society of Biblical Literature program unit Scripture in Early Judaism and Christianity there were several significant papers probing Paul's use of Scripture. The highlight of the 1990 session was a vigorous discussion of Richard B. Hays's *Echoes of Scripture in the Letters of Paul.*[1] This book and the reviews that emerged from the panel's discussion of it have provided the thread that ties the present collection together. These reviews are found in Part One. Part Two is made up of papers which were presented in the 1989, 1990, and 1991 sessions of Scripture in Early Judaism and Christianity. The essay by W.D. Davies is a slightly revised reprint of a chapter contributed to the volume prepared in memory of George B. Caird. The editors are grateful to the Clarendon Press for permission to republish it in this new context.

This is the first book produced by the Scripture in Early Judaism and Christianity section.[2] More will follow. The purpose of these volumes, in keeping with the program unit's stated goal of publishing studies that represent work on the cutting edge, is to present informed and critical scholarship concerned with the function of older Scripture in later Scripture. It is recognized that this is an exciting and promising but complex and problematic field of study. For this reason we believe that these volumes, and more like them, are necessary.

The editors would like to thank the contributors, who have not only made the present volume possible but have made the Scripture in Early Judaism and Christianity section a success; Beverly Roberts Gaventa of Princeton Theological Seminary for assembling and moderating the panel discussion of Hays's book, and David Hill and Stanley Porter of

1. New Haven, CT and London: Yale University Press, 1989.
2. The second is J.H. Charlesworth and C.A. Evans (eds.), *The Pseudepigrapha and Biblical Interpretation* (JSPSup; Sheffield: JSOT Press, forthcoming).

Sheffield Academic Press for their work in the publishing task. Thanks are also due Gerald Bilkes, Thomas R. Hatina, and Ginny Evans for assisting the editors in typing the manuscript.

Fall 1992

Craig A. Evans
Trinity Western University
Langley, British Columbia
Canada

James A. Sanders
School of Theology
Claremont, California
USA

ABBREVIATIONS

AGSU	Arbeiten zur Geschichte des Spätjudentums und Urchristentums
AnBib	Analecta biblica
ANRW	*Aufstieg und Niedergang der römischen Welt*
ANTJ	Arbeiten zum Neuen Testament und Judentum
ASNU	Acta seminarii neotestamentici upsaliensis
BASOR	*Bulletin of the American Schools of Oriental Research*
BFCT	Beiträge zur Förderung christlicher Theologie
BHT	Beiträge zur historischen Theologie
Bib	*Biblica*
BibOr	Biblica et orientalia
BJRL	*Bulletin of the John Rylands University Library of Manchester*
BKAT	Biblischer Kommentar: Altes Testament
BNTC	Black's New Testament Commentaries
BTB	*Biblical Theology Bulletin*
BZAW	Beihefte zur *ZAW*
CBQ	*Catholic Biblical Quarterly*
CBQMS	*Catholic Biblical Quarterly*, Monograph Series
EKKNT	Evangelisch-Katholischer Kommentar zum Neuen Testament
EvQ	*Evangelical Quarterly*
EvT	*Evangelische Theologie*
ExpTim	*Expository Times*
FOTL	The Forms of the Old Testament Literature
FRLANT	Forschungen zur Religion und Literatur des Alten und Neuen Testaments
HeyJ	*Heythrop Journal*
HTR	*Harvard Theological Review*
HUCA	*Hebrew Union College Annual*
ICC	International Critical Commentary
Int	*Interpretation*
ISBE	G.W. Bromiley (ed.), *International Standard Bible Encyclopedia*, rev. edn
JAAR	*Journal of the American Academy of Religion*
JBL	*Journal of Biblical Literature*
JJS	*Journal of Jewish Studies*
JMES	*Journal of Middle Eastern Studies*
JQR	*Jewish Quarterly Review*
JR	*Journal of Religion*
JSHRZ	Jüdische Schriften aus hellenistisch-römischer Zeit

JSJ	*Journal for the Study of Judaism in the Persian, Hellenistic and Roman Period*
JSPSup	*Journal for the Study of the Pseudepigrapha*, Supplement Series
JTS	*Journal of Theological Studies*
KD	*Kerygma und Dogma*
LCL	Loeb Classical Library
NCB	New Century Bible
NICNT	New International Commentary on the New Testament
NovT	*Novum Testamentum*
NovTSup	*Novum Testamentum* Supplements
NRSV	New Revised Standard Version
NTS	*New Testament Studies*
OTG	Old Testament Guides
OTL	Old Testament Library
OTP	J.H. Charlesworth (ed.), *The Old Testament Pseudepigrapha*
OTS	*Oudtestamentische Studiën*
PTMS	Pittsburgh Theological Monograph Series
RB	*Revue biblique*
RevQ	*Revue de Qumran*
SBLDS	SBL Dissertation Series
SBLMS	SBL Monograph Series
SBLSP	SBL Seminar Papers
SBT	Studies in Biblical Theology
SJT	*Scottish Journal of Theology*
SNTSMS	Society of New Testament Studies Monograph Series
SR	*Studies in Religion/Sciences religieuses*
SUNT	Studien zur Umwelt des Neuen Testaments
SVTP	Studia in Veteris Testamenti pseudepigrapha
SWJT	*Southwest Journal of Theology*
TDNT	G. Kittel and G. Friedrich (eds.), *Theological Dictionary of the New Testament*
TGl	*Theologie und Glaube*
TLZ	*Theologischer Literaturzeitung*
TRE	*Theologische Realenzyklopädie*
TS	*Theological Studies*
TWNT	G. Kittel and G. Friedrich (eds.), *Theologisches Wörterbuch zum Neuen Testament*
USQR	*Union Seminary Quarterly Review*
VT	*Vetus Testamentun*
WBC	Word Biblical Commentary
WMANT	Wissenschaftliche Monographien zum Alten und Neuen Testament
WTJ	*Westminster Theological Journal*
WUNT	Wissenschaftliche Untersuchungen zum Neuen Testament
ZAW	*Zeitschrift für die alttestamentliche Wissenschaft*
ZNW	*Zeitschrift für die neutestamentliche Wissenschaft*
ZTK	*Zeitschrift für Theologie und Kirche*

LIST OF CONTRIBUTORS

J. Christiaan Beker,
Princeton Theological Seminary, Princeton, NJ

Linda L. Belleville,
North Park Theological Seminary, Chicago, IL

Stephen G. Brown,
Shasta Bible College, Redding, CA

Nancy L. Calvert,
Wheaton College, Wheaton, IL

W.D. Davies,
Duke University, Durham, NC

Craig A. Evans,
Trinity Western University, Langley, British Columbia, Canada

William Scott Green,
University of Rochester, Rochester, NY

Richard B. Hays,
Duke Divinity School, Durham, NC

James A. Sanders,
School of Theology at Claremont, Claremont, CA

James M. Scott,
Trinity Western University, Langley, British Columbia, Canada

Christopher D. Stanley,
Hastings College, Hastings, NE

Carol K. Stockhausen,
Marquette University, Milwaukee, WI

'IT IS NOT AS THOUGH THE WORD OF GOD HAD FAILED':
AN INTRODUCTION TO PAUL AND THE SCRIPTURES OF ISRAEL

Craig A. Evans

The older Scriptures of the First Testament find expression in the
later Scriptures of both the First and Second Testaments in a variety of
ways. The most obvious expression involves explicit quotations, sometimes with introductory formula (e.g. Hab. 2.4 in Rom. 1.17),
sometimes without (e.g. Ps. 143.2 in Rom. 3.20). In most of these
instances the New Testament writer is trying to show that something
has been 'fulfilled' or that something is in keeping with scriptural
expectation or requirement. At other times New Testament writers
allude to Old Testament passages. These allusions sometimes take the
form of loose paraphrase (e.g. Exod. 34.34 in 2 Cor. 3.16) and other
times consist of the presence of a few key words (e.g. Isa. 45.23 in
Phil. 2.10-11). In some instances it would seem that the very forms
and structures of the Old Testament have influenced the shape of
portions of the New Testament.[1]

1. For introductions to the function of the Old Testament in the New see
C.H. Dodd, *According to the Scriptures* (New York: Charles Scribner's Sons,
1952); J.A. Fitzmyer, 'The Use of Explicit Old Testament Quotations in Qumran
Literature and in the New Testament', *NTS* 7 (1961), pp. 297-333; B. Lindars, *New
Testament Apologetic* (Philadelphia: Westminster Press, 1961); C.K. Barrett, 'The
Interpretation of the Old Testament in the New', in P.R. Ackroyd and C.F. Evans
(eds.), *The Cambridge History of the Bible* (3 vols.; Cambridge: Cambridge
University Press, 1970), I, pp. 377-411; M. Black, 'The Christological Use of the
Old Testament in the New', *NTS* 18 (1971), pp. 1-14; D.M. Smith, 'The Use of the
Old Testament in the New', in J. Efird (ed.), *The Use of the Old Testament in the
New and Other Essays* (Durham, NC: Duke University, 1972); H.M. Shires,
Finding the Old Testament in the New (Philadelphia: Westminster Press, 1974);
R.N. Longenecker, *Biblical Exegesis in the Apostolic Period* (Grand Rapids:
Eerdmans, 1975); B. Lindars, 'The Place of the Old Testament in the Formation of
New Testament Theology', *NTS* 23 (1976), pp. 59-66; E.E. Ellis, 'How the New

Paul himself quoted Scripture some one hundred times and alluded to it many more times.[2] Sometimes his quotations are in verbal agreement with both the LXX and Hebrew, sometimes with one against the other, and sometimes against both.[3] In most of the latter cases the variations are insignificant (e.g. 'God' instead of 'the Lord'). In other cases the differences are much more significant, usually having to do with the interpretation that Paul has given the Old Testament passage. For example, in Rom. 9.25-26 Paul cited two related passages from Hosea (2.23; 1.10) and applied them to the Gentiles. Hosea, however, speaks of an estranged Israel once again restored to her God. Paul's

---

Testament Uses the Old', in I.H. Marshall (ed.), *New Testament Interpretation: Essays on Principles and Methods* (Grand Rapids: Eerdmans, 1977), pp. 199-219; M. Wilcox, 'On Investigating the Use of the Old Testament in the New Testament', in E. Best and R.M. Wilson (eds.), *Text and Interpretation* (Cambridge: Cambridge University Press, 1979), pp. 231-43; S.E. Balentine, 'The Interpretation of the Old Testament in the New Testament', *SWJT* 23 (1981), pp. 41-57; M. Black, 'The Theological Appropriation of the Old Testament by the New Testament', *SJT* 39 (1986), pp. 1-17; J.L. Kugel and R.A. Greer, *Early Biblical Interpretation* (Library of Early Christianity, 3; Philadelphia: Westminster Press, 1986); D.A. Carson and H.G.M. Williamson (eds.), *It is Written: Scripture Citing Scripture* (Cambridge: Cambridge University Press, 1988); C.A. Evans, 'The Function of the Old Testament in the New', in S. McKnight (ed.), *Introducing New Testament Interpretation* (Guides to New Testament Exegesis, 1; Grand Rapids: Baker, 1989), pp. 163-93.

2. See O. Michel, *Paulus und seine Bibel* (BFCT, 2.18; Gütersloh: Bertelsmann, 1929; repr. Darmstadt: Wissenschaftliche Buchgesellschaft, 1972); E.E. Ellis, *Paul's Use of the Old Testament* (Grand Rapids: Eerdmans, 1957); N. Flanagan, 'Messianic Fulfillment in St. Paul', *CBQ* 19 (1957), pp. 474-84; A.T. Hanson, *Studies in Paul's Technique and Theology* (London: SPCK, 1974), pp. 136-278; M.D. Hooker, 'Beyond the Things that are Written? St. Paul's Use of Scripture', *NTS* 27 (1981), pp. 295-309; W.A. Meeks, '"And Rose Up to Play": Midrash and Paraenesis in 1 Cor. 10.1-22', *JSNT* 16 (1982), pp. 64-78; C.A. Evans, 'Paul and the Hermeneutics of "True Prophecy": A Study of Romans 9–11', *Bib* 65 (1984), pp. 560-70; H. Hübner, *Gottes Ich und Israel: Zum Schriftgebrauch des Paulus in Römer 9–11* (FRLANT, 136; Göttingen: Vandenhoeck & Ruprecht, 1984); J.W. Aageson, 'Scripture and Structure in the Development of the Argument in Romans 9–11', *CBQ* 48 (1986), pp. 265-89; J.D.G. Dunn, '"Righteousness from the Law" and "Righteousness from Faith": Paul's Interpretation of Scripture in Romans 10.1-10', in G.F. Hawthorne and O. Betz (eds.), *Tradition and Interpretation in the New Testament* (E.E. Ellis Festschrift; Grand Rapids: Eerdmans, 1987).

3. See Ellis, *Paul's Use of the Old Testament*, pp. 150-52.

point, of course, is that if an estranged people (such as apostate Israel) can become God's people, then so can another estranged people (such as the Gentiles). Many other examples could be offered. In the chapters that follow several will be investigated in detail.

In his day Paul faced a paradox. On the one hand, the Scriptures of Israel have been fulfilled. Israel's long-awaited messiah has come (Gal. 4.4; Rom. 1.1-4). In the death of Messiah Jesus sin has been atoned for (Rom. 3.21-26). In the resurrection of Messiah Jesus death has been overcome (1 Cor. 15.51-57). In the glorious return of Messiah Jesus all Israel will be saved (Rom. 11.25-32) and the kingdom delivered up to God the Father (1 Cor. 15.23-25). This was the good news. Yet there was a problem: relatively few of the apostle's fellow Jews believed this good news (Rom. 9.31-33; 11.1-10; 1 Thess. 2.14-16). How can this disturbing reality be explained?

The paradox is compounded further by the role that Scripture plays. The supreme advantage that the Jewish people have over Gentiles is, according to Paul, their Scripture: 'The Jews are entrusted with the oracles of God' (Rom. 3.2). Yet the Jews apparently do not understand these oracles! For although they have zeal for God, 'it is not according to accurate knowledge' (Rom. 10.2). Herein lies the heart of Paul's dilemma: Israel has an advantage because it has the Scriptures, but it really is no advantage at all because it is unable to interpret them aright. Israel cannot interpret them correctly, and so is unable to recognize in the crucified Christ the Lord of glory. Does this mean that the word of God has failed? This Paul emphatically denies (Rom. 9.6)—something he can do, because he is convinced that the Scriptures foretold Israel's rejection of the gospel and that despite this rejection Israel will nevertheless participate in salvation.[4]

In view of this paradox it is hardly a surprise that the apostle wrestles with the Scriptures of Israel as much as he does. Paul's struggle seems to revolve around two principal themes. Framed as questions they are: (1) where in the Old Testament does the Christian gospel receive support, and (2) what relation does the Christian gospel have to Israel's covenant? Of course, these themes are related. If Paul is able to show that the Christian gospel of faith in the promise of

4. See O. Hofius, '"All Israel Will be Saved": Divine Salvation and Israel's Deliverance in Romans 9–11', in D.L. Migliore (ed.), *The Church and Israel: Romans 9–11* (Princeton Seminary Bulletin, Supplement 1; Princeton, NJ: Princeton Theological Seminary, 1990), pp. 19-39.

God, that through Abraham's single 'seed' (i.e., Christ) Israel and the nations will be blessed, results in the justification of Gentiles, what are the implications for Israel's status as 'most favored nation'? In other words, how does God's covenant with Israel relate to the new covenant in Messiah Jesus? Grappling with this difficult question Paul probes the Scriptures of Israel in quest of answers. Several of the studies contained in this volume are concerned with this problem.

To a great extent the volume revolves around the significant, and in some ways novel, observations and suggestions recently put forward by Richard B. Hays in his book *Echoes of Scripture in the Letters of Paul*.[5] Part One directly discusses and evaluates his approach. It consists of reviews by Craig A. Evans, James A. Sanders, William Scott Green, and J. Christiaan Beker. What is an 'echo' of Scripture? By what criteria can one detect the presence of an echo? How does the observation of putative echoes facilitate interpretation of the Pauline letters (or other writings, for that matter)? Is Paul's hermeneutic ecclesiocentric? Or is it christocentric, or theocentric? It is with these and related questions that the reviews of Part One grapple. Following the reviews Hays offers his response.

Part Two consists of studies concerned with specific passages in which Scripture appears explicitly, as well as allusively. James A. Sanders traces the *Nachleben* of certain parts of Habakkuk, particularly as they find expression in the writings of Qumran and Paul. Sanders hopes not only to shed light on the meaning of particular texts, but to develop a better method of exegesis. Linda L. Belleville and Carol K. Stockhausen tackle the difficult, but crucial, passage in 2 Corinthians 3, a passage which receives special attention in Hays's study.[6] Stockhausen attempts to isolate and describe Paul's exegetical techniques in 2 Corinthians 3. She believes that Paul's exegesis is part of a broader discussion within Judaism concerned with covenant traditions. Belleville seeks to identify the interpretive components linking Paul's exegesis to the story of the giving of the law in Exodus 34. She rightly recognizes that many details in Paul's interpretation do not derive from Exodus, but from later exegetical traditions. James M. Scott surveys some eight different attempts to understand how Deut. 27.26 supports Paul's thesis in Gal. 3.10, that those who are of works of the law are under a curse. Scott then suggests that Paul's elusive assumption in citing this Old Testament

---

5. New Haven and London: Yale University Press, 1989.
6. Hays, *Echoes of Scripture*, pp. 122-53.

text is to be found in a Second Temple tradition which considers Israel under the Deuteronomic curse ever since 587 BCE. Nancy L. Calvert shows how Paul, in interacting with popular views of Abraham as monotheist and anti-idolater, tries to persuade the Galatian Christians that obedience to the law, now that Christ has come, is itself tantamount to idolatry. Craig A. Evans hears an echo of Ps. 47.6 in 1 Thess. 4.16 and ponders the implications for a context in which Paul speaks of the dramatic return of the risen and reigning Christ. He suggests that the apostle has drawn upon the language of Psalm 47 not only to clarify his teaching regarding Christ's second coming, but also to hint at Christ's divine identity. Stephen G. Brown rounds out the collection with an intriguing study of 2 Thessalonians 2 which attempts to unravel the interpretive problems raised by the reference to the 'man of lawlessness' and that which 'restrains' him.

The scholars who have contributed to this collection of studies hope that their work will make a contribution to our understanding of how, on the one hand, the Scriptures of Israel shaped and informed Paul and his churches, and how, on the other, Paul and his churches shaped and informed our understanding of the Scriptures.

CANON AND CHRISTOLOGY IN PAUL

W.D. Davies

Until very recently, when costs increased and computers threatened
their dominance, the abundance and cheapness of paper and writing
materials led to their almost ubiquitous use in our culture. It was a
temptation to contrast this culture with previous more oral ones in
which writing was not so pervasive. However, although the Graeco-
Roman and Jewish worlds of the first century, with which we are concerned, were less 'a papyrus culture' than is ours of the twentieth, this
should not be over-emphasized. Those worlds were 'if not literate,
literary to a remarkable degree; in the Near East in the first century
of our era writing was an essential accompaniment of life at almost all
levels to an extent without parallel in living memory'.[1] The reading of
documents, written on papyrus or skin, was more widespread than is
often acknowledged. Apparently, even in out-of-the-way Nazareth,
Jesus could read, and assumed that his opponents in Galilee also could.[2]

At the same time there was a reserve about the written word among
Greeks and Jews alike. This had long come to clear expression in
Plato, who had urged that the invention of writing was a deceptive
blessing.[3] For Plato's Socrates, so far from helping the memory,
writing militates against it: it is no adequate substitute for living
dialogue between teacher and pupil. It is as if writing confines or even

---

1. C.H. Roberts, 'Books in the Graeco-Roman World and in the New
Testament', in P.R. Ackroyd and C.F. Evans (eds.), *The Cambridge History of the
Bible*. I. *From the Beginnings to Jerome* (Cambridge: Cambridge University Press,
1970), p. 48.

2. E.g. Lk. 4.15-30; Mk 2.25, 12.10. See further W.H. Kelber, *The Oral and
Written Gospel* (Philadelphia: Fortress Press, 1983), p. 78.

3. *Phaedrus* 274c–275a, in which Socrates is given the words, 'You have
invented an elixir not of memory, but of reminding' (LCL translation). Compare
Xenophon's *Symposium* 3.5 and Diogenes Laertius 10.12 (11.541 in the LCL
translation).

ossifies thought; at best what is written only serves as a reminder of what is already known. The most profound truth cannot be encapsulated in writing; living thought needs the give and take of speech in dialogue. How widespread such an attitude was among the Greeks is disputed. However, though emphasized in Plato, it was not a peculiarity of his. This attitude explains why in literary circles in Rome and Alexandria, and probably elsewhere in the Hellenistic age, 'publication' did not signify the appearance of a book or volume but was by public recitation.[4] It was this same attitude, along with other, probably more important, factors, which led in Judaism to the prohibition of the writing of the oral law.[5] That Jesus, like John the Baptist, did not choose to write, even though he apparently could, may be indicative.[6] For Paul his letters were a necessary but, by implication, inferior substitute for his presence (Gal. 4.20; 2 Cor. 13.10; 1 Cor. 11.34). The documents of the early church were only tardily gathered together. Papias, Bishop of Hierapolis (c. AD 60–130), makes clear this attitude in Christian circles. He explicitly preferred oral to written evidence: 'I supposed that things out of books did not profit me so much as the utterance of a voice that lives and survives'.[7]

This ambiguity towards written documents, in which writing was both widely practised and yet often distrusted, raises the question

4. On 'publication', see S. Lieberman, *Hellenism in Jewish Palestine* (Theological Studies of the Jewish Theological Seminary of America, 18; New York: Jewish Theological Seminary of America, 1962), pp. 83-89; Roberts, 'Books in the Graeco-Roman World'.

5. 'That which has been expressed orally [must be transmitted orally] and that which has been expressed in writing [must be transmitted] in writing' (*y. Meg.* 4.1, 74d; compare *b. Giṭ.* 66b; *Tem.* 14b). See Lieberman, *Hellenism*, p. 87. The Talmud contains no reference to a written Mishnah. The interdiction covered Halakah and Haggadah. R. Meyers (*TWNT*, 9.34-35) regards this interdiction as legendary and refuses to press it for the rabbinic period. The interdiction has, moreover, been connected not with the kind of reserve toward writing found in the contemporary Graeco-Roman world, but with the fear that two laws might emerge. The interpretations of the Qumran sectarians were not immediately written down, but some time after the death of the founder. For additional caution about over-emphasizing the literary character of the Hellenistic world, see Kelber, *Oral and Written Gospel*, p. 17.

6. Jn 8.6.

7. Eusebius, *Ecclesiastical History*, 3.39.1-7, 14-17. It is perhaps noteworthy that, much later, on the invention of printing, Islam allowed the printing of secular books, but forbade that of the Qur'an; so W.C. Smith, 'The Study of Religion and the Study of the Bible', *JAAR* 39 (1971), pp. 131-40, esp. p. 137.

whether in the Graeco-Roman world the attitude of Jews towards their Scriptures is to be regarded as peculiar to them. By the first century, religious Jews (it should not be overlooked that most people, even amongst the Jews, were doubtless not religious) regarded their sacred writings—the Pentateuch (which was given pre-eminence), the Prophets, the Writings (although not all were finally fixed as an authoritative canon until the end of the first century, and possibly not even then)—as not simply 'containing' but as 'being' the very words of God himself, and therefore as binding, authoritative, perfect, unchangeable, and eternal. They were conceived to comprise all that Jews know and need to know, a gateway to another, and eternal, world; they represent the eternal breaking into time; the unknowable disclosed; the transcendent entering history and remaining here, available to mortals to handle and appropriate; the divine becoming apparent. To memorize them and even to quote them is to enter into some sort of communion with ultimate reality.[8] And, although recognized to be much in need of interpretation, so that the literal was not their only meaning, the Scriptures were to be understood literally.[9] Immense care was taken to ensure that they were transmitted with strictest accuracy.[10] This Jewish attitude (though not universally held)[11] we shall examine later. At first encounter at least it is very far removed, indeed at the opposite pole, from Plato's attitude. Plato reveals little if any awareness of writings as containing divine truth, as treasures to be handed on to subsequent generations. Contrast the Library of Congress

8.   See my *Setting of the Sermon on the Mount* (Cambridge: Cambridge University Press, 1964), pp. 109-90, esp. pp. 156-90. I here borrow phrases from W.C. Smith, 'The True Meaning of Scripture: An Empirical Historian's Non-Reductionist Interpretation of the Qur'an', *JMES* 1 (1980), p. 491.

9.   Various senses of Scripture were recognized, but the literal sense remained.

10.   See B. Gerhardsson, *Memory and Manuscript*, Part I (ASNU, 22; Uppsala: Almquist & Wiksells; Lund: Gleerup, 2nd edn, 1964 [1961]), pp. 1-191; H.L. Strack and G. Stemberger, *Einleitung in Talmud und Midrasch* (Munich: Beck, 7th edn, 1982), pp. 41-54. For a reply to his critics see B. Gerhardsson, *Tradition and Transmission in Early Christianity* (Lund: Gleerup, 1964); *idem*, *Evangelierna Förhistoria* (Lund: Verbum-Håkan Ohlssons, 1977); ET: *The Origins of the Gospel Traditions* (Philadelphia: Fortress Press, 1979).

11.   The compiler of the Temple Scroll at Qumran (11QTemple) could insert his own halakah in the Pentateuch. See also *b. Yeb.* 79a; *m. Ber.* 9.5. See the chapter 'Law in First-century Judaism' in my *Jewish and Pauline Studies, Collected Essays* (Philadelphia: Fortress Press, 1983), pp. 3-26.

at Washington, which reminds us, each time we enter it, that books were for Milton the precious life-blood of noble spirits and for Thoreau the treasures of the wisdom of the ages; they are not simply 'reminders' but themselves of inestimable worth. Nothing of this is in Plato, nothing of the Jewish sense that in certain writings all truth is to be found, that what is needed is to excavate the inexhaustible mine of the divine revelation contained in the Scriptures and bring to light treasures that lie hidden beneath the surface.[12]

I

Are there parallels in other religious traditions to the use made of Scripture in Jewish and Christian circles? To answer this we must examine briefly a wide range of traditions and texts.[13] This much we can state: it is erroneous to regard all 'sacred texts' as necessarily and automatically 'canonical texts' such as are the Tanak and the Old and New Testaments in Judaism and Christianity respectively.

The Egyptian 'sacred texts' probably owed their sacred character to their hieroglyphic script, not their contents: they were treated with considerable liberty in transmission, and those who read them did not thereby acquire honour as did the readers of the Torah in the synagogue. They do not provide a parallel with the biblical canon.[14]

Somewhat closer parallels may be detected in Hinduism and Islam. The Sanskrit sacred texts were regarded as a unity, as being of divine orgin and possessing supreme authority, and underwent a process of something like canonization. Freedom to interpret these texts— resulting in a well-developed tradition (*Āgama*) which came itself to possess only slightly inferior status—did not imply freedom to modify them, which would entail exclusion from the community of Hinduism. Parallels here with Judaism and Christianity are not hard to find, even

12. Compare A. Cohen, *Everyman's Talmud* (New York: Dutton, 1949 [1932]), p. 132. With this also goes an emphasis on oral learning and memorizing in Judaism; see Deut. 31.19; *Lam. R.* 4.12 §15.

13. In looking at the Egyptian, Near Eastern, and Semitic backgrounds, and at Hindu and Islamic sacred texts, I have no competence in the various original sources involved, and must rely on secondary works. I am particularly grateful to M. Meslin for allowing me to use his unpublished lecture, given at a colloquium at Strasbourg University in 1980 on the theme 'La Bible: est-elle une livre apart?'

14. See the mentions in Herodotus, *History* 11.36; Clement of Alexandria, *Stromateis* 6.4.37, 3; Diodorus Siculus (first century BCE), *History* 11.4.

though the existence of different 'sects' within Hinduism, each with its own claimed sacred texts, warns against such parallels being pressed too far. As for Islam, there are again parallels, this time between the Qur'an with its absolute authority and the Torah in Judaism, with, again, the development of a tradition (*Sunna*) facilitating its interpretation. Despite some difference, then, there are at least partial parallels in Hinduism and Islam to the phenomena of the interpretation of the Bible as a revelation from God, the literary forms which this assumed, the development of an explicatory and supplementary tradition alongside this and the 'canonical' status afforded it, and to the influence which it has exerted on Western culture.[15]

What of the Hellenistic tradition? There is something to be said for applying the predicate 'canonical' to the role of Homer in the Greek world of the first century.[16] Even when the content of poetry was questioned, the belief that poets were 'the schoolmasters of grown men'[17] was unquestioned; and it was based on the conviction that good epic and lyric poets were inspired in a similar way to the Pythia at Delphi or such legendary figures as Bacchus and the Sibyl.[18] As in the case of the latter, the words of the poets were orginally delivered orally, only subsequently being written down and collected. As early as the seventh century BC at the Delian festival, and elsewhere, Greeks assembled to hear their minstrels recite the Homeric poems. There was a public recitation of Homer every fourth year at the Panathenic festival. This, it has been claimed, is 'analogous to the Jewish provision that once in every seven years the Law was to be read at the Feast of Tabernacles in the hearing of all Israel'.[19]

A final possible parallel to the use of the Hebrew Scriptures by Jews and early Christians comes from a later period when the dominance of the epic poets had long been under attack. In the first century or two of the Christian era there was much searching for ancient authority.

15. Smith ('The Study of Religion', pp. 133-34) has urged that the Bible has *not* influenced that culture as much as the Qur'an has influenced Islamic life.

16. See M. Hengel, *Judaism and Hellenism* (2 vols.; Philadelphia: Fortress Press, 1974), I, pp. 66.

17. Aristophanes, *Frogs* 1052-60, compare 1032-35.

18. See Plato, *Phaedrus* 237c-d, pp. 244-245; *Ion* 533b-535e.

19. S.H. Butcher, *Harvard Lectures on Greek Subjects* (London and New York: Macmillan, 1904), p. 105, cited by J. Adam, *The Religious Teachers of Greece* (Edinburgh: T. & T. Clark, 1909), p. 9.

The impulse to appeal to tradition which surfaced at that time in the Graeco-Roman world emerged also in Judaism.[20] The appeal to the Hebrew Scriptures in early Christianity is related to the same impulse.

II

But, when all this has been recognized, is the place of the Tanak in Judaism and the early church adequately accounted for simply as the counterpart to the role played in early Greece especially, but not exclusively, by Homer, and at a later date by the various philosophical traditions? The answer must finally be a qualified but unmistakable negative. There are significant differences between the approach to the Hebrew Scriptures in Judaism and early Christianity and the Greeks' understanding of their ancient poets, and literary and philosophical traditions before and after Plato. The differences can be summarized in one word, 'canon', a word very often too loosely used in comparisons between Greek and Hebrew 'sacred' texts.

A few preliminary considerations are pertinent. First, the Jews' attitude to their sacred writings induced the necessity to reproduce those texts without distortion. The Hebrew texts were transmitted with meticulous and scrupulous care. Although the evidence does not allow certainty, it is probable that such care was exercised before the first century. The texts discovered at Qumran seem to establish that the recension of the Masoretic text existed before the Christian era. Even an imperfect scroll such as 1QIsaiah deviates little from the Masoretic text. Contrast the care which this implies with the freer use and citation of Scripture in the targumim and midrashim.

This is not the place to describe the process whereby Jewish copyists, long before it was fixed by post-Talmud Masoretes, ensured the preservation of the purity of the text of the Torah. There were probably pre-Christian specialists, scribes (*sopherim*) responsible for the official copying of texts.[21] These scribes were at first probably both 'copyists', in the sense of being skilled in the mechanical art of

---

20. Butcher, *Harvard Lectures*, p. 105. A good example is the opening section of the *Pirqe Abot*, for which see my 'Reflections on Tradition: The 'Abot Revisited', in *Jewish and Pauline Studies*, pp. 27-48. Diodorus Siculus (*History* 1.9ff.) is instructive at this point.

21. See Gerhardsson, *Memory and Manuscript*, p. 43.

writing, and persons who knew or were schooled in the Scriptures.[22]
The procedures for copying followed by the scribes probably have
their parallel in the Hellenistic world, as do the rules of argumentation
or of interpretation.[23] How much Jewish scribes owed to Alexandrian
textual critics is hard to assess. As far as I am aware this question has
not been seriously addressed. There *was* certainly an indigenous
scribal tradition in Jewish Palestine. The Wisdom tradition implied a
long-established writing culture. The translators of the LXX could
send to the Temple authorities in Jerusalem for the best text of the
Pentateuch. Most probably the translators of the Scripture into Greek
were influenced by the Alexandrian critical tradition.

Our specific concern is to discover whether the usage of Judaism in
its treatment of the texts of the Tanak points to a qualitatively different attitude towards those texts from that found in the Hellenistic
world towards the sacred texts of Greece. The Hellenistic world, particularly at Alexandria and Pergamum, did seek to preserve its ancient
texts and the mechanical copying processes followed by Jews came to
be similar to those of the Greeks and Romans. But this insistence on
the accurate textual transmission of the Scriptures in Judaism seems to
have become, probably by the first century and certainly later, more
intense, anxious, and exacting than what we find in the Hellenistic
milieu. Alexandrian critics laboured to produce revised texts
(ἐκδόσεις), especially of the poets, and commentaries on them. It was
at Alexandria that Homer first became an object of critical study. But
the attitude of editors to the text of Homer (and, by inference, how
much more to other texts) does not suggest the 'religious anxiety' to
observe the strictest possible exactitude that is clear in the transmission of the Scriptures in Judaism. We can probably claim with
some certainty that the work of Homeric critics such as Zenodotus
(285–247 BCE), Aristophanes (c. 195 BCE), and Aristarchus (180–145
BCE) was simply governed by a textual and literary intent and lacked
the intensity that a religious concern would be likely to have
produced.

22. For the situation after 70 CE, see Gerhardsson, *Memory and Manuscript*,
p. 51.

23. See D. Daube, 'Rabbinic Methods of Interpretation and Hellenistic Rhetoric',
HUCA 22 (1949), pp. 239-64, esp. pp. 239ff., and his 'Alexandrian Methods of
Interpretation and the Rabbis', in *Festschrift Hans Lewald* (Liechtenstein: Topos,
1978 [1953]), pp. 27-44.

But what of the 'canons' (κανόνες) of Alexandria, as they are called? Do they not suggest that the ancient literature of Greece was elevated to a 'canonical' status such as that achieved by the Tanak in Judaism and the Old and New Testaments in Christianity? To answer this question one must note what precisely were the concerns of the Alexandrian critics of the third and second centuries BCE. They aimed at discriminating authentic from spurious writings and at selecting the best writers in each kind from the enormous mass of literature which had come down to them—good, bad, or indifferent. With this end in view they prepared lists (πίνακες) of poets: four heroic (headed by Homer), three iambic, four elegiac, and so on. Crates prepared lists at Pergamum in which the leading writers of prose were given the prominence ascribed at Alexandria to the epic poets.[24] To be included in these lists an author had to achieve a certain excellence in the category concerned. For this reason the lists, so it has often been held, were called 'canons' (κανόνες), and are to be understood as 'canonical'.[25]

First, let it be noted that in fact the πίνακες of Alexandrian scholarship were not called 'canons'. This term is very late as a translation for the πίνακες.[26] But, in addition to this devastating lexicographical point, we may ask whether the critical intention at Alexandria was comparable with that which led to the canonization of the Scriptures of Judaism and Christianity. The fixing of the Alexandrian lists did reveal deep reverence, perhaps especially characteristic of the Hellenistic period, for the literary works of the ancients. But it seems

24. L. Whibley (ed.), *A Companion to Greek Studies* (New York: Hafner, 1963 [1933]), p. 175 (§202).

25. Whibley (ed.), *Greek Studies*, p. 746.

26. See R. Pfeiffer, *History of Classical Scholarship: From the Beginnings to the End of the Hellenistic Age* (Oxford: Clarendon Press, 1968), p. 207. Pfeiffer points out that the term 'canon' was coined for the πίνακες (repertories or lists which we should call indexes) by David Ruhnken in 1768. The use of it for the πίνακες was not Greek, and it was not by the ancient Greek tradition that the use of 'canon' for πίνακες was suggested to Ruhnken, but by the biblical. Eusebius (*Ecclesiastical History* 6.25.3) 'seems to be the earliest evidence for the canon of Scripture' according to Pfeiffer (*History of Classical Scholarship*, p. 207 n. 4). See further J. Barr, *Holy Scripture: Canon, Authority, Criticism* (Philadelphia: Westminster Press, 1983), p. 51, and my article 'Reflections about the Use of the Old Testament in the New in its Historical Context', *JQR* 74 (1983), pp. 105-36 (here, p. 123), to which the reader is referred for fuller treatment of much in the present chapter.

that the criteria for excellence were exclusively literary: the chief responsibility for drawing up the lists was that of the two editors of Homer already mentioned, Aristarchus and Aristophanes. Their interests do not seem to have been the deeply religious ones which governed the Jews in fixing their canon. Primarily by literary discrimination, they were concerned to confirm the fame of the great authors of their people's past, not to provide a literature to govern their people in all the details of their lives in the present. The textual and so-called 'canonical' intentions at Alexandria are perhaps not to be entirely distinguished from those of Judaism and Christianity, but they are certainly not of exactly the same order.

III

This brings us to the question as to the purpose of the fixation of the Jewish canon of Scripture. To begin with, purely literary (as distinct from textual) criteria do not seem to have played a conscious part in the process. The concern of those who elevated the Torah, Nebi'im, and Kethubim to canonicity was not to recognize, confirm, or confer any literary distinction upon them. Equally, the lists of Alexandria and Pergamum do not seem to have been born of a deliberate concern to meet the urgent, immediate, and continuing needs of an ongoing self-conscious religious people or community. The 'new' class of scholars engaged in editing Homer and other Greek writings in Alexandria and Pergamum were called διόρθωται, that is, 'correctors'. Jewish scribes would certainly have resented such a designation as impious: who would dare 'correct' their sacred texts? This contrasts markedly with the concern that led to the fixation of the Jewish canon, as we shall see.

But before we deal further with this concern, the other phenomenon in the Graeco-Roman world to which I referred previously again deserves attention. Does this provide, at least, a partial parallel? As we saw, in the Hellenistic age the founders of schools of philosophy came to be highly revered and their words and works cherished. There were many such schools. What particularly interests us is the attitude each school reveals to the tradition—oral and written—originated by the founder. The tradition was not regarded as of intellectual or 'philosophical' interest only. The tradition of the founder was to provide an inspiring and normative, regulatory, way of life: it provided a 'rule' or 'canon' by which the members of a particular school were to live. This scholastic 'canonization' of a teaching founder's tradition, as we shall see, approaches in part the intent behind the canonization of the Jewish Scriptures, which also were to provide a *halakah*, a way of life.[27] There is, however, an obvious difference. The canon of Judaism was to inform not simply the life of a particular school, although the interpretation of it could and did lead to the emergence of different 'schools' within Israel, but that of a whole people.

This leads to the consideration of the underlying cause for the fixation of the Jewish canon. To grasp this would help to assess how far the Graeco-Roman world offers more than formal parallels to that process.

To begin with, however much veneration for ancient texts and tradition the Graeco-Roman world reveals, it provides only a pale and partial parallel with that implied in the constant, regular, daily reading of the Torah in the synagogue. The history of the synagogue is wrapped in obscurity, but there were synagogues in first-century Palestine and outside. Part of their activity was the reading and study of the Scriptures which, although not altogether formally 'fixed' as a 'canon' until the end of the first century, and possibly not even then, had achieved a prominent (for reasons given later I deliberately avoid the adjective 'normative') role in Jewish life. Certainly in this matter any dogmatism must be suspect, but the claim seems to be justified that by the first century the Torah had become an ubiquitous, ever-present, expression of Jewish religious life. Discussion has centred on whether the whole Torah was read annually or triennially in the first-century synagogues. In any case, the lectionary activity of the synagogue in that period points to an elevation of the sacred Hebrew texts for which there is no fully adequate parallel in the Graeco-Roman world.[28]

27. On the role of philosophy in this connection, see A.D. Nock, *Conversion: The Old and the New in Religion from Alexander the Great to Augustine of Hippo* (Oxford and New York: Oxford University Press, 1933), p. 181; H. Wolfson, *Philo: Foundations of Religious Philosophy in Judaism, Christianity, and Islam* (2 vols.; Cambridge, MA: Harvard University Press, 1947), pp. 8ff.; M. Smith, 'Palestinian Judaism in the First Century', in M. Davis (ed.), *Israel: Its Role in Civilization* (New York: Jewish Theological Seminary of America, 1956), pp. 67-81, esp. p. 80; E.J. Bickerman, 'La chaîne de la tradition pharisienne', *RB* 59 (1952), pp. 44-54, esp. pp. 49-52.

28. For the synagogue, see F. Hüttenmeister, 'The Synagogue', in W.D. Davies and L. Finkelstein (eds.), *The Cambridge History of Judaism*, III (Cambridge:

Only recently has the nature of this elevation begun to be explored in depth. Previously the history of the canon was most often treated chronologically and factually without adequate attention either to the deep forces at work in its fixation or to the significance of the final form of the canon as such. Now it is increasingly urged that the emergence and formation of the canon in Judaism and Christianity was ultimately due to the necessity for the people of Israel, as later for the Christian churches, to define and preserve their identity. The primary impulse behind the elevation of the Torah and the Prophets, as later of the Writings, was the felt need in the disaster of the exile and later to reaffirm the 'story' of Yahweh's dealing with his people. That disaster made the people of Israel—for the sake of their very survival—conceive of themselves increasingly, and more and more emphatically, as a 'chosen people', the record of whose origin and prescribed way of life and destiny they found in their ancient writings. These they revered and tried to preserve and elevate for the sake of their own continued existence. The sacred texts had become necessary to the continuing self-identity of the people of Israel; they became the book of a people and the people became the people of the book. The crises of the sixth century BCE and of the first century demanded the reaffirmation of Jewish identity and this was in part achieved through the development and ultimate fixation of the canon. The understanding of the canon thus crudely set forth here I owe especially to James Sanders and Brevard Childs, who with varying emphases have called for a new canonical perspective.[29]

Despite the partial parallels to which I have pointed, we look in vain for a satisfactory parallel in the Graeco-Roman world. Much as the epic poets, particulary Homer and Hesiod, were revered and regarded as 'inspired', they were never regarded as 'gods', and certainly not as the voice of God, the creator of the universe. Contrast with this the Israelite view that Yahweh had spoken directly to Moses, and not only

Cambridge University Press, forthcoming). Also see J. Mann, *The Bible as Read and Preached in the Old Synagogue* (New York: Ktav, 1971 [1940]). According to Mann (pp. 3ff.) the Palestinian Jewish lectionary was almost certainly triennial.

29. See J.A. Sanders, *Torah and Canon* (Philadelphia: Fortress Press, 1972); *idem, Canon and Community: Canon as Paradigm* (Philadelphia: Fortress Press, 1984); *idem, From Sacred Story to Sacred Text: Canon as Paradigm* (Philadelphia: Fortress Press, 1987); B.S. Childs, *Introduction to the Old Testament as Scripture* (Philadelphia: Fortress Press, 1979).

spoken to him but handed over the tablets on which he himself had written his commandments.

The same contrast applies to the esteem with which the traditions of the founders of the various philosophic schools were held. Some of the great philosophers were conceived of as having prophetic powers. But, as was the case with Homer and the poets, this did *not* connote their divinization: they were not 'gods'. But the tradition of Israel came to be directly traced to Yahweh himself, and, from the outset, its core in the Decalogue was in written form.[30] This placed the Torah outside the categories applied in the Graeco-Roman world to its ancient literature, and its later interpretation in Israel removed it still further from anything in the Graeco-Roman world.

This is reinforced by the way in which Homer was treated. Despite his attachment to Homer, Plato finally had to exclude him from the ideal state because he could corrupt morals.[31] The tragedians often found it necessary to correct Homeric notions of morality and of the gods. In the Hellenistic age, it is not Homer who is the teacher of the Greeks but philosophy. The kind of criticism of Homer and the epic poets which made necessary the rise of the allegorical method in the Graeco-Roman world is not natural in the treatment of the Torah by Jews. Allegory does sometimes occur in Jewish sources but it is more native to the Hellenistic.[32] The approach of the Jews to their Scriptures (which they regarded as of direct divine orgin, though they were in some circles regarded as mediated by angels[33]) was qualitatively different from that of the Greeks to theirs.

Moreover, the kind of historical circumstances which provided the impetus for the formulation and later fixation of the Hebrew canon in Judaism were absent in Greece and in Greek history. The Jewish people came to understand themselves as having been called into being through an act of Yahweh in delivering them from slavery in Egypt.

30. The accounts of the giving of the law to Moses present problems which cannot be dealt with here.

31. *Republic* 607a. A sophist could even call Homer a liar and hold him up to ridicule: so Dio of Prusa, *Discourse* 11.

32. J. Bonsirven, *L'éxégèse rabbinique et l'éxégèse paulinienne* (Paris: Beauchesne, 1939).

33. Gal. 3.19; Acts 7.38; see my *Jewish and Pauline Studies*, p. 7, pp. 84-88, p. 239. See also Wolfson, *Philo*, I, pp. 138ff. For a different interpretation of these New Testament passages see L. Gaston, 'Angels and Gentiles in Early Judaism and in Paul', *SR* 11 (1982), pp. 65-75.

With this they later connected the giving of the Torah on Mount Sinai. The precise way in which the tradition of the exodus and the Sinaitic tradition of the giving of the Torah came to be conjoined does not directly concern us. Those two events came to dominate the memory of Israel. Their emergence and continuance as a people were bound up with these events; their ancient traditions and Scriptures centred on them; the remembrance of these two events provided them with their identity as a people. Later another overwhelming event, the Babylonian exile, engendered the necessity for the collecting of the traditions about those events and the setting in motion of the process which finally resulted in the Hebrew canon. The beginning of the formation of a canon was the means whereby Jewish identity survived the exile in the sixth century BCE. To understand the Hebrew canon, then, well-defined, extra-ordinary, historical memories—of the exodus, Sinai, and the exile—have to be recognized as formative.

When we turn to Greek history, there are no parallels of any comparable magnitude. The Greek identity seems not to have been determined by any outstanding, spectacular historical events. If we follow Herodotus,[34] that identity was forged out of the normal processes of human interaction and exchange, out of an age-long awareness of sharing in the same ethnic character, in the same religious tradition and in the same language. Greek self-awareness was mainly a *cultural* awareness, not a strictly historical one in the sense that it was, as with Israel, the product of specific, overwhelmingly significant historical events. Greeks knew no exodus at their beginnings, nor, in the course of their history, an exile like that of the Jews to Babylon. Certain Greek city states did experience exile and massive, cruel deportations, but the Greeks as a totality never faced such an event. When Persia threatened the existence of Greece, the threat was met and followed, not by exile, but by a period of efflorescence. It is probably significant that there is no one word for exile in classical Greek as there is in Hebrew (גולה, גלות) but rather several words emphasizing various aspects of the experience of exile. In Greek history there were famous 'exiles', such as Odysseus, but no one overwhelming 'exile' in the Jewish sense.

It is equally significant that, as Thucydides 1.3 points out, the term *Hellenes* for all Greeks occurs only late and then simply to distinguish

34. See, e.g. *History*, 8.144.

them from the barbarians, whereas the Jewish people, despite the division between the kingdoms of Judah and Israel, came to think of themselves as constituted of one people from the beginning, through the exodus and Sinai. The Greeks never achieved such a 'politically' unified conception of themselves. The independent city states—not the land or country or people as a totality—were the foci of loyalty, but therefore *ipso facto* also of division and fratricide. Except under very great stress, such as the Persian invasion, the city states hindered the development of a unified Greek world, despite the recognition of its cultural unity. The impulse to the formation of one authoritative 'canon' to justify or preserve that unity was lacking: even reverence for Homer could not provide this. The geographical realities of Greece, as well as Greek history, then, militated against the emergence of anything comparable to the canon of Judaism in the Classical period. In the Hellenistic period the diverse philosophical schools were also not conducive to a common Greek canon, but rather to individual 'canons' for each school. The widespread cultural Hellenic identity does not seem to have required a concentrated literary identification through a 'canon'.

I have suggested that the notion of a 'canon' of Scripture in Judaism and Christianity has no adequate or satisfactory parallel in the Graeco-Roman world. But this presentation has now to be seriously qualified. Two dangers have to be shunned: first, that of reading the role and authority of the Jewish and Christian canons, after they had been fixed, back to an earlier period; and secondly, that of *underestimating* the variety of Judaism at the emergence of Christianity, and so of *overestimating* the role of the Jewish Scriptures in Jewish life at that time. I have emphasized the importance of the Scriptures in first-century Judaism. The probable fixation of the canon at the end of that century confirms this: it recognized what was already fact. But concentration on the written Scriptures alone leads to distortion: this is why I previously rejected the word 'normative' to describe the role of the Tanak in Judaism, and simply used the adjective 'prominent' (see discussion above).

At this point the development of the oral law in Judaism must be emphasized. After the Persian, and particularly in the Greek and Roman periods, Jews who were in Babylon and those who had returned to Palestine confronted new cultures. They faced the new demands and complex dilemmas of those new cultures: for these the ancient Scriptures—important as they were in defining the origins and history, and safeguarding the identity, of the Jews—provided insufficient guidance. This, along with other factors, prompted a renewed development of the oral law alongside the written. For our purposes, contrary to what previous scholars have often asserted, it is strikingly noteworthy that the oral law of Judaism often bears little relation to the written Torah.[35] If the written Torah had enjoyed unswayed and normative authority, this is hard to understand. The strictly mishnaic collecting of oral laws, that is, without reference to Scripture, *may* have preceded the midrashic method of relating the laws to the scriptural text which was also practised and culminated in the later midrashim.[36] The two developments may have occurred side by side. Whether the mishnaic tendency was the prior we cannot ascertain. But the development of the oral law was *often* separate from the written law. According to some of the Sages it came to take precedence over the written law. This indicates that the written law was not as all-dominating as my treatment may have implied. There was a very rich oral legal tradition alongside the written. This oral tradition, rooted in long-established custom, also came to be connected with the giving of the Torah to Moses on Mount Sinai. This meant that it too achieved the authority ascribed to Scripture itself.[37] The relation of Jesus, Paul and the early Church to the Tanak must not be isolated from this phenomenon. In confronting Judaism at the first they faced primarily not only the written Torah, which so controls subsequent Christian thinking on this matter, but also the oral tradition, which was perhaps the more immediately dominant in the Jewish mind.

There is a concomitant factor. As we have seen, the oral law was not always directly or indirectly connected with the Tanak. But it sometimes was. The development of the midrashim points to this. This makes clear what is anyway obvious, that between the Tanak and the

35. The Mishnah (*m. Hag.* 1.8) is particularly illuminating on the connection between the written and the oral tradition. The Scribes, such as Ben Sirach, were not exegetes or midrashists, but expositors of Wisdom.

36. See J.Z. Lauterbach, *Rabbinic Essays* (Cincinnati: Hebrew Union College Press, 1951).

37. This is the implication of *m. Ab.* 1.1. See the chapter on 'The Meaning of Oral Torah' in J. Neusner, *Early Rabbinic Judaism* (Leiden: Brill, 1975), pp. 1-33, and J. Goldin, 'Midrash and Haggadah', and 'The Teachers and their Adherents', and D. Zlotnik, 'Rabbi's Mishnah and the Development of Jewish Law', in Davies and Finkelstein (eds.), *The Cambridge History of Judaism*.

New Testament lies a vast exegetical-interpretative activity within Judaism. This means that in confronting Judaism the early church, like Jesus and Paul, faced not only both a written and an oral Torah but also ways of understanding these, that is, long-standing exegetical-interpretative traditions. They assumed these, and it was to these traditions of exegesis and interpretation rather than to the Tanak itself in its textual nudity that they related. Professor David Daube has long urged this. Recently he claimed that,

> When dealing with the Old Testament in the New we ought to read it as it was read by Jews of that era. The references without exception come from their midst, are founded in their interpretation. If this often clashes with the pristine sense (or what we take to be such) it cannot be helped. We must still stick to it. Unless we do, we may miss parts of the New Testament message conveyed by means of the reference.[38]

Knowledge of varied and complex interpretations of the Tanak in first-century Judaism is a necessary prerequisite for understanding Jesus', and early Christian, engagement with it. To substantiate this claim is not possible here, but examples of the illumination afforded by the recognition of this approach are not hard to find. For the understanding of the use of the Old Testament in the New it matters little what *we* understand by an Old Testament text, but what it meant to Jews with whom Jesus and early Christians were in debate in the first century is of primary importance: this should be one of our exegetical axioms.

Apart, then, from some general considerations pointing to certain parallels, but even greater dissimilarities, the Graeco-Roman attitude to ancient texts helps little in our attempts to understand the early Christian engagement with the Hebrew Scriptures. We are driven to consider anew the oral tradition and the exegetical-interpretative activity within Judaism. The recognition of the complexity of the attitude to the Scriptures in the first-century Judaism suggested here—especially when the mishnaic, midrashic, and exegetical-interpretative developments are given due emphasis—helps to place their use by the writers of the New Testament in better perspective. Most of them wrote in a period of great freedom, and many methods were employed in the approach to the Scriptures even though they were so highly

38. D. Daube, 'The Old Testament in the New: A Jewish Perspective', in Daube, *Appeasement or Resistance and Other Essays on New Testament Judaism* (Berkeley: University of California Press, 1987), pp. 1-38. See especially *m. Sanh.* 11.3; *m. Yad.* 3.2.

regarded. The canon was only in the process of being finally fixed for Judaism, just as the Sages had not yet codified the oral law. From this point of view the New Testament is a document from a transition period in which Judaism had not come fully to terms with either its written or oral Torah. The use of the Old Testament in the New reveals reverence and a daring freedom of exegesis: but in this it was not unique, but probably typical: it was only its christological dimension and approach that was peculiar. Moreover, after the Hebrew canon had been fixed at 22 books with an unimpeachable ancestry, Christians continued to use and quote as Scripture such books as Wisdom and Ecclesiasticus, which they had received as part of the Septuagint. Owing to our familiarity with a fixed, authoritative canon, confined in Protestantism to the Hebrew Bible, it is easy to conceive of the engagement of the early Christian movement, especially before 70 CE, in too simplistic terms. They did use written Hebrew Scriptures which they regarded as sacred: but these were still undefined in detail and had not yet achieved the express authority of '*The* Canon'. Above all, they co-existed with a vast tradition of oral law and subtle and infinitely varied exegetical-interpretative traditions. It is in the light of this, not of any parallels with Hellenism, that the New Testament use of the Tanak is best approached.

Despite his possibly distorting enthusiasm, the words of Josephus, who claimed what I have here reiterated, are probably near the truth:

> how firmly we have given credit to these books of our own nation is
> evident by what we do; for during so many ages as have already passed,
> no one has been so bold as either to add any thing to them, to take any
> thing from them, or to make any change in them; but it is become natural
> to all Jews immediately, and from their very birth, to esteem these books
> to contain Divine doctrines, and to persist in them, and, if occasion be,
> willingly to die for them. For it is no new thing for our captives, many of
> them in number, and frequently in time, to be seen to endure racks and
> deaths of all kinds upon the theatres, that they may not be obliged to say
> one word against our laws and the records that contain them; whereas
> there are none at all among the Greeks who would undergo the least harm
> on that account, no, nor in case all the writings that are among them were
> to be destroyed; for they take them to be such discourses as are framed
> agreeably to the inclinations of those that write them; and they have justly
> the same opinion of the ancient writers, since they see some of the present

generation bold enough to write about such affairs, wherein they were not
present, nor had concern enough to inform themselves about them from
those that knew them...[39]

Perhaps I have been able to suggest additional reasons why classical
antiquity offers no adequate parallel to the 'canon' in Judaism and
Christianity.

IV

What light may these reflections on the nature of the Jewish canon
throw on the topic of Christology? We have seen that there is no
significant parallel to the 'canon' of Judaism in the first century. What
has emerged is that the 'canon' of Judaism is inextricably bound up
with the search for the identity and for the self-preservation and
continuity of the Jewish community. But by itself the 'canon' was not
sufficient to serve this function adequately. It had to be interpreted
and applied to the life of the community. This was achieved by the
perpetuation and development of and obedience to the oral law. (The
use of this expression, 'oral tradition', and its exact connotation have
been minutely examined recently by E.P. Sanders.[40] It might be
advisable not to refer to an undifferentiated 'oral law' but to 'the oral
tradition'.) In this way, the written Torah was minted down to guide
the everday living of faithful Jews. Both Midrash and Mishnah
involved what might be called the Judaization of the Tanak. That is, in
Judaism the Tanak came to be interpreted in order to further and
illuminate the self-understanding of the Jews and to preserve their
identity. The oral law and Midrash served as a 'fence' around the
written law and *ipso facto* around the Jewish community. The Tanak
was interpreted in the interests of elevating the significance of both the
Torah and the relationship of the people of Israel as such to Yahweh.
This process of Judaization has made it necessary to distinguish
Israelite religion and, indeed, the religion of the Tanak, from
Judaism. That process was more chequered before 70 CE (for
example, it is doubtful whether the Sadducees ever fully succumbed to
it) than later. In rabbinic Judaism, strictly so-called, the Judaization of
the Tanak—some go so far as to claim its subordination to the oral

---

39. *Apion* 1.8 §42-46.
40. E.P. Sanders, *Jewish Law from Jesus to the Mishnah: Five Studies* (London:
SCM Press; Philadelphia: Trinity Press International, 1990), pp. 97-130.

Torah (but see Sanders[41])—reached its apogee. The developed rabbinic Judaism which emerged after the first century gave to the oral Torah, originally an accompaniment of the written Torah, an authority equal to that of the latter—if not greater. This helps to clarify the function of the oral Torah. Probably from the time of Ezra on it evolved to make sure that the Tanak was not treated as an isolated deposit, with overweening authority, but was interpreted in the interests of the community. This was why, in time, the oral tradition became Torah, as much as, and according to some even more than, the Tanak.

I suggest that the due recognition of the oral tradition as the interpretative clue to the meaning of the Tanak in Judaism is relevant to our understanding of the Christology of the early church. I here use the term 'Christology' not in its strict traditional sense to denote the doctrine of how God became man in Christ, but in the general sense of doctrine or teaching about Christ. And, in the history of Christian doctrine as in Judaism, the centuries after the first can best illumine the latter. Marcel Simon long ago pointed to the notion of Christ as a New Torah in the Fathers. However, he made no attempt to connect it with the period of the New Testament or with its documents. Later Jean Daniélou was more receptive to such a connection and found anticipations of it in the New Testament. In *Paul and Rabbinic Judaism* I proposed that for Paul Christ had come to fulfil the role of a New Torah, although he never used that phrase.[42] This suggestion has not been generally accepted. Apart from hesitancy, especially on the part of Protestants, to apply 'legal' terms to the Lord of Grace, two reasons were advanced against it: first, the unacceptable appeal to Colossians and Ephesians, which many regard as non-Pauline or at best deutero-Pauline; secondly, the emphasis (which many regard as highly exaggerated and unwarranted) on the words of Jesus as constituting a new law. Moreover, it was often confidently asserted that Paul did not think of Christ in terms of the law, as I had implied, but of the law in terms of Christ, who is not a new Moses in Paul. Neither of these objections is insurmountable. There are pertinent anticipations of Colossians and Ephesians in earlier indubitably Pauline epistles, and the words of Jesus—the role of which I doubtless did underline too

41. Sanders, *Jewish Law*, p. 129.

42. W.D. Davies, *Paul and Rabbinic Judaism: Some Rabbinic Elements in Pauline Theology* (Philadelphia: Fortress Press, 4th edn, 1980), pp. 223-35.

much—do play no mean part in Paul. The role of Moses in Paul's understanding is more difficult to deal with. Here, however, I am not concerned to reassert the interpretation of Christ as a New Torah in Paul without further refinement. Let it simply be noted that in speaking of Christ as Torah I was not thinking primarily of his words as constituting Torah but of the totality of his ministry and person, his cross and resurrection, as having assumed for Paul the ultimate significance which Judaism applied to the Torah.

Such a position is simplistic and needs elaboration and refinement. The words in the Torah, the Tanak, remained authoritative for Paul: he is careful to insist that the life, death, and resurrection of Jesus are 'according to the Scriptures'. The unchangeable 'canon' remains 'canon' for him. But just as, in Judaism, what was deemed to interpret the 'canon' became itself 'canon', so it came to pass for Paul that the life, teaching, death, and resurrection of Jesus became the exegesis of the canon (that is, of the Tanak)—a kind of equivalent of, and hence a substitute for, the oral tradition in Judaism, as the clue to the Scriptures. When he fought against obedience to the law, he was not primarily opposed to the Tanak but to the oral tradition which was already being elevated to the status of the written Torah. In other words, for Paul the identity of the Christian community is preserved by the tradition about Christ: he now fulfils for Christians the role of the oral law in Judaism. But once this had been recognized the further elevation of Christ to part of the 'canon' was natural, as had been the elevation of the oral law to the same status in Judaism. Whether this stage was reached in Paul's mind we need not at this point determine. What I am concerned to suggest again is that, just as the oral Torah in Judaism implied the Judaization of the Tanak, so the elevation of the life, death and resurrection of Jesus by Paul led to its Christianization. Christ, we might claim, has become the 'oral tradition' of Paul, the clue to his understanding of the Tanak.

From a different angle Daniel Patte has recently urged what amounts to the same thing, although he starts out not, as I did, from the canon and oral tradition of Judaism, but from the use of the Scriptures in Paul. I can only refer the reader to his work. For example, of Paul's treatment of Abraham he writes:

> the relation between the believers [the Christian community] and Christ is
> similar to that between the believers and Abraham. More generally, we

may say that the relation of the believers to Christ is the same kind of relation which exists between Scripture and its fulfillments in Christ and the believers. To put it another way, the kerygma about Christ functions in Paul as an *'oral scripture'*. This means that according to Paul's system of convictions, Christ, despite the fact that he is the Fulfillment of Scripture, *has the same status as Scripture* [my emphasis].[43]

A discussion of 1 Cor. 15.3-11 leads Patte to the same conclusion: 'Indeed, for Paul, Scripture is not merely the Old Testament Scripture, but also the kerygma about Christ, and the story of the earlier believers' experience'.[44] In his recent study Richard Hays has come to a similar conclusion: 'the word of God, now present in the Christian gospel, is the same word of God that was always present to Israel in Torah'.[45] Whereas Patte emphasizes Christology, Hays emphasizes ecclesiology: 'What Paul finds in Scripture, above all else, is a prefiguration of the *church* as the people of God'.[46] Although these issues cannot be pursued further in the present essay, various aspects of them will be treated in the essays that make up the balance of the present volume.

Outside the Pauline epistles, too, the New Testament points in other ways to a tradition, a way to be followed, which seems often to be equated with Christ himself. This line of thought later breaks out more explicitly. In short, it is not unlikely that a consideration of

43. D. Patte, *Paul's Faith and the Power of the Gospel* (Philadelphia: Fortress Press, 1983), p. 213.

44. Patte, *Paul's Faith*, p. 227.

45. R. Hays, *Echoes of Scripture in the Letters of Paul* (New Haven and London: Yale University Press, 1989), p. 83.

46. Hays, *Echoes of Scripture*, p. 86 (Hays's emphasis). The position of Hays and that of Patte and myself are not mutually exclusive. This is recognized by N.T. Wright, *The Climax of the Covenant: Christ and the Law in Pauline Theology* (Minneapolis: Fortress Press, 1992). Although Wright avoids writing of a new messianic Torah, this conception is implied in his work. He concludes his study (p. 266) with the following: '...for Paul [Christology] is a means of redefining the people of God and also a means of redefining God himself. Correlated exactly with this double redefinition is his rethinking of Torah... Torah was at one and the same time the charter of the people of God and the full and final revelation of God himself. *If, then, Jesus has taken on this double role, it is no surprise to find him taking on precisely the role of Torah in Paul's understanding of the plan of the one God*' (my emphasis).

Christ in the light of Torah, both written and oral, is still one fruitful way to approach the *mysterium tremendum* of his person.[47]

47. The notion of Christ as the new Torah in Paul has been widely criticized. See e.g. E.P. Sanders, *Paul and Palestinian Judaism* (Philadelphia: Fortress Press, 1977), p. 479; and the studies by S. Westerholm in P. Richardson and S. Westerholm (eds.), *Law in Religious Communities in the Roman Period: The Debate over* Torah *and* Nomos *in Post-Biblical Judaism and Early Christianity* (Studies in Christianity and Judaism, 4; Waterloo, Ontario: Wilfrid Laurier University, 1991), pp. 54-55, pp. 80-85; and F. Thielman, *From Plight to Solution: A Jewish Framework for Understanding Paul's View of the Law in Galatians and Romans* (NovTSup, 62; Leiden: Brill, 1984), p. 11. But D.C. Allison, Jr, in *The New Moses: A Matthean Typology* (Minneapolis: Fortress Press, 1993).

Part I

ECHOES OF SCRIPTURE IN PAUL—SOME REVERBERATIONS

Richard B. Hays

I begin with a warning to the reader: no one should suppose that this abstract can serve as a substitute for reading the book. The real value of *Echoes of Scripture in the Letters of Paul* is to be found in its specific close readings of the texts, which of course cannot be reproduced here. This abstract should be used only as an outline and reminder of the structure of the book's argument.

Chapter One: The Puzzle of Pauline Hermeneutics

Paul repeatedly interprets Israel's Scripture in ways that seem puzzling and idiosyncratic, consistently reading it as a witness to the gospel that he preached. Rom. 10.5-10 is a clear illustration of this tendency: Paul's reading of Deut. 30.11-14 is contrasted to that of the rabbis, who find a prohibition of hermeneutical license at the precise point where Paul finds a warrant for it. Both readings, in fact, demonstrate the way in which interpreters persistently discover latent senses in Scripture through innovative reading practices. The task posed for my investigation is to trace Paul's readings and 'misreadings' of Scripture.

A brief survey of previous investigations concludes that most have been preoccupied with technical questions about the textual form of Paul's citations or about the historical background of Paul's interpretive techniques. Often such studies have been marked by polemical or apologetic concerns, contending for or against the legitimacy of Paul's hermeneutical practices. This is particularly true of studies that have sought to characterize Paul's method as 'midrashic'. In contrast to such methods, I propose to investigate Paul's use of Scripture using an approach to 'intertextuality' derived from literary criticism, particularly John Hollander's work, *The Figure of Echo*.[1] The method is illustrated through a brief reading of Phil. 1.19. This reading demonstrates Paul's use of the rhetorical figure of *metalepsis*, a device that requires the reader to interpret a citation or allusion by recalling aspects of the original context that are not explicitly quoted.

The final section of the opening chapter seeks to clarify the methodological proposal by describing seven tests for identifying and interpreting echoes and allusions. These tests should not, however, be applied in a mechanical fashion: 'texts can generate readings that transcend both the conscious intention of the author and all the hermeneutical strictures that we promulgate' (p. 33). This generative power of the text is exemplified in Paul's readings. Our aim is to become readers attuned to the signifying power of intertextual figuration.

Chapter Two: Intertextual Echo in Romans

Romans is heavily laden with scriptural quotations and allusions. This chapter is a reading experiment which brackets questions about the text's historical occasion and purpose and seeks instead to read Romans as a conversation between Paul and Scripture, attending to the intertextual interplay within the discourse.

The resultant reading shows that Paul is contending for the continuity of God's grace: the gospel, rather than negating God's word of promise to Israel, upholds it. The righteousness of God revealed in the gospel is the same righteousness declared in the Psalms and Isaiah and in the story of the blessing of Abraham. The surprise, the mystery of the gospel is that the righteousness of God is now manifest through Jesus Christ in such a way that uncircumcised Gentiles are included in the promised blessing, while Israel remains in an anomalous state of unbelief. Paul interprets this distressing state of affairs through a complex scriptural argument in Romans 9–11, in which the Song of Moses (Deuteronomy 32) serves as the subliminal subtext, foreshadowing the paradoxical story of God's election of Israel, Israel's rebellion, God's calling of the Gentiles to make Israel jealous, and ultimately the salvation of Israel. Even Deut. 30.11-14, calling for Israel's obedience to Torah, becomes in Paul's hands primarily a

---

1. J. Hollander, *The Figure of Echo: A Mode of Allusion in Milton and After* (Berkeley: University of California Press, 1981).

testimony to the nearness of the word of the Gospel, pointing to the grace of God in Christ's death and resurrection.

Chapter Three: Children of Promise

Through readings of key texts in the Corinthian correspondence and in Galatians, this chapter demonstrates that Paul's hermeneutic is 'ecclesiocentric': it concentrates not on christological prooftexts but on typological prefigurations of the church as the locus of God's saving activity.

The story of Israel in the wilderness is used figuratively by Paul in several key passages in the Corinthian correspondence. In 2 Cor. 8.15, his use of the story is metaleptic: the passing citation of Exod. 16.18 says little but suggests much. In 1 Cor. 10.1-22, however, Paul elaborates a complex typological reading of the exodus story as a prefiguration of the situation of the church. A careful reading of the passage distinguishes Pauline typology from two common misconceptions about it. First, Paul's use of typology does not sponsor a supersessionist hermeneutic; the Gentile Corinthians are taken up into Israel's story rather than vice-versa. Secondly, Pauline typology is not concerned about 'history' in the modern sense; typology is a trope, an act of imaginative correlation between events in a narrative. These points are emphasized by a comparison between Paul's use of the exodus story and that of George Herbert in his poem 'The Bunch of Grapes'.

Paul's ecclesiocentric hermeneutic is shown forth also in Galatians. Gal. 3.8 is a telling hermeneutical marker: 'Scripture prepreached the gospel to Abraham', and the prepreached gospel is that all the Gentiles will be blessed in him through faith. Abraham's story is read as a prefiguration of the church. This conviction is audaciously carried through in Paul's subversive allegorical reading of the Sarah–Hagar story (Gal. 4.21-31). The traditional Jewish reading of the story identified the (circumcised) Isaac, Abraham's true heir, with the Jewish people and Ishmael with the Gentiles. But Paul reverses the polarity, identifying Ishmael with slavery and Law, Isaac with freedom and Spirit. Thus, the climax of Paul's telling of the story (Gal. 4.30: 'Cast out the slavewoman and her son') transforms the word of Scripture into a word spoken directly to the Galatians urging them to expel the 'troublemakers' who are advocating circumcision. Paul's allegorical reading construes Isaac *not* as a type of Christ, but of the church, of all who are 'children of promise'.

Chapter Four: A Letter from Christ

The contrast between *gramma* and *pneuma* in 2 Cor. 3.6 is explored as a key to Paul's hermeneutic. Paul's development of this contrast does not encourage a simple distinction between the literal and the figurative senses of Scripture. Rather, Paul contends that 'in the new covenant incarnation eclipses inscription'. The word that is merely *written* is lifeless until it becomes enfleshed in the community that is being transformed into the image of Christ. Thus, the Spirit is identified precisely with the outward and palpable; the Corinthians are themselves 'a letter from Christ'.

A close reading of 2 Cor. 3.7-18 shows that *telos* in v. 13 refers not to the 'termination' of the fading glory on Moses' face, but to the 'purpose' of the old covenant, which remains concealed until the reader 'turns to the Lord'. Paul employs the story of Exodus 34 as a foil in a *dissimile* (George Lord's term), in which he insists that his ministry is 'not like Moses', all the while appropriating the positive valences of the images of glory that surround the figure of Moses. In the end, the dissimile collapses into a positive metaphor and Moses becomes a figure for the Christian community that stands with unveiled face before the Lord and thus undergoes transformation. Thus, true reading produces the transformation of the readers. Consequently, there can be no dichotomy between hermeneutics and ethics.

Chapter Five: 'The Word is Near You': Hermeneutics in the Eschatological Community

This chapter first summarizes the findings of the previous chapters and then poses some normative questions about how Scripture should be read in the light of Paul's example.

The descriptive findings are summarized under five heads. (1) Paul reads with imaginative freedom, treating Scripture as a generative source for his own metaphorical *poiesis*. (2) Despite the explosive revisionary possibilities inherent in this hermeneutic of imaginative freedom, Paul maintains continuity with Torah through reading Scripture primarily as a narrative of divine election and promise.

(3) Paul reads Scripture ecclesiocentrically, as a prefiguration of the ongoing life of the people of God in history. (4) Scripture for Paul is a living voice that continues to speak in the present time and to call into being the people that it addresses. (5) Paul's hermeneutic is thoroughly eschatological, for he believes himself and his communities to be those 'upon whom the end of the ages have come'.

Using a typology of intertextual relations adapted from Thomas M. Greene's *The Light in Troy* I argue that Paul's strategy of intertextual echo is neither 'sacramental' nor 'eclectic' nor 'heuristic', but *'dialectical'*: it sustains the tension between the world of the ancient text and the world of his own interpretation.

Finally, the closing pages of the book argue that Paul can and should be taken as a model for interpretation of Scripture in the church. Both his readings and his reading strategies should be deemed normative. This recommendation poses enormous difficulties, of course. Are there any operative constraints on hermeneutical freedom if we take Paul as a model? Three are proposed: (1) no reading can be legitimate if it denies the faithfulness of Israel's God to his people; (2) no reading can be legitimate if it denies the death and resurrection of Jesus as the climactic manifestation of God's righteousness; (3) no reading can be legitimate if it fails to shape the readers into a community that embodies the love of God as shown forth in Jesus Christ.

LISTENING FOR ECHOES OF INTERPRETED SCRIPTURE

Craig A. Evans

'How did Paul interpret Israel's Scriptures?'[1] This is the question that animates Richard Hays's scholarly investigation, and the result is a carefully researched and well thought-out work that in my estimation significantly advances the discussion. In this brief review I shall limit my discussion to Chapters 1 and 2, with most of my comments directed to the latter.[2]

In his first chapter Hays assesses Pauline 'intertextuality' in terms of 'metalepsis'. Metalepsis occurs when an older text is echoed in a newer text. It 'places the reader within a field of whispered or unstated correspondences' between these texts.[3] 'Paul's citations of Scripture often function not as proofs but as tropes: they generate new meanings by linking the earlier text (Scripture) to the later (Paul's discourse) in such a way as to produce unexpected correspondences, correspondences that suggest more than they assert.'[4] As an example, Hays argues persuasively that Paul's allusion to Job 13.16 (LXX) in Phil. 1.19 ('will turn out for my deliverance') suggests that Paul wished to portray himself in the role of the righteous sufferer, as paradigmatically prefigured by Job. This exegesis is convincing, not simply because of the verbal correspondence (the *allusion*), but because of several suggestive thematic parallels (the *echoes*) between Philippians and Job.

In my judgment Hays's reasoning in this chapter is sound. What he has identified as 'correspondences' is akin to typology, though implicit, not explicit (as, for example, in 1 Cor. 10.1-13 where Paul compares

---

1. R.B. Hays, *Echoes of Scripture in the Letters of Paul* (New Haven and London: Yale University Press, 1989), p. x.
2. See my review in *CBQ* 53 (1991), pp. 496-98.
3. Hays, *Echoes of Scripture*, p. 20.
4. Hays, *Echoes of Scripture*, p. 24.

the church to Israel in the wilderness).[5] According to typological thinking, these correspondences between biblical contents and the experiences (either real or expected) are written 'for our instruction' (1 Cor. 10.11). Typology is not so much a *method* of exegesis as it is a *presupposition* underlying the Jewish and Christian understanding of Scripture, particularly its historical portions. Typology is based upon the belief that the biblical story (of the past) has some bearing on the present, or, to turn it around, that the present is foreshadowed in the biblical story. Even midrash reflects this understanding of Scripture. J.L. Kugel has recently described midrash as reflecting an 'obsession with past events and the necessity of having them bear on the present'.[6] This is typological thinking, and I think that this is often what lies behind the metalepsis that Hays has rightly observed in Paul's letters.[7]

In his second chapter Hays listens for intertextual echoes in Romans. The result is a truly stimulating and insightful study of this important epistle. According to Hays, Paul has heard the voice of God's righteousness speaking in the Scriptures, a voice that has shaped the apostle's vision of the church. 'Paul rests his case on the claim that his churches, in which Gentiles do in fact join Jews in praising God, must be the eschatological fulfillment of the scriptural vision.'[8] 'God's righteousness, which has now embraced Gentiles among the people of God, includes the promise of God's unbroken faithfulness to Israel. Virtually every text that Paul cites or alludes to is made to circle around this one theme.'[9] Future studies in Romans will have to review the arguments of this chapter carefully.

His exegesis of Rom. 10.5-10, which alludes to parts of Deut. 30.12-14, is insightful: 'the Word of God, now present in the Christian gospel, is the same word of God that was always present to Israel in Torah'.[10] Scripture is certainly heard reverberating in this passage. But Paul has heard more than Scripture itself; he has heard Scripture as it had been interpreted in late antiquity. What suggested to Paul the

5. See vv. 6 and 11 where Paul uses the words τύποι and τυπικῶς, respectively.
6. J.L. Kugel with R.A. Greer, *Early Biblical Interpretation* (Library of Early Christianity, 3; Philadelphia: Westminster Press, 1986), p. 38.
7. For his discussion of typology see Hays, *Echoes of Scripture*, pp. 100-102, pp. 161-62. Hays regards typologies as tropes.
8. Hays, *Echoes of Scripture*, p. 71.
9. Hays, *Echoes of Scripture*, p. 73.
10. Hays, *Echoes of Scripture*, pp. 77-83, quotation from p. 83.

identification of Jesus Christ with the 'word' of Deut. 30.14? Bar. 3.29-30, a passage which Hays does consider,[11] illustrates how the word could be identified with something, or someone, else:

> Who has ascended into heaven
>> and taken her [i.e., Wisdom]
>> and brought her down from the clouds?
> Who has gone across the sea
>> and found her
>> and will buy her with choice gold?

According to Baruch, the word is none other than Wisdom. Since Paul applies wisdom categories to Jesus, indeed, even calls Jesus 'the wisdom of God' (cf. 1 Cor. 1.24, 30), it appears likely that he has resignified Deuteronomy much in the way that the author of Baruch did. Jesus, God's wisdom, has descended from heaven.[12] There is no more need to find someone to ascend to heaven in order to bring Christ down, than there was for someone in the time of Moses to ascend to heaven in order to find God's word.

But Paul speaks of 'descending into the abyss'. This idea is not found in the Hebrew or Greek versions of Deuteronomy 30. Nor is it found in Baruch. Where did Paul get this idea? The word 'abyss' occurs in LXX Jon. 2.6. But that alone would not explain 'descending into the abyss' in place of 'crossing the sea'. The explanation is probably rooted in the Aramaic tradition. Martin McNamara translates *Targ. Neof.* Deut. 30.12-13 as follows (with interpretive additions italicized):[13]

> The Law is not in heaven that one should say:
> *'Would that we had one like the prophet Moses*
> *who would ascend to heaven and fetch it for us*
> and make us hear the commandments that we might do them.'
> Neither is the Law beyond the Great Sea that one may say:
> *'Would that we had one like the prophet Jonah*
> *who would descend into the depths of the Great Sea and bring it up for us*
> and make us hear the commandments that we might do them.'

---

11. Hays, *Echoes of Scripture*, p. 80.

12. See Hays, *Echoes of Scripture*, p. 82.

13. M. McNamara, *The New Testament and the Palestinian Targum to the Pentateuch* (AnBib, 27; Rome: Pontifical Biblical Institute, 1966), pp. 74-75. Portions of this targumic tradition are preserved in the Fragment Targum, esp. the Vatican MS.

The targum's 'descend into the depths' may very well account for Paul's 'descend into the abyss'. Since Jesus may very well have compared himself to Jonah (cf. Mt. 12.40), Paul's preference for the targumic version, indeed, his attraction to the passage itself, may have been due to the presence of the allusion to Jonah.[14] In any case, the echo that we hear in Romans 10 is made up of Scripture *and its exegesis* in late antiquity. It is for this reason that I think that it would be more accurate to speak of the echoes of interpreted Scripture in the letters of Paul.

Those who are inclined to describe the function of Scripture in Paul (and the New Testament in general, for that matter) as *midrash*, should read what Hays has to say.[15] I agree that often 'the label *midrash* tends to bring the interpretive process to a halt, as though it had clarified something'.[16] To identify a passage as midrash does not mean that it has been understood.[17] Hays's point is well taken. Nevertheless, there are studies where the recognition of the presence of midrash in Paul has aided and advanced the interpretive process. William Stegner's study of Rom. 9.6-29 provides a good example.[18] Stegner identifies parallels between Paul and rabbinic interpretation with respect to formal and exegetical details. Recognizing the midrashic features of Paul's use of Scripture clarifies the apostle's technique and argument. The advantage of Stegner's approach is that he takes into account both the echoes of Scripture and the exegetical context against which these echoes should be heard.

There is another area in which I think that Hays could have strengthened his argument. In his treatment of Romans 9–11,[19] Hays

14. The Jonah Targum itself has probably influenced Aramaic Deuteronomy. *Targ. Jon.* 2.4 [2.3E] reads: 'You cast me into the depths'. 'Depths' is the same word as in Neofiti and the Fragment Targum.

15. Hays, *Echoes of Scripture*, pp. 10-14.

16. Hays, *Echoes of Scripture*, p. 14.

17. When J. Drury ('Midrash and Gospel', *Theology* 77 [1974], pp. 291-96) describes the interrelationship of the Synoptic Gospels in terms of 'midrash', what has been clarified? How does this advance synoptic interpretation beyond the results of tradition and redaction criticism?

18. W.R. Stegner, 'Romans 9.6-29—A Midrash', *JSNT* 22 (1984), pp. 37-52. See also W.A. Meeks, '"And Rose Up to Play": Midrash and Paraenesis in 1 Cor. 10.1-22', *JSNT* 16 (1982), pp. 64-78. Hays (*Echoes of Scripture*, pp. 196-97 n. 31) refers to both of these studies as having 'produced helpful insights'.

19. Hays, *Echoes of Scripture*, esp. pp. 66-68.

refers to Paul's 'scandalous inversions' of the scriptural story (e.g., the Jewish people represented by Ishmael and Esau; Gentiles represented by the northern tribes). Accordingly, it is observed that Paul 'deconstructs Scripture's witness to Israel's favored status'.[20] What apparently Hays has not fully realized is that this kind of deconstruction, or 'scandalous' inversion, was frequently practiced by Israel's classical prophets. When in Rom. 11.9-10 Paul cites imprecatory Psalms originally directed against Israel's enemies (Pss. 69.22-23 and 35.8) and applies them against Israel herself, he has employed the hermeneutics of prophetic criticism.[21] He has done what Isaiah did centuries earlier when the seventh-century prophet, for example, alluded to David's great victories, implying that God would once again defeat his enemies—only this time Israel was God's enemy (see Isa. 28.21). When Paul calls his fellow Jews 'enemies' (Rom. 11.28), he has adopted the same hermeneutical mode. His interpretive inversions are no more scandalous than those of Isaiah (though to their respective generations, to be sure, these inversions were indeed scandalous). What Paul engaged in is what many of Israel's prophets and biblical writers engaged in long ago. The Pauline hermeneutic is in fact a biblical hermeneutic.[22]

In sum, I find much in this book that I like. It is refreshing to read work that not only listens carefully to the immediate text, but also listens carefully for the fainter notes of remote text. But this work must take into account the interpretive context. For this reason I think that it would be more accurate to listen for echoes of *interpreted* Scripture, and not just for echoes of Scripture itself.

20. Hays, *Echoes of Scripture*, p. 67.
21. See J.A. Sanders, *Torah and Canon* (Philadelphia: Fortress Press, 1972), pp. 85-90.
22. See P.E. Dinter, 'Paul and the Prophet Isaiah', *BTB* 13 (1983), pp. 48-52; C.A. Evans, 'Paul and the Hermeneutics of "True Prophecy": A Study of Romans 9–11', *Bib* 65 (1984), pp. 560-70.

PAUL AND THEOLOGICAL HISTORY

James A. Sanders

One is so unaccustomed, after Bultmann, to New Testament scholars reading the New Testament scripturally that Hays's work, and especially this book, comes as a welcome surprise. A great deal of New Testament scholarship seems to strive to decanonize the New Testament, reading it synchronically only in terms of its Hellenistic context. In fact, Hays's book is stunning to one who takes the canonical process and canonical hermeneutics seriously.

Hays's approach to Paul is basically intertextual, exploring Scripture as metaphor and its intertextuality as diachronic trope or metalepsis. Taking a clue from Robert Alter, Hays notes that 'literature as language is intrinsically and densely allusive'.[1] With reference to Michael Fishbane's work, Hays notes that within Israel as a reading community all significant speech is scriptural or scripturally-oriented speech.[2] Beyond Fishbane, Hays rightly seeks out the hermeneutics whereby the older word functions in the newer.[3] For Hays that hermeneutic is basically ecclesiocentric. Paul's concern was to establish lines of continuity between Scripture's understanding of Israel as the called people of God and the people in his time being gathered in Christ; these are called now to re-read Scripture in the light of God's just-accomplished work in Christ and continuing work in church and world.

Hays engages early on with the question of who it is that heard or hears the echoes he claims are there, in whom did/does the hermeneu-

---

1. R.B. Hays, *Echoes of Scripture in the Letters of Paul* (New Haven and London: Yale University Press, 1989), p. 20.
2. Hays, *Echoes of Scripture*, p. 21.
3. See my review of Fishbane's *Biblical Interpretation in Ancient Israel* (Oxford: Clarendon Press, 1985) in *CBQ* 49 (1987), pp. 302-305, and of Fishbane, *The Garments of Torah: Essays in Biblical Hermeneutics* (Bloomington and Indianapolis: Indiana University Press, 1989), in *Theology Today* 47 (1991), pp. 433-35.

tical event take place. There are five possible answers to the question: Paul's intention; the perception of the original readers; the text itself; the modern reader's reading; or a community of interpretation. Hays tries to hold them all together in creative tension, and in my mind succeeds remarkably well, largely because this allows him to admit from time to time that the answer to the question may lie in the third or fourth option given above, rather than the first or second. He then offers seven tests for his method but does not pursue them. Instead he rightly notes that

> texts can generate readings that transcend both the conscious intention of the author and all the hermeneutical strictures that we promulgate...To limit our interpretation of Paul's scriptural echoes to what he intended by them is to impose a severe and arbitrary hermeneutical restriction...Later readers will rightly grasp meanings of the figures that may have been veiled from Paul himself.[4]

This comes down to appreciating Scripture not only as historically generated literature but also as canon. What critical scholarship denies to a text the poet, peasant, and preacher may affirm in it. Texts in Scripture did not necessarily make it into the canon because of what an original speaker or writer intended; they might well have made it in because of what the experiences of later communities permitted them to see in the texts. This truth can be affirmed for much of Scripture. Hays does not claim to be dealing with the canonical process in this book; but whether he as its author intended it or not, he does indeed deal throughout the book with aspects of this process.

Hays's insistence that Paul's basic hermeneutic is ecclesiocentric rather than christocentric is enlightening and in part convincing. Hays does not see Paul as claiming that the old Israel κατὰ σάρκα (1 Cor. 10.18) has been replaced by a new spiritual Israel that will never fall into sin and corruption; on the contrary, Paul challenges the church at Corinth for having so fallen (1 Cor. 3.1-4)! Rather, and this is a crux in Hays's argument, 'there always has been and always will be only one Israel...into that Israel Gentile Christians such as the Corinthians have now been absorbed'.[5] For Paul, taking Deuteronomy seriously, there is but one God and one Israel. In all this Hays is basically right.

But one must be careful. Paul's hermeneutic is not ecclesiocentric, it

4. Hays, *Echoes of Scripture*, p. 33.
5. Hays, *Echoes of Scripture*, p. 97.

is theocentric. There is indeed but one God at work throughout
Scripture. As Hays rightly notes, Paul's reading of Scripture is not
typological as that term is normally understood;[6] Paul does not fret
about correspondences between types and anti-types. Rather, Paul's
argument, like Isaiah's and Luke's, and indeed much else in the Bible,
is from theological history. What can we discern about God's current
activity? One turns to (*drashes*) Scripture to discern a pattern of
divine activity and speech and to seek light on what is going on in the
present (whenever that might be). Paul thus affirms God's past work;
it is not superseded. And Paul affirms Scripture; it is the record of
that work. Read in this way, Rom. 9.30–10.4 does not pit faith against
works, but asks in whose works one has faith, God's or one's own.
Hays does not express the idea in quite this way; but he could—or
perhaps should—have done.

Deuteronomy 30 weighs heavily in Paul's (and Hays's) thinking.
Hays cites the well-known passage from *B. Meṣ.* 59b which relates the
dialogue among Rabbis Eliezer, Joshua, and Jeremiah and contrasts it
to Paul's understanding (Rom. 10.5-10). In the former passage Eliezer
calls on heaven to affirm by signs and miracles his halakhic
interpretation of Scripture, and miracles are reported to have
occurred on the spot. But his interlocutors remained unimpressed with
Joshua, citing Deut. 30.12, 'It is not in heaven'. This apparently
amused God considerably and, laughing for joy, he said, 'My children
have defeated me, my children have defeated me'. Hays takes this to
be the opposite of Paul's meaning, which stressed Scripture's 'living
flexibility and capacity for hermeneutical transformation to disclose
God's grace in ways unfathomed by prior generations of readers'.[7]
But the passage from *Baba Meṣi'a* can be read in just the same way,
that is, Scripture's 'right' interpretation is not in some *tavnit* (Idea, or
Form) in heaven, that is, not in God's hands to be confirmed by
miracles from heaven; it is in the hands of succeeding generations of
interpreters who read and re-read Scripture out of ever-changing
community needs. God gave Torah on Mount Sinai, but once he had
done so it belonged to Israel. Modern scholarship may be quite sure
what an Isaiah meant, but once his utterance (or its heir in the
memory of his disciples) became community property (canon), it was

---

6. Hays, *Echoes of Scripture*, pp. 100-104.
7. Hays, *Echoes of Scripture*, p. 3.

out there on its own diachronic and intertextual pilgrimage.[8]

The same passage affirms that 'Yahweh your God will circumcise your heart and the heart of your seed [descendants] to love Yahweh your God with all your heart and with all your being that you may live' (Deut. 30.6). This astounding promise has a history and a context that Hays failed to note; it echoes those passages using the concept of the circumcised heart.[9] In Deut. 10.16 and Jer. 4.4 Israel is exhorted to circumcise its hearts to God. This metaphor rests at the heart of all the prophetic pleas in the eighth and seventh centuries, before the destruction of Israel and Judah, to repent and return to God's ways. Clearly the people could not do it themselves. Then the affirmation is made that, in the very adversity of the destruction and death of old Israel and Judah, and God's subsequent act of restoration (resurrection), God himself will effect the transformation. This had been affirmed already by Hosea (6.1), Jeremiah (30.12-13; 31.31-34), and Ezekiel (36.26-27). What was not effected by human will (through exhortation) will be effected by divine surgery in the adversity itself (Isa. 51.7). The adversity was punishment for sin, no doubt about it; but it had a further, positive purpose. It was a divine operation effecting a new Israel by death and resurrection (Deut. 32.39); and both the death and new life were the work of God.

These echoes become crucial in reading 2 Corinthians 3, where Hays rightly notes that Ezek. 36.26-27 is vital for understanding the passage.[10] There Paul seems to set letter against spirit. But as Hays, again rightly, notes, that is a misreading. It is a question of where and how the writing is done. The church at Corinth is Paul's letter of recommendation; that letter (ἐπιστολή) lives in their hearts. How? By God's act in the judgment/salvation event, God's spirit has been put inside the people (Ezek. 36.27; just like the Torah written inside them on their heart in Jer. 31.33), and God will see to it that they obey. Clearly, as in the Jeremiah passage, God's Torah/Word is no longer only commandments written by God on stone tablets; it is written by

8. See the introduction to J. Rosenblatt and J. Sitterson (eds.), *'Not in Heaven': Coherence and Complexity in Biblical Narrative* (Bloomington: Indiana University Press, 1991); see also my essay, 'The Integrity of Biblical Pluralism', in the same volume.

9. See my essay, 'Deuteronomy', in B.W. Anderson (ed.), *The Books of the Bible*, I (New York: Macmillan, 1989), pp. 89-102, esp. pp. 92-93.

10. Hays, *Echoes of Scripture*, pp. 122-53.

God's spirit on the people's hearts. It is in this sense that the letter (γράμμα) kills and that God kills (ἀποκτείνειν/κτείνειν—Deut. 32.39; 2 Cor. 3.6); and it is in this sense that God brings to life (ζῆν ποιεῖν/ζῳοποιεῖν—Deut. 32.39; 2 Cor. 3.6). God is the God of death and of life. To rest with reading Scripture in the old way, only by God's letter given and granted on Mount Sinai, is to miss its significance revealed by this further act of God in calling an unboundaried people through Christ. This next chapter in God's theological history forces a re-reading of the old texts, both to affirm that God has once more acted in consonance with the record of previous divine work and to insist that every new chapter throws light on those that precede it.

Echoes of Scripture is a remarkable book. For those of us who read the literature of the Tanak and of Early Judaism diachronically as well as synchronically, from inception through to the fall of Rome in 70 CE, it is like a beacon of light and a breath of fresh air. The point of these reflections on it is that more can be affirmed of Scripture's intertextual depths than even Hays has seen; it is a question of the ongoing canonical process.

The crucial question is, wherein lie the constraints, if one thus dares to move beyond historical/critical (ever-changing) determinations of 'original' or authorial intentionality? Addressing that question is a part of the canonical process; it is an exercise of canonical criticism. The rules of Hillel, as well as those of Ishmael and the classical 32, arose as constraints on a process already under way of adapting Torah and canon to ever-changing cultural and social situations and problems. But they failed to constrain the vibrant convictions that Scripture was canonical (of continuing relevance and not purely historical); all sorts of hermeneutic devices were, and continue to be, brought to bear on the adaptive process.[11]

In a recent seminar of mine Hays's book was scrutinized with the following question in mind: what difference would comparative midrash make to each of Hays's claims about intertextual echoes in Paul. How did the very same First Testament passages and concepts 'echo' in Jewish literature prior to Paul? What flexibility or fluidity of application of the older word in the stream of newer words is evident from inception in the Tanak down to Paul? And by what hermeneutic did the tradent in each case effect changes to the older concept by

---

11. See, e.g., my discussion in *From Sacred Story to Sacred Text* (Philadelphia: Fortress Press, 1987), pp. 9-39, pp. 125-51.

means of the newer? Tracing the pilgrimage from inception within the Tanak itself (following Fishbane's emphasis, but also going beyond Fishbane) through the Septuagint and its descendants, the Dead Sea Scrolls, Apocrypha, Pseudepigrapha, Philo, Josephus, Tannaic literature, and the Vulgate, provides a clear view of the breadth of function that Scripture and tradition had in a stream of communities of interpretation before its function in Paul or the Gospels; discerning the intertextual hermeneutics all along the way provides a clear view of what kinds of constraints, if any, were operative in the canonical process.

DOING THE TEXT'S WORK FOR IT:
RICHARD HAYS ON PAUL'S USE OF SCRIPTURE

William Scott Green

Anyone who chooses to specialize in the writings of Paul had better be a masochist—or so the late Oxford professor George Caird used to warn his graduate theology students. The primary materials are so meager, and the secondary literature so extensive, that the effort to say something new threatens a career of frustration and suffering. Caird's gloomy assessment has proven only a modest deterrent. The atavism of scholarship as a profession notwithstanding, the energetic persistence of Pauline studies shows that the epistles raise issues that continue to be important and unresolved—perhaps important because unresolved—in the study of early Judaism and Christianity.

Richard Hays's *Echoes of Scripture in the Letters of Paul* attempts both to examine Paul's letters in a novel way and to resolve some long-standing issues in Christian theology, particularly concerning the status of 'Israel's Scripture'. (This is as good a term as any. It reminds us that we cannot call Paul's Bible the Old Testament, because for him it was not. We also cannot call it the Hebrew Scriptures, since it was Greek. And, as D. Moody Smith remarks, for various textual reasons it is more accurate to say that Paul's use of Scripture is 'septuagintal' than to say that he uses the Septuagint.[1])

Hays's book argues on two fronts: theological and literary. On the theological front, it seeks to disprove the vulgar assertion that Israel's Scripture was unimportant in the shaping of Paul's teaching, and the more subtle assertion that Paul's use of Israel's Scripture was supersessionist, which is to say, apologetic and self-serving. On the literary front, the book supplies a textual analysis to show that Israel's

---

1.   D.M. Smith, 'The Pauline Literature', in D.A. Carson and H.G. Williamson (eds.), *It is Written: Scripture Citing Scripture: Essays in Honor of Barnabas Lindars* (Cambridge: Cambridge University Press, 1988), pp. 265-91, esp. p. 273.

Scripture had a 'constitutive role' in the formation of Paul's writing. In the intellectual design of the book, the literary argument is supposed to clinch the theological one.

The book's claim to novelty is less in the content of these positions than in the scope of its literary attention and its mode of literary argument. Hays uses the concept of 'intertextuality' and carries forward the insights of John Hollander, Thomas Greene, Herbert Marks, and, to a lesser extent, Harold Bloom to show that Israel's Scripture pervades Paul's writing and influences it viscerally, almost ubiquitously, far beyond the level of mere formal citation. To make that case, the book pays special attention to the way Paul's letters allude to Israel's Scripture, the way that Scripture is echoed subtly, delicately and often subliminally in the epistles' language.

In particular, the book elaborates Herbert Marks's suggestion[2] that Paul's writing appropriates Israel's Scripture with a trope called metalepsis or transumption, a kind of typology in which, according to Harold Bloom, 'a word is substituted metonymically for a word in a previous trope'. In Bloom's view, 'when properly accomplished', this trope 'produces the illusion of having fathered one's own fathers'.[3] In Hays's book, metalepsis refers especially to the 'unstated or suppressed (transumed) points of resonance between...two texts', to 'a field of whispered or unstated correspondences',[4] and is a primary mode of Pauline hermeneutics.

The book employs a minimalist notion of intertextuality, using it to mean simply the presence of an older text in a newer one. The philosophical and ideological arguments that often accompany discussions of intertextuality, particularly concerning the inherent instability of all texts, are barely mentioned here. Likewise, the book eschews a 'systematic distinction'[5] between allusion, which usually connotes a conscious authorial act and perhaps a knowing audience, and echo, which requires neither. This sometimes blurs the focus of the book's analyses.

Nevertheless, the demonstrations of scriptural allusion and echo that

2. H. Marks, 'Pauline Typology and Revisionary Criticism', *JAAR* 52 (1984), pp. 71-92.

3. Marks, 'Pauline Typology', p. 75.

4. R.B. Hays, *Echoes of Scripture in the Letters of Paul* (New Haven and London: Yale University Press, 1989), p. 20.

5. Hays, *Echoes of Scripture*, p. 29.

make up the bulk of the book are the best part of the work, and it is a pleasure to admire the literary sensitivity and erudition that they display. By so turning up the volume on these echoes, the book gives Paul's letters a depth, a richness, a biblical texture that most readers probably could not apprehend unaided. These demonstrations also slow the letters down and make them seem less shrill—more thoughtful, more reflective.

The demonstrations usually work by noting a verbal correspondence between an epistle and a biblical text, which then leads to a more elaborate examination of the larger literary and theological context of the biblical text and a demonstration of the new meaning that results when that context is applied to Paul's circumstances. Thus, let us select a particularly accessible example, part of a verse from Job 13.16. 'Even this will turn out for my deliverance, for deceit shall not enter in before him', echoes in Phil. 1.19: '...through your prayers and the help of the Spirit of Jesus Christ this will turn out for my deliverance'. After describing the larger setting of the verse from Job, and the different circumstances of Job and Paul—for both of whom the image of prisoner is fitting—Hays concludes, 'Job's tenacious assertion of his own rectitude becomes in Paul's mouth a triumphant affirmation of trust in the power and faithfulness of the God who raised Jesus from the dead. Those who have ears to hear will detect the contrapuntal effect and delight in it.'[6]

The book's demonstrations of scriptural echoes in Paul's epistles are relentlessly—indeed, exclusively—textual. The book's argument neither presents them as historical nor requires that they be understood as historical. The presence of these echoes, to say nothing of their plausibility or credibility, in no way depends—indeed cannot depend—on Paul's intention to make them, or on any reader's ever having actually understood them. In a pointed juxtaposition of two rabbinic images, Hays claims that, 'Despite all the careful hedges that we plant around texts, meaning has a way of leaping over, like sparks. Texts are not inert; they burn and throw fragments of flame on their rising heat'.[7] For this reason, the book asserts, 'later readers will rightly grasp meanings of the figures [of speech] that may have been veiled from Paul himself'.[8]

6. Hays, *Echoes of Scripture*, p. 22.
7. Hays, *Echoes of Scripture*, p. 33.
8. Hays, *Echoes of Scripture*, p. 33.

Despite its admirable efforts at historical sensitivity, and its awareness of five 'distinguishable possibilities' of the locus of 'intertextual
meaning',[9] this book cannot but display the thoroughgoing extent to
which intertextuality really is the reader's work, not the writer's.
Consequently, we can only understand such historically-descriptive-
sounding phrases as 'no reader familiar with the psalter could possibly
fail to hear the resonance...'[10] or 'anyone who had ever prayed Psalm
143 from the heart would instantly recognize...'[11] as referring
neither to Paul nor even to his contemporaries but to the learned
author of this book—anxious to share his scholarly discoveries. The
same applies to the book's discussion of 'Paul as reader of Scripture'.

These necessary qualifications and clarifications aside, the book's
demonstrations of scriptural echo—even when speculative—are
responsible, disciplined, well within the range of textual plausibility
and imaginative possibility, and presented with artful suggestion. They
strongly suggest that in the Pauline epistles, to use Herbert Marks's
language again, Israel's Scripture was more than 'expository', likely
'constitutive', and perhaps even 'initiatory'.[12] On the basis of these
demonstrations of echo, it is reasonable to think—speaking metaphorically now—that Paul 'spoke Scripture'. The question is: what did he
make it say?

Hays's book uses the demonstration of the thick scripturality of
Paul's writing to confound the claim of supersession. It argues that
Paul saw in Israel's Scripture a coherent narrative of election and
promise, that his allusions 'conjure up...narratively ordered patterns
of connotation',[13] and that, as a consequence, 'Paul's great struggle is
not a struggle to assert his own authority over Scripture; it is, rather,
a dialectical struggle to maintain the integrity of Scripture in relation
to that proclamation to justify his startling claims about what the God
of Israel had elected to do in Jesus Christ'.[14] Paul does not 'wrest the
Scriptures from Israel';[15] he does not 'subordinate Scripture' to his

9. Hays, *Echoes of Scripture*, pp. 26-27.
10. Hays, *Echoes of Scripture*, p. 49.
11. Hays, *Echoes of Scripture*, p. 52.
12. Marks, 'Pauline Typology', p. 74.
13. Hays, *Echoes of Scripture*, p. 158.
14. Hays, *Echoes of Scripture*, p. 159.
15. Hays, *Echoes of Scripture*, p. 95.

own 'belated conceptions'.[16] Rather, 'Paul's urgent hermeneutical project...is to bring Scripture and gospel into a mutually interpretive relation in which the righteousness of God is truly disclosed'.[17]

This part of the book's argument is less than convincing. Even if we grant, for the sake of argument, the book's claim that in Paul's writing Scripture and gospel are in tensive and dialectical relationship, does it follow that the literary is co-essential with the theological? Does a literary relationship between two texts necessarily imply a comparable theological one?

Hays grants that the constraint on Paul's interpretation of Scripture is Paul's 'conviction that the Law and the Prophets bear witness to the gospel of God's righteousness, now definitively disclosed in the death and resurrection of Jesus Messiah'.[18] If so, does this not mean that the narrative of election and promise that Paul sees in Israel's Scripture is completed by something outside Scripture, something non-scriptural? If so, then in what does the 'integrity' of Scripture consist? If the narrative of election and promise is incomplete in itself, what does the notion of the 'integrity' of Scripture mean? It is not clear how this argument exempts Paul from the charge of supersession, made in various ways by Harnack, Bultmann, and Herbert Marks.

The claim that Paul maintains the 'integrity' of Israel's Scripture allows Hays to assert that Paul's writing is continuous with that Scripture. The book argues that, at the deeper level of the narrative unity between law and gospel,

> Paul can hardly be accused of imposing his own conceptions on the earlier tradition. Rather, he has selected fundamental themes of the biblical story as hermeneutical keys to the meaning of the tradition. The selection of key themes differs in important ways from the selection made in rabbinic Judaism, but Paul's claim of hermeneutical continuity is grounded no less thoroughly in the texts themselves.[19]

The assertion of a Pauline hermeneutic 'grounded...in the texts' of Israel's Scripture is not presented as a consequence of theological conviction or ideological necessity. Interestingly—and surprisingly in a book shaped by intertextuality and devoted to figuration—it is presented literally, as a matter of brute textual fact: 'The extraordinarily

16. Hays, *Echoes of Scripture*, p. 95.
17. Hays, *Echoes of Scripture*, p. 176.
18. Hays, *Echoes of Scripture*, p. 161.
19. Hays, *Echoes of Scripture*, p. 157.

interesting feature of Paul's hermeneutical strategy...is his reverence for Scripture's own indirect and allusive mode of revelation, which he honors by imitating...Paul's own discourse recapitulates the allusive complexity of his great subtext'.[20]

This slip into literalism and objectivity results from the minimalist notion of intertextuality Hays uses to interpret Paul's letters. As a technique, intertextual analysis aims to display the varied connections between any piece of writing and its textual predecessors. It does so to undercut the notions of an autonomous author or a self-contained text—ideas especially important in creative writing, which celebrates and derives power from a claim of authorial originality. The larger purpose of intertextual analysis is to undergird and underscore an ideological position about the fluidity of textual meaning. Hays uses intertextuality more as a technique than as an ideology and does not push much beyond the domain of the text itself. Hence, in this book, the application of intertextuality to Paul's writings—which are polemical and self-consciously exegetical—reveals, and in fact reinforces, just what the letters want hearers and readers to apprehend: that Christian teaching is 'grounded...in' Israel's Scripture rather than imposed upon it.

In literary analysis, if the texts under study are constructed to do precisely what the analytical method seeks to expose, then the method does the text's work for it. The language of analysis loses its critical force and falls into mere descriptiveness, as if it were simply telling us how things are. So it is in this book's argument: Paul's writing is presented as continuous with Israel's Scripture because it reads that Scripture the way that Scripture reads itself. The old theological claim of Paul's continuity with Scripture—with new subtlety, to be sure—re-emerges here as a matter of literary fact, rather than of doctrine or faith. This sort of argument is less an analysis of religion than a specimen of it.

20. Hays, *Echoes of Scripture*, p. 155.

ECHOES AND INTERTEXTUALITY:
ON THE ROLE OF SCRIPTURE IN PAUL'S THEOLOGY

J. Christiaan Beker

I would like to address three areas of inquiry, which in my mind have raised several questions. I shall consider them under the following headings: (1) literary-critical and historical questions; (2) exegetical questions; and (3) theological questions.

Literary-Critical and Historical Questions

In terms of Hays's overall scheme, I would like to know what the constraints are that curtail both Paul's imaginative freedom and that of Hays. For instance, when are echoes whispers, when trumpets, when muffled, subliminal sounds? To use a Dutch image, how is anyone to know from where the sounds of foghorns are coming amidst their plaintive voices in the fog? In other words, how can 'echoes' serve as constraints,[1] when they are muffled, subliminal, or 'latent'?

It seems to me that one of Hays's main spokesmen, Michael Fishbane, is much clearer about constraints for intertextuality when he specifies as the two major criteria for haggadic exegesis first explicit citation, and secondly density of occurrence.[2] Therefore, to cite an example, the essay by Gail O'Day on intertextual relations between Jer. 9.22-31 and 1 Cor. 1.26-31 strikes me as much more convincing than many of Hays's echoes, because she adheres to Fishbane's density of occurrence criterion.[3] Compare her approach to Hays's fanciful reading of Phil.

---

1. R.B. Hays, *Echoes of Scripture in the Letters of Paul* (New Haven and London: Yale University Press, 1989), esp. pp. 190-91.

2. M. Fishbane, *Biblical Interpretation in Ancient Israel* (New York: Oxford University Press, 1985).

3. G.R. O'Day, 'Jeremiah 9.22-23 and 1 Corinthians 1.26-31: A Study in Intertextuality', *JBL* 109 (1990), pp. 259-67.

1.19 in which he hears an echo from Job 13.16.[4] Consider also his statement that 'another echo murmurs unbidden in the ear'.[5] This echo supposedly resonates from Job 19.25-26: 'For I know that my Redeemer lives...' In fact, Hays's references to 'faint echoes', a 'synthetic hermeneutical act', a 'teasing datum',[6] and especially his reading of Rom. 8.36[7] seem to me quite unconvincing.

What actually is the communication-structure in Paul's hermeneutic of Scripture?[8] How many echoes of specific scriptural passages are solely in *Paul's* head—and how many does he presuppose in his *hearers*? Moreover, since Paul intends to *persuade* his audience, he may well skip details by his scriptural argument—as we all do—*or* he may simply use Scripture to impress his audience with his profundity, while the contours and context of a specific fragment of the Old Testament passage are in fact not the necessary presupposition for the validity of his argument.

In this context I would have expected a more detailed critique of the shortcomings of the pesher and midrashic methods. Is it not true that a midrashic exegete selects that piece from a *traditum* which suits his immediate purpose, without resonating the total text?

In what specific way does Hays conceive of the relation between historical and literary criticism? Notwithstanding his remarks about the issue in the preface[9] and elsewhere, intertextual echoes seem necessarily to produce an ahistorical conception of Paul's letters. Hence my question: how is an intertextual method able to maintain one of the most important features of these letters, the confluence of coherence and contingency?

Exegetical Issues

In what way is the flow of Paul's argument clarified, for example, in Romans, by the many over-arching echoes of Scripture, especially

---

4. Hays, *Echoes of Scripture*, pp. 21-24.
5. Hays, *Echoes of Scripture*, pp. 23-24.
6. Hays, *Echoes of Scripture*, p. 24.
7. Hays, *Echoes of Scripture*, pp. 57-63.
8. Cf. Hays, *Echoes of Scripture*, p. 24.
9. Hays, *Echoes of Scripture*, p. xi.

those in Romans 9–11, which according to Hays form the climax of the whole letter? According to Hays, 'Deuteronomy 32 contains Romans *in nuce*',[10] a statement which he backs up by two considerations:

1.   Rom. 10.19 and 15.10 cite respectively Deut. 32.21 and 32.43 in an explicit fashion.
2.   The overall scheme of the Song of Moses 'describes God's election of and care for Israel (Deut. 32.6-14), Israel's inexplicable rebellion (Deut. 32.15-18, cf. 32.5), God's judgment upon them (Deut. 32.19-35), and—ultimately and mysteriously—God's final deliverance and vindication of his own people (Deut 32.36-43)'.[11]

However, apart from the fact that the overall scheme of Deuteronomy 32 does not seem to apply to *all of Romans*, but only to the movement of Romans 9–11, what should the reader do with the other explicit citation of Deuteronomy 32 in Rom. 12.19 (Deut. 32.35; cf. also Deut. 32.4 in Rom. 9.14)? There one can hardly claim the presence of an overall salvation scheme, because Paul uses in this text an isolated prooftext from Deuteronomy 32. In other words, how can Deuteronomy 32 contain Romans *in nuce*, when the total of explicit citations from Deuteronomy 32 is limited to three occurrences (10.19; 12.19; 15.10)? How can one claim in the face of this evidence that the rest of Deuteronomy 32 is present as a 'pervasive echo'?

Moreover, how pervasive actually is the intertextual scriptural echo in Romans? How can Hays maintain the crucial importance of the Old Testament Scriptures in all of Romans, when a superficial glance at the letter shows that, whereas scriptural references abound in chs. 1–4 and 9–11, they are almost completely absent in the crucial chs. 5–8 and sharply reduced in chs. 12–14, in order to reappear as the conclusion of the letter in ch. 15 (cf. vv. 9, 10, 11, 12, 21)?

Although Rom. 15.1-13 is crucial for Hays's argument, it seems arbitrary to call these verses the climax of the letter, since Paul's description of his apostolic office in Rom. 15.14-21 is much more climactic. The peculiar appearance and disappearance of Scripture in Romans can only be explained if we pay attention to the social

---

10. Hays, *Echoes of Scripture*, p. 164.
11. Hays, *Echoes of Scripture*, p. 164.

situation of the Roman church, that is, to the relation of coherence and contingency in the letter.

Furthermore, is it not remarkable that—Hays's bold claims about the crucial theological importance of Scripture for Paul notwithstanding—citations from the Old Testament are rare in some of Paul's other letters (for example, Philippians, 1 Thessalonians, Philemon)? Is it not true that Paul basically concentrates on the use of Scripture only when he is engaged with Judaism and Judaizers, that is, when the contingent situation forces him to do so? And finally, if indeed intertextuality and scriptural resonance are so crucial for Paul, do we then have to conclude that his pupils in the New Testament completely misunderstood him, by practically ignoring Scripture? (See, for example, the Pastoral Epistles, Colossians, and 2 Thessalonians, with Ephesians in some ways an exception.) It seems that where the Jewish question is no longer an issue in the Gentile church, the hermeneutic of Old Testament Scripture is left behind.

A crucial text for Hays is Rom. 10.5-10, whose discussion he saves for the conclusion of his chapter on Romans[12] and implicitly returns to in his final chapter, entitled 'The Word is Near You'.[13] I am surprised at the apodictic manner in which Hays, first, rejects the adversative conjunction in v. 6 (Rom. 10.5 and 10.6 '*must* not stand in antithesis to one another'[14]); secondly, claims that the righteousness from the law (10.5) and that from faith (10.6) are used 'synonymously', because Paul 'quotes Moses in both verses'; and thirdly, subsequently paraphrases Rom. 10.1-6, 8-9 in a way which fuses Lev. 18.5 with Deut. 30.14.[15]

I would argue that the interpretation of τέλος νόμου (v. 4) is determined by vv. 5 and 6. In other words, the conjunction δέ (v. 6) must be adversative, because it contrasts Moses in Lev. 18.5 not with Moses in Deut. 30.11-14, but rather with the personification of ἡ δὲ ἐκ πίστεως δικαιοσύνη (v. 6), that is, with a term that actually forms the theme of the whole letter (i.e. the Habakkuk citation in

12. Hays, *Echoes of Scripture*, pp. 73-83.
13. Hays, *Echoes of Scripture*, pp. 154-92.
14. Hays, *Echoes of Scripture*, p. 76, my emphasis.
15. Hays, *Echoes of Scripture*, p. 77.

Rom. 1.17) and is the equivalent of Christ and the gospel (Hab. 2.4).

Indeed, the argument in Romans (cf. also Galatians) has already determined—*before* we read ch. 10—that the νόμος, embodied in Lev. 18.5, can only condemn us (Rom. 3.9, 10-20). In other words, Paul *presupposes* the *negative* element of Lev. 18.5 in order to highlight the ῥῆμα of the gospel (v. 8), a move similar to the one he makes in Gal. 3.11. Moreover, the emphasis in Deuteronomy 30 with respect to the Torah (three times: 'to do it') is omitted by Paul in the climactic v. 8, because Paul underscores—contrary to Deuteronomy— πίστις and not the *mizwoth* of the Torah.

Thus, I claim that Hab. 2.4 is *the* crucial Old Testament text for Paul. This text is not only contrasted to Lev. 18.5 in Gal. 3.11, but it also determines his reading of Deuteronomy 30 and may well be the 'echo' which guides Paul.

Some Theological Questions

My previous discussion of the issues involved in Rom. 10.4-10 is related to some theological questions that I want to raise, albeit in a succinct manner.

Hays's emphasis on one basic continuity in Paul between Israel and Christianity, that is, between law and gospel, is certainly important, especially as a corrective of the views of Martin Luther and Rudolf Bultmann. However, does Hays pay enough attention to the discontinuity within the continuity, that is, to the fact that Paul's interpretation of the Old Testament rejects the ethnocentricity of the law (as inherent in the Jewish understanding of the law) for the sake of the inclusion of the Gentiles into the Jewish heritage? In other words, the fusion of law and gospel in Paul does not seem to be as smooth as Hays suggests. This discontinuous aspect is clearly evident in comparing Paul's interpretation of Scripture during his Pharisaic period with his Christian interpretation (cf., for example, the *diastases* between law and gospel in Rom. 7.7-25).

We might wonder whether the work of Krister Stendahl and E.P. Sanders influences our treatment of Judaism so heavily these days that their important contributions are unduly exaggerated and—as it were—considered to be dogmatic, unassailable truth.

Hays's notion of an ecclesiocentric hermeneutic is appealing and intriguing, and he makes a compelling case for it. However, at least two questions arise that relate to this matter:

1. How is an ecclesiocentric hermeneutic related to a christo-centric hermeneutic? Can they really be separated from each other, since Paul's concept of the σῶμα Χριστοῦ is strictly christocentric?

2. How in turn is an ecclesiocentric hermeneutic related to Paul's apocalyptic perspective, a perspective which Hays correctly emphasizes?

Let me discuss the second question at greater length. If Paul's apoca-lyptic perspective has a *theocentric* focus and climax, in terms of which the church is only a *proleptic* sign, does this mean that Hays actually makes the ecclesiology of Ephesians normative for Paul's theological construal? And if that is true in some way, does not the claim for an ecclesiocentric center of Paul's theology actually propose a form of realized eschatology for Paul's theology, because—according to Hays—*all the promises of God* in the Old Testament are fulfilled in the transformed community of the church. In this context, I do not think that Rom. 15.1-13 focuses in a one-sided way on the *church* of Jews and Gentiles, but rather on the δοξάζειν and praise of *God* (cf. vv. 6, 7, 11), climaxing in the hope of God's final theophany (v. 13).

Finally, the way in which Hays relates Scripture/Word of God to the Spirit, embodied in the transformed community, remains unclear to me. Is he here imposing a Methodist hermeneutic on Paul with the result that the Word is now fully fused with the gift of the Spirit? Does this mean that the Word has now lost its critical function, because it has reached its true fulfillment in a transformed church—a church which embodies the Spirit completely? Does this possibly suggest to the reader that the church no longer needs to hear the 'written Word' in its *critical* function, that is, in its *'overagainstness'* to the church?

ON THE REBOUND:
A RESPONSE TO CRITIQUES OF *ECHOES OF SCRIPTURE IN THE
LETTERS OF PAUL*

Richard B. Hays

It is a distinct honor to have my work given a careful reading by Craig A. Evans, James A. Sanders, William Scott Green, and J. Christiaan Beker. I have found their responses instructive, and I am grateful for the opportunity to carry forward the discussion initiated by *Echoes of Scripture in the Letters of Paul*. The book was conceived not as a definitive treatment of its topic but as a probe, an attempt to pose some new questions about familiar but intractable texts. Consequently, it is fitting for the conversation to continue. I welcome the opportunity to respond to the discerning critiques of my colleagues.

1. *Response to Craig A. Evans*

Craig Evans has rightly focused attention on my plea for greater care in our use of the terms 'midrash' and 'typology'; the latter is—as Evans puts it—'not so much a *method* of exegesis as it is a *presupposition* underlying the Jewish and Christian understanding of Scripture', and the former is not so much a *literary form* as it is an *activity*, whose hermeneutical strategies and results require close investigation in each actual instance. I am pleased that Evans finds my cautionary words apt. His substantive response to my interpretations demonstrates the value of pushing beyond these labels to consider in more careful detail how Paul reads Scripture.

Evans raises two important matters for discussion, both of which I take to be friendly suggestions for further development of my proposals. First, Paul the Apostle does not come as a *tabula rasa* to the reading of Scripture; he interprets within a Jewish hermeneutical tradition. 'Paul has heard more than Scripture itself; he has heard

Scripture as it had been interpreted in late antiquity.' Thus, 'it would be more accurate to speak of the echoes of interpreted Scripture in the letters of Paul'. (Sanders makes a similar point: see further discussion below.) Secondly, Evans suggests that Paul's revisionary interpretations that subvert Israel's favored status before God are less startling than my discussion would make them appear: Paul is practicing a 'hermeneutics of prophetic criticism' already well developed in Israel's classical prophets.

The first of these points is the weightier challenge to the working method of *Echoes*. The phenomena of intertextuality in Paul are more complex, Evans contends, than my interpretations allow. His example offers a useful illustration: the reference in Rom. 10.7 to a 'descent into the abyss' must be understood as an echo of *Targ. Neof.* Deut. 30.13. (Or perhaps the echo is not of the Targum itself but rather of an interpretative tradition attested independently by the Targum; I assume that Evans means the latter.) In this case, we must reckon with at least a four-part polyphony: Deuteronomy (as mediated through the LXX), Baruch, Neofiti, and Paul.

This example is useful for several reasons. As Evans notes, my interpretation of the passage had already drawn attention to the importance of the Baruch passage as a middle term between Deuteronomy 30 and Romans 10: the traditional identification of Torah with Wisdom allows Paul, presupposing a Wisdom Christology, to interpret 'the word' of Deuteronomy as a figurative pointer to Christ.[1] Thus, Evans and I have no disagreement in principle about the necessity of discerning multilayered intertextual echoes. Indeed, Evans's challenge allows me to reiterate a point perhaps insufficiently emphasized in the book: my discussion of Paul's intertextual hermeneutics in no way forecloses the possibility of extrabiblical echoes and influences in Paul's letters. I have no stake in arguing for an unmediated encounter between Paul and Scripture. (The methodological difficulty, of course, is to know how to distinguish between traditions already known to Paul and those that emerged later, either independently or even in reaction against Paul's exegesis.) Whether the non-scriptural echoes

1. This suggestion is not, of course, original; my discussion was significantly informed by M.J. Suggs, '"The Word Is Near You": Romans 10.6-10 within the Purpose of the Letter', in W.R. Farmer, C.F.D. Moule, and R.R. Niebuhr (eds.), *Christian History and Interpretation: Studies Presented to John Knox* (Cambridge: Cambridge University Press, 1967), pp. 289-312.

come from Greco-Roman culture or from the traditions of Jewish biblical interpretation, Paul's discourse is performed within the linguistic symphony (or cacophony, as the case may be) of his culture. As critical listeners, we can identify some of the major parts in the score, but none of us at this historical distance can hope to recover all the resonances that a competent listener contemporary with Paul would have heard. We do the best we can.

So where do Evans and I differ? I had proposed that the 'abyss' motif in Rom. 10.7 is derived from texts like Sir. 24.5, which speaks of Wisdom making the circuit of the vault of heaven and walking in the depths of the abyss. This still seems to me to be a valid reading, in view of the close affinities between Sir. 24.5 and Bar. 3.29-30. Evans, however, has offered a more compelling suggestion—a clearer echo— by pointing to *Targ. Neof.*, where the 'abyss' motif is explicitly employed in the interpretation of Deut. 30.12-13. It seems entirely likely that Paul knew (or even presupposed that his readers knew) this tradition.[2]

In this instance, Evans has offered a better reading because he is a more competent hearer: that is, he brings to the hearing of Romans an ear tuned to a tradition that was not 'in the ear' for me. His reference to the Targum enriches our hearing of the text of Romans without invalidating my identification of Sirach as one overtone also present here. Now we have at least five parts in the polyphony.

This is exactly the sort of complex reading that is urged upon us by the example of John Hollander, whose work on literary echo was catalytic for my study of Paul: in *The Figure of Echo*, Hollander seeks to trace the way in which motifs and images are passed along through literary traditions in such a way that they gather significations through time. For example, in the invocation of Book III of *Paradise Lost* Milton coins a simile comparing his own poetic activity to the singing of a nightingale: '...as the wakeful Bird/ Sings darkling, and in shadiest Covert hid/ Tunes her nocturnal note...' Keats in 'Ode to a Nightingale' subliminally evokes Milton's language, but transmutes it so that he, the poet, now *listens* 'darkling', rather than sings. Thomas Hardy, in turn, in 'The Darkling Thrush', evokes both Milton and Keats in such a way that the effect of his poem depends on the hearer's aural memory of both predecessors and recognition of the tension

2. This is a case where the evidence of Paul's letters might help to confirm the early dating of a Targum tradition.

between them.[3] The discerning reader will hear the different voices at play. I welcome Evans's contribution to a similarly nuanced hearing of Romans 10.

On the other hand, I am skeptical of Evans's further proposal that Paul was drawn to the Deuteronomy text because he knew the tradition that Jesus had compared himself to Jonah (Mt. 12.40) and because *Targ. Neof.* Deut. 30.13 also refers to Jonah's descent into the abyss. This is not impossible, of course, but I see no evidence for it in the text, and Evans's contribution to our understanding of Romans 10 hardly requires this speculation. This seems to me an instance of what I called the 'vanishing point' problem:

> As we move farther away from overt citation, the source recedes into the discursive distance, the intertextual relations become less determinate, and the demand placed on the reader's listening powers grows greater. As we near the vanishing point of the echo, it inevitably becomes difficult to decide whether we are really hearing an echo at all, or whether we are only conjuring things out of the murmurings of our own imaginations.[4]

The important point here is that I see no fundamental disagreement between Evans and myself about the proper method to employ in our efforts to read Paul. Evans calls us to attend to certain traditions of scriptural interpretation within Judaism that might thicken our perception of Paul's readings of Scripture. I say that is a laudable goal, where appropriate evidence exists. I continue to insist, however, that the work of interpretation must include careful attention to the manner in which Paul puts his own distinctive spin on the inherited traditions. In the case of Deut. 30.12-13, the Targum explicitly understands the passage as a reference to the commandments of the Mosaic law. Paul, by identifying the 'word' with Christ, reads the reference to bringing the word up 'from the abyss' as an ironic reference to Christ's resurrection. So, even if Paul is hearing Deuteronomy 'as it had been interpreted in late antiquity' by the Targum tradition, he is at the same time also reading it through his own distinctive hermeneutical filter.

Evans's other point about the 'hermeneutics of prophetic criticism'

3. For a more nuanced discussion of this example, see J. Hollander, *The Figure of Echo: A Mode of Allusion in Milton and After* (Berkeley: University of California Press, 1981), pp. 89-91.

4. R.B. Hays, *Echoes of Scripture in the Letters of Paul* (New Haven and London: Yale University Press, 1989), p. 23.

is one that I am happy to acknowledge. The powerful instance that he cites (Isa. 28.21) could, of course, be multiplied: one thinks, for example, of the way in which Amos's oracles against the nations culminate dramatically in revisionary oracles of judgment against Judah and Israel (Amos 2.4–3.2): 'You only have I known of all the families of earth; therefore I will punish you for all your iniquities'. So, yes, as Evans indicates, 'the Pauline hermeneutic is in fact a biblical hermeneutic'.[5] Clarification is necessary, however, on three points.

First, it should be emphasized that Evans's comment supports, rather than challenges, my argument. In the final chapter of *Echoes*, where I sum up my conclusions about Pauline hermeneutics, I observe that Deuteronomy and Isaiah in particular are Paul's hermeneutical precursors: he has adopted their device of reading the history of God's past dealings with Israel as 'a prefiguration of a larger eschatological design'. Thus, Paul's 'reading strategy extends a typological trajectory begun already in the texts themselves'.[6] This remark is made precisely with reference to the dialectic of judgment and salvation that appears in Paul's precursors as well as in Romans. Consequently, I find it puzzling when Evans writes that 'apparently Hays has not fully realized. . . that this kind of deconstruction, or scandalous inversion, was frequently practiced by Israel's classical prophets'. One who has written, as I have, that 'Deuteronomy 32 contains Romans *in nuce*'[7] hardly needs to be pressed to admit that Paul's hermeneutic is biblical. One suspects that Evans, by concentrating his remarks on my analysis of Romans in Chapter 2 of *Echoes*, may have given insufficient weight to my conclusions in the book's final chapter.

Secondly, Paul's hermeneutic is selective: from among various canonical models, he adopts the highly dialectical hermeneutic of judgment and salvation that appears in Deuteronomy and Isaiah, rather than—for instance—the straightforwardly triumphalist ideology of 2 Samuel 7. This dialectical hermeneutic is, to be sure, homologous with the *kerygma* of the cross. Indeed, one might put it the other way around: the *kerygma* of the cross becomes the hermeneutical lens

5. For elaboration of Evans's point, see his helpful article, 'Paul and the Hermeneutics of "True Prophecy": A Study of Romans 9–11', *Bib* 65 (1984), pp. 560-70. I regret that this essay had not come to my attention during the time of the writing of *Echoes*.

6. *Echoes of Scripture*, p. 164.

7. *Echoes of Scripture*, p. 164.

through which Paul refocuses the classical 'hermeneutics of prophetic criticism'. It is precisely in this respect that Paul's reading of Scripture differs dramatically from most other Jewish traditions of scriptural interpretation: one could scarcely find a construal of Isaiah more dissonant with Pauline hermeneutics than the Isaiah Targum.

Finally, Paul's gospel transposes 'the hermeneutics of prophetic criticism' into a new key by proclaiming God's embrace of Gentiles *on the same terms as Israel* (i.e., through the grace of Jesus Christ), οὐ γάρ ἐστιν διαστολή (Rom. 3.23). One may contend—as Paul did—that this message was already latent in Scripture and/or in the very logic of monotheism,[8] but at the same time, it must be acknowledged that no Jew before Paul, so far as we are able to tell, drew the same conclusions from the prophetic texts that Paul drew. Paul's Gentile mission creates a new hermeneutical context within which the classical prophetic hermeneutic is metaphorically reconfigured. That reconfiguration is what I mean to emphasize when I say that Paul '*extends* a typological *trajectory* begun already in the texts themselves': Paul's hermeneutic is *analogous* to the prophetic hermeneutic, not a simple continuation of it.[9]

2. *Response to James A. Sanders*

James A. Sanders helpfully places *Echoes* within the discipline of biblical studies, recognizing it as a counterproposal both to the sort of New Testament scholarship that reads the New Testament 'synchronically only in terms of its Hellenistic context' and to Michael Fishbane's

---

8. The point is elegantly put by J.A. Sanders, *Torah and Canon* (Philadelphia: Fortress Press, 1972), p. 87: 'For the prophets were true monotheists, and nothing they said so stressed their monotheism as the idea that God was free enough of his chosen people to transform them in the crucible of destitution into a community whose members could themselves be free of every institution [sc. 'Law'] which in his providence he might give them.'

9. In this last point, I find myself in agreement with Sanders, who speaks of 'this *further* act of God in calling an unboundaried people through Christ' and perceives that this act 'forces a re-reading of the old texts, both to affirm that God has once more acted in consonance with the record of previous divine work and to insist that every new chapter throws light on those that precede it'. (I suspect that Evans would not find this emphasis on the newness of God's act in Christ and its hermeneutical consequences to be uncongenial, but he does not articulate it so clearly as Sanders.)

exclusion of the New Testament from the continuing stream of Israel's 'inner-Biblical interpretation'. Sanders's own sensitivity to 'the canonical process' also disposes him favorably towards my emphasis on the power of texts to engender unforeseen interpretations that may transcend the original authorial intention and historical setting. The book 'succeeds remarkably well', in his judgment, in holding together in creative tension the various possible loci for the hermeneutical event.

While I am grateful for Sanders's gracious and discerning remarks, I find it necessary to qualify his suggestion that 'whether [Hays] as its author intended it or not, he does indeed deal throughout the book with aspects of the canonical process'. This sentence can be accepted as an account of my work, rather than as an account of what Sanders believes I should have written, only if one emphasizes the word 'aspects'. Unlike Sanders, I am not engaged in tracing the *'process'* of tradition and canon formation; herein lies a significant distinction between my project and his desideratum. My study of Paul as reader of Scripture might be employed in the larger project that Sanders envisions,[10] but my focus is on the 'hermeneutical event' that occurs in Paul's applications of Scripture. Thus, I aim at a deep reading of a single text (or handful of Pauline texts) rather than at a comparative or developmental treatment of motifs 'from inception within the Tanak itself...through the Septuagint and her daughters, Dead Sea Scrolls, Apocrypha, Pseudepigrapha, Philo, Josephus, Tannaitic Literature and the Vulgate...' Sanders's question about the history of the canonical process is both important and interesting, but it is not quite mine. Having said that, I wish I could have been a participant in the seminar that Sanders describes: no doubt his working procedure would have illuminated the texts and taught me many things. It seems to me that my approach and Sanders's are complementary; still, it is important not to confuse one with the other.

While I am quibbling with Sanders's characterization of my work, I should also note that he misreads my comparison of Rom. 10.5-10 to *B. Meṣ.* 59b. Sanders cites a passage from p. 3 of *Echoes* in which I set the two interpretations of Deut. 30.12-14 in opposition to one another, and then objects that 'the *B. Meṣ.* passage can be read in just the same way, that is, Scripture's "right" interpretation is not in some

---

10. Indeed, I describe my inquiry into Paul's use of Scripture—largely conducted without reference to the diachronic trajectories that Sanders emphasizes—as 'a valid and necessary (even if preliminary) task' (*Echoes of Scripture*, p. 11).

tavnit (Idea or Form) in heaven…it is in the hands of succeeding generations of interpreters who read and re-read Scripture out of ever-changing community needs.' Sanders's point is certainly correct, but I find it a puzzling objection to my treatment of the passage, since I say substantially the same thing on the page following the one that Sanders cites:

> Both sides… presuppose the legitimacy of innovative readings that disclose truth previously latent in Scripture… [T]he rabbis gain leverage on the text by appealing to majority opinion within an interpretive community. The rabbinic story, therefore, exposes the quest for hermeneutical closure as an illusion. Texts will always demand and generate new interpretation, as this halakhic dispute demonstrates.[11]

It seems to me that Sanders has reacted against a provisional formulation in the middle of my unfolding comparison without following the comparison through to its conclusion. Thus, contrary to his suggestion that we might have a difference of opinion here regarding the character of rabbinic hermeneutics, I think in fact that we do not.

The most significant, in my judgment, of Sanders's constructive responses to *Echoes* is his insistence that Paul's hermeneutic is not ecclesiocentric, as I had argued, but theocentric. It is *God* who promises to circumcise the hearts of his people, *God* who kills and makes alive, *God* who keeps faith with the promises of Israel; in short, God, not the church, is the center and protagonist of Scripture as Paul reads it. Sanders's point is very well taken, and the letter to the Romans is eloquent testimony for his case. I am content, then, to accept this word of correction and say that Paul's hermeneutic is, in an important sense, theocentric.

But what then of the considerable body of evidence that led me to identify an ecclesiocentric hermeneutic in Paul?[12] That evidence still stands and must be granted its force, as Sanders is willing to do. Perhaps we need a new term, such as 'ecclesiotelic'. Granting that Scripture tells the story of *God's* activity, we must say in the same breath that God's activity is directed towards the formation of a *people*.[13] God reveals himself precisely through his activity of

---

11. *Echoes of Scripture*, p. 4.

12. See *Echoes of Scripture*, pp. 84-121. My aim in choosing the deliberately provocative term 'ecclesiocentric' was to call attention to Paul's relative lack of interest in christological prophecy-fulfillment schemes, in contrast to Matthew and John.

13. Cf. the emphasis placed by N.T. Wright on monotheism and election as the

choosing and saving Israel.[14] It is then impossible to speak of a theocentric hermeneutic without simultaneously recognizing that the God disclosed through Scripture read theocentrically is the God whose activity drives towards the creation of the eschatological ἐκκλησία; likewise, it is impossible to speak of an ecclesiocentric hermeneutic without recognizing that the ἐκκλησία disclosed through Scripture read ecclesiocentrically has its life only in and through the merciful action of the one God.

Perhaps the difficulty lies in the spatial metaphor of 'center'. If Paul's theological hermeneutic is fundamentally narrative in character —as both Sanders and I have argued elsewhere[15]—then it is artificial to single out one motif as the 'center' of everything else. The distinctive character of the hermeneutic can be displayed only in its capacity to incorporate all of the community's experience into the *story* of God's redemptive righteousness.

So far I think Sanders and I would agree. But is it correct to describe Paul's hermeneutic as 'argument...from theological history'? Here caution is necessary. The history in question, the history of God's dealings with Israel, is always read by Paul retrospectively through the lens of God's act of reconciling the world to himself through the death of Jesus Christ. The 'pattern of divine activity' that Paul discerns in Scripture is not a simple one that can be read off the surface of the text; it appears only through the dialectical encounter between Scripture and gospel in the missionary situation in which Paul finds himself. Furthermore, for Paul, ἡ γραφή is not simply the source for constructing a historical outline of God's past activity; rather, Scripture addresses the community in the present directly.[16]

In all this, I suspect that Sanders and I are in reasonably close agreement. I am concerned only that his emphasis on categories such as

fundamental twin organizing themes of Pauline theology, in 'Putting Paul Together Again', in J. Bassler (ed.), *Pauline Theology*, I (Minneapolis: Fortress Press, 1991), pp. 183-211.

14. Indeed, so intimately are these motifs linked throughout Scripture that we must join Karl Barth in confessing that God is the one whose being is known only in his act.

15. See, e.g., J.A. Sanders, 'Torah and Christ', *Int* 29 (1975), pp. 372-90; R.B. Hays, *The Faith of Jesus Christ: An Investigation of the Narrative Substructure of Galatians 3.1–4.11* (SBLDS, 56; Chico: Scholars Press, 1983); *idem*, 'Crucified with Christ', in Bassler (ed.), *Pauline Theology*, I, pp. 227-46.

16. For extended discussion of this, see *Echoes of Scripture*, pp. 154-78.

'process' and 'history' might lead to an underestimation of the dramatic discontinuities introduced by Paul's revisionary readings of Scripture,[17] and to a simultaneous underestimation of the metaphorical aspects of his reading strategies. The test of such concerns, of course, can be conducted only in the detailed exegesis of particular texts; consequently, I gladly anticipate the continuation of this collegial discussion.

3. *Response to William Scott Green*

The sorts of questions posed by William Scott Green, however, are not susceptible to adjudication at the exegetical level. Green poses fundamental questions about the theoretical underpinnings of my work and about the way in which my own theological commitments may color, or even determine, the results of my analysis. I am grateful to him for posing the issues in such an incisive fashion. To formulate an adequate answer to his astute methodological challenge, I would have to write another book. For the present, however, I offer a brief response to three closely related points: (1) the character of intertextual analysis as a critical method; (2) the relation between literary and theological analysis of Paul's letters; and (3) the issue of my critical stance *within* the tradition that I am seeking to explicate.

1. Green regards what he calls my 'minimalist notion of intertextuality' as problematic, because I fail to take on board the ideological baggage carried by most recent literary critics who use the buzzword: 'The larger purpose of intertextual analysis', Green asserts, 'is to undergird and underscore an ideological position about the fluidity of textual meaning.' Since Green cites no authority for his pronouncement, I can only assume that he has in mind the work of poststructuralist semiotic theorists such as Roland Barthes and Julia Kristeva,[18] or perhaps Harold Bloom's theorizing about 'misreading'.[19] While I am well aware of the philosophical context in which these

17. For a strong word of warning against the assumption of linear continuities between Scripture and Paul's theology, see now J.L. Martyn, 'Events in Galatia: Modified Covenantal Nomism versus God's Invasion of the Cosmos in the Singular Gospel: A Response to J.D.G. Dunn and B.R. Gaventa', in Bassler (ed.), *Pauline Theology*, I, pp. 160-79.

18. For bibliographic citations, see *Echoes of Scripture*, p. 198 n. 50.

19. For discussion and bibliographic references, see *Echoes of Scripture*, pp. 16-19 and p. 199 n. 58.

theorists employ intertextual analysis, I fail to see why my interest in intertextual echo should compel me to accept their ideological framework. As I argued in a long footnote in *Echoes*, the literary-critical operation of tracing the meaning-effects created by Paul's intertextual figurations is 'in principle neutral with regard to metatheories about language and truth'.[20] In fact, one possible outcome of analyzing intertextual phenomena would be to demonstrate the persistence of certain semantic constraints imposed by precursor texts on their later interpreters; if so, the method could disclose not only 'the fluidity of textual meaning' but also, if I might turn the trope again, its solidity. In fact, that is one of the findings of my analysis in *Echoes*: the Scriptural texts keep imposing at least part of their original sense on Paul's argument, even if only subliminally, even when Paul is trying to employ them for new purposes. That is what I mean when I propose in the book's final chapter, using Thomas M. Greene's typology, that Paul's hermeneutic is 'dialectical'.[21]

As Green correctly notes, the major theoretical influences on my working method are John Hollander and Thomas Greene—and Michael Fishbane should be duly noted as well. None of these critics espouses the ideological perspective that William Scott Green believes to be the necessary concomitant of intertextual analysis. I thought I had made all this reasonably clear in *Echoes* from the moment in Chapter 1 where I first introduced the term 'intertextuality'.[22]

Similarly, contrary to Green's statement, my use of the synonymous terms 'metalepsis' and 'transumption' is dependent neither on Harold Bloom nor on his student Herbert Marks but directly on Hollander. The distinction is important, because Hollander's usage of these terms is rooted in his extensive historical account of the definition of this trope by ancient and medieval rhetoricians.[23] One of the stated purposes of Hollander's long appendix on this terminology is to *distinguish* his usage from Bloom's idiosyncratic appropriation of it.

One other matter concerning the definition of intertextuality requires comment. When Green asserts that 'intertextuality really is

20. *Echoes of Scripture*, p. 227 n. 60.
21. *Echoes of Scripture*, pp. 173-78.
22. *Echoes of Scripture*, pp. 14-21.
23. 'Appendix: The Trope of Transumption', in Hollander, *Figure of Echo*, pp. 133-49.

the reader's work, not the writer's',[24] he seems to abolish by fiat one side of the dialectical interaction that occurs in Paul's wrestling with Scripture and again in our wrestling with Paul. If Green means to suggest that my work, despite its 'historically-descriptive-sounding phrases' actually reveals *only* my own creativity in discovering intertextual correspondences and that such discoveries can be attributed neither to Paul nor to the reading experience of his original readers, then Paul falls mute. His reading of Scripture contributes nothing to the phenomena of intertextual echo; the echoes are only inside our heads. (Can one read Joyce's *Ulysses* and suppose that the Homeric intertextual resonances are only the product of the reader's ingenuity? Can we read Dante without supposing that he intended to echo Virgil?) Apparently, however, Green does not go so far as to endorse this sort of hermeneutical solipsism; he deems my discussions of scriptural echo to be 'responsible, disciplined, well within the range of textual plausibility and imaginative possibility'. Thus, his comment that 'intertextuality really is the reader's work' must be taken as a cautionary note, rather than as an embargo on the importation of authorial meaning.

In any case, Green finds fault with my work because, despite my focus on intertextual allusion, I fail to fall in line with the currently fashionable skepticism about the stability of meaning in texts. I can only respond that I am indeed operating with a notion of intertextuality that is 'minimal' by Green's canons, and that I have chosen consciously to do so. If Green should insist on denying me permission to use the term 'intertextuality' (since my work does not properly reverence its 'larger purpose'), I will surrender it with a shrug. Nothing is at stake for me in the use of the term.

2. Green asks, penetratingly, 'Even if we grant...the book's claim that in Paul's writing Scripture and gospel are in tensive and dialectical relationship, does it follow that the literary is co-essential with the theological? Does a literary relationship between two texts necessarily imply a theological one?' The specific matter at issue here is the question of supersessionism: does Paul's theology annihilate Torah and replace it with a new religion?[25]

24. For a similar critique, see the review of *Echoes of Scripture* by D.B. Martin in *Modern Theology* 7 (1991), pp. 291-92.
25. Incidentally, when Green says that the 'the charge of supersessionism' was 'made in various ways by Harnack, Bultmann, and Herbert Marks', his formulation

Green correctly states that my book seeks to show that Paul's theology is *not* supersessionist. More significantly, he correctly poses the issue by asking whether 'the literary is co-essential with the theological'. Green rightly perceives that the argumentation of *Echoes* moves from a description of the complex literary linkages between Paul's letters and Scripture to an assertion of a corresponding theological coherence. From Green's point of view, this assertion is problematic, both materially and methodologically.

Green argues[26] as follows: because, for Paul, Scripture's 'narrative of election and promise...is completed by something outside Scripture' (the death and resurrection of Jesus), Paul's position is *theologically* discontinuous with Scripture, no matter how many literary allusions and echoes Paul may create. In other words (mine, not his), Green would describe Paul's hermeneutic—using Thomas Greene's typology again—as *heuristic*: Paul evokes the symbolic world of Scripture precisely to reconfigure it systematically into his own symbolic world.

The complaint is as old as Paul's letters themselves. The letter to the Romans in particular bears witness to Paul's vigorous debate with his contemporaries over precisely these issues. Paul insists that his gospel, despite its evident revisionary relation to Israel's law, stands nonetheless in an authentic relation of continuity with it.

> But now, apart from Law, God's righteousness has been revealed—
> though it is attested [μαρτυρουμένη] by the Law and the prophets—
> God's righteousness, revealed through the faithfulness of Jesus Christ,
> for all who believe...Do we then abolish the Law through this faith? By
> no means! On the contrary, we confirm the Law (Rom. 3.21, 31).

Should Paul's claim be credited, or should we share Green's dubiety? About one point, Green is certainly correct: the mere presence of

---

is slightly misleading, because it suggests that these critics *disapproved* of supersessionism. In fact, Harnack and Bultmann were enthusiastic Christian supersessionists seeking to enlist Paul in support of their position. Marks is a very different case: his Paul is 'a dogmatist—affirming the priority of his own conceptions by imposing them on the earlier tradition'. But that makes Paul a 'strong misreader', which is, in Marks' critical universe, a *good* thing to be; Marks is actually defending Paul against Bloom's judgment that he is a weak conventional reader.

26. To be precise, I should note that Green casts his remarks in the interrogative mode: 'Does this not mean that...' For the sake of simplicity, I have taken the liberty of treating Green's rhetorical question as though it were an assertion. I do not believe that I have thereby misrepresented his position.

scriptural citations, allusions, and echoes in Paul's discourse cannot settle the question. If that were the burden of my argument in *Echoes*, Green's skepticism would be fully warranted.

In fact, however, my argument is far less simple than Green makes it sound. Everything rides on the *character* of the intertextual relation between Paul's writing and what was written in Israel's Scripture. If, as I have tried at some length to show, the intertextual relation is genuinely *dialectical*, if Scripture really does retain its own voice and power to challenge and shape Paul's unfolding discourse, then indeed Paul's stance is not supersessionist, at least not as that term is ordinarily understood. But the determination of whether Scripture's voice continues to be heard rather than suppressed is, in significant measure, a literary judgment about how the text's tropes work. Thus, if the literary is not co-essential with the theological, it is at least organically fused.

A truly supersessionist Christian theology would steamroller the Scriptural text, flatten it out into a pavement to 'prepare the way of the Lord [Jesus]'. A non-supersessionist theology will necessarily grapple in a more anguished and loving way with Scripture. The difference will manifest itself not only in the 'bottom-line' theological position but also in the specific character of the literary nexus between old text and new. Thus, in response to Green's question, I would say, yes, there is *some* correlation between the literary relation of two texts and their theological relation. The correlation is not one-to-one identity; nonetheless, intertextual literary linkages both reflect and create theological convictions.

3. Finally, Green accuses me of 'doing the text's work for it', of becoming the tool manipulated by Paul's rhetoric. Because my 'minimalist notion of intertextuality' is insufficiently suspicious of Paul's readings, my analysis 'loses its critical force and falls into mere descriptiveness', with the result that the book 'reinforces just what [Paul's] letters want hearers and readers to apprehend: that Christian teaching is "grounded...in" Israel's Scripture rather than imposed upon it'. In short, the book functions, albeit subtly, as a piece of Christian theology. Thus—the final jab—the argument of *Echoes* is 'less an analysis of religion than a specimen of it'. A specimen!

> And when I am formulated, sprawling on a pin,
> When I am pinned and wriggling on the wall,
> Then how should I begin?

Green is exactly right: my book is written ἐκ πίστεως εἰς πίστιν. It is consciously and explicitly an attempt to write a work of scholarly analysis that seeks to do what my last chapter says Christian thinkers and writers should do: to take Paul as a hermeneutical model. In the closing pages of the book, I suggest *inter alia* that, 'If we learned from Paul how to read Scripture, we would read it in the service of proclamation'.[27]

Thus, I take Green's critique as unintended praise, confirmation that I accomplished what I set out to do. If my book 'reinforces just what [Paul's] letters want hearers and readers to apprehend', then it has served faithfully as an instrument of the word. (I note with interest that Green chides me for precisely the same things that Sanders lauds: 'appreciating Scripture not only as historically generated literature but also as canon'.) To say that the book is a 'specimen' of religion is to say, in the putatively value-neutral argot of the 'religious studies' sub-culture, that it stands in confessional continuity with its subject matter, that it carries forward Paul's theological trajectory. If so, this is—for me—cause to rejoice.

Still I find the dichotomy disturbing: why are the confessional and the analytical deemed antithetical? Does a scholar's hermeneutical stance within a particular faith-tradition preclude critical reflection about that tradition?[28] On the contrary, I would suggest that *Echoes* seeks to enact a mode of sympathetic reading that may be possible only for interpreters who know the tradition and its struggles from the inside.[29] By reflecting the text's message faithfully, but in a slightly new idiom, this kind of reading tries to make the text come alive for readers who otherwise would not be able to hear it. That is not the only thing that scholarly analysis can or should do, but it is surely one legitimate aim of study. Does Green want to foreclose such readings?

4. *Response to J. Christiaan Beker*

As I turn to J. Christiaan Beker's critique of *Echoes*, I find myself back on familiar terrain. Beker's most pressing questions address the

27. *Echoes of Scripture*, p. 184.

28. For an eloquent rebuttal to such assumptions, see R.L. Wilken, 'Who Will Speak *For* the Religious Traditions?', *JAAR* 57 (1989), pp. 699-717.

29. In the infelicitous, but perhaps useful, terminology current in anthropology, the book's account of Pauline hermeneutics is 'emic' rather than 'etic'.

exegesis of particular texts; his criticisms are not about the propriety of a theological reading of Paul but about the theological contours of the reading I have given. His challenges are particularly important for me to answer, because they express the sorts of objections that many traditional New Testament critics might have to my book. Beker divides his response into three sections: literary-critical and historical questions, exegetical issues, and theological questions. I shall consider briefly the first category of questions before giving more detailed discussion to the exegetical and theological concerns.

a. *Literary-Critical and Historical Questions*

What are the constraints, Beker wants to know, on imaginative freedom, both Paul's and mine? There are two distinct questions here, I think: what constraints limit our critical assertions about the presence and significance of scriptural echoes in Paul's writings, and what constraints limit our own constructive theological uses of biblical texts? I have already answered both of these questions in *Echoes* as well as I know how.

Regarding the first question, I refer my colleague to pp. 29-33, where I propound seven tests for assessing the possible presence of particular echoes in Paul's letters. Beker may not find the criteria proposed in my seven tests to be sufficient, but it is hard to see how they are less clear than Fishbane's; if anything, my criteria are more extensive and nuanced.[30]

Regarding the second question, I have offered three hermeneutical constraints on pp. 190-91: our creative interpretations of Scripture must affirm that God remains faithful to the promises made to Israel, must confess the death and resurrection of Jesus as the decisive manifestation of God's righteousness, and must drive towards shaping the community of readers into a community that embodies the love of God as shown forth in Christ. Beker cites this passage in a footnote, but—mysteriously—he seems to think that it proposes that 'echoes' themselves somehow serve as constraints on hermeneutical whimsy. I urge him to go back and read these pages again.

Likewise, I think that Beker has simply misunderstood my treatment of Job 19.25-26 in relation to Phil. 1.19. I cite the passage as a

30. I agree with Beker that Gail O'Day's 'Jeremiah 9.22-23 and 1 Corinthians 1.26-31: A Study of Intertextuality' (*JBL* 109 [1990], pp. 259-67) is a splendid example of fruitful intertextual analysis.

limiting case, a possible echo so faint that it has no semantic
significance. It is employed as an illustration of the sort of echo that I
do *not* intend to discuss in the book.[31] I am forced to conclude that
Beker was not reading very carefully at this point.

More weighty is Beker's question about the 'communication-
structure' in Paul's allusive uses of Scripture, its persuasive value for
his readers. If these letters are pastoral communications addressing
contingent situations, as Beker rightly insists, how effective are Paul's
indirect echoes of a text that his readers, mostly Gentile converts, may
not know very well in the first place? The question is an important
one. The answer, of course, is that the effectiveness of Paul's communication strategy varies with different situations and with different
readers/hearers. Each case must be considered individually. It would
be wrong, however, to assume that Paul was always a consummate
communicator. The evidence suggests otherwise: he was trying, with
mixed results, to resocialize his converts into a new symbolic world
that was still in process of formation even in his own mind. There
were some successes, some failures. Often it appears that his readers
found him baffling. One reason for their incomprehension may have
been that he was not able to fill in all the gaps left for his hearers by
his allusive references to Scripture; he may have been consistently
presupposing knowledge that he ought not to have presupposed.

The basic point, however, is this: the fact that Paul was trying to
communicate in contingent situations does *not* mean that he could not
have used allusive echoes in his letters. When they are understood,
allusions are potent strategies of communication. On the other hand,
many uses of echoes and allusions are unpremeditated, subconscious;
they are grasped consciously, even by their author, only sometimes.

Beker also remarks that he would have expected a more detailed
discussion of 'pesher and midrashic methods'. Of course, we can hardly
assume that Paul's original audience would have been acquainted with
such methods. Beker's point is that midrashic exegesis selects prooftexts
without evoking the wider context of that citation. Actually, I doubt
the adequacy of this characterization of the midrashists' use of
Scripture,[32] but in any case Paul's own hermeneutical practices are

---

31. *Echoes of Scripture*, pp. 23-24.
32. See D. Boyarin, *Intertextuality and the Reading of Midrash* (Bloomington:
Indiana University Press, 1990) on the allusive character of the biblical references in
rabbinic midrash.

sufficiently different from theirs to demand independent investigation. (I note with some satisfaction that Green, whose own expertise is in the field of formative Judaism, endorsed my methodological decision to explicate Paul's readings of Scripture without using formal categories derived from rabbinic midrash.[33])

b. *Exegetical Issues*
Beker's exegetical critique identifies four loci for discussion.

1. He challenges my declaration that 'Deuteronomy 32 contains Romans *in nuce*'. He notes that 'the overall scheme of Deuteronomy 32 does not seem to apply to *all of Romans,* but only to the movement of Romans 9–11'. This strikes me as an odd objection coming from Beker, who has published an article arguing persuasively that God's faithfulness to Israel is the central theme not only of chs. 9–11 but also of the letter as a whole.[34] Indeed, according to Beker, Rom. 11.32 is 'the climax and crown of Paul's argument'.[35] If the contingent character of Romans appears most clearly in Romans 9–11, then whatever governs the movement of these three chapters is surely to be deemed generative for the entire epistle.

Consequently, Beker's protest that there are only three explicit citations of Deuteronomy 32 in Romans misses the point: Paul's meditation on the mystery of Israel's election, rejection, and restoration finds its theological genesis in Deuteronomy. The importance of Deuteronomy 32 is shown not only by explicit citations, but also by allusions in Rom. 9.14 and 11.11-14. Beker quotes me—without citing a reference —as claiming that Deuteronomy 32 is present as a 'pervasive echo' in Romans, but I cannot find any such statement in my text. My suggestion, rather, is that Deuteronomy 32 is generative, not that it is pervasive. To say that Deuteronomy 32 contains Romans *in nuce* is to say that Deuteronomy is to Romans as the acorn is to the oak tree.

Let me try to put the point another way: Deuteronomy provides a fundamental theological resource for Paul's attempt to explain the puzzling experience of his own missionary activity. Gentiles believe, Jews do not. What is happening here? Deuteronomy offers Paul not

33. *Echoes of Scripture*, pp. 10-14. Green's written response passes over this matter without comment; his agreement with my approach emerged in a group discussion.
34. 'The Faithfulness of God and the Priority of Israel in Paul's Letter to the Romans', *HTR* 79 (1986), pp. 10-16.
35. 'The Faithfulness of God', p. 14.

only the explanatory narrative pattern (covenant election, Israel's unfaithfulness, God's judgment, followed by God's ultimate gracious act of reconciliation/new creation), but also the 'jealousy' theory, based on Deut. 32.21, as an explanation for God's surprising decision to bring many Gentiles to salvation before reclaiming unfaithful Israel.

This is not to deny the comparable generativity of other scriptural sources. Genesis, Psalms, and Isaiah appear in Paul with regularity, and, as Beker notes, Hab. 2.4 is given a place of special importance in the rhetorical structure of Romans. One might note, however, against Beker, that Habakkuk is quoted only *once* in Romans. How then, using Beker's criterion of frequency of citation, can it be claimed to be '*the* crucial Old Testament text for Paul'?[36]

2. Beker questions whether intertextual scriptural echo actually is as pervasive in Romans as I have claimed: 'a superficial glance at the letter shows that, whereas scriptural references abound in chs. 1–4 and 9–11, they are almost completely absent in the crucial chs. 5–8 and sharply reduced in chs. 12–14, in order to reappear in the conclusion of the letter in ch. 15'. The operative word here is 'superficial'.

One implication of my work is that we cannot confine our investigation of Pauline intertextuality to passages in which there is an explicit quotation (καθὼς γέγραπται) of a source. In fact, if we look not just for citations but for allusions to Old Testament figures and motifs, it is not difficult to show that the chapters Beker singles out contain fundamental features that would be incomprehensible apart from their relation to Old Testament subtexts. In Romans 5 we have Moses and—especially—Adam as key figures whose identity and stories are treated by Paul as *déjà lu*; furthermore, Rom. 5.19 echoes Isa. 53.11 artfully. In Romans 7, we find a complex analysis of the impact of the commandments of the Mosaic Torah on those who hear it, with Exod. 20.17/Deut. 5.21 taken as a paradigmatic illustration (Rom. 7.7). In Romans 8, we find several pivotal scriptural allusions: the sin-offering[37] (8.3), τὸ δικαίωμα τοῦ νόμου (8.4), the fallen creation subjected to decay (8.20-21), the echo of Gen. 22.12, 16 ('did not spare his own son') in Rom. 8.32, the citation of Psalm 44 in

---

36. See further discussion of Rom. 10.6, below.

37. See now the compelling argument of N.T. Wright that περὶ ἁμαρτίας in its context in Rom. 8.3 must be a metaphorical reference to the Torah's offering for unwilling sin: *The Climax of the Covenant* (Edinburgh: T. & T. Clark, 1991), pp. 220-25.

Rom. 8.36 and the many echoes of Isaiah 50 in the surrounding verses.[38]

I have cited here only the most obvious evidence in Romans 5–8. Does Beker really want to maintain that references to Scripture are 'almost completely absent' in these chapters? Such a position can be maintained only by focusing narrowly on direct quotations and ignoring the Scripture-laden language that Paul employs in his own discourse. To be sure, Paul is not arguing *about* the interpretation of particular biblical texts in these chapters, as he is in other parts of the letter. But I never claimed that he was. Again, Beker's criticism simply suggests to me that he has misunderstood my discussion.

A book that begins with the assertion that the gospel was 'promised beforehand through [the] prophets in holy Scriptures' (Rom. 1.2) and concludes its train of argument with the glad affirmation that 'whatever was written in former days was written for our instruction, so that by steadfastness and by the encouragement of the Scriptures we might have hope' (Rom. 15.4)—with at least 51 direct Scripture quotations and dozens more allusions in between—can surely be claimed to be pervasively concerned with Scripture and its interpretation.[39] Can this be a controversial claim? As Paul might say, 'I am astonished!'

Beker also contests my description of Rom. 15.1-13 as the climax of the letter, claiming instead that 15.14-21 should be read as the climax. I believe that an analysis of the letter's rhetorical structure will support my view, but there is insufficient space here to set forth the argument. I note that my analysis is in agreement with J.D.G. Dunn, who treats 15.7-13 as a 'concluding summary...intended to round off the body of the letter'.[40]

3. Still arguing that Scripture does not play a constitutive role in Paul's thought, Beker contends, following the lead of Adolf von Harnack, that Paul cites Scripture only when he is forced into it by the contingency of refuting Judaizing opponents. (One might well doubt whether this is an appropriate description of the use of Scripture in

38. I have discussed the biblical texture of Rom. 8.31-39 in *Echoes of Scripture*, pp. 57-63.

39. I leave aside the matter of Rom. 16.26, which might not be an original part of the letter. Even if this is a conclusion added by a later editor, it shows that the letter was understood at a very early date as fundamentally concerned with the role of 'prophetic writings' in making the gospel known.

40. *Romans 9–16* (WBC, 38B; Dallas: Word Books, 1988), p. 844.

Romans, but I let that pass for now.) The evidence for this position is supposed to be that Paul rarely cites Scripture in Philippians, 1 Thessalonians, and Philemon.

One of the last places I would have expected to find Chris Beker is in alliance with Harnack! Surely Beker's own programmatic case for the apocalyptic character of Pauline theology would be far better served by acknowledging the biblical roots of Paul's proclamation of the universal triumph of God than by attributing Paul's use of Scripture to purely contingent factors. I am, consequently, puzzled by Beker's decision to pursue this line of argument.

In any case, 1 Corinthians stands as the decisive refutation of the Harnack/Beker position. Here, where there is no 'Judaizing' problem, Paul repeatedly employs biblical citations (e.g. 1.19; 1.31; 2.16; 3.19-20; 5.13; 6.16; 9.9; 10.7; 14.21, 25; 15.32; 15.54-55) and allusions, and he unreflectively addresses his Gentile converts as part of the covenant community (see especially 5.13, 10.1, 12.2).[41] In none of these cases is Paul arguing *about* the interpretation of Scripture or contending that some 'Judaizing' tendency is to be rejected; rather, he simply takes Scripture as an authoritative or illuminating warrant in his argumentation. Furthermore, he assumes that his readers will acknowledge the force of such arguments.

It is noteworthy that the three letters claimed to show that Paul uses Scripture 'only when the contingent situation forces him to do so' (Beker) are the three shortest of the letters generally acknowledged to be authentic. Thus, the absence of explicit citation is not so striking as it might be in a longer letter. In any case, the diction of these letters continues to reflect Paul's immersion in the language of Scripture. As I have noted elsewhere,[42] there are a number of biblical allusions in these letters: for example, Phil. 1.19/Job 13.16; Phil. 2.10-11/Isa. 45.23; 1 Thess. 3.9/Ps. 115.3 LXX; 1 Thess. 3.13/Zech. 14.5 (?); 1 Thess. 5.8/Isa. 59.17.

Even more peculiar is Beker's suggestion that the deutero-Pauline and pastoral epistles ought to be taken as evidence that Scripture was not crucial for Paul, because they rarely cite Scripture. Are we to conclude, Beker asks, 'that Paul's pupils completely misunderstood

---

41. For discussion of this rhetorical strategy in 1 Corinthians, see *Echoes of Scripture*, pp. 91-104.

42. *Echoes of Scripture*, p. 195 n. 16; R.B. Hays, 'Crucified with Christ', in Bassler (ed.), *Pauline Theology*, I, p. 246.

him'? This argument can cut both ways. It is usually alleged that Paul's pupils did indeed misunderstand him, or at least that they developed the traditions of his teaching in directions quite foreign to the distinctive character of his own thought. That is how these later epistles are usually distinguished from the 'authentic' ones. Why then should we find it surprising that second- or third-generation followers should have allowed Scripture to recede to a more peripheral position? That might be one more theological litmus test applied in conjunction with others (e.g., eschatology, ecclesiology) to demonstrate the inauthenticity of these letters. Surely this argument backfires on Beker.

4. Finally, we come to the matter of the exegesis of Romans 10. Beker correctly identifies this as a crucial text for my enterprise, and his remarks make it evident that we are in substantive disagreement about its proper interpretation. The passage is, on any showing, a very difficult one. A full discussion of the problems is impossible within the scope of this essay; I offer here only a response to some of Beker's specific criticisms.

I am surprised that Beker describes my manner of argumentation as 'apodictic'. My claim that 'Rom. 10.5 and 10.6 must not stand in antithesis to one another'[43] is not arbitrary: it is based on the evidence adduced in the foregoing paragraph (note that my sentence begins with a 'therefore'), which Beker apparently overlooks. I shall restate the salient points: the whole argument of Romans insists repeatedly that the law bears witness to the righteousness of God (3.21), and that the gospel of righteousness through faith confirms rather than abolishes the law (3.31). The appeal to the story of Abraham (Romans 4) functions to support the claim that the law (i.e., Scripture) calls its hearers to receive righteousness through faith. 'The mind set on the flesh' (τὸ φρόνημα τῆς σαρκός) does not submit to the law of God (τῷ γὰρ νόμῳ τοῦ θεοῦ οὐχ ὑποτάσσεται—8.7); this is synonymous with Paul's lament that his kinfolk κατὰ σάρκα have not submitted to the righteousness of God (τῇ δικαιοσύνῃ τοῦ θεοῦ οὐχ ὑπετάγησαν —10.3). Those, however, who walk κατὰ πνεῦμα now fulfill τὸ δικαίωμα τοῦ νόμου (8.4); that is why Paul can affirm—based on the empirical evidence of his Gentile mission—that Christ is τέλος νόμου. 'The sum and substance of Torah . . . is righteousness through

43. *Echoes of Scripture*, p. 76.

faith.'[44] Otherwise, what possible function does the γάρ in 10.4 have? It would appear that, if Paul had meant what Beker proposes, he should have written ἀλλά instead.

In view of these considerations, I am amazed by Beker's assertion, on the basis of Rom. 3.9-20, that 'the argument in Romans...has already determined—*before* we read ch. 10—that the νόμος, embodied in Lev. 18.5, can *only* [emphasis mine] condemn us'. Rather, I would suggest, this Reformation-era construal of Romans is so firmly fixed in Beker's mind before he reads ch. 10 that he ignores Paul's massive effort to assign a far more positive revelatory function to the Torah. As I propose in an important footnote (*Echoes*, p. 208 n. 83), the burden of proof lies strongly on Beker and other interpreters who read τέλος as 'termination'. The strength of the interpretation of τέλος as 'goal, aim' is underscored by the convincing studies of Badenas and Meyer, cited in that note.[45]

To be sure, this means that Paul is interpreting Lev. 18.5 in Romans in a way different from his negative construal of it in Gal. 3.12. That is one of the difficulties for my interpretation of the passage. Nevertheless, I would suggest that this shift in the reading of Lev. 18.5 is consistent with the larger shift between Paul's relentlessly negative treatment of the law in Galatians and his more dialectical interpretation of it in Romans.

When Beker notes that 'Paul underscores—contrary to Deuteronomy—πίστις and not the *mizwoth* of the Torah', I would agree, with the qualification that *Paul* himself does not at all think that his emphasis on πίστις is contrary to Deuteronomy. Indeed, he finds in Deuteronomy a decisive witness for ἡ ἐκ πίστεως δικαιοσύνη. This surprising revisionary reading, I have argued, is made possible in part by the hermeneutical focusing of Deuteronomy 32, in which God (in Moses' song) condemns Israel as 'a perverse generation, sons in whom there is no πίστις' (Deut. 32.20).[46]

Rom. 10.5-10 remains a vexing passage because Paul so daringly co-opts the voice of Moses. Paul's rhetorical strategy is one of

---

44. *Echoes of Scripture*, p. 76.

45. In addition to the references cited in *Echoes of Scripture*, p. 208 n. 83, see also C.T. Rhyne, *Faith Establishes the Law* (SBLDS, 55; Chico: Scholars Press, 1981) and G.N. Davies, *Faith and Obedience in Romans* (JSNTSup, 39; Sheffield: JSOT Press, 1990), pp. 185-204.

46. For discussion, see *Echoes of Scripture*, pp. 82-83.

revision rather than rejection. Despite our discomfort about his reading, we cannot escape acknowledging that Paul is subjecting Deuteronomy to a hermeneutical transformation that makes the law bear witness to the gospel. The Reformation reading of the passage (defended by Beker), on the other hand, plays down the hermeneutical scandal by factoring law and gospel out into the very antithesis that Paul (in Romans) is determined to preclude.

c. *Theological Questions*

Beker's first theological question is an outgrowth of his last exegetical one: does my reading of Paul underestimate the discontinuity between 'Israel and Christianity, that is, between law and gospel'?[47] Certainly this issue of continuity versus discontinuity is one of the central issues raised by my book. Beker acknowledges that my argument is an important 'corrective to the views of Martin Luther and Rudolf Bultmann'; reciprocally, I will acknowledge that my work might occasionally overstate the case for continuity. If so, I have done so in the effort to redress what I perceive to be a drastic imbalance in the literature of the discipline. The task for all of us who seek to interpret Paul is to do justice to both aspects of his thought: he insists on the one hand that the gospel of Jesus Christ is a decisive and radically new manifestation of God's saving power and, at the same time, that this manifestation is fully consistent with—and adumbrated by—God's past gracious dealing with his people Israel. I think that Beker and I are generally in agreement about this; the disagreements go back to matters of the exegesis of particular passages.

Secondly, Beker questions my description of Paul's hermeneutic as 'ecclesiocentric'. The question has two prongs. Beker asks, first, whether an ecclesiocentric hermeneutic can be separated from a christocentric one, since Paul understands the church as σῶμα Χριστοῦ. Here, as with regard to Beker's first theological question, I believe that whatever disagreements may exist are matters of emphasis. Many readers of *Echoes* seem to have reacted to my catch-phrase 'ecclesiocentric hermeneutics' without noting the conclusion of Chapter 3:

47. This is the same issue raised, in slightly different terms, by William Scott Green's objection that I misconstrue literary intertextual linkage as theological continuity. See my discussion of this matter, above.

[C]hristology is the foundation on which his ecclesiocentric counter-readings are constructed...Gal. 3.29 finally unlocks the riddle of the relation between Paul's ecclesiocentric hermeneutic and his christological convictions...[T]hese aspects of Pauline thought are complementary rather than contradictory: Paul's understanding of Jesus Christ as the one true heir of the promise to Abraham is the essential theological presupposition for his hermeneutical strategies, though these strategies are not in themselves christocentric.[48]

My emphasis on the ecclesiocentric character of Paul's hermeneutic is the result of seeking to ask in a disciplined manner, 'What is Paul actually *doing* with Scripture when he appeals to it in his arguments?' The striking result of such an inquiry is to reveal the scarcity of christologically-interpreted Old Testament passages in Paul. My explanation for this phenomenon is to propose that Paul's christological convictions belong to a foundational 'substructure' of his thought; apart from his christological presuppositions, his ecclesiocentric (or, as I suggested above, *ecclesiotelic*) readings make no sense. To formulate the issue in these terms, however, still leaves room—and, indeed, necessity—for a more careful study of the few passages in which Paul does interpret the scriptural text christologically (e.g., Rom. 15.3).[49]

The second prong of Beker's question, however, precisely skewers my work: 'How...is an ecclesiocentric hermeneutic related to Paul's apocalyptic perspective?' As I reread *Echoes* in light of Beker's complaint that my ecclesiocentric focus yields a reading of Paul as having a 'realized eschatology', I must acknowledge the force of the objection. Most of my attention is given to the way in which past narratives find their meaning in the present reality of Paul's churches, to whom he proclaims, 'Now is the day of salvation' (2 Cor. 6.2). By identifying the apocalyptic context of Paul's ecclesiocentric hermeneutic, I intended to locate his interpretative activity within the 'already/not yet' dialectic that pervades his thought, but in fact my discussion fails to do justice to the 'not yet' pole. In order to remedy this deficiency, my analysis ought to place more emphasis on two key points. First, when Paul writes that the words of Scripture were written 'for our

48. *Echoes of Scripture*, pp. 120-21. Cf. the exegesis of Galatians 3 in my earlier work, *The Faith of Jesus Christ*; see especially pp. 193-209, pp. 225-35.

49. I have begun to work on this problem in a paper entitled 'Christ Prays the Psalms: Paul's use of an Early Christian Exegetical Convention', presented at the SNTS meeting in Madrid, 1992.

instruction, upon whom the ends of the ages have met' (1 Cor. 10.11), he identifies the church as standing precisely at the temporal juncture in which the old age has lost its claim upon us but in which the new age is present only proleptically. That, in fact, is precisely the force of his use of the story of the exodus generation: let the one who thinks he stands (the 'strong' in the Corinthian church) take heed lest he fall (1 Cor. 10.12). The story is not over yet, and the church should imagine itself to be, analogously to Israel in the wilderness, a pilgrim people that has not yet arrived at its promised destination. Secondly, Romans 9–11 clearly underscores the provisional character of the experience of salvation in the church. Just as those who have received the first fruits of the Spirit still groan and suffer along with the unredeemed creation (Rom. 8.18-25), so the present community that confesses Jesus as Lord remains anomalous and incomplete, in anguish over Israel's unbelief until the eschatological consummation in which 'all Israel shall be saved' (Rom. 11.26). These 'unrealized' aspects of Paul's eschatology must be acknowledged as integral to his hermeneutical perspective. I regret that my discussion did not illuminate this aspect of Paul's thought—which I myself consider of central importance for Pauline theology—more adequately.[50]

Beker's final theological question, however, seems to me to miss the mark. He accuses me of 'imposing a Methodist hermeneutic on Paul', by which he means that 'the Word is now fully fused with the gift of the Spirit' in such a way that the church 'embodies the Spirit completely', with the result that written word loses its critical function, its ' *"overagainstness"* to the church'. No doubt my insistence on the embodiment of the word in the real-world obedience of the faithful is influenced by my own Wesleyan heritage, but I categorically reject the charge that my interpretation of Paul leads to an abandonment of the critical function of the word over against the church. On the contrary, it seems to me that Paul conceives of the word as alive and dangerous, always at work to shape and transform the community in ways that could not have been predicted. That is the explicit import of my use of Thomas Greene's category of 'dialectical imitation' to describe Paul's reading strategy: 'two symbolic worlds are brought into collision so

---

50. With regard to Beker's insistence that Paul's apocalyptic perspective has 'a theocentric focus and climax', I refer the reader back to my response to Sanders's similar point, above.

that each is vulnerable to criticism and interpretation by the other'.[51] I argue that 'Paul's allusive manner of using Scripture leaves enough silence for the voice of Scripture to answer back... The word that Scripture speaks where Paul falls silent is a word that still has the power to contend against him'.[52]

To follow Paul's example, then, as I have urged, would mean to stand with him in this life-or-death wrestling with the word, recognizing that all our claims about God's activity in our lives must be subjected to the scrutiny of Scripture and—simultaneously—that our readings of Scripture must always be subject to the test of enactment:[53] 'No reading of Scripture can be legitimate, then, if it fails to shape the readers into a community that embodies the love of God as shown forth in Christ'.[54] If Beker wants to call that a 'Methodist hermeneutic', so be it. In such a hermeneutic, has the word lost its critical function? μὴ γένοιτο. On the contrary, we uphold the word's critical function by upholding its living power.

5. Conclusion

Despite my emphatic rejoinder to Beker's final theological question, I deeply appreciate his asking it. This is precisely the sort of ultimate theological question that we exegetes ought to ask each other. That we do it so seldom is an indictment of our discipline. The present forum, however, has been an occasion for considering issues that matter profoundly. Our elder brother Paul would be pleased, I think, with the theological gravity of our debate. My thanks again to Evans, Sanders, Green and Beker for their careful and provocative responses. May this round of discussion help us all to a better understanding of the way in which Paul heard Scripture and the ways in which the word is near also to us.

51. *Echoes of Scripture*, p. 174.
52. *Echoes of Scripture*, p. 177.
53. See G. Steiner's fine account of hermeneutics as 'the enactment of answerable understanding' in *Real Presences* (Chicago: University of Chicago Press, 1989) p. 7-11.
54. *Echoes of Scripture*, p. 191.

Part II

FUNCTIONS OF SCRIPTURE IN PAUL—SELECTED STUDIES

HABAKKUK IN QUMRAN, PAUL, AND THE OLD TESTAMENT*

James A. Sanders

The Qumran expositor of Habakkuk firmly believed that Habakkuk spoke to Qumran's day and time, to the situation and to the crisis which the Qumran sect believed marked the beginning of the divine eschaton. He was a modernizer in the ageless sense of the term. He sought the meaning of Scripture and the word of God for his time. With the best will in the world, he wanted to know what God was saying to his people through his ancient prophet.

What the Qumran commentator was doing was normal and, even in some secondary sense within his own group of fellow believers, inspired. He brought Habakkuk to his people in their time and in terms which they undoubtedly understood clearly.

The type of exegesis found at Qumran is largely the same as is found in the New Testament.[1] They each employ a kind of historical typology. They find in ancient Scripture a situation analogous to their own, a crisis described much as they would describe their own, and they proceed to link the two, the old and the immediate, in a pattern of ancient 'type' and present 'antitype'. Once such an analogy is established, then a present situation can be illuminated by an older. Typology, however, goes much further and tends thus to interpret not only present facts but also the future. Nor does it stop there; it goes on to cloak the new situation in an imaginary aura which finally responds more to the factors of the old than to those of the new. The result is

---

* This study originally appeared in *JR* 39 (1959), pp. 232-44. It has been slightly revised for this volume.

1. Cf. J.M. Allegro, *The Dead Sea Scrolls* (Baltimore: Penguin Books, 1956), p. 137; and W.D. Davies, 'Paul and the Dead Sea Scrolls: Flesh and Spirit', in K. Stendahl (ed.), *The Scrolls and the New Testament* (New York: Harper, 1957), pp. 157-82.

frequently a report of the new so couched in terms of the old that an innocent eyewitness would not recognize the account when finally recorded. For example, the Second Isaiah's account of the new exodus from Babylon would be unrecognizable to the poor straggling Jew who wandered home in the reign of Cyrus or Darius.

Typology as a means of modernizing has the other, opposite, effect as well, where the antitype dominates and enhances the type, or older event. For instance, Matthew, who frequently employs typology as a means of stating the church's claim to Old Testament faith, quotes Hos. 11.1, 'Out of Egypt have I called my son'. In so doing, the first evangelist attributes to an Old Testament passage a meaning it did not originally have. Hosea speaks of the event of the exodus using the father–son figure to describe the relationship of God and Israel (cf. Exod. 4.22). Matthew uses the same father–son figure in describing the relationship of God and Jesus and thereby enhances the Hosea passage with the aspect of prediction or foreshadowing of Jesus' trip with Mary and Joseph to and from Egypt. Since the father–son figure dates from the earliest days of the church, the Hosea passage was tailor-made to Matthew's purpose.

Many other examples could be given of the uses of typology and of the other principal exegetical method—promise and fulfillment—to show the interaction which takes place between the Old and New Testament statements.[2] Invariably, each will give a little to and take a little from the other.

A crucial instance of this interaction is Paul's use in Rom. 1.17 and Gal. 3.11 (cf. Heb. 10.38) of a phrase in Hab. 2.4, 'The righteous

2. For recent discussions of the problem see especially W. Eichrodt, 'Ist die typologische Exegese sachgemasse Exegese?', *TLZ* 81 (1956), pp. 641-54 [ET: 'Is Typological Exegesis an Appropriate Method?', in C. Westermann (ed.), *Essays on Old Testament Interpretation* (London: SCM Press, 1963), pp. 224-45]; *idem*, 'Les Rapports du Nouveau Testament et de l'Ancien Testament', in J. Boisset (ed.), *Le Problème biblique dans le Protestantisme* (Paris: Presses Universitaires de France, 1955), pp. 105-30; G.W.H. Lampe and K.J. Woollcombe, *Essays on Typology* (SBT, 22; London: SCM Press, 1957); G. von Rad, 'Typologische Auslegung des Alten Testaments', *EvT* 12 (1952), pp. 17-33; D. Patte, *Early Jewish Hermeneutic in Palestine* (SBLDS, 22; Missoula, MT: Scholars Press, 1975), pp. 159-67; J.W. Drane, 'Typology', *EvQ* 50 (1978), pp. 195-210; L. Goppelt, *Typos: The Typological Interpretation of the Old Testament in the New* (Grand Rapids, MI: Eerdmans, 1982); G.R. Osborne, 'Type', *ISBE*, IV, pp. 930-32; and C.A. Evans, 'Typology', in *Dictionary of Jesus and the Gospels*, forthcoming.

[person] will live by his faith'. Paul, of course, says, 'He who by faith is righteous will live'.

The Habakkuk passage is used by Paul to bolster his theological doctrine of justification by faith, that is to say, his contention as thoroughly set forth in Rom. 3.21-26, Phil. 3.9 and elsewhere that our righteousness comes of God through faith in Christ, and not by our works. While the emphasis in Habakkuk is on acceptance of the divine judgment and commitment to the sovereignty of God in adversity, the emphasis in Paul is on faith in the person of Christ. For Paul, to say 'righteous' was to say 'God in Christ', the cornerstone of the Christian (particularly Pauline) faith. This is an example of a New Testament use of Old Testament Scripture, though not strictly typological, where the New Testament is at a distinct advantage. Paul develops his meaning and use of the phrase to the point of total clarity; Habakkuk is at a great disadvantage, in that his meaning of the phrase is almost totally without explanation in its context.

The Qumran understanding of the same phrase (Hab. 2.4b) has its affinities to that of Paul as well as its marked differences: 'This means all doers of the law in the house of Judah, whom God will deliver from the house of judgment because of their labor and their faith in the Teacher of Righteousness'.[3] The method of exegesis, however, is the same. The 'righteous' for Paul's counterpart in Qumran means all who in the house of Judah practice the law. All such will be spared the final judgment. Thus in Qumran, as in the other expressions of Judaism in this period, righteousness has to do with works. 'Faith' or 'faithfulness' means those who maintained through their labors and affliction their faith in the Teacher of Righteousness. Here we see, as in Paul, that faith is centered in a person. This certainly is not a person similar to Paul's 'God in Christ', but it is a person, the leader of a sect. Nor is it the same faith, the belief which involves commitment and perseverance in the face of adversity and suffering.[4]

---

3. 1QpHab 7.14–8.3. For critical commentary see W.H. Brownlee, *The Midrash Pesher of Habakkuk* (SBLMS, 24; Missoula, MT: Scholars Press, 1979), pp. 125-29; and M.P. Horgan, *Pesharim: Qumran Interpretations of Biblical Books* (CBQMS, 8; Washington: Catholic Biblical Association, 1979), pp. 10-55.

4. That '*amalam* here implies labor of pain and adversity was recognized as early as in A. Dupont-Sommer, *Aperçus préliminaires sur les manuscrits de la Mer Mort* (L'Orient Ancien Illustré, 4; Paris: Maisonneuve, 1950), p. 56, and H.E. del Medico, *Deux manuscrits hébreux de la Mer Mort: Essai de traduction du 'Manuel de*

The Major Premise

What must not be lost sight of in our understandable excitement over how Qumran and Paul used Habakkuk is the abiding necessity to let Habakkuk speak for himself.[5] To deny to Habakkuk his problems and his own solution to those problems is to commit an error almost as great as that of Marcion and the early Gnostics, whom the early church condemned as heretics. Marcion attempted to deny the Old Testament as valid for Christian faith. Just as erroneous is the attempt to force the Old Testament to be seen solely through the eyes of New Testament faith. The church has wisely and constantly through the ages insisted on the 'whole Bible' as the valid rule or canon of faith.

If the Old Testament is to be read only as the New Testament reads it, we will have to admit that we are cheating the New Testament itself of the very basis of its arguments and claims, which, as Krister Stendahl has pointed out, rest solidly and solely on Old Testament faith:

> In the New Testament the major concern is to make clear that all is 'old', in accordance with the expectations of the prophets... Thus the issue between the Essenes and the early Christians was not one of 'originality', but a searching question about who were the legitimate heirs to the prophetic promises and who could produce the most striking arguments for fulfillment.[6]

In marked agreement, his colleague Frank Cross states that 'the New Testament faith was not a new faith, but the fulfillment of an old faith... The New Testament does not set aside or supplant the Old Testament. It affirms it and, from its point of view, completes it'.[7]

If this position is an accurate one—and I am convinced that it is—then it follows logically and convincingly that the faith which the Old Testament itself propounded must never be permitted simply to be

Discipline' et du 'Commentaire d'Habakkuk' avec notes et commentaires (Paris: Geuthner, 1951), p. 114.

5. R.B. Hays (*Echoes of Scripture in the Letters of Paul* [New Haven and London: Yale University Press, 1989], pp. 39-41) has recently and rightly underscored this very point.

6. K. Stendahl, 'The Scrolls and the New Testament: An Introduction and a Perspective', in Stendahl (ed.), *The Scrolls and the New Testament*, pp. 1-17, quotation from p. 6.

7. F.M. Cross, Jr, *The Ancient Library of Qumran and Modern Biblical Studies* (Garden City, NY: Doubleday, 1958), pp. 183-84.

seen in the light of the New Testament's understanding of it. *The Old Testament was the New Testament's major premise.* If that be so, then the Old Testament case for faith must be seriously examined on its own terms. To do anything less makes the New Testament claim a sham and a farce!

The minor premise in the New Testament's argument is its own claim to the fulfillment, in Christ and his church, of the promise of the Old Testament (the major premise). To put it otherwise, both the Old Testament statement of faith referred to in the New, and the New Testament claim based on that statement, must be taken equally seriously.

However, biblical faith is not finally proved or disproved on the basis of the rational logic of a syllogism. To claim such a criterion would be to submit logic as superior to faith, which is a position bearing its own contradiction in terms and its own inherent fallacy. To stay on the plane of faith, suffice it to say that the New Testament lays a claim based on Old Testament faith; therefore, to deny the major premise of that claim would be to deny the faith of the New Testament itself. Furthermore, to force an Old Testament statement into a position other than its own, in order to bolster a New Testament argument, not only would be a logical fallacy but would be evidence of a lack of faith. The Old Testament can best serve the New Testament by standing on its own two feet.

To call the Old Testament a 'torso', as does Otto Procksch in his *Theologie des Alten Testaments*, damages the New Testament argument.[8] Procksch further says that Christ cannot be understood without the Old Testament and that the Old Testament cannot be understood without him. Simple statements such as these can be greatly misleading. What we can say is: to understand Christ as the New Testament would have us understand him, the Old Testament is the *sine qua non*, the only stance from which one must perceive the New Testament statements about him. Other stances, other bases, are also needed to appreciate the full New Testament picture, such as the Hellenistic mystery cults (and social/cultural setting) or, indeed, one's own life situation. To lose sight of the variety of New Testament perspectives does not become the Old Testament student.

8.   O. Procksch, *Theologie des Alten Testaments* (Gütersloh: Bertelsmann, 1950), p. 8; cf. pp. 1-19, pp. 45-47. See G.E. Wright's view of any futile separation of the Testaments and his different use of the word 'torso' (*IB*, I, p. 389).

But Procksch's other dictum concerns us more: the Old Testament cannot be understood without Christ. Such a statement cheats the New Testament of the forcefulness of its argument. If Procksch is right, then the New Testament is wrong, and the minor premise becomes the major.

The New Testament seems to say something like this: the Old Testament itself is the only single criterion to determine the validity of a claim to fulfill its promise; Christ meets the test of that criterion; therefore, Christ is the fulfillment of that promise. Procksch and many other recent biblical theologians would turn the syllogism around to read: Christ is the only single criterion to determine the validity of a claim to be the divine promise; the Old Testament claims to contain the divine promise; therefore, only Christ validates the Old Testament.

Christ is our criterion and, figuratively, our crisis as well. Christ is our judge and our judgment. He, by Scripture and the Holy Spirit, is the canon of our faith and our lives. And, in some sense, all that historically preceded must submit to his judgment. He is the Christian's canon of what in the Old Testament is relevant and valid to the life of faith. But the Old Testament stands in a special relationship to Christ which nothing else can claim. Before it, too, finally came under his judgment, the Old Testament was the criterion by which to identify the Christ, the only single criterion. The Old Testament was not only Jesus' Scripture, hence *his* canon of faith, but, in the end, the major premise of the church in its claim that Jesus was the Christ. All the while that we insist that nothing is exempt from the judgment of Christ—even our faith-understanding of the Old Testament—we must remember that the Old Testament was and, in some sense, is the criterion whereby Christ is Christ. Without the Old Testament, Christ is innovator, not fulfillment.

Any attempt to do away with the Old Testament, as in the Marcionite sense, is therefore to do away with the peculiar New Testament image of Christ. Furthermore, any attempt to take away from the Old Testament its unique relation to the New Testament as the New Testament itself accepts it—namely, as the only single criterion of its claim—is to reduce the Old Testament to nothing more than any other literature or phenomenon of history. While Christ is the *krisis* of all things for the life of faith of the Christian, the Old Testament stands in a peculiar relation to the New Testament and hence to Christ. Not only does it submit, for the Christian, to the canon of Christ for what is valid in Christian faith; it also has the unique and distinct role of forever standing in judgment over our understanding of Christ. The New Testament image of Christ, by its own admission and insistence, depends on the Old Testament; and the New Testament claims about him submit uniquely and only to the Old Testament judgment of them.

To argue that the Old Testament no longer enjoys this distinction or has lost its significance as canon for the New Testament is to declare the New Testament argument outdated and, in some sense, therefore, to destroy the whole concept of the canon of Scripture. When one denies to the Old Testament this dual relationship to the New Testament, one has denied to the first-century argument of the New Testament any abiding significance. In so doing, one has denied the relevance of Scripture altogether. The New Testament accepts no other criterion than the Old Testament in its claims for Christ and his church. If we rid the Old Testament of that role of criterion to the New Testament, we have pulled the teeth out of the New Testament argument and claim. If we rid the New Testament of the power of its claim, we discard it altogether, or we find ourselves in the position of the child unwilling to believe his balloon is burst who keeps trying to blow air into scraps of rubber.

Emending Procksch, I assert that for the Christian the Old Testament cannot be accepted as canon of faith without Christ. But we must with equal force assert that, without the Old Testament, the New Testament image of Christ and the New Testament claims made for him and his church are without foundation, without context, without force, and without meaning. In other words, without the Old Testament, Christ is not Christ at all in the New Testament sense. It is, therefore, not just a question of understanding Christ, it is a question of having him at all. The New Testament is the New Testament because of the Old Testament, in some sense both absolute and relative. Therefore, I assert: *Christ cannot be the New Testament Christ without the Old Testament, and the Old Testament cannot be the Christian Old Testament without Christ.* Out of such an assertion the Old Testament looms forth as critical to the New Testament in an absolute sense inapplicable to any other claim. The Old Testament is subject to New Testament judgment, as are all other phenomena of the Christian experience, but the New Testament is subject to Old Testament judgment as is nothing else in the Christian experience.

The question immediately arises as to whether New Testament

revelation surpasses Old Testament revelation. For the Christian it does, since the Old Testament does submit to the Christ *krisis* or judgment. It is the faith of the Christian that nothing is exempt in all history from the judgment of this one historical figure we call the Christ. For the Christian the Old Testament is Christian because of Christ, and it is to be understood as canon from the Christian perspective. Christ judges the Old Testament in all its parts. But this does not mean that the New Testament has superseded the Old Testament. Revelation is not progressive in the sense of superseding all that historically precedes. That would render not just history but the passage of time as superior to all revelation. No such idea is to be seriously entertained by the thinking Christian. Revelation and history stand in such a relationship to one another that, though history does affect revelation in its form and content, revelation stands forever in judgment on history. The greatest hurdle of the whole story that the Christian has to tell is the Incarnation, where revelation itself entered nature and became history. Not only does the Christian tell that story, he believes it. But commitment to it involves the admission and recognition that revelation is dynamic, vital, and alive and that it is subject to the nature it entered and the history it became at the same time that it stands in judgment on that very history. Faith is affected by history all the while it stands in judgment on history.[9]

New Testament faith, therefore, surpasses, but does not supersede, Old Testament faith. The Old Testament, like nothing else in the Christian experience, has a unique and special relationship to the New Testament; for without the major premise of its own argument, there is no biblical foundation to the New Testament claim.

Faith and History

The very crux of the Christian faith, the very heart of the incredible story that Christians have to tell the world, is at the point of the relationship of faith to history. In a review in the *New York Times* of

---

9. See the still pertinent article by J.P. Hyatt, 'The Ministry of Scholarship', *Crozer Quarterly Review* 28 (1951), pp. 212-16, esp. p. 215. Note J. Jeremias's discussion of the implications of the incarnation for historical research in 'The Present Position in the Controversy concerning the Problem of the Historical Jesus', *ExpTim* 69 (1958), pp. 333-39.

Edmund Wilson's *Scrolls from the Dead Sea*,[10] Frank Cross put it suc-
cinctly by stating that it is the Christian's belief not that God has from
time to time suspended history but that he has given significance to it.
That faith affects history is the Christian statement to the world. If
this is so, then it is plausible to think that the opposite holds: history
affects faith. For both statements there is ample evidence. If this be
the case, then there is as much spirit of faith as historicism in the lib-
eral attitude that the biblical historian in his or her work should let the
chips fall where they may. To put it theologically, it would seem that
there is more faith in the sovereignty of God as Lord of history in
evidence among the historians than among some existentialist theologians who would discount historical research as important to faith.

If faith affects history and history affects faith, and if this faith and
this history are truly dynamically related and not abstracted one from
another, then, though the faith expressed in one historical circum-
stance can be modernized or made relevant to a later historical cir-
cumstance, that expression of faith must be fully examined in its own
Sitz im Leben, within the problems to which it first responded. That is
to say, specifically, that, while we must allow Paul his use of Hab.
2.4b and the Qumranian expositor his use of the same, we must also
allow Habakkuk his meaning in his situation.

However, to use Habakkuk's meaning as the sole criterion of the
validity of a later application would simply be to ignore the problem
of the relevance of the canon. Neither Qumran nor the New Testament
can be expected simply to echo Old Testament faith. While both the
Qumran and the New Testament exegetes were committed to the then
extant Old Testament's functioning as canon, they were certainly not
limited to a simple rehashing of Scripture. The problem of the relevance of the canon is at best complex, certainly exceeding the simple
problem of finding analogous historical situations in which to reiterate
exactly the canonical faith. As stated above, New Testament faith surpasses, but does not supersede, Old Testament faith—by its own commitment to it. The same was true of the faith professed at Qumran.
For at Qumran it is quite clear that, while there was a commitment to
the Old Testament as canon, there was certainly no hesitancy in
asserting the peculiar election of the sect and its particular role within
Israel in its own day. In a sense equal to that we have seen for the

10. E. Wilson, *The Scrolls from the Dead Sea* (New York: Oxford University
Press, 1955).

New Testament, the faith of the Qumran community was a faith surpassing that of the Old Testament, though not superseding it. The difference, it would appear, was the same for both, namely, the belief that each was heralding the eschaton. Both Qumran and the early church firmly believed itself the chosen evangelist of the good news of the inbreaking eschaton, of the divine intervention in history which would mean the immediate sovereignty and reign of God and his will on earth.

The task of each was conceived as crucial to world history, not just to the ongoing life of the sect. Their task was to proclaim the eschaton and to prepare for it. To execute the task, each made use of its Scripture, the Old Testament as it was known to them. Both groups felt not only free to modernize Habakkuk but obliged to do so. If, in so doing, Habakkuk's historical situation was obscured, it was because of the belief that the eschaton would consummate and affirm, not deny, prior history. For, surely, not only Habakkuk's history but all history was about to be fulfilled. The relevance of Habakkuk was in what the prophet had to say to the most crucial and important event of all history, the immediate and inbreaking eschaton. Qumran and the early church believed that Habakkuk was addressing himself primarily to that moment in history to which each community believed itself to bear witness. However, there is no evidence whatever to think that they denied a meaning in Habakkuk to Habakkuk's own situation. Their belief was that Habakkuk's faith was a canonical faith, and, if canonical, then its application was not limited to its original expression; indeed, it had an especial application to the eschaton.

Contemporary Hermeneutics

The *rapprochement* of New Testament and Qumranian hermeneutics has been an object of study since the Habakkuk scroll was first published.[11] It is beyond doubt that the closest link between the scrolls and the New Testament is their hermeneutics. This is so much the case that we now describe the principal exegetical method of Qumran, of Matthew, and even Paul, as the *midrash pesher*, taking the word *pesher* from the scrolls themselves. The use of the word *pesher* was

11. One of the earliest of such studies was that of B.J. Roberts, 'Some Observations on the Damascus Documents and the Dead Sea Scrolls', *BJRL* 34 (1951-52), pp. 366-87, esp. pp. 367ff.

hardly noticeable before the discovery of the scrolls but, since Krister Stendahl's dissertation, is freely applied to the New Testament, where the hermeneutics resemble that of Qumran Habakkuk.

Stendahl deals particularly with variant readings and the differing quotations of the Old Testament, especially of Habakkuk, found in Qumran and the New Testament.[12] One observation which has emerged from such comparative studies is outstanding: there was no established authoritative text of the Old Testament before the Masoretic collations beginning in the second century AD.[13] Paul's usual vade mecum was the LXX, while the Qumran commentator's was chiefly a pre-MT Hebrew text very close to the MT. Stendahl's interest in 1QpHab centers on the variants between it and the MT. He says, 'We must...presume that [1QpHab] was conscious of various possibilities, tried them out and allowed them to enrich its interpretation of the prophet's message, which in all its forms was fulfilled in and through the Teacher of Righteousness.'[14] Such, Stendahl feels, was also the case for Matthew. Earle Ellis applies the same reasoning to Pauline hermeneutics and states:

> Taken as a whole, the Pauline citations reflect in substantial measure a *pesher* type moulding of the [Old Testament] text which in some cases is determinative for the New Testament application of the passage. While this at times involves a choosing and rejecting between texts and/or targums known to the apostle, more often the interpretive paraphrase appears to be created *ad hoc* by Paul or by the early church before him.[15]

To illustrate this point further, consider the diversity of readings of Hab. 2.4b, some from texts that obviously preceded Paul's time, some from later periods which may reflect earlier readings, and some from the apostle himself:

1. MT:	וְצַדִּיק בֶּאֱמוּנָתוֹ יִחְיֶה
2. Targum:	וצדיקיא על קושטהון יתקיימון
3. LXX:	ὁ δὲ δίκαιος ἐκ πίστεώς μου ζήσεται
4. Vulgate:	*iustus autem in fide sua vivet*

12. K. Stendahl, *The School of St Matthew and its Use of the Old Testament* (Lund: Gleerup, 1954), esp. pp. 185-90.

13. See W.F. Albright, 'New Light on Early Recensions of the Hebrew Bible', *BASOR* 140 (1955), pp. 27-33; and Cross, *Ancient Library of Qumran*, pp. 124-45.

14. Stendahl, *The School of St Matthew*, p. 190.

15. E.E. Ellis, 'A Note on Pauline Hermeneutics', *NTS* 2 (1955-56), pp. 127-33, esp. pp. 131-32.

5. 8HevXIIgr 17.30: καὶ δίκαιος ἐν πίστει αὐτοῦ ζήσεται
6. Paul (Rom. 1.17): ὁ δὲ δίκαιος ἐκ πίστεως ζήσεται
7. Paul (Gal. 3.11): ὁ δίκαιος ἐκ πίστεως ζήσεται
8. Heb. 10.38 (Π⁴⁶ ℵ A): ὁ δὲ δίκαιός μου ἐκ πίστεως ζήσεται
9. Heb. 10.38 (D* itᵈ,ᵉ): ὁ δὲ δίκαιος ἐκ πίστεώς μου ζήσεται
10. Heb. 10.38 (Π¹³ D²): ὁ δὲ δίκαιος ἐκ πίστεως ζήσεται

The diversity is plainly evident. What is also of interest is to observe that Habakkuk's theology influences targumic readings elsewhere. For example, *Targ. Zech.* 2.17 reads, at least according to one MS (Parma 555), 'The righteous and the meek shall live by their upright deeds'. It is likely that this targumic reading has been directly influenced by Hab. 2.4. What we have, then, are variant readings *and exegeses*; and it is not always possible to distinguish them.

Hence, while we are faced with the freedom of Qumran and the early church to choose and select among equally viable Old Testament readings in their period, these variants do not limit the problem. They both felt free to adapt the prophet's message to their respective situations and, as I have shown above, on the grounds of simple logic, to let the prophetic word be thereby enriched. In other words, they were not constrained only to quote the prophet and modernize; they had the freedom to modernize first and then to quote the adapted version.

This would be a dangerous, even frightening, observation without the sort of wisdom to accompany it which T.W. Manson affords:

> We are long accustomed to distinguish carefully between the text which—in more senses than one—is sacred, and the commentary upon it and exposition of it. We tend to think of the text as objective fact and interpretation as subjective opinion. It may be doubted whether the early Jewish and Christian translators and expositors of Scripture made any such sharp distinction. For them the meaning of the text was of primary importance; and they seem to have had greater confidence than we moderns in their ability to find it. Once found it became a clear duty to express it; and accurate reproduction of the traditional wording of the Divine oracles took second place to publication of what was held to be their essential meaning and immediate application. Odd as it may seem to us, the freedom with which they handled the Biblical text is a direct result of the supreme importance which they attached to it.[16]

16. T.W. Manson, 'The Argument from Prophecy', *JTS* 46 (1945), pp. 129-36, citation from p. 135, as quoted in Ellis, 'Pauline Hermeneutics', p. 132.

The modern critical student is faced not only with the first-century hermeneutics of modernization but with the freedom of the early exegetes to quote the Old Testament in the light of modernization.

Contemporary Interpretations

We are now prepared to accept these two interpretations as legitimate exegetical attempts to modernize what is equally canonical for both in the Old Testament prophetic corpus. Their respective interpretations are amazingly similar. As has been noted, they both expound upon faith in, or fidelity to, a person: for Paul, Christ; for 1QpHab, the Teacher of Righteousness. However, whereas Paul denies works or obedience as a means of salvation, Qumran insists on the necessity of obedience to the law to escape the judgment.

Erich Dinkler has more or less convincingly shown the conjunction of the doctrines of predestination and individual responsibility in both Romans and the Dead Sea Manual of Discipline.[17] But the value of Dinkler's discussion is more distinct in his work on Paul than on Qumran. The documents from Qumran give abundant evidence of the general election of Israel and the peculiar election of the sect, as well as the necessity of responsibility and obedience. It is good to realize, with Dinkler, Paul's insistence on responsibility and obedience for the person already under grace in Christ. The difference is not in the call to obedience, it is in Qumran's view that obedience to the law will put off the day of judgment; or, rather, the distinction here, in view of the varieties of Judaism of the period, is Paul's.

However, one of the most exciting facets of recent study has been that of discovering Paul's doctrine of the righteousness of God in at least one of the psalms of Qumran, the closing hymn of praise appended to the Manual of Discipline. Sherman Johnson has said, 'How startling it is that a narrow and harsh law ends on such a note of hope and justification'.[18] The following is a fresh translation of a few selected lines from the Manual of Discipline:

17. E. Dinkler, 'The Historical and the Eschatological Israel in Romans Chapters 9–11', *JR* 36 (1956), pp. 109-27, esp. pp. 120-25.
18. S.E. Johnson, 'Paul and the Manual of Discipline', *HTR* 48 (1955), pp. 157-66, quote from p. 165.

... And in his righteousness will my sin be blotted out...

For the truth of God, that is my stepping stone ...

... A source of righteousness... God has given to whom he has chosen.

As for me, if I should slip, the loving faithfulness of God is my salvation
  forever,

And if I should stumble because of the sins of the flesh,[19]

My vindication will be forever established through the righteousness of
God...

In his mercy he has drawn me near

And by his loving deeds my vindication approaches.

In the righteousness of his truth has he judged me

And in his abundant goodness he forever atones for all of my iniquities.

And by his righteousness he cleanses me from human filth and sin

In order that I may thank God for his righteousness and the Most High for
his beauteous majesty (1QS 11.3-7, 11, 12, 13-15).

Johnson goes on to say, 'The new materials show, furthermore, that
the issue of justification and the means whereby God accepts the
sinner, are not creations of Paul's brain, above all not *ad hoc* creations
for occasional sermons to the Galatians and Romans, but real issues
about which people were concerned, at least in sectarian circles.'[20] It
seems fairly certain that the theologians of Qumran and Paul have
many thoughts in common relating humanity's sin and God's righteousness. Very cautiously Johnson says that it would be tempting to
think of our phrase in 1QpHab to Hab. 2.4b as meaning 'faith in the
Teacher of Righteousness'. Johnson rightly recoils from such a meaning and translates the phrase 'fidelity to the Teacher of Righteousness'.

Let us look again at the two *pesher* interpretations of the Habakkuk
passage. Obedience and responsibility are to the point for both. The
great distinction lies in Paul's interest in responsibility after justification by faith, not as a necessity for justification. Furthermore, Paul's
universalism and general struggle against the Petrine church distinguishes him clearly from Qumran's 'all who fulfill the law in the
house of Judah'. But in the matter of justification itself, Qumran and

19. On the meaning of 'flesh' here and elsewhere in the scrolls see K.G. Kuhn,
'New Light on Temptation, Sin, and Flesh in the New Testament', in Stendahl (ed.),
The Scrolls and the New Testament, pp. 94-113, esp. pp. 101-103; Davies, 'Paul
and the Dead Sea Scrolls', in Stendahl (ed.), *The Scrolls and the New Testament*,
pp. 159-71; and cf. J.P. Hyatt, 'The View of Man in the Qumran "Hodayot"', *NTS*
2 (1955-56), pp. 276-84.

20. Johnson, 'Paul and the Manual of Discipline', p. 165.

Paul have many affinities. In Paul faith in Christ seems to make the difference.

Here, then, are two similar, yet distinct, applications of one Old Testament verse in two approximately contemporary writers, each firmly believing the eschaton to be at hand. Each views the Old Testament phrase from his eschatological perspective. Neither could ever be convinced that he had done any injustice to Habakkuk. Each believed that he had drawn from Habakkuk its true meaning, each using what we have seen as a *pesher*-type interpretation.

Not only does the recovery of the ancient library of Qumran afford us a comparison of the beliefs and arguments of two contemporary eschatological denominations in Judaism, but it also affords us a comparison of their use of what for both was equally sacred and canonical —their Scripture, the Old Testament. In all probability, a comparison of their beliefs will ultimately force us to a simple statment of what the essential difference between them really is.

Krister Stendahl has issued the simple statement that, 'It is Jesus that makes the difference'.[21] He is compelled to state that the fundamental distinction between them is not one of kind but one of degree. They were both eschatologically oriented. They both lived in anticipation of the fulness of the eschaton. Stendahl says:

> The Teacher of Righteousness suffered persecution and injustice and the community held a high doctrine about its Council as the ones chosen to atone for the people. But in the light of the resurrection, the death of Jesus was transformed into an atoning suffering of an ultimate and cosmic significance. Thus, it was the higher degree of anticipation, i.e., a relative difference.

He later adds, 'The relative difference in anticipation led to what appears to us an absolute difference in ideas'.[22] What he means by this relative difference being really and finally absolute can only be, it seems to me, again, that the atoning Christ makes the difference.

The real difference between Paul's exegesis of Hab. 2.4 and Qumran's is Paul's application of the passage to Christ's atoning death.[23] This,

21. Stendahl, 'The Scrolls and the New Testament', p. 17; cf. J. Jeremias, 'The Qumran Texts and the New Testament', *ExpTim* 70 (1958), pp. 68-69.

22. Stendahl, 'The Scrolls and the New Testament', p. 17.

23. See O. Cullmann, 'The Significance of the Qumran Texts for Research into the Beginnings of Christianity', *JBL* 74 (1955), pp. 213-26, esp. pp. 225-26. However, see the results of work on recent finds from Cave 4 by J. Allegro,

then, *is* the distinction between Qumran's 'fidelity to the Teacher of Righteousness' and Paul's 'righteousness of God through faith in Jesus Christ...whom God put forward as an expiation...' (Rom. 3.22, 25).

Habakkuk Himself

Now let us look once more at Habakkuk himself. What was the faith of which Habakkuk spoke? Was it only a faithfulness to divine will or law? Was it only a fidelity to Yahwism? Rather, Habakkuk was speaking of faith in God—the startling, shocking faith that God does not die; that Marduk, the principal god of the Babylonians, had not defeated Yahweh, but that Yahweh had used the Babylonians to judge and discipline his own people (Hab. 1.12). Habakkuk meant more than fidelity or obedience, he meant a radical faith in the sovereignty of God, not only over Judah, but over the Babylonians as well—indeed, the whole world. This was the kind of faith that Isaiah preached; and it seems to me that Habakkuk's famous phrase means precisely the same thing as an equally famous phrase of Isaiah's: 'The person of faith need not haste' (Isa. 28.16).[24] Habakkuk's faith was in the universal sovereignty of God. The righteous person was distinguished by his faith in God's lordship over the current events of history. This was not just a fidelity to Yahweh as against Marduk; it was a faith-perception that God was in full control of the situation, the judge of his own people by means of another. If he judged them, he was not just their god, he was God.

Such an assertion was too commonplace for either Paul or our Qumranian exegete. They both applied it to their time, to the inbreaking eschaton of which they were both certain. For Paul it meant faith in God's work in Christ, in God's righteousness through Christ. For the Qumran exegete it was quite as likely also faith in God's work in the Teacher of Righteousness. The difference, as noted above, was the

---

'Further Light on the History of the Qumran Sect', *JBL* 75 (1956), pp. 89-95, pp. 174-87, and the criticism of them by H.H. Rowley, '4QpNahum and the Teacher of Righteousness', *JBL* 75 (1956), pp. 188-93, and *idem*, 'The Teacher of Righteousness and the Dead Sea Scrolls', *BJRL* 40 (1957), pp. 114-46.

24. Cf. S.H. Blank, *Prophetic Faith in Isaiah* (New York: Harper, 1958), pp. 37-39, where Blank, too, suggests, though with different emphasis, that Isa. 28.16 informs the meaning of Hab. 2.4b.

atoning death of Christ, the relative difference which has for Christians today become absolute.

Habakkuk was modernized by both and rendered messianic, or at least eschatological, by both. But the faith of Habakkuk, and of the Old Testament in general, while surpassed by the work of God in Christ's expiatory death, was not superseded, not is it yet superseded. It is the foundation faith of all our faith. It is Isaiah's precious cornerstone of a sure foundation: God is lord; he lives and he reigns.[25] Just as the first assertion of faith for the exiled Jews of the sixth century BC was that God had not died but yet lived, so it was the first assertion of the followers of Jesus after the crucifixion: he lives; and, just as the fulness of the sovereignty of God was revealed to the Second Isaiah a few years later (Isa. 52.7), so the fulness of the reign of the grace of God in Christ (Rom. 5.21) was revealed to Paul.[26]

But Habakkuk did not have this Christ, nor did he consciously point to him. He consciously pointed to and witnessed to his God, the living and reigning God whose power was universal and whose judgment of his people was a righteous judgment.[27] To say that Habakkuk unconsciously witnessed to Christ is a burden for Paul and the modern theologian to bear. To say that Habakkuk witnessed to the judging and redeeming God—hence, by definition, Christ—is to deny the historical aspect of the incarnation. We cannot say with J.K.S. Reid, 'If God saves in the time of the Old Testament, Jesus Christ is there, by whom He saves'.[28] Trying to hold to the historical aspect of the incarnation and also to Christ doing God's work of salvation in a history prior to that incarnation is more than a dynamic paradox; it violates the monotheizing process.

The Old Testament Today

The Old Testament does not need such desperate handling to belong to the church. The Old Testament stands on its own two feet. Old Testament faith bears witness to God within the history of a people, which history has become the prehistory of the church and whose

25. Cf. J.A. Sanders, 'Thy God Reigneth', *Motive* (February, 1956), pp. 28-31.

26. By simple analogy, not typology.

27. I agree with Hays (*Echoes of Scripture*, pp. 39-41) that the basic issue to which Habakkuk addressed himself was theodicy.

28. J.K.S. Reid, *The Authority of Scripture* (London: Methuen, 1957), p. 257.

faith is the foundation of the Christian faith. While there are parts of the Old Testament which are an embarrassment to the church and would never have formed the phraseology of the major premise of the Christian argument and claim for Christ, there are equally embarrassing parts of the New Testament which do not speak to our modern day. Such portions of either Testament are good only for allegorization, and if we must resort to allegory to save them, we might as well canonize all the world's literature and allegorize Rabelais' *Gargantua*, as well as the Song of Songs.

Paul picked and chose. He chose as his text for his most thorough treatment of the Christian soteriology and Christology Hab. 2.4b, a passage well suited to his purpose. He did not give a historical exegesis of the passage; he proclaimed its relevance to the work of the same God in Christ. The claim that the Old Testament bore witness to the righteousness of God formed the basis of his argument. To this extent, it seems to me, as it seemed to Professor Ropes of Harvard back in 1903, that Paul's idea of the righteousness of God arose from the Old Testament itself, where Paul had his firmest roots.[29] To say that Paul gives us a *pesher* quotation of the verse and an application relevant to the work of God in Christ is to say that he has at least done more than rehash his Old Testament text; he has seen its dynamic relevance to what he firmly believed was a historical event surpassing the event to which Habakkuk himself spoke—namely, the eschaton of God's saving history. In other words, Paul said something more than Habakkuk said.

But because he added to Habakkuk, is Habakkuk therefore to be denied the meaning his own statement had for him, and can also have for us? Never. Habakkuk and the Old Testament in general (though not equally in every part) must be permitted to say what they say, to stand on their own two feet. Only then does the New Testament stand a chance to state its claim and propound its argument. The Old Testament is the Old Testament to the Christian because of Christ. But the New Testament is the New Testament, and Christ is Christ, because the Old Testament is its foundation and its major premise. To deny to the Old Testament its faith in its time is to deny that God acted in that time, which is equally to deny the basic New Testament argument of the eschaton of that divine activity and history.

29. J.H. Ropes, ' "Righteousness" and "The Righteousness of God" in the Old Testament and in St Paul', *JBL* 22 (1903), pp. 211-27.

Christ is the Christian's criterion of what in the Old Testament is relevant. But the Old Testament must forever remain the only single criterion of the New Testament claim that Jesus is the Christ; for the Old Testament can and must be understood apart from Christ, that it may fulfill its role as witness to the New Testament argument. For the Christian the Old Testament must continue to play this dual role. If not, then Christ becomes solely innovator, not fulfillment, and hence no longer the New Testament Christ.

If these conclusions are correct, then it follows that the task of historical research, of close study of the facts and factors of the history to which God has given significance, must be pursued as objectively as possible, letting the chips fall where they may. Only then is our faith real and not a sham.

Stendahl with candid force has said that,

> The task of biblical studies must be confined to the presentation of the original. To be a good historian in this field is not only to give date and theories of authorship. It includes the empathic descriptive analysis of the ideas and the synthetic description of the patterns of thought. The task of biblical studies, even of biblical theology, is to describe, to relive and relate in the terms and presuppositions of the period of the texts what they meant to their authors and their contemporaries.[30]

Millar Burrows makes the same point equally well:

> Objectivity does not mean treating another person like a laboratory specimen, to be dissected and described; it means respecting his dignity and freedom, allowing him to be himself and to say what he wants to say: without that kind of self-denying objectivity genuine exegesis is impossible. The exegete must treat Paul or Isaiah with respect and allow him to be himself.[31]

Archaeology is the exegete's most essential tool and certainly the most valuable. To furnish the original, as Stendahl says, or to practice

---

30. K. Stendahl, 'Implications of Form-Criticism and Tradition-Criticism for Biblical Interpretation', *JBL* 77 (1958), pp. 33-38, quote from pp. 37-38. In the same issue see the similar points made with different emphasis by J. Muilenburg ('Preface to Hermeneutics', pp. 18-26, esp. pp. 21-24), and by J.C. Rylaarsdam ('The Problem of Faith and History in Biblical Interpretation', pp. 26-32, esp. pp. 31-32). 'Original' here means what extant texts permit of recovery of early understandings of events.

31. M. Burrows, 'Thy Kingdom Come', *JBL* 74 (1955), pp. 1-8, quotation from p. 3.

objectivity, as Burrows insists, the biblical exegete and theologian are obligated to archaeology. However, contrary to popular opinion, archaeology is not going to prove (or disprove) anything in matters of faith. To make archaeology or any other method of historical research the criterion of faith is to assert commitment to history, and that is precisely what faith frees us from.[32] Nonetheless, archaeology can and does help clarify that which is history or myth or legend, and to clarify the details of each. Even if archaeology should show the Bible to be mostly good history, that would not prove the priority of the Christian faith as over against, say, the priority of the Qumranian faith, though it might make us feel better about how things have turned out. If it should show the Bible to be mostly poor history, that would not disprove Christian faith, though it might in our Western minds increase the risk we normally run by being committed to our Christ and increase the doubt that inevitably accompanies faith. Archaeology and historical research have acheived both these things. In the one case we heave a sigh of relief, and in the other we are forced to dig deeper into what faith really means. The latter has often been the healthier eventuality, and we should never cease to welcome the challenging study or the daring work of the historian. Only when we are willing to run the risks of doubt is our faith relevant, dynamic, and alive. Anything less is not worthy of Paul's faith or Habakkuk's faith, or, for that matter, the faith of the ancient theologians of Qumran.

32. Cf. F.R. Steele, 'Archaeology and the Bible', *Christianity Today* 2.4 (November 25, 1957), pp. 15-17; also G.E. Wright, 'Archaeology and Old Testament Studies', *JBL* 77 (1958), pp. 39-51.

'THE REDEEMER WILL COME ἐκ Σιων':
ROMANS 11.26-27 REVISITED

Christopher D. Stanley

In his recent book, *Echoes of Scripture in the Letters of Paul*,[1] Richard B. Hays examines Paul's handling of his ancestral Scriptures from the vantage point of modern literary criticism. Central to Hays's analysis is the phenomenon of 'intertextuality', defined here as 'the study of the semiotic matrix within which a text's acts of signification occur'.[2] The primary aim of such an approach is to expose the dynamic interplay between Paul's explicit quotations and allusions and 'the symbolic field created by a single great textual precursor: Israel's Scriptures'.[3] As a literary critic, Hays makes use of 'a style of interpretation that focuses neither on the poet's [i.e., Paul's] psyche nor on the historical presuppositions of poetic allusions but on their rhetorical and semantic effects'.[4] Paul appears in this interpretation as 'a prophetic figure, carrying forward the proclamation of God's word as Israel's prophets and sages had always done, in a way that reinterpreted past revelation under new conditions'.[5]

Though he does not eschew historical inquiry, Hays relegates the kinds of questions that investigators have traditionally asked about Paul's quotations to a decidedly secondary role. Whereas historical studies can determine, for example, whether a given interpretive tradition might have been available to Paul in the first century CE, the evocative effects of a quotation ultimately transcend all historical limitations.[6] What Hays aims to uncover is not what Paul 'meant' by

1. New Haven and London: Yale University Press, 1989.
2. *Echoes of Scripture*, p. 15
3. *Echoes of Scripture*, p. 15.
4. *Echoes of Scripture*, p. 19.
5. *Echoes of Scripture*, p. 14.
6. To be sure, Hays does include historical factors among his seven 'tests' for

appealing to this or that passage of Scripture (an 'author-centered' approach), but rather 'the poetic effects produced for those who have ears to hear'.[7]

That Hays himself has 'ears to hear' is evident from his results. Time and again his sensitive analysis lays bare the subtle interplay between text and subtext that typifies Paul's repeated appeals to Scripture. But what about those passages where the biblical text is only indirectly the focus of Paul's interpretive activities? Numerous instances can be cited where Paul quotes a verse that shows signs of an earlier (Jewish or Christian) history of interpretation.[8] In these cases, the interpreter must be alert to the possibility that it is the *tradition* that is being reconfigured in the Pauline context, and not the language of Scripture itself. The problem is especially acute in those passages where Hays posits a 'metaleptic' relationship between the Pauline quotation and the original biblical context.[9] How is the interpreter to know whether it is the voice of Paul or some unknown predecessor that is being revived in such instances? The question remains moot so long as the discussion is limited to purely literary matters. But when the investigation turns to historical and exegetical issues, the problem of sources must be squarely faced. Otherwise the interpreter might be tempted to build an argument around some minor aspect of a quotation that bears little relation to the broader rhetorical context. A clear example is Rom. 9.33 (= Isa. 28.16 and Isa. 8.14), where a failure to

---

assessing an interpreter's claim to find 'echoes of Scipture' in the letters of Paul (pp. 29-31). These 'tests', however, function only as 'rules of thumb', not actual constraints, as Hays himself acknowledges (p. 29). In the final analysis, says Hays, 'Texts can generate readings that transcend both the conscious intention of the author and all the hermeneutical strictures that we promulgate' (p. 33).

7. *Echoes of Scripture*, p. 19. Hays offers a refreshingly honest appraisal of his own stance as a reader in pp. 25-29.

8. See especially B. Lindars, *New Testament Apologetic* (Philadelphia: Westminster Press, 1961), pp. 222-50, and D.-A. Koch, *Die Schrift als Zeuge des Evangeliums* (Tübingen: Mohr [Paul Siebeck], 1988), pp. 239-47.

9. Following J. Hollander (*The Figure of Echo: A Mode of Allusion in Milton and After* [Berkeley: University of California Press, 1981], pp. 133-49), Hays defines 'metalepsis' (also called 'transumption') as a 'diachronic trope' in which 'the figurative effect of the echo can lie in the unstated or suppressed (transumed) points of resonance between the two texts' (*Echoes of Scripture*, p. 20). The task of the critic in such cases is to explicate the 'field of whispered or unstated correspondences' that links the two texts (*Echoes of Scripture*, p. 20).

distinguish between a pre-Pauline interpretive tradition (cf. 1 Pet. 2.6-8) and Paul's own adaptation of that tradition could cause an unwary exegete to exaggerate the christological dimensions of Paul's argument.[10]

Another passage where questions of this sort come bubbling to the surface is Rom. 11.26-27, a passage not treated in Hays's study. In what has become a *crux interpretum*, Paul offers a brief glimpse into his own expectations regarding the eventual outcome of his all-absorbing mission to the Gentiles. Once 'the fulness of the Gentiles has come in', says Paul, then 'all Israel will be saved' (vv. 25-26a). In support of his position, Paul presents what appears to be a running quotation from the authoritative Jewish Scriptures (vv. 26b-27). What he gives instead is a 'conflated citation' in which a single clause from Isa. 27.9 has been merged into a longer excerpt from Isa. 59.20. Though the precise link between assertion and citation is by no means obvious,[11] a suitable rationale for Paul's appeal to these particular passages is not hard to find. Both Isaiah 27 and Isaiah 59 portray Yahweh as a military hero who comes to rescue his people from a state of 'darkness' and 'captivity'. Both passages include references to the forgiveness of Israel's sin, the judgment and subjection of her enemies, and the return of her dispersed children from the surrounding nations. Clearly a person who has 'ears to hear' could discover a multitude of resonances between the Pauline context and the original Isaianic oracles. But do any of these 'echoes of Scripture' help to clarify the relationship between the 'quotation' and Paul's own assertions about Israel's future in vv. 25-26a? If so, which ones? And what about the unusual wording of Paul's biblical text at this point? Do his divergences from the Greek Septuagint (his usual *Vorlage*)[12] say anything about his interpretive agenda in the present passage? Or are they

10. For a thorough examination of the evidence, see the discussion of Rom. 9.33 in my detailed study of Paul's citation technique, *Paul and the Language of Scripture* (SNTSMS, 69; Cambridge: Cambridge University Press, 1992).

11. For a thoughtful survey of recent scholarship on the subject, see R. Hvalvik, 'A "Sonderweg" for Israel: A Critical Examination of a Current Interpretation of Romans 11.25-27', *JSNT* 38 (1990), pp. 87-107. Additional materials are cited by R.D. Aus, 'Paul's Travel Plans to Spain and the "Full Number of the Gentiles" of Rom. XI 25', *NovT* 21 (1979), p. 233 n. 6.

12. On the question of Paul's *Vorlage*, see most recently Koch, *Die Schrift als Zeuge*, pp. 48-83.

merely careless slips of memory, or even pre-Pauline adaptations that reveal an earlier (Jewish or Christian) use of the verses in question? Only a careful sifting of the evidence can determine the origins of the various 'echoes of Scripture' that the modern reader is sure to hear whispering throughout the passage.

Whose Voice?

The first question to be examined is how this 'quotation' came to be shaped into its present form. Most interpreters assume that Paul himself selected and combined the two verses from Isaiah on the basis of their similar ideas and language, so that any further changes reflect Paul's own interpretive concerns. Some would trace both the conflation and the altered wording to the vagaries of memory quotation, while others would credit the apostle with a more active editorial role.[13] The differences are easily identified when the verses are placed side by side (brackets in the Pauline text signify omissions; other differences in bold):

Paul: [ ] ἥξει ἐκ Σιων ὁ ῥυόμενος, [ ] ἀποστρέψει ἀσεβείας ἀπὸ Ἰακωβ. καὶ αὕτη αὐτοῖς ἡ παρ' ἐμοῦ διαθήκη, + ὅταν ἀφέλωμαι τὰς ἁμαρτίας αὐτῶν.

Isa. 59.20-21 LXX: καὶ ἥξει ἕνεκεν Σιων ὁ ῥυόμενος καὶ ἀποστρέψει ἀσεβείας ἀπὸ Ἰακωβ. καὶ αὕτη αὐτοῖς ἡ παρ' ἐμοῦ διαθήκη, [εἶπεν κύριος· τὸ πνεῦμα τὸ ἐμόν, ὅ ἐστιν ἐπὶ σοί, καὶ τὰ ῥήματα ἃ ἔδωκα εἰς τὸ στόμα σου.]

Isa. 27.9 LXX: [διὰ τοῦτο ἀφαιρεθήσεται ἡ ἀνομία Ἰακωβ, καὶ τοῦτό ἐστιν ἡ εὐλογία αὐτοῦ] ὅταν ἀφέλωμαι αὐτοῦ τὴν ἁμαρτίαν, [ὅταν θῶσιν πάντας τοὺς λίθους τῶν βωμῶν κατακεκομμένους ὡς κονίαν λεπτήν].

Besides the conflation itself, the Pauline text differs from the primary LXX tradition in the following ways:

---

13. Perhaps the best known champion of the 'memory quotation' explanation is O. Michel, *Paulus und seine Bibel* (Darmstadt: Wissenschaftliche Buchgesellschaft, 1972 [1929]). For the view that Paul actively adapted the wording of his quotations to reflect his own exegetical and rhetorical concerns, see Koch, *Die Schrift als Zeuge*, pp. 102-90, and my *Paul and the Language of Scripture*, pp. 73-79, 259-64.

1. Omitting an initial καί;
2. Placing ἐκ rather than ἕνεκεν before the proper noun Σιων;
3. Omitting καί in the second clause of the quotation;
4. Pluralizing ἁμαρτίαν and its modifiers ('their sins' versus 'his sin'); and
5. Shifting the possessive pronoun in the last clause to final position.

Of these differences, only the omission of the initial καί (a standard Pauline practice)[14] can be traced with any degree of confidence to Paul himself. While many interpreters have strained to discover a Pauline motive behind the shift from ἕνεκεν to ἐκ Σιων,[15] few have even attempted to explain why Paul would have wanted to replace an original ἕνεκεν ('the Redeemer will come *for the sake of* Zion') in the present context. As Berndt Schaller puts it, 'Dem Apostel geht es doch um den Nachweis, dass Israel, dass Gottesvolk, vom eschatologischen Heil nicht ausgeschlossen ist. Dass das Heil vom Zion kommt, spielt in diesem Zusammenhang keine Rolle'.[16] The total absence of any 'Zion' theme elsewhere in Paul's letters (the word occurs only here and in Rom. 9.33, both in quotations) points in the same direction.[17] As for the second καί, while the omission clearly improves the parallelism between the first two clauses (after the

---

14. In fully a quarter of his citations Paul leaves out an initial καί, while other particles (mostly δέ and ὅτι) are omitted in another 10 per cent of the cases. Introductory particles are retained in only a handful of instances (Rom. 4.17; 8.36; 9.26; 11.35; 2 Cor. 6.17; Gal. 3.16), and in fully half of these the conjunction plays a vital role in linking the two parts of a composite quotation. See the discussions of the individual verses in my *Paul and the Language of Scripture*, pp. 83-251.

15. Typical is Ernst Käsemann, who sees here a reference to 'the return of the exalted Christ from the heavenly Jerusalem of Gal. 4.26' (*Commentary on Romans* [trans. G.W. Bromiley; Grand Rapids, MI: Eerdmans, 1988], p. 314). For a summary of the standard options for reading the change as a Pauline adaptation, see J.D.G. Dunn, *Romans*, II (WBC; Dallas: Word Books, 1988), p. 682. The arguments for a pre-Pauline (Jewish or Christian) alteration or a text-based explanation will be examined below.

16. 'ΗΞΕΙ ΕΚ ΣΙΩΝ Ο ΡΥΟΜΕΝΟΣ: Zur Textgestalt von Jes. 59.20-21 in Rom. 11.26-27', in A. Pietersma and C. Cox (eds.), *De Septuaginta: Studies in Honour of John William Wevers on his Sixty-Fifth Birthday* (Missisauga, Ontario: Benben, 1984), p. 203.

17. So J. de Waard, *A Comparative Study of the Old Testament Text in the Dead Sea Scrolls and in the New Testament* (Leiden: Brill, 1965), p. 12 n. 1.

omission of the initial καί), the frequency of such minor variants throughout the manuscript tradition makes it hazardous to search for an editorial purpose in every instance.[18] The conversion of the pronoun from singular to plural in the final clause ('his' to 'their') is an obvious result of the conflation (to conform to the preceding αὐτοῖς), and should be assigned to whoever brought the two texts together in the first place (see below). Whether the different placement of the pronoun goes back to the same source remains entirely unclear.[19] Finally, the more substantive shift from 'sin' to 'sins' in the final line is hardly Pauline. The plural form of ἁμαρτία is uncommon in Paul's letters, appearing mostly in quotations (Rom. 4.7-8) or traditional formulae (1 Cor. 15.3; Gal. 1.4; Col. 1.14), while the idea of 'taking away sins' finds almost no place in his theology.[20] Though Paul uses a variety of terms to describe Israel's 'problem' in Romans 9–11 ('hardness' [11.7, 25], 'unbelief' [10.16; 11.20, 23, 30-32], reliance on 'works of law' [9.32; 10.2-3], 'transgression' [11.11-12], and so on), not once does he refer to 'sins' that need to be 'taken away'. That Paul should have modified the text of his quotation at this point appears highly unlikely.

But what about the actual conflation? Several lines of evidence suggest that the combination of Isa. 59.20 and Isa. 27.9 into a unified 'quotation' was not original with Paul. In the first place, there is

18. The problem corresponds to the free-floating placement of the letter *waw* in the underlying Hebrew tradition. Whether intentional or not, the omission also forecloses the possibility that the second clause might be understood as following somehow temporally or logically after the first. This in turn agrees with an interpretation that would see the 'turning away of ungodly deeds from Jacob' as taking place in the very 'coming' of the 'Redeemer'. Whether this was the actual reason for the omission, however, can no longer be determined.

19. Shifts in word order are common throughout the manuscript tradition of antiquity. A similar reversal occurs in the LXX tradition in the Hexaplaric MS 88, the Syrohexapla, and the Catena MS 377, all of which follow the 'standard' text for the remainder of the verse. The change has no evident effect on either the meaning or the rhetorical impact of the verse.

20. The idea is implied (but not stated) in 1 Cor. 15.17 and Eph. 2.1. In other places, the plural is used to describe the actions of those outside the faith, with no direct mention of 'forgiveness' (Rom. 7.5; 1 Thess. 2.16; cf. 1 Tim. 5.22, 24; 2 Tim. 3.6). The same is true of the word ἀσέβεια, which appears only in Rom. 1.18 (cf. 2 Tim. 2.16; Tit. 2.12). Koch overlooks this point when he traces both the changed wording and the conflation itself to Pauline editorial activity (*Die Schrift als Zeuge*, pp. 113, 177, 241).

nothing especially 'Pauline' or even 'Christian' about the merging of the two texts. The close verbal similarity between the two verses would have drawn the attention of any reader familiar with the text of Isaiah,[21] while the extensive parallels between their respective contexts would no doubt have reinforced this association.[22] The stress placed here on the word διαθήκη also argues against a Pauline origin, since the word plays almost no role in Paul's theology.[23] The fact that not one of the deviations from the LXX in Rom. 11.27 can be traced with confidence to Paul himself likewise hints at an earlier round of redactional activity. Finally, it seems unlikely that Paul would have broken off his quotation of Isa. 59.20 at precisely the point where the divine 'covenant' is linked with the coming of the Spirit, an association that seems tailor-made for Paul's theology.[24]

So where did the text come from? Some have argued that Paul was simply quoting a passage that was familiar to him from earlier Christian usage. Several arguments can be cited in favor of this position. From the perspective of early Christian appeals to Scripture, the language of Isa. 59.20 fairly seethes with possibilities for a Christian soteriological interpretation. Once 'the Redeemer' is identified as Jesus Christ, a Christian typological/allegorical re-interpretation of the verse follows almost as a matter of course. Modern interpreters differ over whether the pre-Pauline community would have applied this

---

21. Isa. 59.20-21: ἀποστρέψει ἀσεβείας ἀπὸ Ἰακωβ. καὶ αὕτη αὐτοῖς ἡ παρ' ἐμοῦ διαθήκη...

Isa. 27.9: ἀφαιρεθήσεται ἡ ἀνομία Ἰακωβ, καὶ τοῦτό ἐστιν ἡ εὐλογία αὐτοῦ...

22. The close thematic parallels between Isa. 26.7–27.13 and Isa. 59.12–63.7 will be discussed below.

23. The notion of a 'new' covenant in Christ comes to expression in Paul's letters only in 1 Cor. 11.25 (where it reflects traditional language), 2 Cor. 3.6, 14 (where the idea is presupposed rather than developed), and Gal. 4.24 (again presupposed). The legal analogy in Gal. 3.15, 17 does not enter into consideration here, while the plurals in Rom. 9.4 and Eph. 2.12 refer to the biblical covenants with Israel. Moreover, as Koch notes, '[Paulus] sonst nie von einer (künftigen oder Neuen) διαθήκη *mit Israel* spricht' (*Die Schrift als Zeuge*, p. 178; italics his).

24. The relevant portion of the text reads: καὶ αὕτη αὐτοῖς ἡ παρ' ἐμοῦ διαθήκη, εἶπεν κύριος· τὸ πνεῦμα τὸ ἐμόν, ὅ ἐστιν ἐπὶ σοί, καὶ τὰ ῥήματα, ἃ ἔδωκα εἰς τὸ στόμα σου. It would have been quite typical of Paul to end the quotation after τὸ πνεῦμα τὸ ἐμόν (cf. Rom. 3.11; 4.8; 10.6; etc.)—indeed, it is hard to see how he could have missed the opportunity.

verse to the first or second 'coming' of Christ.[25] Many of the 'non-Pauline' elements in the quotation also become more comprehensible under this explanation: the stress on the word διαθήκη, the repeated references to turning away 'sins' (including the adapted language of the final clause), even the apparently irrelevant (to Paul) substitution of ἐκ for ἕνεκεν before Σιων.[26] If the conflation with Isa. 27.9 stems from the same source, then the shift away from Isa. 59.20 just before the reference to 'my Spirit' likewise ceases to be a problem, since the original users were (so it appears) more interested in soteriology than ecclesiology.

But this explanation, too, has its problems. While it is indeed possible that someone in the pre-Pauline community read Isa. 59.20 in the manner indicated, the literary sources offer no evidence for any early Christian use of the passage outside of Romans 11. Moreover, nothing in the wording of Paul's quotation in Rom. 11.26-27 actually requires a Christian origin. Though the description of the divine διαθήκη as a 'taking away of sins' accords well with early Christian soteriological formulations, the presence of similar language in Jer. 38 (31).31-34 and Ezek. 37.23-26 cautions against any automatic assumption that the conflation (and the corresponding shift to the plural in the final clause) must have arisen in Christian circles.[27] The same can be said for the apparent shift from ἕνεκεν to ἐκ Σιων in the first line of the

25. The standard arguments on both sides of the question are summed up by F. Refoulé, '...*Et ainsi tout Israël sera sauvé*': *Romains 11.25-32* (Paris: Cerf, 1984), pp. 56-61. While it seems clear that Paul viewed the events described here as still future (note ἄχρι οὗ in 11.25 and σωθήσεται in 11.26), it requires little imagination to see how an earlier Christian reader could have found in this same passage an anticipatory reference to the soteriological effects of Jesus' death. Koch (*Die Schrift als Zeuge*, pp. 175-77, 241-42) argues that Paul has taken an earlier 'backward-looking' tradition and applied it to the future restoration of Israel.

26. Though the idea of a 'new covenant' plays a central role only in the book of Hebrews, its presence in the traditional eucharistic formula (Mt. 26.28/Mk 14.24/Lk. 22.20; 1 Cor. 11.25) would have made it a familiar concept throughout early Christianity. The idea that Jesus' death somehow took away the 'sins' of humanity is common throughout the literature. The change from ἕνεκεν to ἐκ Σιων (if that is indeed what happened) could be taken as a reference to the place of Jesus' birth ('Zion' = Palestine or the Jewish people), his death ('Zion' = Jerusalem), or his expected return (as in 2 Thess. 2.4, 8; Rev. 14.1; 16.12-16; 20.11-21).

27. Not to mention the many places in Isaiah where forgiveness of 'sins' is a vital aspect of the divine visitation upon Israel—see Isa. 1.18; 43.25; 44.22; 55.7; cf. 4.4; 33.24; 40.2; 53.4-6, 12; 57.17-18.

quotation. The idea that Jesus came (or will come) 'out of Zion' to deal with sins is without parallel in early Christian soteriological expressions, while the expectation that Yahweh would come 'out of Zion' to 'redeem' his people (especially those in the Diaspora) from their pagan overlords was common in early Judaism.[28] The inherent ambiguity of the title 'Jacob' (v. 26b) as a designation for the pre-Pauline community (a self-reference by Jewish Christians? an implicit assertion of continuity with physical Israel?) likewise disappears when the quotation is placed on the lips of contemporary Jews who took the term in its usual sense.

Thus it seems likely that Paul has drawn his quotation in Rom. 11.25-26 not directly from the Jewish Scriptures, but rather from a Jewish oral tradition in which Isa. 59.20 and Isa. 27.9 had already been conflated and adapted to give voice to a particular interpretation of Yahweh's coming intervention on behalf of his oppressed people Israel. To understand how Paul reconfigures this tradition in Romans 11, one must first develop an appreciation for the specific Jewish tradition that Paul presupposes in his quotation.

The 'Text' Behind the Text

The book of Isaiah employs a bewildering variety of images and narratives to express the hope that Yahweh would eventually come to deliver his people from foreign oppressors and establish them in peace in their own land. Later writers combined these images with others drawn from both Jewish and pagan sources to produce the rich diversity of eschatological views that characterizes Jewish apocalyptic literature.[29] The simplest form of expectation offered by Isaiah is the 'political' hope that Yahweh, having forgiven his people's sins, would rise up in judgment against the surrounding nations (Babylonia, Assyria, Syria, Moab, and so on) on account of their ungodliness and their oppressive treatment of Israel. In most cases the instrument of judgment is another foreign nation (Medes, Persians, Arabians, and so on). Once Yahweh's enemies have been defeated, so the story goes,

28. The evidence for the latter point will be set out further below.
29. On the biblical roots of Jewish apocalyptic expectation, see P.D. Hanson, *The Dawn of Apocalyptic* (Philadelphia: Fortress Press, rev. edn, 1979). On the importance of non-Jewish elements, see J.J. Collins, *The Apocalyptic Imagination* (New York: Crossroad, 1984).

Israel will rest secure in its own land, free from all foreign tyranny.

Alongside this simple hope for political restoration stand at least three relatively complete narrative scenarios in which the 'historical' dimension has been modified or even transformed by the intrusion of various 'mythical' elements.[30] (1) In a broadening of the 'political' theme, Yahweh is portrayed as first arising to rescue his own territory (Palestine) from foreign domination, then marching forth as a warrior to defeat the surrounding nations and return his captive people to their land. Sometimes the agent of victory is the army of Israel or a revived Davidic monarchy, but more often it is Yahweh's own 'hand' that destroys his enemies, often in a theophany. Life in the restored Israel is depicted in glowing terms, with peace and prosperity, superabundant harvests, and the subservience of the nations to Israel as recurrent themes. Passages in which this view of the future come to expression include Isa. 10.12–12.6; 26.20–27.13; 33.1–35.10, and 59.12–63.7.[31] (2) The second scenario is almost the opposite of the first. Instead of Yahweh going forth to defeat the nations on their own territory, the nations now gather together in a massive alliance to attack and destroy Jerusalem. Once the city is surrounded, however, Yahweh suddenly bursts forth in theophanic power to destroy all his foes. Little is said about life beyond this battle, except that the victory is clearly final, that is, the nations will never again trouble Jerusalem. Places where this expectation predominates include Isa. 9.11-12; 29.1-8; and 41.2-28.[32] (3) Yet another distinctive view emerges in several passages where the nations are depicted as coming peacefully to Israel with the goal of submitting to their rule, worshipping their God, and obeying their law. Despite an occasional reference to some form of

30. Modern interpreters would of course trace these different scenarios to multiple authors or to the complexity of what J.J. Collins calls 'the apocalyptic imagination' (see previous note). Ancient readers, on the other hand, approached Isaiah as a unified book of Scripture, which meant that selective reading and harmonization became a vital part of their interpretive agenda. On the tension between myth and history in Second Isaiah, see Hanson, *Dawn of Apocalyptic*, pp. 61-63, 132-34, 206-207.

31. The thematic unity of each of these sections is clearer in the Septuagint, where the translator has rendered several passages quite loosely (10.20-23, 26-28; 26.18; 27.2-6) to improve the continuity of the narrative. It is this version of the text that would have been read and studied by Paul and other Jews in the Diaspora.

32. Here again the wording of the Septuagint offers a more coherent and explicit narrative in the passages cited: see Isa. 9.11; 29.6; 41.2, 25-28.

judgment on the ungodly, peace is established among the nations without conflict, after which Yahweh rules forever in the midst of his people. Sometimes the narrative includes the peaceful return of the exiles to Israel, often carried on the shoulders of their former captors. Such an optimistic view of the future is reflected in Isa. 2.2-4; 14.1-3; 25.6-9; 49.1-13; 51.4-11; 54.1–55.5; and 56.3-8.[33]

Each of these scenarios is developed further in the literature of Second Temple Judaism. It is the first one, however, that promises to shed light on the Jewish tradition presupposed by Paul in Rom. 11.26-27. Of the four passages cited under this heading (Isa. 10.12–12.6; 26.1–27.13; 33.1–35.10; and 59.12–63.7), the unit that begins in Isaiah 59 offers the clearest and most consistent narrative of what will happen when Yahweh comes to restore his people.[34] The passage begins (59.1-11) with a lengthy catalogue of Israel's sins, followed by a prayer of confession (59.12-15) in which the validity of this divine indictment is acknowledged. In response to this humble confession, Yahweh rises up as an angry warrior to defend and deliver his people from all their foes (59.15-19). Included in this response is the removal of Israel's ungodliness (59.20, quoted by Paul in Rom. 11.26-27) and the instigation of a new covenant that includes the eternal presence of Yahweh's Spirit and word among his people (59.21), a presence that shines forth as a light over all the world (60.1-3). In the next scene (60.4-22), the dispersed children of Israel are seen returning from the four corners of the earth, accompanied by the wealth of

33. Places where the Septuagint presents a clearer and/or more consistent narrative include Isa. 14.3; 25.7 (though v. 8 is actually better in the MT); 49.6; 51.5, 9; 54.15; and 55.5. R.D. Aus ('Paul's Travel Plans') argues that a re-interpretation of this latter tradition lies at the heart of Paul's insistence that 'the full number of the Gentiles' must 'come in' (to Jerusalem) (v. 25) before the messiah could 'come' (in Christian terms, 'return') to redeem his people. Among other problems with this argument is the fact that the coming of a 'messiah' figure (where one appears at all) actually precedes the so-called 'pilgrimage of the Gentiles' in every passage that the author cites as a parallel.

34. Hanson, working from a schema of prophetic typology, would divide this unit into three sections (59.1-20; 60.1–62.12; 63.1-6) composed by three (or perhaps only two) different authors (*Dawn of Apocalyptic*, pp. 59-64, 126-34, 204-8). On the narrative level, however, these divisions appear overly subtle. While Hanson may be right in his historical analysis, it is difficult to imagine that an ancient reader would have recognized any notable breaks in this relatively coherent narrative, especially as it stands in the Septuagint.

the nations (vv. 4-8, 13, 16-17), while nations that refuse to submit to Israel are destroyed by Yahweh himself (vv. 11-12, 14). Finally injustice itself is banished from the earth, as Yahweh takes up visible residence among his righteous people (vv. 18-22). In this era, suffering and mourning will be replaced by joy (61.1-3), the old waste places will be restored (61.4), and all Israel will serve Yahweh as priests (61.6), sustained by their former captors (61.5). All the nations will declare that this is a people blessed by God (61.8–62.5), and eternal praise will be offered to Yahweh on account of his mercies toward his people (62.6-12). The unit ends where it began (63.1-6; cf. Isa. 59.16-19), with a backward-looking coda that exults in the divine warrior's victory over the nations. A doxology praising Yahweh for his mercies toward Israel (63.7) rounds off the whole.

The value of such an optimistic portrait of the future for an 'oppressed' people can hardly be overstated. The same is true whether the people in view are the sixth-century Hebrew exiles of Babylon or first-century Jews who chafed under Roman rule. It should therefore come as no surprise to see an unknown Jewish reader of Scripture giving special attention to a verse (Isa. 59.20) that occupies a crucial position in one of the most significant biblical depictions of this future hope. The same can be said for the conflation of this verse with Isa. 27.9 in Rom. 11.27.[35] While it may well have been their close verbal similarities that caused the two verses to be viewed together in the first place, the scenario played out in Isa. 26.7–27.13 offers a ready parallel to that found in Isa. 59.12–63.7. In both passages the description of Yahweh's deeds is preceded by an indictment of sin and a prayer for divine intervention, though in Isa. 26.7-19 it is the plea of the righteous rather than the confession of the sinner that finally moves Yahweh to action. The action begins with an injunction to 'my people' to 'hide yourself for a little while', since 'the Lord is bringing forth wrath from the holy place [ἀπὸ τοῦ ἁγίου] upon the inhabitants of the earth' (26.20-21). The verses that follow depict the fulfillment of this promise on both the mythical and historical planes. The first scene shows Yahweh marching forth as a mighty warrior against the mythical 'dragon' (Hebrew 'Leviathan'), whom he destroys with his

---

35. Conflating two or more texts to create an artificial 'citation', whether for rhetorical or interpretive purposes, was a rather common way of quoting texts in the ancient world—see *Paul and the Language of Scripture*, pp. 289-91, 304-306, 321-23, 333-37, 341-42.

mighty sword (27.1-2). Next follows a parabolic narrative in which
the people of Israel achieve a similar victory over a representative
'besieged city' in execution of the divine judgment (27.2-6).[36] The
same victory is universalized in vv. 7-11, where a forgiven Israel is
sent out by Yahweh to wreak havoc on its enemies, with a special
concern for destroying their 'idols'.[37] The final scene shows Yahweh
gathering the dispersed children of Israel from the surrounding
nations to worship him in Jerusalem (27.12-13).

Though the story is not identical, the obvious parallels between this
passage and Isa. 59.20–63.7 make it easy to see why an ancient reader
(who worked from the premise of a unified Scripture) might have felt
compelled to interpret the one passage in the light of the other. Even
today, reading the two passages with a view to harmonization produces a stereophonic effect that could hardly be missed by a reader
attuned to the cadences of both passages. In one ear sounds the woeful
confession of sinful Israel; in the other, the impassioned plea of the
'righteous' for vindication. Yahweh's 'coming' answers to both of
these needs, not only removing the ungodliness of his people but also
rescuing them from their oppressors. The picture of the divine
warrior marching forth from his sanctuary to destroy his foes
becomes a cipher for the armies of Israel advancing in the power of
Yahweh against their ungodly neighbors. In both scenes the victory is
complete: the nations and their rulers submit not only to the armies of
Israel but also to Israel's God. Both passages reach their climax in the
return of the dispersed children of Israel to their land, in the one case
by the supernatural activity of Yahweh himself, in the other by the
hand of the defeated nations. The final scene shows the fulfillment of

36. The Septuagint translator has entirely reversed the sense of the 'parable' in
Isa. 27.1-6. In the MT, the passage recalls the 'vineyard' parable of Isaiah 5, with
Yahweh now committed to nurturing and protecting his restored 'vineyard' (= Israel)
until it brings forth luscious fruit. The echo of this earlier passage is lost in the LXX,
where Israel is cast in an offensive rather than a defensive mode (note v. 6, 'those
who are coming are the children of Jacob') under the rule of Yahweh.

37. The Greek of vv. 7-8 is unclear. Verse 7, with its awkward grammar and
ambiguous pronouns, seems intended to justify Israel's assault on its neighbors as a
case of *lex talionis* (i.e., αὐτός refers to the representative enemy in vv. 2-6). Verse
8 then converts this indictment to direct speech to narrate the divine commission to
Israel: 'Fighting and rebuking, he [Yahweh] sends them [Israel] out, [saying:]
"Weren't you [Israel's enemies] hardheartedly planning to destroy them [Israel] with
an angry spirit?" '

all the dreams and aspirations cherished by Yahweh's people over the years: eternal peace and security in their own land, immeasurable wealth and prosperity, the rule of justice and righteousness in every sphere of life, honor and tribute from the surrounding nations, and above all the visible presence of Yahweh among his holy people. What Jew could fail to find hope and reassurance in such a glorious future?

Reverberations

In fact, the evidence indicates that precisely this portrait of future events played an important role in at least some circles of Judaism in the years prior to the rise of Christianity. Already in the Septuagint there are places where the wording of the translation itself reveals a contemporary interest in these ancient traditions. From the text of Isaiah alone one could cite 10.17-23, where a word of judgment against Israel and the nations becomes a scene in which the people of Israel go forth as a 'fire' to destroy their foes; 11.11, 16, where the names of the places from which the exiles will return have been 'modernized' to suit a later period (cf. 49.12); 35.8-10, where loose renderings allow the people who walk on the 'holy way' to Zion to be called 'those who were dispersed' (οἱ διεσπαρμένοι, v. 8) and 'those who were redeemed and gathered on account of the Lord' (v. 10; cf. 56.8); 42.1, where gratuitous references to 'Israel' and 'Jacob' identify the people of Yahweh as the 'Servant' who will execute judgment on the nations; 49.6, where this same 'Servant' is designated a 'covenant of a race', a 'light of the nations', one who bears 'salvation to the end of the earth' (cf. 42.6), with a mission that includes restoring the διασπορά of Israel; and 66.12, where a description of the returning exiles is intruded into a passage that promises comfort to Jerusalem.[38]

The same motif is developed in a variety of directions in the literature of Second Temple Judaism. In *1 En.* 91.7-17, the seer looks for the day when 'the holy Lord shall emerge with wrath' to execute his judgment against the pagan oppressors of his people and inaugurate a new world in which goodness and righteousness reign forever.[39] In

38. These examples are in addition to those noted above for Isaiah 27 and 59.

39. As in Isaiah, the punishment of the oppressors is carried out in one instance by Yahweh himself (vv. 7-9), in another by the 'righteous' among his people (vv. 11-13).

Bar. 4.21–5.9, a sorrowful Jerusalem assures her scattered children that Yahweh will indeed come to avenge himself against their foreign captors and restore them to their land. In Sir. 36.1-17, the author pleads with Yahweh to reveal his power by destroying the pagan rulers who oppress his people, culminating in a prayer that he 'gather all the tribes of Jacob together' (v. 13a). In *Pss. Sol.* 17.21-32, the cry arises for a 'son of David' who will not only purge Jerusalem of 'sinners' and rescue his people from foreign rule, but also smash the power of the nations and resettle the captives of Israel in their land (so also 8.23-28; 11.1-6). A number of the speeches in the *Test. XII Patr.* include promises to the dispersed children of Israel that Yahweh will hear their prayers of repentance and forgive their sins, after which he will liberate them from the forces of Beliar and lead them back to a glorified Israel (*T. Zeb.* 9.7-8; *T. Dan* 5.9-13; *T. Naph.* 8.2-3). In *T. Mos.* 10.1-10, the author looks forward to the day when Yahweh 'will go forth from his holy habitation with indignation and wrath on behalf of his sons' (v. 3) to wreak vengeance on the nations and exalt Israel to the heavens. Finally, the Qumran War Scroll (1QM) contains an extended description of a final battle in which the 'sons of light' (the members of the community) advance against the 'sons of darkness' (the surrounding nations and their Jewish allies) to execute Yahweh's judgment against his enemies, in direct fulfillment of the prophecy of Isaiah (11.11-12).

Despite their differences, the texts cited thus far make it clear that the picture of Israel's future outlined in Isaiah 26-27 and Isaiah 59-63 remained current within at least certain circles of Second Temple Judaism. The basic elements of this tradition can be summed up in a few words: in response to the prayers of his people, Yahweh will come to Zion (or arise in Zion) to free his land from foreign domination, after which he will march forth from Zion to execute judgment on his enemies and restore his captive people to their land.[40] It is noteworthy, however, that not all of the texts cited embrace both sides of this formula with equal fervor. In some texts, the stress is on the coming deliverance of Israel from pagan rulers who mistreat Yahweh's people and defile his land with their foul practices. In others, it is Yahweh's conquest of the nations and the accompanying

40. Cf. W.D. Davies, 'Paul and the People of Israel', *NTS* 24 (1978), p. 27 n. 3. Of course, not all of the texts cited use either the 'Zion' language or the 'to/from' dichotomy suggested here.

restoration of his dispersed children to their land that occupies the
spotlight. In each case, external evidence supports the obvious inference
that the first group of texts arose in Palestine and reflects the interests
of people who continued to live in the land, while the second group
originated in the Diaspora and gives voice to the concerns of certain
Jews who regarded life in a pagan world as a temporary 'exile' from
their true home.[41] For them, it was the coming of Yahweh 'out of Zion'
that took precedence—if not temporally, then at least existentially.

The closeness of these sentiments to the tradition that Paul presupposes in Rom. 11.26-27 should not be overlooked. In addition to
the evidence for a Jewish background cited above, it can now be noted
that the shift from ἕνεκεν to ἐκ Σιων in the first line of the text is
likewise best understood as a Jewish adaptation. For years investigators have tried to make sense of this seemingly insignificant and
unmotivated change, but with little success. Problems surround every
attempt to discover a Pauline (or pre-Pauline Christian) motive for
the alteration.[42] The possibility of a memory slip can never be ruled
out, but the evidence that Paul drew most of his quotations from some
sort of written source argues against this explanation.[43] A variety of
ingenious attempts have been made to trace the present wording to a
textual corruption of some sort, but none of these solutions can be said
to carry weight.[44] When the quotation is viewed within the broader

41. Documents in which the liberation of Palestine occupies center stage include
1 En., T. Mos., and the Qumran War Scroll. In Sirach and *Ps. Sol.*, a fundamentally
Palestinian outlook is united with a plea for the restoration of Yahweh's dispersed
children to their land. Texts that reflect a Diaspora point of view include Baruch (see
especially 4.25-26, 31), *Test. XII Patr.*, and of course the Septuagint. It goes without saying that many Diaspora Jews felt quite at home in Greek society, particularly
in the large Jewish community in Alexandria, Egypt. But even here the voice of
tradition can be heard on occasion, as in *3 Macc.* and parts of *Sib. Or.*

42. See the discussion above.

43. See ch. 3 of my *Paul and the Language of Scripture*. The form ἐκ Σιων
appears in the LXX tradition in the miniscules 22c-93 564* 407 534, the Bohairic
Coptic version, and quotations by Epiphanius, Hilary and Jerome, all of which
follow the primary LXX tradition for the remainder of the verse.

44. The explanations can be divided into two groups according to whether the
investigator sees the corruption occurring in the underlying Hebrew tradition or in the
Greek text before it reached Paul. (1) The simplest solution would see behind the ἐκ
of Paul's Greek text a Hebrew *Vorlage* that read מציון rather than לציון. This

framework of Israel's hopes for the future, on the other hand, the reason for an exegetical adaptation becomes clear. While the Jews of

explanation, suggested by B. Duhm, *Das Buch Jesaja* (Göttingen: Vandenhoeck & Ruprecht, 1892), pp. 417-18, was included by G. Kittel as a conjecture in his *Biblia hebraica*. The phrase מציון is in fact rendered ἐκ Σιων in every place where it occurs in the MT (Ps. 13 [14].7; 49 [50].2; 52.7 [53.6]; 109 [110].2; 127 [128].5; 133 [134].3; Amos 1.2; Mic. 4.2; Joel 4 [3].16; Isa. 2.3). At the same time, the lack of evidence for a Hebrew text with a מ and the paucity of witnesses with ἐκ in the LXX tradition (see previous note) make the originality of this reading highly unlikely. A different solution is offered by J. de Waard, who suggests that the reading אל ציון (found in 1QIsaᵃ) lies behind both Greek readings. According to de Waard (*Comparative Study*, pp. 11-12), both the LXX translator and Paul's Greek *Vorlage* interpreted this אל in the sense of על, 'on account of, because of', echoing the common confusion between אל and על in the Hebrew tradition. What one translator sought to express by ἕνεκεν, the other rendered by ἐκ (BAGD 2f). Apart from the unnecessary complexity of this explanation, it is difficult to imagine why any translator would have rendered an original אל in a sense other than the obvious 'to' (εἰς, πρός, etc.) within the context of Isa. 59.20. It is also worth noting that neither אל nor על appears with ציון anywhere else in Isaiah, and that nowhere in the LXX does ἐκ Σιων translate the Hebrew אל/על ציון.

(2) Solutions that posit a corruption in the Greek text generally assume that the present Hebrew text (לציון) stands behind the original Greek rendering of Isa. 59.20. Perhaps the simplest approach would argue that the original text read simply Σιων (an indeclinable dative), as in Isa. 41.27, 51.16, and 52.7, the only other places where the phrase appears in Isaiah. The insertion of both ἐκ and ἕνεκεν is thus a later development, arising either as an exegetical gloss (ἐκ) or as an attempt to give some account of the original ל (ἕνεκεν). Despite its initial attractiveness, this explanation falters on the cold realities of the textual evidence: if such a version of Isa. 59.20 ever existed, it has left no traces in the manuscript record. Another solution, suggested by F. Godet (*Commentary on St Paul's Epistle to the Romans*, II [trans. A. Cusin; Edinburgh: T. & T. Clark, 1895], p. 257), would assume that an original ἕνεκεν (itself a loose rendering of a Hebrew ל) was contracted at some point in the transmission process to ἐκ, whence it entered Paul's quotation in Rom. 11.26-27. Though it would be difficult to disprove such a hypothesis, Godet cites no other place in the manuscript tradition of antiquity where such a contraction of ἕνεκεν actually appears. More plausible is the explanation that an original ἕνεκεν was somehow modified in the course of transmission to conform to a Hebrew text that read מציון (see above). Here again, however, the lack of Hebrew evidence with מציון leaves this solution as no more than a conjecture. Perhaps the most recent attempt at a solution comes from Berndt Schaller, who argues that an original εἰς (itself a Hebraizing 'correction' of the LXX's ἕνεκεν) was somehow corrupted to ἐκ in the course of transmission (in uncial characters, EIC—>EK). Despite its initial attractive-

Palestine were crying out to Yahweh to deliver his people from
Roman rule, the Jews of the Diaspora were looking forward to the
day when Yahweh would come forth 'out of Zion' to rescue his
dispersed children from their pagan overlords and return them to
their land. In addition to the texts cited above, there are a number of
passages in the Septuagint where this expectation is described specifically as a deliverance ἐκ Σιων:[45] Ps. 13.7, where a cry for salvation
ἐκ Σιων centers on the return of Yahweh's captive children to their
land (cf. 52.7); Ps. 109.2, where Yahweh promises to arise ἐκ Σιων
to crush kings and nations on behalf of his anointed one (vv. 5-6);
Joel 4.16, where Yahweh comes as a mighty warrior ἐκ Σιων to judge
the nations and restore his people to their land (vv. 1-3, 7, 12, 19);
Amos 1.2, where Yahweh lifts his voice ἐκ Σιων against the nations
who have afflicted Israel; Obad. 1.21, where the people of Israel are
depicted as a 'fire' that goes forth ἐκ Σιων to destroy their neighbors
who have mistreated them (vv. 15, 18); and Mic. 4.2, where Yahweh
is pictured as ruling ἐκ Σιων over 'many nations' who stream to 'the
mountain of the Lord' after Yahweh has exalted it from an earlier
devastation.[46] The phrase ἕνεκεν Σιων, on the other hand, appears
only here in the LXX.[47] With these ideological and linguistic factors in
mind, it requires little imagination to see how a conservative Diaspora

ness, Schaller's explanation founders on two counts: the lack of any other 'Hebraizing'
features in the wording of Paul's quotation in Rom. 11.26-27 (the second colon
especially remains quite different from the MT), and the observation that לציון is never
translated by εἰς Σιων in the entire LXX. In the three other places where it appears in
Isaiah, לציון is rendered simply as Σιων (see above), with no preposition or article.
Aquila and Symmachus follow a similar practice in translating the phrase as τῇ Σιων
in Isa. 59.20.

45. The general expectation derives from the Hebrew tradition (the Greek ἐκ
Σιων translates מציון in every case), but the ubiquity of the phrase in the Greek text
facilitated its influence on later generations.

46. The wording of Isa. 2.3 is identical to that of Mic. 4.2, but the idea of an
earlier restoration of Zion is less visible there. The same can be said for Ps. 49.2,
where Yahweh is said to arise ἐκ Σιων to vindicate his 'holy ones' (v. 5) against the
'sinners' within Israel (v. 16). Elsewhere in Isaiah the phrase ἐκ Σιων appears in
codex B at Isa. 24.23 and in a minority tradition at Isa. 51.11, neither of which is
relevant to the present study.

47. The preposition ἕνεκεν translates several Hebrew words in Isaiah (eight
times למען, but also עקב, כ, בלי, יען, and לבלתי one time each), but never ל. The sole
occurrence of למען ציון (Isa. 62.1) is rendered διὰ Σιων. What this says about the
Hebrew *Vorlage* of the LXX in Isa. 59.20 remains unclear.

Jew might have (consciously or unconsciously) replaced the less useful phrase ἕνεκεν Σιων with the more common ἐκ Σιων as part of the same interpretive process that molded Isa. 27.9 and Isa. 59.20 into a focused statement of the future hopes of his community.

Echoes of Tradition

So what does all this mean for the interpretation of Paul's quotation in Rom. 11.26-27? In the first place, it means that care must be exercised in looking back to Isaiah 27 and Isaiah 59 for clues as to what Paul meant in adducing this conflated text. The precise link between Paul's 'quotation' and the statements that it is intended to support (vv. 25-26a) is already rather obscure, and the intrusion of shadowy voices from the past (via the interpretive tradition) clouds the issue still further. On the literary level, the 'metaleptic' effect of the earlier conflation fairly forces its way onto the later passage. The tradition can no more silence these 'echoes of Scripture' than a tourist can halt the reverberations of a shout released into the Grand Canyon. On the historical level, on the other hand, what matters most is the interplay between Paul and the tradition, not between Paul and the biblical text. When Paul appeals to a traditional formulation in place of a specific verse of Scripture, he implicitly adopts the voice of tradition as his own, even as he struggles to reconfigure that tradition to reflect his new 'Christian' horizon of understanding. In this way the tradition continues to speak through the apostle, albeit with a Christian accent. So long as the tradition retains its own voice, the extent of the Pauline reinterpretation remains open for all to see. But in a day when the original tradition has been effectively silenced, the first task of the interpreter must be to revive that ancient voice.

A second implication of this approach is that one must listen for the voice of Paul not only where he diverges from the tradition, but also where he allows it to stand unchallenged. In the present case, Paul's repetition of a traditional formula evokes not just the specific passages in Isaiah from which these excerpts were taken, but the entire narrative about the future of Israel that has grown up around these passages over the centuries.[48] The broad outlines of this narrative have been set

48. Norman Perrin discusses a similar phenomenon in his *Jesus and the Language of the Kingdom* (Philadelphia: Fortress Press, 1976). In attempting to explain the way the term 'kingdom of God' functions in the preaching of Jesus,

forth above, and need not be repeated. Despite differences in detail, the basic story-line remains so thoroughly fixed that the whole would no doubt spring to the mind of a person familiar with the tradition at the mention of one of its parts. In the same way, the reader who would understand Paul's use of Scripture in Rom. 11.26-27 must learn to listen for the cadences of the tradition as a whole—not only those elements that occupy center stage at the moment, but also those parts that stand whispering in the wings.

In practical terms, this means that the voice of tradition must be allowed to speak through Paul except where it can be shown that Paul has consciously sought to remold that tradition. This has important implications for the way one understands Paul's use of Scripture in Rom. 11.26-27.

1. In view of the lack of evidence for a christological interpretation in the broader context, one should assume that Paul read the term ὁ ῥυόμενος in its traditional sense, as a designation for Yahweh himself.[49] Including the passage currently under discussion, the phrase occurs nine times in the book of Isaiah (5.29; 44.6; 47.4; 48.17; 49.7; 49.26; 54.5; 54.8; 59.20), always as a title for Yahweh and always in connection with his promise to deliver his people from foreign oppressors.[50] The weight of the postbiblical tradition also supports

Perrin argues that the term has no fixed content, but rather evokes a complex 'myth' about the creative, sustaining, and redeeming activity of Yahweh on behalf of his people. As Perrin puts it, 'The symbol functions by evoking the myth, and in turn the myth is effective because it interprets the historical experience of the Jewish people in the world' (p. 22). This is precisely the position that is being argued here in connection with Paul's appeal to tradition.

49. Refoulé ('...Et ainsi tout Israël sera sauvé', p. 54) cites T. Zahn, P. Althaus, C.K. Barrett, K.H. Schelkle, B. Mayer, C. Müller, H. Ridderbos, K. Stendahl, and P. Benoit as affirming this view. Supporters of a christological interpretation often cite E.P. Sanders's dictum: 'It is incredible that [Paul] thought of "God apart from Christ", just as it is that he thought of "Christ apart from God"' (Paul, the Law, and the Jewish People [Philadelphia: Fortress Press, 1983], p. 194). This statement, however, fails to take into account the traditional Jewish background of Paul's quotation here. The unity of Paul's thought on this subject is well stated by Martin Rese: 'So wie Gott das Subjekt ihrer Verstockung war (vv. 7-10), so wird er auch das Subjekt der Aufhebung ihrer Verstockung sein' ('Die Rettung der Juden nach Römer 11', in A. Vanhoye [ed.], L'Apôtre Paul (Leuven: University Press/Peeters, 1986], p. 428).

50. The form with the aorist participle (ὁ ῥυσάμενος) is actually more common; the present participle appears only here and in Isa. 5.29. Other forms of the verb are

this view: it is Yahweh, the God of Israel, who will come to free his people from captivity and reverse their present state. The voice of the modern interpreter must not be allowed to silence the voice of tradition on this critical point.

2. The future verb 'will come' (Greek ἥξει) is clearly vital to Isaiah, to the tradition, and to Paul himself. In each case the hope that Yahweh will indeed 'come' at some time in the future plays a crucial role in determining how the community understands and relates to its present position in the world and in history. On this point the voices of Scripture, tradition, and Paul the Christian speak as one.

3. The orientation of the phrase ἐκ Σιων within the tradition is clearly spatial. Since Jewish belief typically pictured Yahweh as residing in the Temple on Mount Zion, it is only natural that a first-century Jew would expect Yahweh to arise 'out of Zion' when he comes to rescue his people from their oppressors. From the perspective of Diaspora Judaism, 'Zion' carries a wider sense, as a designation for the land of Israel as against the pagan territories.[51] Since Paul makes no effort to recast this part of the tradition, one can only presume that he shared the view of his compatriots that any move by Yahweh to 'redeem' his people would require him to come forth from his normal place of residence in 'Zion'.

4. The remainder of Paul's quotation is concerned with what will happen when Yahweh at last arises to visit his people Israel. The fact that Yahweh's 'coming' is described here solely in terms of 'turning away ungodliness' and 'taking away sin' is probably more significant for Paul than for the tradition. Readers familiar with the tradition could easily supply what comes next: after forgiving his people for the waywardness that led to their present low estate, Yahweh would arise as a mighty warrior to deliver his people from their pagan overlords and restore them to their land in peace and prosperity. For Paul's Gentile Roman readers, on the other hand, this latter portion of the tradition has been effectively silenced. This selective stifling of the voice of tradition turns out to be crucial to Paul's interpretive strategy

used throughout Isaiah (14 times) to describe Yahweh's actions on behalf of his people.

51. So also W.D. Davies, *The Gospel and the Land* (Berkeley: University of California Press, 1974), p. 196, who speaks of 'a distinction without a difference'. According to Davies, 'Just as Jerusalem became the quintessence of the land, so also the Temple became the quintessence of Jerusalem' (p. 152).

in the present passage. The key to Paul's reconfiguration of the tradition appears in the way he uses the word σωθήσεται (v. 26a) to sum up his understanding of Israel's future hope. In the tradition, as in Scripture, the verb σώζειν and its cognates (σωτήρ, σωτηρία, and so on) are used often to describe what Yahweh will do when he comes to restore his people.[52] In this case the reference is to Yahweh's anticipated victory over 'the nations' that will allow his people to rest securely in their own land. In Romans 11, on the other hand, the word takes on a whole new meaning. Already in 1.16 Paul offers his unequivocal judgment that '[the gospel] is the power of God for salvation to all who believe, to the Jew first and also to the Greek'. In 10.1 he speaks of praying earnestly for the 'salvation' of his Jewish brethren, while in 11.14 he describes his strategy of preaching the Christian gospel to non-Jews in order to provoke his fellow Jews to jealousy, 'in order that I might save some of them' (cf. 1 Cor. 9.20). In 10.9-13 he sets forth the terms of this 'salvation' more fully: 'For if you confess with your mouth "Jesus is Lord!" and believe in your heart that God raised him from the dead, you will be saved' (v. 9). Here again he leaves no doubts about his belief that this condition applies equally to Jews and non-Jews (v. 12). A similar judgment is presupposed in 11.23-24, where Israel's restoration is described as the reversal of a present state of 'unbelief' (ἀπιστία), and in 11.28-31, where the 'disobedience' (ἀπείθεια) of Yahweh's covenant people is said to place them on a par with the Gentiles. Paul's assertion that Israel will ultimately 'obtain mercy' from Yahweh (11.31) cannot be understood apart from this broader context. What Paul meant by this statement is light years away from what Jewish tradition anticipated would happen when Yahweh once again turned his 'mercy' upon his people.[53]

---

52. This sort of language is especially common in Isaiah: seven times Yahweh is styled 'the Savior' (ὁ σωτήρ) of Israel, while the words σώζειν, σωτηρία, and σωτήριον occur some 57 times in passages that speak of Yahweh's activity on behalf of his people.

53. This much is conceded (implicitly for the most part) by all the parties to the present debate. The argument that Paul anticipated an eschatological redemption of Israel apart from faith in Christ, set forth most recently by Franz Mussner ('Ganz Israel wird gerettet werden [Röm. 11.26]', *Kairos* 18 [1976], pp. 241-55) and somewhat differently by Krister Stendahl (*Paul Among Jews and Gentiles* [Philadelphia: Fortress Press, 1976], and 'A Response', *USQR* 33 [1978], pp. 189-91) simply fails to do justice to this evidence. Recent responses to Mussner and Stendahl include

On the other hand, Paul offers few details about his own 'Christian' understanding of the future of Israel. For instance, nothing in either the quotation itself or Paul's interpretive comments links Israel's 'salvation' with either the first or second 'coming' of Christ. The only way to construct such a link is to read ὁ ῥυόμενος as a veiled reference to the exalted Christ, a move whose legitimacy I have here been at pains to deny. Further, there is nothing explicitly 'eschatological' about Paul's hopes for Israel insofar as they come to expression in Rom. 11.25-32. While it is clear that he anticipates a concrete intervention by Yahweh in the life of his people at a specific point in history ('when the fulness of the Gentiles has come in', v. 25), there is nothing to indicate that he connects this intervention with the 'end' of the present age.[54] By quoting a passage that casts Yahweh's 'coming' in exclusively 'spiritual' terms ('turning away ungodliness'/ 'taking away sins'), Paul has effectively silenced the 'eschatological' dimension of the tradition that he invokes.[55] While it may be true that

---

E.P. Sanders, 'Paul's Attitude Toward the Jewish People', *USQR* 33 (1978), pp. 175-87; F. Hahn, 'Zum Verstandnis von Römer 11.26a: "...und so wird ganz Israel gerettet werden"', in M. Hooker and S.G. Wilson (eds.), *Paul and Paulinism: Essays in Honour of C.K. Barrett* (London: SPCK, 1982), pp. 221-36; S. Hafemann, 'The Salvation of Israel in Romans 11.25-32: A Response to Krister Stendahl', *Ex Auditu* 4 (1988), pp. 38-58; Refoulé, '...*Et ainsi tout Israël sera sauvé*', pp. 183-89; and especially Hvalvik, 'A "Sonderweg" for Israel'. W.D. Davies offers a helpful corrective to the 'either/or' tone that has come to dominate recent debate on the issue ('Paul and the People of Israel', p. 27): 'Paul was not thinking in terms of what we normally call conversion from one religion to another but of the recognition by Jews of the final or true form of their own religion'.

54. For a review of the arguments for and against an 'eschatological' reading of the present passage, see Refoulé, '...*Et ainsi tout Israël sera sauvé*', pp. 56-61, and Hvalvik, 'A "Sonderweg" for Israel', pp. 92-95. Like most commentators, Refoulé assumes that the only alternative to a purely 'eschatological' reference is a link to the first 'coming' of Christ. The possibility that Paul might have looked forward to a future, non-eschatological event has been overlooked by modern investigators.

55. Even Paul's use of the term μυστήριον (v. 25) to characterize his message in these verses would have carried no 'eschatological' overtones for a non-Jewish audience, where the most natural frame of reference would be the so-called 'mystery religions' (cf. 1 Cor. 2.1, 7; 4.1; 13.2). Paul himself uses the word almost exclusively to refer to something once 'hidden' but now made manifest (cf. *TDNT*, IV, pp. 819-24). The only places where Paul speaks of a μυστήριον that remains to be realized in the future are 1 Cor. 15.51 and (possibly) 2 Thess. 2.7. On the nature and

the tradition still speaks in its fulness to 'those who have ears to hear', one could assume that few in Paul's Gentile Roman audience actually fit into that category. Just as the tradition sought to reshape the voice of Scripture to communicate a particular understanding of the present and future circumstances of Israel, so now Paul truncates the voice of both Scripture and tradition in order to enlist their support for his 'Christian' understanding of Yahweh's purposes in history. The limiting factor in Yahweh's intervention on behalf of Israel is now something entirely outside the history of Israel, that is, the 'fulness of the Gentiles' (v. 25). Precisely what this phrase signifies and how its fulfilment is to be recognized is never clarified.[56]

This leads finally to the question of Paul's purpose in adducing this particular passage in the context of Romans 11. The only thing that can be said for certain about Paul's expectations regarding the future of Israel—apart from a rather ill-defined link with the preaching of the gospel to the Gentiles (vv. 12-15, 25, 30-32)—is that Paul anticipated a radical change in Israel's attitude toward the Christian gospel. This much can be deduced both from the temporal limitation (ἄχρι οὗ) that he places on the present 'hardening'[57] of Israel in v. 25 (cf. 11.7) and from several other statements where he voices optimism about an eventual change of heart on the part of his fellow countrymen (11.1, 12, 15, 23, 31). Because he was convinced that Yahweh would never abandon his people (11.1), Paul could not accept the weak Jewish response to his divinely ordained message of salvation as a permanent reality. His solution was to incorporate this rejection into

extent of the 'mystery' in Romans 11, see Hvalvik, 'A "Sonderweg" for Israel', pp. 96-101.

56. The usual presumption that the phrase refers to the completion of Paul's own Gentile mission is probably too specific—at least, Paul offers no clear statement to that effect. Since the simultaneous 'unhardening' of Israel (*not* the Parousia) is cast as an act of the divine will, it seems more likely that Paul simply refrained from speculating on the details and timing of this combined event (cf. Rom. 11.33-36). In this case, 'the fulness of the Gentiles' becomes a cipher for 'all the Gentiles who will (in actuality) be saved (prior to Yahweh's intervention)'.

57. The actual wording is πώρωσις ἀπὸ μέρους, which could refer either to a 'partial hardening' of the whole of Israel or a substantial 'hardening' of a 'part' of Israel. That the latter reading is to be preferred is apparent from 11.5, 7, 12-15, where the basis for the distinction seems to be the response of individual Jews to the Christian gospel. From the predominantly Gentile tone of Paul's congregations, one can infer that the minimizing reference to a 'part' of Israel is a gross understatement.

a broader interpretation of Yahweh's purposes in history, an interpretation that included a period of 'hardening' for the bulk of Israel as a precondition for the (already experienced) extension of Yahweh's 'mercy' to those outside the Jewish community. Eventually, however, this phase of Yahweh's program would run its course, at which time Yahweh would 'come' to his people in a way that would both pardon their 'sins' and remove their present 'hardness' to the Christian gospel.[58] In this way (a way that differs markedly from traditional Jewish expectation), Yahweh's plans for his people would at last be realized.

Thus Paul waits eagerly for the day when Yahweh will arise 'out of Zion' to 'redeem' his people Israel. Though he offers no hint as to when this event might take place, he feels certain that the result will be a new responsiveness to his own message about Yahweh's act of salvation in Jesus Christ. In this way (οὕτως, v. 26a), and only in this way, 'all Israel will be saved' (Rom. 11.26).

---

58. Though he is simply quoting traditional language at this point, the significance of the parallel references to 'turning away ungodliness' and 'taking away sins' could not have escaped either Paul or his readers. The two phrases are not synonymous: in the New Testament as in Isaiah, the word ἀσέβεια and its cognates refer consistently to an attitude that denies and/or rejects Yahweh and his purposes (cf. Rom. 1.18; 4.5; 5.6), while the word ἁμαρτία is used (alongside ἀνομία in Isaiah) to describe those deeds by which the people of Israel fall short of the expectations of Yahweh and thus bring down divine judgment upon themselves. As Paul viewed the situation, simple 'forgiveness' would not be enough; something must be done to reverse Israel's present 'ungodly' rejection of Yahweh's act of salvation in Jesus Christ.

2 CORINTHIANS 3 AND THE PRINCIPLES OF PAULINE EXEGESIS

Carol K. Stockhausen

Introduction

This paper has a dual goal: to isolate from Paul's argument in 2 Corinthians 3–4, as a set-piece of such Pauline argumentation, several exegetical principles or procedures which appear to be central for Paul here and elsewhere, and to illustrate them further from the Epistle to the Galatians in order to show that 2 Corinthians 3 is not a unique, or even a non-Pauline, departure from ordinary practice dictated either by his opposition or the text of Torah operative in that particular case.[1] Several remarks are appropriate at the outset. First, the material serving as backdrop for the present study is taken from my book, *Moses' Veil and the Glory of the New Covenant*.[2] I will not be able to present the argument and documentation to support the conclusions about 2 Corinthians 3–4 with which I will begin here, but will simply draw from and refer to that earlier work. Secondly, I am not approaching 2 Corinthians 3 as uniquely programmatic for Paul's exegesis because it includes specifically hermeneutical statements such as '...where the spirit of the Lord is, there is freedom' (2 Cor. 3.17)

---

1. In a sense this article serves to counteract Richard Hays's assertion that, 'Our account of Paul's interpretive activity has discovered no systematic exegetical procedures at work in his reading of scripture', and the following discussion in *Echoes of Scripture in the Letters of Paul* (New Haven and London: Yale University Press, 1989), pp. 160-61. Although I would agree with Hays that 'Paul's hermeneutic is narratively oriented' (*Echoes of Scripture*, p. 161), we understand that statement quite differently. In fact, considering his earlier work with narrative (*The Faith of Jesus Christ* [SBLDS, 56; Chico, CA: Scholars Press, 1983]), I find Hays surprisingly negligent in the detailed consideration of narrative sources in the later volume.

2. C.K. Stockhausen, *Moses' Veil and the Story of the New Covenant: The Exegetical Substructure of II Cor. 3.1–4.6* (AnBib, 116; Rome: Pontifical Biblical Institute, 1989).

or '...the written code kills, but the spirit gives life' (2 Cor. 3.6).[3] Instead, in my opinion, 2 Corinthians 3 is valuable for the discovery of the principles of Pauline exegesis because it is an obvious and easily agreed upon example of an exegetically centered passage, rather than because it has a specifically hermeneutical intent. Finally, it does not seem to me that the primary text of Torah being interpreted—Exodus 34—is itself at all well suited for such hermeneutical reflection, so it is unlikely that the exegetical principles should have arisen from literary or theological features intrinsic to Exodus 34.[4]

To summarize my conclusions in advance, Paul's most important exegetical procedures are five in number, although three are primary and will be treated at length here. First, Paul takes as the basis for his interpretative task the Torah; that is to say, narrative texts from the Pentateuch are usually (perhaps always) at the core of his arguments. In interpreting selected Pentateuchal narratives, he is usually (perhaps always) extremely concerned with the stories themselves—that is, with plot-line, character, narrative event and especially the inexplicable, unusual or unmotivated character or action.[5] Secondly, it is Paul's usual procedure to apply prophetic and occasionally sapiential texts to bring the Torah into the proper contemporary focus.[6] These secondary interpreting texts are usually (perhaps always) linked to each other verbally and linked to the fundamental Torah verbally— forming a network of mutually-interpreting texts which creates a new synthetic meaning at once scriptural and Pauline. These two basic

---

3.   All biblical quotations in this paper are taken from the *Revised Standard Version: The New Oxford Annotated Bible with the Apocrypha* (New York: Oxford University Press, 1973) unless otherwise noted, since that was in use in many of the studies cited here.

4.   This is again in deliberate dialogue with Hays's recent work. He works throughout as if Paul were stimulated to his own poetic creation by the particular texts he chooses, but not characteristically further limited or determined by them. For Hays, then, Exodus 34 stimulated a reflection on hermeneutics in 2 Corinthians 3, but not for any specific reason now discernable and, having stimulated it, Exodus 34 had no further active role in the interpretive process (Hays, *Echoes of Scripture*, pp. 132, 140, 147). For me, however, Exodus 34 did not stimulate the discussion of hermeneutics, if indeed there is one, in 2 Corinthians 3, because Exodus 34 in itself has nothing to do with the interpretive process; but, once chosen by Paul, Exodus 34 did exercise a continuous and dynamic influence on Paul's discussion.

5.   Stockhausen, *Moses' Veil*, pp. 96-101.

6.   Stockhausen, *Moses' Veil*, p. 41 n. 19.

principles are fundamental, I would argue, in Paul's exegesis, which is not to say that they are present in his arguments as they now stand in his correspondence. I have argued that Pauline exegesis often structures the arguments of Pauline letters but is not on that account to be expected to be exhausted by them. Quite the contrary; Paul's interpretations of Scripture are often only to be recovered from behind or beneath his text as it stands. Paul does not describe his exegetical process. We see only its results, as the shape of his arguments express his hermeneutic. His exegetical process will always remain a more or less hypothetical abstraction from and beneath his tantalizingly obscure 'text as we have it', which provides some visible brush strokes but does not yield a full portrait of the exegete.[7]

A third favorite occupation of Paul's in relation to the Scripture, in particular the Torah, is the location and solution of contradictions or uneasily reconciled passages. As Dahl argued some time ago, and as Beker also reminds us,[8] there is a strong element of discontinuity in Pauline thought, for example, in Galatians. It seems to me that this discontinuity is due, not only to the disjunction between Paul's way of life in the customs of his fathers and his new life in Christ, but to his tendency in response to locate and exegetically reconcile passages in his traditional Scriptures which express this disjunction. This sort of argumentation is present in 2 Corinthians 3, and might be illustrated with the antitheses of 2 Cor. 3.3, 'not with ink but with the Spirit of the living God, not on tablets of stone but on tablets of human hearts'; or 2 Cor. 3.6, 'not in a written code but in the Spirit; for the written code kills, but the Spirit gives life'; 2 Cor. 3.9 (dispensation of condemnation/dispensation of righteousness) and 2 Cor. 3.11 (fading/permanence), as well as in the ambivalent comparison and contrast with Moses drawn throughout these chapters.

A fourth element of Paul's use of both focus and related texts is his consistent attention to the context of cited passages. It seems to me that this is an extension of his narrative interest as described earlier. Finally, the fifth exegetical method, used occasionally in Paul's letters, and present in 2 Cor. 3.17 ('Now the Lord is the Spirit') is the *pesher-*

---

7. Stockhausen, *Moses' Veil*, pp. 38-41.

8. N.A. Dahl, 'Contradictions in Scripture', in *Studies in Paul* (Minneapolis: Augsburg, 1977), pp. 159-77; J.C. Beker, *Paul the Apostle* (Philadelphia: Fortress Press, 1980).

like contemporization discussed extensively by Dunn and others.[9] It must also be noted that certain rhetorical/exegetical forms are present in Paul's arguments, such as the *kal va-homer* or *a minore ad maius* arguments in 2 Cor. 3.7-11, Romans 5 and elsewhere.[10] I will not touch on this since these forms are part of Paul's general rhetorical equipment and so aid and inform exegesis as well as persuasion, but are not exclusively interpretive in application.

Part One

In this first segment of my study, I will illustrate the first of my five principles—Paul's concern with extended narratives *as* narratives—first briefly from 2 Corinthians 3–4 and then from Galatians. In 2 Corinthians 3–4 Paul displays a serious and sustained interest in the narrative of the life of Moses. His interest peaks at the episode of the veiling of Moses' face, but it is not limited to that episode.

For example, the summary statement of the nature of the new covenant in contrast to the Mosaic covenant of 2 Cor. 3.6bc is introduced in 2 Cor. 3.6a by the statement that God has also made Paul competent to minister a new covenant ([θεός, v. 5] ὃς **καὶ** ἱκάνωσεν ἡμᾶς διακόνους [καινῆς διαθήκης]). 2 Cor. 3.5 refers to competence as well: **οὐχ** ὅτι ἀφ' ἑαυτῶν ἱκανοί ἐσμεν λογίσασθαί τι ὡς ἐξ ἑαυτῶν, ἀλλ' ἡ ἱκανότης ἡμῶν ἐκ τοῦ θεοῦ ('Not that we are competent of ourselves to claim anything as coming from us; our competence is from God'.) Only one parallel use of ἱκανός occurs in the Septuagint, and that is at Exod. 4.10. This is a most unusual biblical use of the term because it refers to the competence of a specific person, Moses. I have argued that it is this use of ἱκανός which determines Paul's use of the word in 2 Corinthians 3.[11]

The story of the burning bush begins in Exodus 3, including the vision which first makes the Lord's name known to Moses (Exod. 3.14) and which commissions him to bring Israel out of Egypt to receive the covenant (Exod. 3.10-12). Moses lacks the confidence to

9. J.D.G. Dunn, '2 Corinthians III.17—"The Lord is the Spirit"', *JTS* 21 (1970), pp. 309-20; see Stockhausen, *Moses' Veil*, pp. 130-50 for further discussion with regard to 2 Corinthians 3 and additional bibliographical information.

10. Hays, *Echoes of Scripture*, p. 132; Stockhausen, *Moses' Veil*, pp. 109-11, pp. 113-22.

11. Stockhausen, *Moses' Veil*, pp. 82-85.

take on this task, however, and in Exodus 4 he argues with the Lord about it, denying his ability. God's answer to Moses' humility is the assurance in vv. 11-12 that God will tell him what to say. The competence that Moses admits he lacks in himself will be supplied to him by God. The situations reported in the two texts are quite similar. In Exodus 3-4 Moses is commissioned to minister to Israel, ultimately to minister what Paul will call in 2 Cor. 3.14 the 'old covenant'. Although Moses claims that he is incompetent even to accomplish the release from Egypt, God assures him that he will receive the power to do so. 2 Cor. 3.5-6 echoes Moses' attitude in this scene from Exodus. Exod. 4.10-12 is appropriated and paraphrased in the Pauline version: 'Not that we are competent in ourselves so as to reckon anything as coming from ourselves'—like Moses in Exod. 4.10; 'rather our competence is from God'—like Moses in Exod. 4.11-12.

Paul is obviously interested in more than one episode in the Moses narratives, including one from its very early chapters, although he generally focuses on the later Sinai events. Moses as the minister of the old covenant in contrast to Paul as minister of the new covenant is a theme explicitly treated at length in the following section, 2 Cor. 3.7-18, and implicit also in 2 Cor. 4.1-6. Just as Moses was commissioned by God and recognized in humility that his competence to fulfill that commission came, not from himself, but from God, so Paul declares that he has boundless confidence because his competence to fulfill his commission as the minister of the new covenant stems from God also.

But is Paul like Moses? 2 Cor. 3.13 and 3.18 both answer this important question. Paul is both like Moses and not like Moses. Paul is not like Moses because he may be bold and does not need to veil himself in either shame or humility. Paul is like Moses because he also has a share in the glory given to the minister of God's covenant with Israel. Like Moses, who received visions on the mountain and in the tent, Paul's glorification in 2 Cor. 3.18 is also visionary.

2 Cor. 3.13 and 3.18 are not alone in addressing the comparison with Moses; they simply provide summary statements. 2 Cor. 3.1-4.6 as a whole explains just when and how the new covenant minister resembles his Old Testament model, as well as how, when and *why* he does not. The presence of Jeremiah's promised new covenant is the basis for both the similarities and the differences, and resolves the tension between Moses' glory and his veil. Because Paul is the

minister of a superior new *covenant*, he shares in Moses' glorification. Because Paul is the minister of a *superior* new covenant, he does not need to veil his glory.[12] To explore all of the ways in which Paul's similarity to and difference from Moses are developed in 2 Cor. 3.7-18 is not only to interpret this text itself but also to touch on Paul's practice in dealing with a narrative tradition.

Paul's reference to Exodus 34, his argument's primary narrative focus, is explicit in 2 Cor. 3.7. The beginning of Moses' ministry of the covenant in glory and the reluctance of the children of Israel to approach him is a direct and unmistakable reference to the narrative account of Moses' second descent from the mountain with the stone tablets of the law and the events which followed in Exod. 34.29-35. It is important to remember, however, that Exod. 34.29-35 is a *story* about what happened to Moses as he came down from Mount Sinai, about the reaction that the people had to his theophanic appearance, and about further actions that Moses regularly performed in mediating the covenant. This story has all the elements that every story has, at least potentially. It has actors (Moses, the children of Israel). It has props (the stone tablets, the veil). It has action (Moses descends the mountain; he calls the people to him and communicates the commandments to them; he veils his face). It has motivation (Moses is ignorant of the glorious appearance of his face; the people are afraid to come near him because of that appearance).[13]

2 Cor. 3.7-18 evidences numerous verbal contacts with this Exodus narrative. Because of the nature of story and its power, however, one should consider that very likely those verbal echoes call to mind the *whole* story, not just isolated snatches of it, and indicate dialogue with it. I have argued that the props, actors, action and motivation of this particular Pentateuchal narrative enter into Paul's own composition as they are verbally recalled by him. He accepts and enters into the story as he retells and interprets it. As story, Exod. 34.29-35 lacks one important narrative element. Moses' motivation for the veiling of his face is left unexplained, or at least implicit. It is ultimately this problem in the story that Paul exploits in 2 Cor. 3.13 when he explicitly assigns a motivation to Moses not present, even implicitly, in the original story.[14] Numerous examples detailed in my previous work

12. Stockhausen, *Moses' Veil*, pp. 85, 94.
13. Stockhausen, *Moses' Veil*, p. 96.
14. Stockhausen, *Moses' Veil*, pp. 96-101.

illustrate the depth and extent of Paul's appropriation of the story of Moses. He shares some of his narrative interests with others in his milieu, but some portions of his re-narration appear to be his own, especially the devaluation of Moses' covenant, and the movement of Moses' veil, and these are the heart of his argument in 2 Corinthians 3–4. Before discussing these from the perspective of Paul's second major exegetical method—intertextual analogy—I would like to illustrate the principle of narrative interest from another part of his correspondence.

The Narrative Interest in Galatians

Paul displays a sustained interest in the Genesis Abraham narrative in his Epistle to the Galatians which is comparable to his interest in the Moses narrative in 2 Corinthians. The citation of Genesis 12 and 15 early in Galatians 3 is obvious and receives great emphasis as the locus of the definitive statement of, and scriptural proof for, his 'doctrine of justification by faith', so called. His clear reference to Genesis 12, 15 and 22 in Gal. 3.16, when he introduces the important concept of the seed of Abraham, is undisputed and ties the beginning and ending of Abraham's story to Paul's argument. Finally, Paul clearly refers to the stories, recounted in Genesis 16 and 21 respectively, of the birth of Abraham's two sons, Ishmael and Isaac, as he allegorizes their mothers in Galatians 4 and establishes the lineage of those who are in Christ, born according to the promise. Arguably, therefore, Paul has in mind and refers to the entire length of the story of Abraham through his brief citations and clear allusions. His references run roughly in order from the beginning of Abraham's story to its end, with emphasis on the beginning and end. He begins, we realize, as Abraham begins, with promises, and he ends, we realize, as Abraham ends, with sons. Yet we rarely say that the story itself is therefore of considerable importance to him, or recognize his brief references to it as connected to each other sequentially following the order of the narrative, or as structurally indicative of his thesis and intention. Instead we customarily presume that Paul offers, at selected points, proof of a theological argument essentially independent of the story of Abraham through occasional reference to the text of Genesis. Furthermore, the story of Abraham is not generally recognized as relevant to the argument of Galatians *except* where it is explicitly cited. On the contrary, however, I would argue that a fundamental awareness of the

constitutive presence of Abraham's story in Paul's argument requires
that Paul's arguments in the whole of Galatians be seen, not as isolated
'arguments from Scripture', but as a connected series of statements,
which have the primary goal of correctly interpreting the story of
Abraham itself and concomitantly show the relationship between that
story, the gospel and contemporary events and persons.

In Paul's view Abraham's story was surely unitary, historical, and
authoritative. If this is granted, then segments of Galatians not generally seen to relate to Paul's scriptural argument, for example Gal.
4.12-20, may become less isolated and problematic. Rhetorical
analysis of 4.12-20 as a 'string of topoi belonging to the theme of
friendship',[15] for example, might be amplified from this perspective.
Although the narratives of Genesis 18 and 19 are sometimes noted as
Jewish parallels to the appearance of divine or angelic beings, nothing
is made of the fact that the action of the Galatians in welcoming Paul,
as an angel or even as the Lord himself, reflects an important aspect
of Abraham's story, sets the Galatians in a parallel with Abraham in
offering hospitality to Paul and implies that they have fallen away
from this imitation of Abraham and have lost their resemblance to
him in rejecting Paul and 'his gospel'. The ambiguity of Gal. 4.14c,
'[you] received me as an angel of God, as Christ Jesus', may even
reflect the ambiguity of Gen. 18.2, 9-10, 13 and so on between the
angelic figures and the Lord alone. One might also be tempted to think
about the theological question of the power of the few righteous to
save multitudes of sinners which is debated in Genesis 18–19 as it
might be related to Christ's death discussed in Gal. 3.13-14. For now,
however, I wish only to emphasize the power of the Abraham story,
when it is placed in the proper focus, to offer new and renew old
possibilities for understanding the unity and intention of Galatians, as
well as the theological interests of all its parts.

Several scholars have stressed that the autobiographical material
provided by Paul in the early chapters of Galatians, in common with
similar kinds of personal information provided in letters and moral
treatises by numerous Greek authors of antiquity, served the primary
function of example in a paraenetic context and that, therefore, Paul's
personal remarks should be seen within this perspective vis-à-vis the
theological argument and moral exhortation of Galatians.[16] Paul

15. H.D. Betz, *Galatians* (Philadelphia: Fortress Press, 1979), pp. 220-33.
16. B.R. Gaventa, 'Galatians 1 and 2: Autobiography as Paradigm', *NovT* 28

emerges as the one who willingly abandoned his former way of life (Gal. 1.13-17), following the will of God toward a new and unexpected mission to the Gentiles. Following this paradigmatic reversal, Paul shows himself to be consistent in one way especially—he alters his course when it is God's will that he should (Gal. 2.2) but he refuses to do so when it is not the will of God but merely human provocation which urges it (Gal. 1.16-17; 2.4-9, 11-14).

The paradigm which Paul has so skillfully presented functions in both positive and negative directions with respect to the behavior of the Galatians. It is positive insofar as Paul provides reinforcement for their abandonment of their former lives in paganism for the sake of the gospel. It is strongly negative insofar as they are abandoning their new adherence to that gospel message which came from God (Gal. 1.15, 17; 2.6-10) in favor of another gospel that is merely human (Gal. 1.6-7, 11-12).

As helpful as this particular scholarly perspective on Galatians is, however, it seems to me that an important part of the paradigmatic function of the portrait of Paul has received little attention. If it is true, as I am arguing here, that in Galatians Paul shows an interest in the whole story of Abraham, is it not possible to investigate whether or not that story is relevant even at this early point in the letter? If the story of Abraham is relevant, has not its theological force become Paul's own?

The first episode in the story of Abraham is his encounter with God and resultant migration out of the land of his fathers into a new land of promise in obedience to the command of God (Gen. 12.1, 4). A promise of blessing is attached to this migration (Gen. 12.2-3) and Paul refers to it in Gal. 3.8. This episode is of extraordinary importance in the roughly contemporary writings of Philo, for example, who devotes a great deal of time to Abraham's migration as a type of the migration of the soul toward true knowledge. It is of course true that we find no trace in Galatians of Philo's particular allegorical use of this portion of the narrative, although we do encounter a similar allegorization with a different intention in Gal. 4.21-31. What is of significance is that although Philo, possibly the most important of Paul's contemporaries in terms of exegetical methods and interests, found the episode so important, scholars frequently do not see the

(1986), pp. 309-26; G. Lyons, *Pauline Autobiography* (SBLDS, 73; Atlanta: Scholars Press, 1985).

migration, but only the *promise*, as important for Paul, without
further inquiry. We have generally seen those verses from the story
which Paul *cites* as the only ones with which he is concerned, and I
would suggest that this methodological presupposition may have provided too narrow a focus on the letter. I would like to explore the
possibility that the very first part of Abraham's story is also important
for Paul at the very beginning of his letter to the Galatian Christians.

It is true that he does not cite the text of Genesis in Galatians 1 or 2.
It is true that he does not mention Abraham's name. However, it is
also true that the story of Abraham is a remarkable parallel at its
earliest point to Paul's own story and to the pattern which the
Galatians have followed and to which Paul writes to exhort them to
remain constant. Both elements of this parallelism—place in the narrative sequence and similarity of content—are important for my purposes in much the same way that similar order and similar wording
are important for the source critic working with the Synoptic Gospels,
and as order and wording were important to my analysis of Moses
traditions in 2 Corinthians 3–4. It seems to me, on the basis of these
two kinds of correspondence, that the figure of Abraham and his story
are the most powerful level of the paradigmatic narration of Galatians
1–2. Abraham is the revered model who first abandoned his heritage,
his home, and the ways of his fathers to follow the will of God. It is
his authority that lends a profound authority to Paul's self-portrait, in
its turn intended to be paradigmatic for Paul's readers. The following
of this paradigm is the first theological recommendation made in the
letter.

However, the stories of Paul and Abraham are not identical. In fact,
they differ in one highly explosive way which is directly related to the
central issue of the epistle. Abraham followed God out of paganism to
become the father of Israel and the model for Gentiles to do the same.
It seemed, at least to some, that Paul strayed out of Israel to become
the apostle to the Gentiles. Paul's claim that he and Abraham both
trusted and followed the same God is obvious throughout the letter.
Yet it is at this point that Paul's paradigm is most in jeopardy. It is at
this point that the Galatians' certainty of their own resemblance to
Abraham their father is most upset. Just as in 2 Corinthians 3–4 Paul
is both like and unlike Moses, in Galatians Paul is both like and unlike
Abraham. Furthermore, in both cases Christian disciples are called upon
to make choices ultimately mediated by an exegetical manipulation of

a narrative scriptural tradition. This is the issue that calls forth and creates Paul's argument about sonship, an argument that is central in Paul's letter concerning events which are central in Abraham's story, just as the paradigm tension in 2 Corinthians 3–4 called forth the argument about covenant which finally solves it.

Galatians research remains haunted by the shadowy figures who 'preached a different gospel' (Gal. 1.7), whose bewitching of his Galatians Paul has set out to refute.[17] The important question for my purposes is the way in which Galatians might reveal these opponents' concept of the relationship between Abraham's story and the gospel, which Paul found disturbing enough to be called a perversion and which he sets out to refute. If the significance of the whole Abraham narrative for Paul's argument is taken into account, a very simple rationale for his opponents' position is immediately clear. From Galatians itself we learn that the feature of the opposing gospel that Paul found particularly repellent was the practical attempt to circumcise his Gentile converts. Interpreters regularly emphasize the consequences of circumcision for the Galatians—real, but ultimately self-defeating obligation to the whole law of Moses. But, when he mentions this consequence (Gal. 5.3-4), the concern appears to be Paul's own. The opponents focused on circumcision alone (Gal. 6.12-13) and the thrust of Paul's argument is against circumcision primarily. Why should this be so? It seems to me that such a procedure—circumcision as a perfection of what was begun with belief in Jesus Christ on the part of Gentiles[18]— arises from a consistently linear and exclusive reading of the narrative of Abraham. First, Abraham abandons his pagan past (Genesis 12), then Abraham comes to faith (Genesis 15), then Abraham receives the command to walk blamelessly and circumcise the males of his household in perpetuity (Genesis 17), then Abraham has a son as God promised (Genesis 21), then Abraham is tested (Genesis 22). The

17. See B.H. Brinsmead, *Galatians—Dialogical Response to Opponents* (SBLDS, 65; Chico, CA: Scholars Press, 1982) for a lengthy discussion of Paul's opposition in Galatia from the perspective of their 'Abraham theology', and J.H. Neyrey, 'Bewitched in Galatia: Paul and Cultural Anthropology', *CBQ* 50 (1988), pp. 72-100, revised and reprinted in *Paul in Other Words* (Louisville, KY: Westminster Press/John Knox, 1990), pp. 181-206 for a social sciences perspective on these issues.

18. As discussed for example by R. Jewett, 'The Agitators and the Galatian Congregation', *NTS* 17 (1971), pp. 198-212.

opponents have a perfectly straightforward case, drawn from Scripture, for the procedure that they advocate for the Gentile Christians of Galatia. Paul mounts an exegetical argument of considerable difficulty and sophistication to counter a position that itself has very strong scriptural warrant.

In sum, although this line of argument might be pursued further, we have seen, in two of Paul's letters, a considerable, detailed and wide-ranging reference to two Pentateuchal narrative texts focused on two scriptural characters and the events of their lives. Each of us could probably multiply examples. It seems to me, then, that great interest in and attentive treatment of narrative is shown to be a fundamental principle of Paul's exegesis.

Part Two

The second fundamental method Paul typically uses is the application of verbally linked, usually prophetic, texts to the appropriated narrative to create a contemporary understanding of the Torah. My work on 2 Corinthians has been primarily devoted to analyzing and presenting this dimension of Paul's argument in 2 Corinthians 3.

First, I have argued particularly against a reading of 2 Cor. 3.1-6 which sees Paul as sliding from one topic to another, mixing his metaphors, or as guilty of repeated non sequiturs. On the other hand, I am willing to acknowledge the ambiguity and density of the text.[19] I have offered an exegetical background which enables an appreciation of the coherence of Paul's thought, and which was, presumably, sometimes available to the original readers of the letter. It is an exegesis resting on verbal links which could be mediated in an aural culture and created by following simple rules of analogy common in Paul's Hellenized Jewish milieu.[20] Perhaps in this case brief examples drawn from my earlier work will best illustrate the principle.

There is discoverable from the vocabulary of 2 Corinthians 3 a text-complex from Scripture centered around Jer. 38.31-34 (LXX)

---

19. Stockhausen, *Moses' Veil*, pp. 35-38.

20. Hays (*Echoes of Scripture*, pp. 128-29) recognizes these verbal clues, but does not follow through with any careful methodological analysis of Paul's treatment of the recovered texts. This is the primary difference in our treatments of this particular text and Paul's exegesis in general, not conclusions or theology.

which consists in hook-word connections. This text-complex forms an indispensable background apart from which 2 Cor. 3.1-6 is not understandable. This is so because Paul's metaphors in this section are dependent on, and are in fact *pointers to*, the vocabulary of the scriptural texts which undergird his argument.

Several key expressions in 2 Cor. 3.1-6 lead quickly into this background. These are,

1. New Covenant (καινὴ διαθήκη); v. 6
2. Hearts of flesh (...καρδίαις σαρκίναις); v. 3
3. Stone tablets (...πλαξὶν λιθίναις); v. 3
4. Engraved on the heart (ἐγγεγραμμένη ἐν ταῖς καρδίαις); v. 2

The Old Testament (LXX) texts to which this unusual vocabulary points are, respectively,

1. Jer. 38.31-34 (LXX)
2. Ezek. 11.19/36.26
3. Exod. 34.1-4, 27-28
4. Jer. 38.31-34 (LXX)[21]

It is not unusual for commentators or editors of 2 Corinthians to be aware of these scriptural references. One can find them in the notes of any critical edition. What is important, however, is what one does with them once one has them. It is necessary to understand not only *that* Paul alludes to these various texts but *why*, and how he uses them.

Each of the texts in the group can be associated with one or more of the others through a significant hook-word. All of the prophetic texts in the group can be associated with one another *verbally* through καρδία. The primary *thematic* link within this system of texts (constructed via the hook-word links) is between the covenant of Jeremiah and the spirit of Ezekiel. Without the link between the texts διαθήκη and πνεῦμα are not necessarily connected. The texts cited from Exodus do not share this verbal link through καρδία. Hence the spirit is denied to the written διαθήκη. Exod. 34.27-28, however, does contain the word διαθήκη in common with Jer. 38.31-34 (LXX), so these texts from the prophets are validly used to interpret the Torah covenant story.

The links between the prophetic texts in the group are positive. On

21. Stockhausen, *Moses' Veil*, pp. 43-52.

the other hand, the relationships of the Jeremiah/Exodus texts and of the Ezekiel/Exodus texts are a set of contrasts through the links γράφω and λίθος. The Jeremiah/Exodus texts are contrasted and set in a contradictory juxtaposition on the basis of two different types of writing, just as Ezekiel's spirit and flesh are contrasted with the stones of Exodus as writing materials.[22]

The individual texts unearthed on the basis of the Pauline vocabulary in 2 Cor. 3.1-6 form a cohesive group in themselves on the basis of hook-word linkage. All of the key linking words are present in Paul's text, but they have also become integral parts of his own composition. The hook-word links exist between the texts which form the background of his text. The structure of Paul's own text hangs on a single link with the text-group, γράφω, and consists of an argument which relies heavily on ideas drawn from the group.[23]

The exegetical procedure (*gezera shava*) as it is illustrated in the works of the rabbis is usually performed on legal texts, but does also occur in the interpretation of prophetic or narrative texts to the extent that such texts captured the interest of those interpreters. Hook-wording itself is a common ancient mnemonic technique. In Jewish exegetical texts the verbal linkage between two or more texts is often performed for the sake of interpretation. What one text lacks in detail, or in clarity, is supplied from the other, or others, with which it shares specific verbal affinity. Once a chain of scriptural texts has been established through such a hook-word procedure as I have suggested for the Jeremiah/Ezekiel texts, a further exegetical operation, the rabbinic *hekkesh*, may be performed upon them. The texts, now related through specific verbal links, may be further related through any of their themes. They become mutually explanatory as a whole. Each text may be used to expand the interpreter's understanding of any of the others. If this procedure were to be performed in all of its possible variations on a particular set of texts, a pool or family of terms and the concepts which they express could be formed, drawn from all of the texts in the set. The individual texts become a mutually interpreting group and their individual aspects form a pool around their leading concept, the notion of greatest interest to the interpreter in each case. In the case of 2 Cor. 3.1-6 that notion is 'covenant'. This is admittedly an abstraction of Paul's exegetical procedure from

22. Stockhausen, *Moses' Veil*, pp. 54-59.
23. Stockhausen, *Moses' Veil*, p. 59.

evidence encountered in his argument and later articulations of specific exegetical rules. The value of the model, however, is that it has worked very well for me in explaining Paul's otherwise illogical jumps in 2 Cor. 3.1-6.[24]

One example: in 2 Cor. 3.6 Paul says that he is a minister of a new covenant, not a written one, but a spiritual one. Although the phrase 'new covenant' stems from Jeremiah, the deceptively familiar covenant theology which knows that the new covenant is 'spiritual' cannot really be drawn from Jer. 38.31-34 (LXX) or its context alone. I have suggested that the combination of the notions καινὴ διαθήκη and πνεῦμα is the result of the mutual interpretation of Jer. 38.31 (LXX) and Ezek. 11.19/36.26-27 based on their verbal links. The pool developed through the association of these texts contains both 'new covenant' and 'new spirit' and so the ideas have been combined.[25]

Another example: the notion of 'writing' could legitimately be associated with the Ezekiel texts from Jeremiah 38 (LXX) on the basis of their established connection, even though Ezekiel does not talk about writing. There is evidence in 2 Cor. 3.3 that this application has been made, even though the process itself is not articulated in Paul's text. In 2 Cor. 3.3 Paul speaks of a letter written on tablets which are hearts of flesh. It is clear that the phrase 'hearts of flesh' stems from Ezekiel. In Ezekiel, however, nothing is to be written on them; they are to receive the spirit. It is in Jer. 38.33 (LXX) that something is to be written on a heart. Paul's expression is not a mixed metaphor. It is an interpretation of Ezek. 11.19/36.26 by Jer. 38.33 (LXX). The pool of concepts which their text-group creates includes both 'written-on hearts' and 'hearts of flesh', and the two notions have been combined.[26]

A reading of 2 Cor. 3.1-6 reveals that the terms and concepts appearing most frequently are those having to do with writing and written things. In addition, continuity between the narrative and prophetic texts on which Paul depends is established by the key verbal and conceptual link, διαθήκη, shared by Exod. 34.27-28 and Jer. 38.31-34 (LXX). But Paul has engaged his scriptural background in support of his argument precisely at the point at which the Exodus covenant can be compared unfavorably with the new covenant of

24. Stockhausen, *Moses' Veil*, pp. 60-62.
25. Stockhausen, *Moses' Veil*, p. 62.
26. Stockhausen, *Moses' Veil*, pp. 62-63.

Jeremiah—the way that they are written. The tone of his text is
entirely positive to the prophetic side of this contrast and, with only
two exceptions—its original and inviolable status as διαθήκη and the
divine commission of Moses as covenant minister—negative to the
Exodus side. Thus the Torah narrative is brought into Paul's contemporary world in such a way that Paul can pass a critical judgment on it
on the basis of other scriptural passages and accepted interpretive
procedures.

Textual Interrelationship in Galatians

A similar hook-word association is obvious, and indeed has often been
noted, in Gal. 3.10-14, with Deut. 27.26 being connected to Deut. 21.23
through the hook-word 'cursed', and Hab. 2.4 connected to Lev. 18.5
by the word 'live'. Such hook-word structures can be found every-
where in the authentic letters.[27] However, these texts in Galatians 3
are also used by Nils Dahl as the most obvious instance of Pauline
reconciliation of contradictions.[28] The curse of the law stands in
contradiction to the life available through faith, yet both are
scriptural. Rather than delving into the already well-turned turf of
this surface hook-word association, I propose a second, deeper, level
of contradiction in Galatians, also involving interpretive verbal
analogy, but more closely connected to the narrative interest in Part
One of this chapter and illustrative of Paul's tendency to pose and
solve exegetical questions in this manner.

I would like to suggest that the contradiction with which Paul is
concerned is one which he has posed himself in order to counter the
'twisted' gospel of his opponents and offer an alternative reading of
the narrative of Genesis 12–22. Paul proposes to read the narrative
not in a linear way, but as containing a pair of contradictory episodes.
The first of these contradictory episodes is the vision of Abram containing the dialogue with God concerning Abram's lack of an heir,
seed (σπέρμα) (Gen. 15.3), God's promise of a 'seed' of Abram's
own to inherit (κληρονομία) (Gen. 15.4-5), and Abram's response of
belief (πιστεύω) with God's reckoning (λογίζομαι) of righteousness
(δικαιοσύνη) (Gen. 15.6) cited by Paul in Gal. 3.6. The promise of
heir and inheritance is confirmed by a covenant (διαθήκη) between

27. Rom. 2.27-29; 3.10-18; 9.33; 11.8-10; 1 Cor. 15.24-28, 45; 2 Cor. 6.16-18
are obvious on the surface.

28. Dahl, 'Contradictions', pp. 169-75.

Abram and God following in Gen. 15.7-18, alluded to by Paul in Gal. 3.15-18. The second episode can only be the second vision of Abram containing the divine speech commanding him to be pleasing and blameless (Gen. 17.1), the establishment of a covenant (διαθήκη) between God and Abraham (Gen. 17.2-10) which carries the promise of numerous descendants, fatherhood of many nations and of kings, and possession of the land. This covenant is signified and established by circumcision (περιτομή) in the flesh (σάρξ) (Gen. 17.10-11). Any male who is not circumcised on the eighth day is cut off from the people and has broken the covenant (Gen. 17.14). I would argue that Paul has posed this very fundamental contradiction—between the absolute promise and covenant in Genesis 15 and the conditional promise and covenant in Genesis 17—in order to relate the Abraham narrative properly to the gospel of Jesus Christ, in order to counter his opponents' preaching of a gospel requiring circumcision, and in order to clarify the Galatians' status as sons of God and sons of Abraham with reference to the text of Scripture itself. The pair of verbally linked contradictory texts more familiar to us, Lev. 18.5 and Hab. 2.4, is in fact introduced into the argument following the citation of the primary text to be defended as relevant to Paul's context in Gal. 3.6 in order to support Paul's preference for the Genesis 15 narrative episode, just as their contradiction is ultimately solved with reference to Deuteronomy 22/27 and the death of Christ as the source of life and righteousness. The procedure is very similar, although not identical, to the case of the Jeremiah and Ezekiel texts in 2 Corinthians 3 after explicit mention of the Exodus 34 Moses episode.

The interplay of Genesis 15 and 17 is not limited to the first part of Galatians 3, but informs Paul's argument directly at least through the end of Galatians 4. A contradiction as serious as this within a single traditional narrative is a matter of profound theological significance. That is, the question of the divine intentionality and integrity is immediately raised, as Gal. 3.19-20 shows, a question to which the later Romans quite properly responds.

However, a serious objection can be raised immediately against this preliminary outline of the structure of Paul's argument. Paul has not cited the text of Genesis 17 with a formula anywhere in Galatians 3 or 4. Surely citation is the most reliable way to indicate and thus to determine sources. In the absence of citation modern critics demand unique repetition of vocabulary from the proposed source and similar usage such as I have outlined for 2 Corinthians 3.[29] In defense, then, of my suggestion that Galatians 3 and 4 (not to mention the paraenetic chapters 5 and 6) are primarily intended to reconcile a contradiction within the Abraham narrative, I would like to point out some preliminary lexical indicators of the presence of this pattern.

It is remarkable, but not coincidental, how much of the key vocabulary of Galatians is to be found in the story of Abraham, and precisely as key terms in the older story. Faith, righteousness, seed, inheritance, covenant, circumcision and flesh all appear in the saga of Abraham and are used as Paul uses them.[30] At this point I would like to distinguish myself from the school of thought which sees this phenomenon of common vocabulary as an extraordinary coincidence of Pauline theological concepts and real historical events reported by a particular Old Testament text, an oddity which allows Paul to proof-text his theological position. I mean quite the opposite, that these terms represent his theological concepts and these issues are historical issues for him precisely *because* they are the key terms and ideas in Abraham's story. Notice, then, that the terms which are used positively by Paul come from Genesis 15 (faith/righteousness/inheritance) and do not occur in Genesis 17. Similarly, the terms about which Paul is extremely and notoriously negative (circumcision/flesh) occur in Genesis 17 and do not appear in Genesis 15. The term 'seed', interestingly, occurs in both, having the role of verbally linking the two texts, and is central for Paul, as most analysts of his argument here would agree.

In search of evidence for the negative presence of Genesis 17 in Paul's argument as a whole, one could stress the phenomenon that both texts contain references to covenants and that Paul becomes quite concerned with the existence of two covenants in Gal. 4.21-31. Commentators are sometimes unclear about which 'two covenants' Paul can mean here, or suppose Paul to be referring to the Mosaic

29. Hays (*Echoes of Scripture*, p. 30) has this as his 'second test' of proposed intertextual echoes, although he makes relatively little use of it in the actual case-discussions which make up the bulk of the book. I am in agreement with him, however, in rejecting citation with formula as the only way reliably to determine intertextuality.

30. Of course, Paul's use of the term σπέρμα in Gal. 3.16 is exegetical, and I do not mean to assert, for example, that here or elsewhere Paul is replicating the authorial intention of Genesis passages. I only mean to say that there is a general correspondence in the use of the terms, i.e. seed = child or inheritor.

covenant as one of these and the 'new covenant' in Christ as the other, but a reference to the two covenants contained in the Abraham narrative itself cannot be ruled out. If either of these two covenants can be seen as anticipatory of the Mosaic covenant and the 'whole' law, it is surely Genesis 17 and the covenant of circumcision which Paul connects with the flesh. It is this covenant which carries with it the threat of being 'cut off' from God's people (cf. Gal. 5.2-4; Gen. 17.14). The obscurities of the allegory are not thereby expelled and it is not my intention to provide a full explanation here. I wish to point out only that a reference to the two covenants with Abraham keeps the text closer to the story with which the argument is clearly connected by the references to Sarah, Hagar and Isaac and indicates that the same two foci—Genesis 15 and Genesis 17—are in view and in a contradictory way. It appears then that the second and third primary exegetical principles—verbal association and resolution of contradictions—can be linked to the first principle—narrative interest—in Galatians as in 2 Corinthians and do help to explain Paul's arguments there as well.

Part Three

Finally, to touch briefly on the attention to context that is typical of Paul's exegesis, I will note the relevance of context in the allusions in 2 Cor. 3.6 and Gal. 3.13. We have already seen that a group of Septuagint texts is reflected in the vocabulary of 2 Cor. 3.1-6 and that several unusual phrases present there, rather than being mixed metaphors, are in fact evidence of the dynamic exegetical structure of that text-group. One of those unusual phrases previously discussed was καινῆς διαθήκης, οὐ γράμματος ἀλλὰ πνεύματος of 2 Cor. 3.6. Several of the elements of this highly significant phrase have already been explained. For the moment, I would like to concentrate on the final segment of the verse, τὸ γὰρ γράμμα ἀποκτέννει, τὸ δὲ πνεῦμα ζῳοποιεῖ. I have argued that this statement is also traceable to the complex of texts undergirding Paul's argument. In this case, the second member of the parallelism is a direct recalling of a passage from the context of Ezek. 36.26, that is, Ezek. 37.6, 10 and 14.[31]

31. Stockhausen, *Moses' Veil*, pp. 67-70. It is interesting, and quite typical, that Hays also invokes Ezekiel 37 to explain the life-giving quality of the new covenant (*Echoes of Scripture*, p. 129) but provides no argument to support his assertion that

Chapter 37 of Ezekiel opens with the famous 'dry bones' vision, linked with the material Paul uses from Ezekiel 36 through the word 'spirit' (πνεῦμα). Ezek. 37.1-14 is a narration depicting the realization of the promise of Ezek. 36.26b-27a ('...and I will give you a new spirit...' καὶ πνεῦμα καινὸν δώσω ἐν ὑμῖν '...and I will put my spirit in you...' καὶ τὸ πνεῦμά μου δώσω ἐν ὑμῖν). Ezekiel 37 echoes with the phrase, 'I will put my spirit within you, and you shall live'. In this text, in vv. 6, 10 and 14, the promise of Ezek. 36.26, 27 is repeated in an only slightly modified form: v. 6 καὶ δώσω πνεῦμά μου εἰς ὑμᾶς; v. 10 καὶ εἰσῆλθεν εἰς αὐτοὺς τὸ πνεῦμα; v. 14 καὶ δώσω πνεῦμά μου εἰς ὑμᾶς. Each time the promise is followed by the same qualification: καὶ ζήσεσθε v. 6; καὶ ἔζησαν v. 10; καὶ ζήσεσθε v. 14. The result of the gift of the spirit is life—'And you (they) will live'. Therefore, the spirit gives life. This is a direct conclusion from Ezek. 37.6, 10, 14, but it is also exactly what Paul says in 2 Cor. 3.6c—τὸ δὲ πνεῦμα ζῳοποιεῖ. My vocabulary analysis has shown that Paul is in contact with Ezek. 36.26, 27 in this section of his text. Its context, and interestingly a narrative episode, has just as surely provided Paul with his concluding remark. The concept of life and its association with the spirit is thereby added to the pool of covenant characteristics Paul has developed.

In Galatians 3, Paul's citation of Deuteronomy 21 is a clear reference to the crucifixion and this, in addition to the hook-word 'cursed', is commonly thought to be enough to account for the presence of the reference in Gal. 3.13. A glance at the context of the passage in Deuteronomy, however, suggests a more profound reason for Paul's use of it, one related directly to his narrative interest in the letter. Deut. 21.15-17 discusses the proper behavior of a man with two sons born to two wives, one of whom is beloved and the other disliked. The text is concerned to confirm the right of the first-born in spite of the father's preference for a younger son. Deut. 21.18-21 discusses the fate of the stubborn and rebellious son, whose parents must reject him and give him up to the punishment of all the people. There follows Paul's cited text, concerning the curse of execution. The relevance of the question of the elder and younger son, the right of inheritance, the relative status of two mothers, as well as the rebellion of the elder son and the need for punishment, to basic issues in the

the 'dry bones' vision is in fact relevant here, either for Paul or for us.

Genesis narrative background of Galatians as well as the Christian gospel story cannot be missed. The central issue in Galatians is the inheritance of the sons of Abraham, their mothers are explicitly mentioned (Gal. 4.21-31), and the Jew–Gentile question provides a reasonable *Sitz im Leben*. Numerous New Testament texts, and not only Pauline ones, express this issue of Jews and Gentiles in Christ using the older brother/younger brother image.[32]

Conclusion

What has emerged from this study is only a sketch of the exegete at his work in the Pauline letters. This portrait in embryo begins to reveal a man with identifiable preferences and interests, with predictable procedures and ways of dealing with his Scriptures. In short, we see a man of his times, a man with *methods*. Driven to the Scripture by his religious tradition and environment as well as the shattering experience of Jesus Christ in Israel, Paul created a new scriptural expression in his letters. But, like the original tellers of the biblical stories and the long chain of tradents of the scriptural narratives, Paul did so in the ways of this world—with a fascination with stories, how they turn out in the end and how the pieces of a single story, matching or not, puzzling as they might be, fit together to explain this life and offer a pattern to follow to a new life in Christ, the one seed in whom all inherit the blessing of Abraham, the one image in whom all behold the glory of God, and the beloved and guiltless son who died so that none of God's children would ever carry the burden of a curse.[33]

32. Consider, for example, the story of the prodigal son in Lk. 15.11-32, or the parable of the laborers in the vineyard (Mt. 20.1-16 par.) and the parable of the vineyard (Mt. 21.33-44 par.) for variations on the same theme. One might ponder why Paul chooses to explore it through the Abraham story directly or why John chose to deny Abraham's paternity of the rebellious son (Jn 8.31-59) in an argument more similar to Paul's.

33. It is interesting to ponder, in closing, how close to the theological concept of 'salvation history' this chapter on Paul's interpretive methodology, or Hays's work on Pauline intertextuality, come, especially in view of our emphasis on Paul's narrative interest. It is clear to me at least that Hays is very close to it indeed, particularly when he discusses typology as a major Pauline technique (*Echoes of Scripture*, pp. 75-102) and describes Paul's hermeneutic as the drawing out of Scripture the story of God's righteousness as it expressed itself in all stages of the scriptural witness (*Echoes of Scripture*, pp. 155-57, 171) and the contemporary church. I fancy

The paradox of Pauline exegesis is the creation of these profound theological insights into God's ways with the world through the world's own ways.

myself to be farther away, but, however unfashionable, this classic theological idea is inescapable. I would, however, locate the creative force in this 'salvation history' in *Paul's* interpretive work with the Moses and Abraham narratives, rather than in the texts or in the divine will. The former only witness to the process and provide grist for its mill, and the latter is imponderable, while it is humans who create history.

TRADITION OR CREATION? PAUL'S USE OF THE
EXODUS 34 TRADITION IN 2 CORINTHIANS 3.7-18

Linda L. Belleville

Introduction

Merrill P. Miller, in a 1971 article, asserted that now is not the time for further comprehensive treatments of the use of the Old Testament in the New Testament, but that what is needed are detailed analyses of limited passages—analyses that concern themselves not merely with relationships between the Testaments but with the body of Jewish exegetical tradition that had grown up around the Scriptures by the time of the New Testament.[1] One passage that is still in need of such an analysis is 2 Cor. 3.7-18. For it has long been noted that Paul's use of Exod. 34.28-35 does not sufficiently account for his exegetical comments in 2 Cor. 3.7-18. There is, for example, no mention in the Exodus narrative of the fading glory of Moses' face,[2] no reference to

---

1. M.P. Miller, 'Targum, Midrash and the Use of the OT in the NT', *JSJ* 2 (1971), pp. 37-39; pp. 74-76.

2. Richard Hays in his recent work *Echoes of Scripture in the Letters of Paul* ([New Haven and London: Yale University Press, 1989], pp. 130-42) argues for a transitory as opposed to a fading glory based on his claim that the semantic field of the term καταργέω is the realm of legal process ('to nullify') rather than of visual image ('to fade'): 'the old covenant glory... was done away by the greater glory of the new covenant in Christ' (p. 135). The basic idea of καταργέω in Hellenistic Greek, however, is not 'to do away with' but 'to render powerless' or 'ineffective' (κατά = causative and α privative + ἔργον = 'not working', 'to cause to not work'; 'to render idle', 'ineffective'). That the semantic field is broader than the legal realm is clear from usage in the papyri: for example, *P.Oxy.* 38.17: 'Syrus hinders me (καταργοῦντός με) in my trade.' The decay or diminishment of Moses' facial glory is a familiar idea in the rabbinic materials (see below). Paul's consistent use of the present tense in 2 Cor. 3.7, 11, 13 and 14, and the shift to neuter in vv. 11ff., suggests the idea of the Mosaic ministry with its attendant glory as being in the process of diminishment or decay and not 'done away with', which would require the aorist.

the Israelites' inability to gaze at Moses' face, no connection between the Israelites' gazing at Moses' face and his donning of a veil, and no motive for the veiling—yet Paul assumes his readers' knowledge of these features and builds his argument on them.[3] This matter is further complicated by the fact that the glory of Moses' face and the donning of a veil are not explicitly recalled anywhere else in the Old Testament.

The intent of this study is, first, to review current form-critical approaches to 2 Cor. 3.7-18, and secondly to examine extrabiblical usage of Exod. 34.28-35 with a view to determining the extent to which Paul is making use of Jewish exegetical traditions and where he is providing a fresh interpretation.

Form-Critical Approaches
2 Cor. 3.7-18 has been analyzed formally in a number of ways. Some think in terms of a midrash that finds its material source in Paul's own fanciful thinking.[4] Others suppose that Paul is Christianizing a midrash already formed within Judaism.[5] Of late it has been suggested that vv. 7-18 are in essence a midrash composed by Paul's opponents, which he modifies and uses against them to his own advantage.[6] The

---

There is also a problem of consistency in Hays's interpretation of καταργέω. He argues that in vv. 7 and 11 the glory reflected on Moses' face (i.e., the glory of the old covenant) was a glory that is now, through God's act in Christ, 'nullified' and 'done away' (pp. 134-35), while he states that in vv. 12-18 the Mosaic veil conceals the presence of the glory of God (pp. 138, 146).

3.   Brevard Childs in his 1974 commentary on the book of Exodus makes a similar observation (*The Book of Exodus* [Philadelphia: Westminster Press, 1974], p. 624).

4.   For example, C.K. Barrett states that Paul's exegesis is probably not based on traditional Jewish themes but is a new Christian interpretation, and that there is no reason to think of it as anything but Paul's own work (*The Second Epistle to the Corinthians* [New York: Harper & Row, 1973], p. 115). Cf. W.D. Davies, *Paul and Rabbinic Judaism* (Philadelphia: Fortress Press, 4th edn, 1980), p. 107 n. 2; R. Le Déaut, 'Traditions targumiques dans le Corpus Paulinien? (Hebr. 11,4 et 12,24; Gal. 4,29-30; II Cor. 3,16', *Bib* 42 (1961), p. 44 n. 5. Hays prefers to think in terms of 'an allusive homily based on biblical incidents' the interpretive details of which Paul 'conjures into existence' (*Echoes of Scripture*, pp. 132, 141).

5.   E.g. M. McNamara, *Targum and Testament* (Grand Rapids, MI: Eerdmans, 1972), p. 112.

6.   E.g. S. Schulz, 'Die Decke des Moses: Untersuchungen zu einer vor-paulinischen Überlieferung in II Cor. 3:7-18', *ZNW* 49 (1958), pp. 1-30; T. Saito,

bases for this judgment are perceived terminological, stylistic, and conceptual tensions that point to two distinct and diverse strands of thought. For instance, it is maintained that an inordinate number of Pauline *hapax legomena* exist side by side with genuine Pauline terms and phrases.[7] It is also argued that the style is uneven at a number of points, suggesting secondary modification.[8] It is further claimed that a number of ideological tensions exist, indicating the juxtaposition of conflicting points of view.[9] Consequently, it is maintained that these inherent tensions point to the existence of a midrashic document that enshrines an understanding of the role of the Mosaic covenant and a view of Moses that Paul is at pains to correct by means of additions and modifications.[10]

Die Mosevorstellungen im Neuen Testament (Bern: Peter Lang, 1977), pp. 3ff.; D. Georgi, *Die Gegner des Paulus im 2 Korintherbrief* (WMANT, 11; Neukirchen–Vluyn: Neukirchener Verlag, 1964), pp. 274-82; M. Theobald, *Die überströmende Gnade. Studien zu einem paulinischen Motivfeld* (Würzburg: Echter, 1972), pp. 204-208. Cf. G. Friedrich, who thinks that 2 Corinthians 3 represents a reworked Jewish-Christian theological tractate of Paul's opponents, which Paul recast through a number of additions and modifications ('Die Gegner des Paulus im 2 Korintherbrief', in O. Betz [ed.], *Abraham unser Vater: Juden und Christen im Gespräch über die Bibel* [AGSU, 5; Leiden: Brill, 1963], p. 184).

7.   E.g. ἀτενίζω, παλαιὰ διαθήκη, ἡνίκα ἄν, ἄχρι τῆς σήμερον ἡμέρας, κάλυμμα, ἀνακαλύπτω, ἐπιστρέφειν πρὸς κύριον. See Schulz, 'Die Decke des Moses', pp. 2-3.

8.   Verse 7b has no parallel in vv. 7-11; vv. 15-16 are a repetition of v. 14. See, e.g., Saito, *Die Mosevorstellungen*, p. 3.

9.   For example, it is asserted that contrary statements regarding overpowering splendor, on the one hand, and the diminished glory of Moses' face, on the other hand, exist side by side in v. 7b. Also, two contradictory functions of the veil occur in vv. 14b-15: in v. 14b the veil serves to conceal that the power of the Torah has been set aside, while in v. 15 the veil prevents Israel from understanding the Torah. In addition, κύριος suddenly appears in v. 16, whereas in the context Χριστός is the christological title. Further, references to both the glory of the old covenant and the covenant of death are juxtaposed in vv. 7-11. Finally, there are conflicting motives given for the veiling of Moses' face: v. 7b implies that Moses veiled his face out of consideration for the people, while v. 13b states that he sought to prevent recognition of the transient nature of the old covenant and of his own facial glory. Saito, *Die Mosevorstellungen*, pp. 4, 10-11; Schulz, 'Die Decke des Moses', pp. 3, 8-9; Theobald, *Die überströmende Gnade*, pp. 205-207.

10.   See, e.g., Georgi, *Die Gegner des Paulus*; Schulz, 'Die Decke des Moses'; Saito, *Die Mosevorstellungen*; Theobald, *Die überströmende Gnade*; Friedrich, 'Die Gegner des Paulus'.

The primary difficulty with such an analysis is that it overlooks the extent to which Paul's terminology and ideology can be accounted for on the basis of Septuagintal and extrabiblical dependence, and the degree to which his style is attributable to the haggadic character of his sources and method.[11] In particular there is a tendency in current form-critical approaches to ignore the more basic question of whether there is any evidence for the existence of parallel traditions—or even a pre-Pauline *Vorlage*—in the Jewish exegetical literature of Paul's day.[12]

So there is a need at this point to explore extrabiblical usage of the Exodus 34 narrative and Paul's relationship to existing exegetical materials. Because Paul's argument revolves around the Exodus 34 Septuagintal tradition of the veiling and unveiling of the glory of Moses' face,[13] the focus of this investigation will be usage of this Moses-*Doxa* tradition.

11. E.g., the semantic equivalent of ἀτενίζω is also found in the Philonic tradition (see below); ἡνίκα ἄν and κάλυμμα occur in the Exodus 34 narrative; and ἄχρι τῆς σήμερον ἡμέρας, ἐπιστρέφειν πρὸς κύριον, and ἀνακαλύπτω are common terms and phrases in both the LXX and extrabiblical literature.

12. Many of these tensions, in fact, disappear on closer examination. The over-powering splendor of Moses' face in v. 7b is part and parcel of an *a minori ad maius* argumentation in vv. 8-11 that all attribute to Paul himself. Also, Paul's shift from the articular τὸ κάλυμμα in v. 14 to an anarthrous use of κάλυμμα in v. 15 points to not one but two different veils: one that stands over the face of Moses/Torah (vv. 13-14); another that lies over the heart of Israel (vv. 15-16). Furthermore, the use of κύριος in v. 16 is a moot point if a citation of Scripture is involved. In addition, it is important to observe that Paul distinguishes between the positive nature of the old covenant ('came in glory') and its negative effects ('death', 'condemnation')—a distinction not sufficiently noted. Finally, the perception that vv. 7-18 include contradictory motives for the veiling of Moses' face involves reading into the text something that is plainly not there. All v. 7 explicitly states is that the Israelites were unable to gaze intently at the face of Moses because of the brilliance.

13. A comparison of terminology and phraseology in Exod. 34.28-35 and 2 Cor. 3.7-18 shows that Paul is dependent on a text closer to the LXX than the MT.

The Moses-Doxa Tradition

The Targumim[14]

Both the Babylonian and Palestinian Targumim show familiarity with
the Moses-*Doxa* tradition, as evidenced by the departures from the
MT. For example, Codex Neofiti has 'splendor' (זיו) for the MT 'skin'
(עור) and has added the term 'glory' (איקרהון) in line with what occurs
in the LXX and in Paul:

MT: ומשה לא־ידע כי קרן עור פניו

    And Moses did not know that the skin of his face shone.

TN: משה לא הוה ידע ארום נהר זיו איקרהון דאפוי

    And Moses did not know that the splendor of the glory
    of his face shone.

A number of elaborations of this Moses-*Doxa* tradition occur in the
Targumim. In Pseudo-Jonathan it is the 'image' of Moses' face that
shines: ומשה לא חכים ארום אשתבהר זיו איקונין דאנפוי ('And Moses did not
recognize that the splendor of the image [= features] of his face
shone'; cf. Paul's concept of transformation into the 'same image' in
v. 18). And a source for the splendor is specified as the glory of the
Shekinah of Yahweh himself: דהות ליה מן זיו איקר שכינתא דה ('which
came to him from the splendor of the glory of the Shekinah of
Yahweh'). Targum Onkelos and the Fragmentary Targum go further
to state that Moses' face not merely 'shone' but that the splendor of his
face 'increased':[15]

14. The Palestinian Targum is of particular importance, since its formation
probably began as early as the pre-Christian era. A. Díez Macho dates Neofiti 1 as
early as the first or second century CE. M. Kasher dates this codex in its origins in
the period of the Second Temple. For discussion, see McNamara, *Targum and
Testament*, pp. 79-85 and S.A. Kaufman, 'On Methodology in the Study of the
Targums and Their Chronology', *JSNT* 23 (1985), p. 123.

15. 'The glory of his face increased' is clearly the sense here and not 'they
praised the glory of his face' as M. McNamara would translate (*Neophyti* [5 vols.;
Madrid: Consejo Superior De Investigaciones Cientificas, 1968–78], I, nn. 6-7). The
verb is plural to agree with the noun זיווהון. Compare Deut. 34.7 where this same
plural noun–verb combination requires a third person singular translation. See
M.L. Klein's translation 'had increased' (*The Fragment-Targums of the Pentateuch*,
I, II [Rome: Biblical Institute Press, 1980]). German translations generally translate
the verb as *war gross*, yet the primary meaning of שבח is 'to grow'. See M. Jastrow,
A *Dictionary of the Targumim, the Talmud Babli and Yerushalmi, and the Midrashic*

ומשה לא ידע ארי סגי זיו יקרא דאפוהי :TO

And Moses did not know that the splendor of the glory of his
face increased.

ארום שכחו זיוותהון דאפוי :FT

... that the splendor of his face increased

In contrast to Paul, who speaks of a fading glory, the Targumim
assert that Moses' face did not fade during his years of ministry. This
is clear, for instance, from the commissioning of Joshua in Num.
27.20, where the Targumim interpret the command given to Moses to
place his הוד[16] on Joshua as a command to confer the splendor of his
glory. In Targum Onkelos, for example, Moses confers on Joshua
some of his splendor (מזיוך); in Targum Neofiti he is commanded to
put [the garment][17] of his dignity (ית מן רבותך) on him; and Targum
Pseudo-Jonathan has 'you will confer some of the splendor of your
glory (מזיו יקרך) on him'.

That Moses' splendor was thought never to have weakened right to
the end of his life is further suggested by the targumic interpretations
of Moses' death and burial in Deut. 34.7. For where the MT has 'his eye
was not dim nor was his natural force abated' (לא־כהתה עינו ולא־נס לחה)
both the Babylonian and Palestinian recensions refer to the unaltered
splendor of Moses' face:[18]

ולא שנא זיו יקרא דאפוהי :TO

And the splendor of the glory of his face did not change

ולא אשתנייו זיווהון דאפוי :TN

And the splendor of his face had not altered

ולא אישחנו זיויהון דאפוי :FT

And the splendor of his face had not altered

Literature (New York: Shapiro, Vallentine, 1926), s.v.

16. הוד can mean 'splendor', 'dignity', 'authority' or 'vigor'. The LXX, in line
with the Targumim, understands הוד to be a reference to Moses' glory: καὶ δώσεις
τῆς δόξης σου ἐπ' αὐτόν.

17. McNamara (in *Neophyti*, I) reads מין ('garment') instead of מן ('part of'). He
also suggests the possible reading זיו רבותך ('the splendor of your majesty').

18. The last clause of v. 7 in the LXX reads οὐδὲ ἐφθάρησαν τὰ χελύνια
αὐτοῦ. For discussion, see R. Le Déaut, 'Un phénomène spontané de
l'herméneutique juive ancienne: le "targumisme"', *Bib* 52 (1971), p. 511.

Like Paul, then, the Targumim preserve the tradition that the giving of the law was attended by the glorified face of Moses. They also, like Paul, refer to the transformation of Moses' facial 'image'. But unlike Paul the Targumim speak of Moses' glory as increasing rather than decreasing and as a permanent possession rather than a passing phenomenon.

Philo

References to the Moses-*Doxa* tradition are found primarily in Philo's three-volume work *De Vita Mosis*.[19] Of particular importance is his description of the changed appearance of Moses on his descent from Mount Sinai at the second giving of the law in *Vit. Mos.* 2.70. For Philo states that after forty days:

κατέβαινε πολὺ καλλίων τὴν ὄψιν ἢ ὅτε ἀνῄει ὡς τοὺς ὁρῶντας τεθηπέναι καὶ καταπεπλῆχθαι καὶ μηδ' ἐπὶ πλέον ἀντέχειν τοῖς ὀφθαλμοῖς δύνασθαι κατὰ τὴν προσβολὴν ἡλιοειδοῦς φέγγους ἀπαστράπτοντος.

He [Moses] descended with a countenance far more beautiful than when he ascended, so that those who saw him were filled with awe and amazement; nor could their eyes continue to stand the dazzling brightness that flashed from him like the rays of the sun.[20]

Philo's first two statements follow fairly closely the biblical narrative: Moses descends with a countenance far more beautiful than when he ascended; those who see him are filled with awe and amazement. Philo's third statement, however, is not found in the biblical narrative. For not only did those who saw Moses stand in awe, but his brightness was so dazzling that they were unable to continue gazing at him. Paul, it is to be noted, makes a similar statement in 2 Cor. 3.7.

There is nothing in Philo's account to suggest the notion found in

19. *De Vita Mosis* is largely an interweaving of written and oral traditions, as Philo himself states: 'the story of Moses as I have learned it both from the sacred book... which he [Moses] left behind him and from some of the elders of the nation; for I always interwove what I was told with what I read' (*Vit. Mos.* 1.4). See the numerous parallels between Philo and Palestinian traditions adduced by E. Stein, *Philo und der Midrash* (BZAW, 57; Giessen: Töpelmann, 1931) and B. Bamberger, 'Philo and Aggadah', *HUCA* 48 (1977), pp. 153-55.

20. The comparison of Moses' glory with that of the sun, as will be seen, is one that occurs as well in Pseudo-Philo, the Samaritan documents, and the rabbinic materials.

the Targumim of the permanent possession of this dazzling splendor. In fact, *Vit. Mos.* 2.69 suggests that this facial splendor was tied to the Sinai ascent. For in this passage Philo identifies the source of Moses' altered appearance as the 'better food of contemplation sent from heaven above' (τροφὰς ἔχων ἀμείνους τὰς διὰ θεωρίας αἷς ἄνωθεν ἀπ' οὐρανοῦ) so that those who saw him afterwards 'could not believe (ἀπιστεῖν) their eyes'.

The non-permanence of this facial transformation is further indicated by Philo's linking of the splendor of Moses' face with his office as lawgiver. For Philo, it is as Moses functions as God's spokesperson that he becomes 'another man changed both in outward appearance and mind and filled with the Spirit' (*Vit. Mos.* 2.271). Inspiration comes on him and he is 'transformed into a prophet' (*Vit. Mos.* 2.280). Philo can thus refer to Moses in *Abr.* 23 as 'the Lawgiving Word'. This is comparable to the link Paul makes in vv. 7-11 between the glory of Moses' face and the glory of the old covenant.

While there is no explicit reference in Philo to the veiling of Moses' face,[21] there is one passage that could very well be an allusion to Moses unveiling his face on entering the Tabernacle. In *Spec. Leg.* 1.270 Philo states:

> ὁ μὲν οὖν τούτοις διακεκοσμημένος ἴτω θαππῶν εἰς οἰκειότατον αὐτῷ τὸν νεών...δ' ἐγκάθηνται καὶ ἐλλοχῶσιν αἱ πλεονεξίαι καὶ ἐπιθυμίαι τῶν ἀδικιῶν ἐγκαλυψάμενος ἠρεμείτω τὴν ἀναίσχυντον ἀπόνοιαν.

> He who is adorned with these [the virtues of wisdom] may come with boldness to the Sanctuary as his true home but anyone whose heart is the seat of lurking covetousness and wrongful cravings should remain still and hide his face in confusion.

The contrast that Philo makes in this passage between boldly entering the sanctuary and hiding the face is similar to the one Paul makes between veiling the heart and the removal of that veil on turning to the Lord in 2 Cor. 3.15-17.

---

21. While this omission is surprising, it is understandable given that veiling in Philo generally holds a negative connotation (e.g., *Gig.* 53; *Spec. Leg.* 2.11; 4.7). Moses in particular is eulogized for his frankness of speech and boldness of discourse with God (*Rer. Div. Her.* 2) and presented as one for whom 'nothing is unknown since he has within him a spiritual sun and unclouded rays to give him a full and clear apprehension of things unseen by sense but apprehended by the understanding' (*Spec. Leg.* 4.192).

A number of parallels between Philo's and Paul's use of the Moses-*Doxa* tradition can thus be found. First, both refer to the inability of the Israelites to continue gazing at Moses' face. Secondly, both contrast the actions of openly coming before the Lord and hiding the face (or heart). Thirdly, Philo, like Paul, draws an important link between the concept of facial transformation and the office of lawgiver. And fourthly, both consequently admit the possibility of the impermanence of this glory.

Yet, while Philo's treatment of Moses' shining face can admit the possibility of fading and termination, the step that Paul takes in vv. 13-14 to speak, as well, of the paling of the law's glory is foreign to Philo. For Philo the law is 'firm, unshaken, immovable; stamped as it were with the seals of nature herself and secure from the day when it was first enacted and will remain for all future ages as though immortal' (*Vit. Mos.* 2.3).

Pseudo-Philo[22]

The particular importance of Pseudo-Philo for a consideration of the Moses-*Doxa* tradition stems from the fact that it contains a commentary on Exod. 34.28-34 that includes references to both the splendor of Moses' face and his act of veiling. In *LAB* 12.1 Moses descends from Mount Sinai 'covered with invisible light' (*et cum perfusus esset lumine invisibili*)—a light so great that it 'overcame the brightness of both the sun and the moon' (*vicit lumen faciei sue splendorem solis et lune*).[23] Further, the transformation of Moses' face was so complete that the Israelites 'saw him and knew him not [*videntes non cognoscebant eum*], but when he spoke then they knew him'. The account then concludes with the comment, 'when Moses realized that his face had become glorious, he made a veil for himself with which to cover his face' (*Moyses quoniam gloriosissima facta fuerat facies eius, fecit sibi velamen unde cooperiret faciem suam*).

That this facial transformation was ephemeral is clear from *LAB*

---

22. G.W.E. Nickelsburg (*Jewish Literature between the Bible and the Mishnah* [Philadelphia: Fortress Press, 1981], pp. 267-68) and M.R. James (*The Biblical Antiquities of Philo* [London: SPCK, 1917], pp. 29-33) date this work to the closing decades of the first century CE. P.-M. Bogaert, however, dates it prior to the Jewish War, possibly as early as Pompey (in C. Perrot, P.-M. Bogaert, and D.J. Harrington, *Pseudo-Philon: Les Antiquités Bibliques*, II [2 vols.; Paris: Cerf, 1976], pp. 66-74).

23. A frequently appearing tradition. See next note.

19.16, where the author speaks of Moses' death as the time when his countenance 'was changed gloriously and he died in glory' (*et mutata est effigies eius in gloria et mortuus est in gloria*).[24] The reason for the temporal nature of this transformation can be inferred from the author's attachment of the shining face tradition to the first Sinai descent and the golden calf episode to the second descent (the reverse of the biblical account)—an order suggesting that the passing of Moses' glory was thought to be a direct consequence of the sin of Israel.[25]

That the author is drawing a connection between the passing nature of the Mosaic glory and the sin of Israel is also suggested by his treatment of the Mosaic veil. The Exodus 34 commentary concludes with the statement that 'when Moses knew that his face had become glorious he made a veil to cover his face'. Since the author follows this statement with an account of the sin of the people (the reverse of the biblical narrative) and does not refer prior to Moses' death to either to facial glory or any future activity of veiling or unveiling (as the biblical account does), the implication is that Moses covered his face to prevent a sinful people from gazing on the divine glory.

Pseudo-Philo's use of the Moses-*Doxa* tradition offers some interesting parallels with the Pauline account. Both share the concept of a passing glory. For both the act of veiling is an effort to prevent gazing; and in both a reference to the veiling of Moses' face is followed by a negative response on the part of Israel (in Paul's case, a 'dulling of the perceptions', in Pseudo-Philo's, the sin of the golden calf).

Yet there are some important differences. First, Pseudo-Philo does not link Moses' veiling with the need to cover a fading glory, as Paul does (2 Cor. 3.13). Secondly, whereas Pseudo-Philo refers to the reinstatement of Moses' glorious face at death (*LAB* 19.10-16), Paul envisages no such renewal. Thirdly, Pseudo-Philo does not make the further connection that Paul makes between the fading glory and the waning of the covenant (2 Cor. 3.11, 13). The author stands rather with the Targumim and Philo in maintaining the eternality of the law.

24. For discussion on the shining face of Moses as a passing phenomena see Perrot, Bogaert and Harrington, *Pseudo-Philon*, II, p. 135, and M. McNamara, *The New Testament and the Palestinian Targum to the Pentateuch* (Shannon: Irish University Press, 1972), p. 174.

25. On the transposition of material in *LAB*, see Perrot, Bogaert and Harrington, *Pseudo-Philon*, II, p. 114.

At Mount Sinai God established 'the law of an everlasting covenant with the children of Israel' (*LAB* 11.5), 'prepared from the creation of the world' (*LAB* 32.7), and 'gave to them an eternal commandment that would not pass away' (*LAB* 11.5).

The Qumran Scrolls

Although no commentary on Exodus 34 exists in the Qumran Scrolls published to date, exodus and wilderness terminology and imagery play a prominent role in these documents. The Qumran community takes up the exodus imagery and applies it to its own special circumstances, with the result that what was once applied to Moses and the Israelites is now applied to the Teacher of Righteousness and the Covenanters.[26]

The Moses-*Doxa* imagery of an illumined countenance and facial splendor, in particular, is taken up by the Teacher of Righteousness and applied to his role within the community as the revealer of God's mysteries and interpreter of Scripture. For instance, in 1QH 7.23-25 the Teacher claims: 'Thou my God hast. . . lifted up my horn on high and I will shine with a seven-fold li[ght] in the [light which] thou hast [est]ablished for thy glory'; and in 1QH 4.5 the Teacher declares: 'I give thanks, O Adonai, for thou hast illumined my face by thy covenant and as the sure dawn for [per]fect illu[mination] hast thou appeared to me'.[27]

---

26. 1Q34 2.5-8 demonstrates this transfer quite well:

> Thou hast chosen for thyself a people
> in the time of thy good will
> for thou hast remembered thy covenant.
> Thou hast [appointed] them to be set apart
> from all the peoples
> as a holy thing for thyself [cf. Exod. 19.5-6].
> And thou hast renewed for them thy covenant
> (founded) on the vision of glory [cf. Exod. 24.16-17]
> and the words of thy holy Spirit
> on the works of thy hands
> and the writing of thy right hand [cf. Exod. 32.16]
> causing them to know the glorious teachings
> and everlasting ascensions [cf. Exod. 34.4-7, 29-35]
> . . . [and thou hast raised up] for [them]
> a faithful shepherd. . . [cf. Exod. 3.1].

27. For 1QH 4.5-6 as an allusion to the radiant face of Moses when he descended from Mount Sinai with the tablets of the law, see W.H. Brownlee, *The Meaning of*

The idea noted earlier of the waning of facial glory when divine communication ceases is also found in the Scrolls. For example, in 1QH 5.29-32 the sealing up of the law within the Teacher of Righteousness results in the light of his face 'dimming into darkness' and his 'brightness' changing into 'blackness'. Here too, the fortunes of this glory are tied to the Teacher's role as mediator of divine revelation and teacher of the Torah. So closely, in fact, is the Teacher associated with the Torah that when he is forced by his opponents into hiding he can claim that the Torah also went into hiding (1QH 5.11-12).[28] This close association is further evident in the easy shift that is made in 1QH 16.9 and 6.12 between the splendor of the Teacher and the glory and splendor of the covenant.[29]

Several parallels between the Moses-*Doxa* imagery in the Scrolls and in 2 Cor. 3.7-18 are to be observed. Both the Scrolls and Paul refer to the dimming and cessation of facial splendor. Also, the prophet and the law are intimately linked in both, so that the hiding of the prophet's glory results in the hiding of the law and the cessation of the prophet's light is equivalent to the cessation of the Torah. Then too the Scrolls, like Paul, can readily shift between the splendor of the prophet and the glory and splendor of the covenant.

Yet two differences are to be noted. First, the cessation of the law's light in the Scrolls is only temporary. When the Teacher of Righteousness comes out of hiding the light of the law once more shines forth. Secondly, for the Covenanters, as with all the materials thus far considered, God has established his 'covenant with Israel forever' (1QSb 1.1; cf. CD 3.13)—a covenant that has been engraved for them with the 'burin of life' (1QM 12.3) and established with their seed 'for everlasting ages' (1QM 13.7).

---

the Qumran Scrolls for the Bible (New York: Oxford University Press, 1964), pp. 139-40. For a treatment of the enlightened face of the Teacher of Righteousness, see J.A. Fitzmyer, 'Glory Reflected on the Face of Christ (2 Cor. 3.7–4.6) and a Palestinian Jewish Motif', *TS* 42 (1981), pp. 639-44, and A.R.C. Leaney, *The Rule of Qumran and its Meaning* (Philadelphia: Westminster Press, 1966), p. 130.

28. For an analysis of 1QH 5.11-12 and 29-32, see W. Grundmann, 'The Teacher of Righteousness of Qumran and the Question of Justification by Faith in the Theology of the Apostle Paul', in J. Murphy-O'Connor (ed.), *Paul and Qumran* (Chicago: Priory, 1968), pp. 93-94.

29. Compare 1QH 6.12, 'Thy glorious [covenant]' with 1QH 16.9, 'Thou hast favored me with the [brightness] of thy glory'.

The Samaritan Documents[30]

The Sinai ascents and the giving of the law represent in Samaritan thinking the high points of Moses' career. Consequently, reference to these events is frequent and the shining face of Moses is given particular prominence.[31]

The Samaritan documents refer, like Philo, to the Israelites' inability to stand before Moses' glorious appearance. *Memar Marqa* 6.3 states that God's form (manuscript A has 'face') 'dwelt on him [Moses]' (צלמה שרה בה), 'terrifying all who beheld' (בלד כל חזוי), and 'no one was able to stand before it' (ולא אבש יקום קבלה). For Moses had drawn 'near to the holy deep darkness, where the Divine One was'.

There is no indication in these documents that the light on Moses' face ever lessened during his lifetime. On the contrary, his face 'shone up to the day of his death' (והוה מניר על צלמה עד יום מותה, *MM* 5.4). In fact, the Samaritan documents go beyond all the materials thus far examined in ascribing this light to Moses as an eternal possession. *MM* 5.4, for example, states that 'the shining light which abode on his face is with him in his tomb. It will not abide ever again on another's face' (קרן אורה דהוה שרי על צלמה עמה לגו קבורתה ליתו שרי על צלם חורנה לעלם).

The close association found in the previously-considered literature between Moses and the law is found in these materials as well. For example, *MM* 3.6 states: 'I commanded Moses to expound the law and revealed to him its secrets'; and *MM* 6.3 exclaims: 'See him go up to the Glory so that he was magnified by the proclamation of his mouth'. So closely, in fact, are the law and Moses associated that *MM* 6.9 can state that to withhold Moses from any generation is to withhold light.

---

30. The Samaritan materials have been largely neglected until recently as a source for shedding light on the New Testament. This is partly because these documents cannot be dated with certainty much earlier than the third or fourth century AD. The earliest Samaritan writings, however, contain a wealth of haggadic material that almost certainly stems from an earlier period, and must, therefore, be considered as providing potentially relevant background for Paul's use of the Moses-*Doxa* tradition. See J. Macdonald, *The Theology of the Samaritans* (London: SCM Press, 1964), pp. 11-13, 41-44. The focus here will be on the earliest Samaritan documents, viz., *Memar Marqa, Defter*, and *The Death of Moses*.

31. See, e.g., *MM* 2.9, 12; 4.1, 4, 6; 5.3, 4; 6.11; *Defter* 1.40-41 (in A.E. Cowley, *The Samaritan Liturgy* (2 vols.; Oxford: Clarendon Press, 1909]); *The Death of Moses* fol. 7a.

Reference to the veiling of Moses occurs in an important passage at the conclusion of *Memar Marqa*:

אה בר בית אלה אה הבר קיאמה אה מהימן אלהותה אה מן אחימן
כסיאתה ואתיקר בגליאתה ודער לנו עננה ולבש קרן אורה ואתעתד לה
מסו גדיל מן רומה למרבאתה מכלד מדעי ישראל עד אן לא עמו צלמה

O Son of the House of God, O companion of the covenant, O faithful of the Divine One. O you who were entrusted with the mysteries and honored in the things revealed, who dwelt in the cloud and wore the shining light for which was prepared a great veil from on high to magnify it, terrifying the minds of Israel so that they might not look upon the face; where is there a prophet like you... (6.11)

Here, Moses' veil is given a heavenly origin and results in his shining light being magnified rather than hidden or extinguished. Moreover, the Israelites' inability to look on the shining face of Moses is connected with the presence of a heavenly veil, which serves to increase the brilliance of the light. Also to be noted is the close connection between the shining light and the revelation of mysteries, suggesting that the light on Moses' face had its origin in the divine, esoteric communication he received during his sojourn in heavenly realms.

There are several important points of similarity between the Samaritan documents and Paul. Both refer to the Israelites' inability to look upon Moses' shining face. Both connect the donning of a veil with the intent to prevent further gazing. Also in both so close a connection is drawn between Moses and the law that they can be used interchangeably.

Yet, while there are important similarities, there are also some notable differences. In the Samaritan documents, Moses' glory does not fade or cease as it does in the Pauline account. Further, the Mosaic veil serves to enhance rather than hide the glory, and is of heavenly origin rather than human divining. Then, too, where Paul speaks of a waning covenant, the Samaritan materials, in line with the other materials thus far considered, emphasize the eternal and life-giving character of the law. The law is 'a perpetual memorial giving increase of life' (*MM* 4.12) and 'containing life for all generations' (*MM* 4.3).

Rabbinic Literature[32]

The rabbinic writings offer by far the most extensive and diverse use of the Moses-*Doxa* tradition. Almost all of the Mosaic traditions found in the literature already considered also appear in the rabbinic materials. This includes the tradition of the Israelites' inability to look on Moses' face due to the brilliance of the light. *Pes. R.* 10.6, for example, states: 'Even as no one can look at the sun as it rises, so no one could look at Moses' (220–250 CE). Indeed, *Cant. R.* 3.7 §5 claims that even angels 'were not able to look steadily at the face of Moses' (200–220 CE).[33]

The rabbinic materials go beyond other Jewish sources in specifying the reason for this inability. R. Hiyya b. Abba (c. 280 CE) claims that it was due to the fact that Moses wore the Divine Light.[34] Others attribute it to Moses' divinization on Mount Sinai.[35] The vast majority, however, ascribe Israel's inability to the sin of the golden calf. The tradition most frequently found is that before Israel sinned they had been able to bear without fear the glory of God on Mount Sinai; but after they sinned they could not even bear the reflection of the divine glory on the face of Moses.[36]

Concerning the durability of this facial glory the rabbinic materials contain divergent traditions. One line of tradition goes beyond even the Samaritan documents in its almost polemical stress on the eternal

32. While it is true that this literature embraces a period covering several hundreds of years, it is nonetheless important to recognize that much of it is based on earlier sayings and traditions. It is therefore necessary to be critical in dealing with the rabbinic writings, yet open to the possible relevance of the wide range of traditions found here as background for Paul's use of the Moses-*Doxa* tradition.

33. See also *Sifre Num.* §1 (on 5.1-4) and *Midr. HaGadol* כי תשא 30.

34. As Moses and Elijah could not endure the light when the Lord passed by the cave, so the Israelites were not able to bear the Divine Light on the face of Moses (*b. Meg.* 19b).

35. See e.g. *Death of Moses*, in A. Wünsche, *Aus Israels Lehrhallen* (2 vols.; Leipzig: E. Pfeiffer, 1907), I, p. 143, where 'I am God and you are God' is applied to the Israelites' inability to look on Moses as he descended from Mount Sinai; cf. *Gen. Rabbati* 129, where 'you have made him a little lower than אלהים' (Ps. 8.5) is referred to Moses.

36. See e.g. *Sifre Num.* §1 (on 5.1-4); *Cant. R.* 3.7 §5; *Midr. Sam.* 17. In *Cant. R.* 3.7 §5 this tradition is attributed to R. Levi (c. 280 CE). For an analysis, see S. Schechter, *Aspects of Rabbinic Theology* (New York: Schocken Books, 1961 [1909]), pp. 236-37.

permanence of Moses' shining face, even in the grave. *Seder Eliyahu R.* 18, for instance, states, 'lest you suppose after he died, the radiance vanished, it entered with him into his eternal abode and remains with him forever'.[37] Another line of tradition denies that this splendor was a permanent possession. This is especially clear in the claim that Moses transferred his glory to Joshua rather than taking it with him to the grave.[38] Indeed some texts maintain that Moses' splendor was not even constant during his lifetime.[39] This is particularly true of those texts that link the durability of Moses' glory with either Moses' office as lawgiver or the fortunes of Israel. For example, R. Abihu states that after Israel sinned, Moses was not able to look in the face of even the most ordinary of them (the angels), whereas before Israel sinned the angels had fled from Moses' face (*Cant. R.* 3.7 §5); and R. Eleazar (80–120 CE) claims that when Israel sinned, God said to Moses on Mount Sinai: 'Have I given you greatness save for the sake of Israel? Hence descend from your greatness, for Israel has sinned and why do I want you'. Then 'straightaway Moses became powerless and had no strength to speak' (*b. Ber.* 32a).[40]

It is commonly assumed and often stated by New Testament scholars that there are no traditions in rabbinic literature regarding the veiling of Moses. This assumption is in large part based on the statement in Strack–Billerbeck that, 'At no place in the ancient rabbinic literature do we find reference made to the "covering of Moses" of Exod. 34.33ff'.[41] But traditions on the veiling of Moses can, in fact, be

37. Cf. R. Simeon b. Yohai (140–165 CE): 'if an opening were to be made in the grave of Moses the entire world could not endure the light' (*Pes. R.* 21.6).

38. E.g., R. Yudan (c. 330 CE) states that all of Moses' glory was conferred on Joshua at the Jordan: 'for it is written, "they feared him as they had feared Moses"' (*Ps. R.* 21.4).

39. See, e.g., *b. Bat.* 75a: 'Alas for such shame! The countenance of Moses was like that of the sun but the countenance of Joshua was like that of the moon.' The implication is that the light of the moon is much inferior to that of the sun, and hence much deterioration had occurred in the transfer from Moses to Joshua.

40. *b. Ta'an.* 30b and *b.B Bat.* 121a-b also reflect this notion when they claim that so long as the generation of the wilderness continued to die out, there was no divine communication to Moses.

41. H.L. Strack and P. Billerbeck, *Kommentar zum Neuen Testament aus Talmud und Midrash.* III. *Die Briefe des Neuen Testaments und die Offenbarung Johannes erläutert aus Talmud und Midrash* (Munich: Beck, 1926), p. 516.

found.[42] A brief reference to Moses' veil occurs in *Pes. R.* 10.6, which
states, 'when Moses came down to meet Israel they saw his radiance
surpassing and brilliant...so that no one could look at Moses until
Moses put a veil over his face' (וכיון שירד משה לקראת ישראל ראו אותו דבר
מעולה ומשובח...כשהוא עולה כך לא היה אדם יכול להביט במשה אלא
א"כ נותן סודר על פניו); attributed to R. Jonathan of Beth Gubrin (220–
250 CE). Here, the motive for the veiling—that the brilliance of
Moses' face was too great for human sight—is based on a tradition
commonly found in the other materials considered.[43]

Reference to the veiling of Moses' face also appears in *Midr.
HaGadol* (to Exod. 34.33) where the statement is made: 'As soon as he
noticed [the brilliance] in himself, he immediately placed a veil on his
face' (כיון שהרגיש בעצמו מיד ויתן על פניו מסוה). While Moses' motive for
veiling his face could be one of embarrassment or a desire to protect
Israel, this text could be implying what Paul himself suggests, namely,
that Moses' behavior lacked a certain openness. Indeed, this is
supported by the fact that the text goes on to emphasize Moses' boldness in removing his veil on entering the tabernacle.

There are also a number of texts that speak of the unveiling of
Moses on entering the tabernacle. One, in *Midr. HaGadol* (to Exod.
34.34), interprets this unveiling as a gesture of boldness and highlights
the 'extraordinary greatness given to Moses', since even the ministering angels 'covered their faces before the Shekinah' (שנתן לו הקב"ה
גדולה יתירה על מלאכי השרת...מכסין פניהם כלפי שכינה...אבל משה רבינו
אינו כן מגלה פניו ועומד לפני שכינה שנאמר יסיר את המסוה עד צאתו). Another
reference in *Mishnath Rab Eliezer*[44] states that when Moses removed
the veil in coming before Yahweh, the brightness of his face was so

---

42. What is surprising, though, is that there are so few references. Given the
amount of speculation concerning the glory of Moses' face, one would have expected
a similar interest to be shown in the veiling and unveiling of Moses' face. This comparative silence can be explained, in part, by the fact that rabbinic interpretation is
built on an association of words, phrases and concepts found throughout Scripture.
מסוה, the word for veil, however, occurs only in Exod. 34.33-35, and apart from
references to the veil of the tabernacle even the idea of a veil rarely appears in the Old
Testament.

43. As has been seen, this is a tradition that has wide currency, occurring in
Philo, Pseudo-Philo, the Samaritan documents, other rabbinic literature, and, as will
be seen, in the Jewish mystical writings as well.

44. Cf. H.G. Enelow, *The Mishnah of Rabbi Eliezer* (New York: Bloch, 1933),
pp. 150-51.

great that the ministering angels turned away in fear (ראה ער היכן)
...ער שנתן עליו הוד שהיו מלאכי השרת יראין מפניו שנ' ויהי ברדת משה מהר סיני
וגו' ומנ' שהיו מלאכי השרת יראין מפניו שנ' ובבא משה לפני ייי יסיר את המסוה
ולמה היה מסירו אלא שהיה זיוו מבהיק וכשהיה מבקש ליכנס היה מסיר את המסוה
והמלאכים רואין את זיוו ונפנין ממנו). This text also gives as a motive for
Moses' unveiling his face the fact that 'his bright countenance was
shining'.[45]

Rabbinic use of the Moses-*Doxa* tradition offers a number of
significant parallels with Paul. Both refer to the inability of the
Israelites to 'gaze intently at' the face of Moses because of its splendor. Also, in both there is the claim that the glory of Moses' face
deteriorated. Indeed, some rabbinic texts go beyond Paul in claiming
that this glory was lost at the point Israel sinned. Then, too, both
closely link the glory of Moses' face and his office as lawgiver.

Of particular importance are the veiling and unveiling parallels.
One parallel is the notion that Moses veiled his face when he noticed
the brilliance. Along similar lines, Paul states that Moses veiled his
face so that the Israelites might not gaze further on his brilliance
(2 Cor. 3.13). A second parallel is the claim that the removal of the
veil was an act of boldness. Paul likewise asserts that the removal of
the veil before the Lord is an act of 'freedom' (2 Cor. 3.16-17).

Yet there are notable differences between the rabbinic materials and
Paul. First, there is no rabbinic text that connects Moses' act of veiling
with the concept of a fading glory (as does 2 Cor. 3.13). Secondly,
there lacks any reference to contemporary Israel wearing a veil over
their hearts or of the law being veiled when it is read (2 Cor. 3.14-15).
And finally, there is no parallel to Paul's linking of the fading of Moses'
splendor and the waning of the covenant (2 Cor. 3.13-14). Indeed,
here, as in all of the Jewish sources examined, the Torah is eternal and
life-giving (*b. Šab.* 30a). It is also pre-existent, having been 'hidden by
God for 974 generations before the world was created' (*b. Šab.* 88b).

---

45. The *hiphil* of בהק can mean: (1) to be bright, to shine, or (2) to make bright,
to brighten. See Jastrow, *A Dictionary of the Midrashic Literature*, *s.v.*; cf.
M.H. Segal, *A Grammar of Mishnaic Hebrew* (Oxford: Clarendon Press, 1978
[1927]) § 146. The difficulty with this text is that it is not specific enough. If מבהיק
bears the sense 'became bright', this would seem to suggest that the glory of Moses'
face began to fade once he left the tabernacle. But it is probably more natural to
assume that he unveiled an already shining face when entering to speak with God
'face to face', otherwise the fact of the veil is left unexplained.

The Zohar[46]

Many of the previously examined references to the Moses-*Doxa* tradition find their parallel in the *Zohar*. One parallel is reference to the inability of the Israelites to look on Moses' fading splendor. 3.58a, like Paul, claims that Israel's inability was due to the brightness of Moses' facial splendor which prevented 'the children of Israel from looking steadfastly at the face of Moses'. 1.52a-b goes beyond Paul, in attributing this inability to Israel's sin regarding the golden calf, stating that 'before they [Israel] sinned, they saw God by the Red Sea and did not fear... but after they sinned they were not able to look even on the face of the deputy'.

A second parallel is found in a number of texts that speak of the deterioration of or end to Moses' facial splendor. One text in 3.58a ascribes this deteriorated glory to the 'Holy One' who 'took away from Moses 1000 parts of his splendor' because of Israel's sin regarding the golden calf. Other texts speak of Moses' glory coming to an end at death. For example 1.31b claims that Moses' splendor 'was with him until the end of his life'; and 1.21b states that Joshua derived prophetic inspiration from the glory that Moses conferred on him. Of special interest is 3.58a which, in language very similar to Paul's, speaks of the deteriorated state or 'remnant' of the splendor on Moses' face, which, nonetheless, was still glorious enough to prevent the Israelites from looking steadfastly at the face of Moses:

> Now if merely because of this remnant of brightness the children of Israel could not look steadfastly at the face of Moses, how glorious must the splendor have been in its original state.

> ומה בהחי דאשתאר ביה לא הוי יכלין לאסתכלא באנפוי בההוא דאסתלק
> מיניה עאכ"ו[47]

There is only one place in the *Zohar* where mention of Moses' veil is made. 1.31b states, in contrast to the Exodus account, that 'the

46. Commonly grouped with the *Kabbalah* (the Jewish mystical writings), the *Zohar* is essentially a reshaping of ancient traditional material. See W.O.E. Oesterley, *A Short Survey of the Literature of Rabbinical and Medieval Judaism* (London: SPCK, 1920), pp. 236-38. The greater part of this material purports to be the utterances of the fourth generation Tanna, Simeon b. Yohai.

47. Despite the existence of this and other Jewish texts (see above) that refer either implicitly or explicitly to the deterioration of Moses' facial glory, Hays claims that 'there is no direct evidence for the existence of any such tradition within Judaism' (*Echoes of Scripture*, p. 133).

Israelites could not approach Moses until he put a veil over his face'
(ולא יכלו בני ישראל למקרב בהדיה עד דיהב מסוה על אנפוי).[48]

The similarities between the *Zohar* and Paul are striking. Like Paul
the *Zohar* refers to the Israelites' inability to gaze steadfastly on
Moses' face because of the glory. Both refer to the deteriorated state
of Moses' splendor. Both associate this glory with Moses' role as
covenant mediator. And both similarly understand the veiling of
Moses' face as a response to Israel.

Conclusions

The foregoing examination has shown that there is a substantial background of Moses-*Doxa* haggadah on which Paul could have drawn for
his use in 2 Cor. 3.7-18. Reference in Philo to the Israelites' inability
to gaze intently at Moses' face demonstrates the currency of this interpretation of the Exodus 34 narrative in the first century CE. Its
appearance in the Samaritan documents, the rabbinic materials, and
the *Zohar* indicates that this interpretation was widely known.

It was also seen that most of the literary materials examined include
one line of interpretation that suggests that Moses' glory experienced
some deterioration or that it was lost either during his lifetime or at
death. The *Zohar*, in particular, preserves a tradition that closely
approaches Paul's concept of a fading glory. This suggests that Paul
was not an innovator at this point.

References to the veiling of Moses' face appear as early as the first
century CE. The connection that Paul makes between the Israelites'
gazing at Moses' face and the donning of a veil is a common and early
one. The motive that Paul gives for the veiling, namely to prevent
further gazing, occurs in both Pseudo-Philo and the Samaritan documents, and is implied by at least one rabbinic text.

Speculation concerning the unveiling of Moses' face is found solely
in the rabbinic materials. Yet Paul's specific connection between
unveiling the face and boldness or freedom occurs in both Philo and

---

48. This is contrary to the sequence of events in Exod. 34.29-30, where Moses
descends, the people see his shining face, they are afraid to draw near to him, he
calls to them and they return, he communicates God's commands to them, and then
he places a veil over his face. Compare *Pes. R.* 10.6, which states that the Israelites
could not look at Moses until he veiled himself.

rabbinic haggadah; and his further link between covering the face and a lack of openness appears in Philo.

All the Jewish literary materials examined closely associate the glory of Moses' face with the glory of the law and tie this glory to his office rather than to his person. Even the Qumran Scrolls make this connection, albeit on the level of allusion.

What remains distinctively Pauline is the following. Paul alone links the fading of Moses' glory with the waning of the covenant. In addition, he is the only one to specify that the veil was put in place to prevent the Israelites from gazing right up to the end of this fading glory. He is also the only writer who explicitly links Moses' actions with a lack of openness, although the precedent is already there in Philo for identifying the act of veiling with negative motives. The contemporizing of the Mosaic veiling in the present veiling of the old covenant, and the corollary of the dulled perceptions and veiled heart of the Jew, are also uniquely his, although a similar interpretive move can be found in the Qumran Scrolls. Distinctively Pauline, also, is the association of the Spirit with the act of unveiling.

What this analysis demonstrates is that there is no real uniqueness to the Moses-*Doxa* material in 2 Cor. 3.7-18. Parallels clearly exist for what is commonly attributed to Pauline creativity. It is, rather, in the application of these traditions to the Mosaic covenant itself and to his contemporary situation that Paul's original contribution is made.

The preceding examination also indicates that it is unlikely, as some have suggested, that an extended midrash of Exod. 34.28-35 existed, which Paul simply modified to his own specification. The most that can be claimed is a familiarity with certain lines of interpretation. The picture in the literary materials examined is of a mosaic of traditions rather than a single, unified Moses-*Doxa* tradition or midrash. A comparison of 2 Cor. 3.7-18 and extrabiblical interpretations of Exodus 34 suggests that Paul is interweaving fragments of the Exodus 34 narrative with a number of extrabiblical traditions and his own distinctive contributions, rather than making modifications to an already existing midrashic unit.[49]

49. One of the major difficulties with the hypothesis of an existing midrashic unit is its unprovable character. Interaction with an alternative position by means of additions and modifications to a representative document is a method which is simply not attested in the literature of Paul's day. The pattern in the rabbinic materials is dissent by means of a clearly defined alternative opinion. In the Nag Hammadi texts a contrary position is introduced by the phrase 'and not as so-and-so said'. In the Samaritan materials one finds the phrase 'but according to the true tradition' (e.g., the commentary *Pitron*). Models for this type of subtle manipulation of an existing text are totally lacking. There is also the difficulty of accounting for how such a document came into Paul's possession.

'FOR AS MANY AS ARE OF WORKS OF THE LAW ARE UNDER A CURSE' (GALATIANS 3.10)

James M. Scott

Introduction

Gal. 3.10 forms part of the answer to the rhetorical questions which Paul puts to the Galatians in Gal. 3.1-5: 'Did you receive the Spirit by works of the law or by the hearing of faith?' (v. 2) and 'Does he who supplies you the Spirit... do so by works of the law or by the hearing of faith?' (v. 5). In answer, Paul sets forth chiastically in Gal. 3.6-14 the contrast between 'those of faith' (vv. 7, 9) and 'those of works of the law' (v. 10). Those who are of faith (οἱ ἐκ πίστεως) are blessed along with Abraham (v. 9), whereas those who are of works of the law (ὅσοι ἐξ ἔργων νόμου) are under a curse (v. 10).[1] The latter assertion is substantiated (γάρ) in v. 10b by a citation from Deut. 27.26 (+29.19b) LXX: 'For it is written: "Cursed is every one who does not abide by all things written in the book of the law, to do them"'.[2] After additional scriptural support for v. 10a in vv. 11-12, Paul advances his argument a step further in v. 13: 'Christ redeemed

---

1. The γάρ in v. 10a does not introduce substantiation for an argument from the previous context (*e contrario*); it facilitates a connection which carries the argument forward. For this use of γάρ, see Rom. 2.25; 5.7; 14.5, 15; 1 Cor. 10.1; 2 Cor. 1.12; 3.14b; 10.12; 11.5; Gal. 1.11; 5.13 (cf. O. Hofius, 'Gesetz und Evangelium nach 2 Korinther 3', in *Paulusstudien* [WUNT, 51; Tübingen: Mohr (Paul Siebeck), 1989], pp. 75-120 [here p. 117 n. 241]).

2. For the epexegetical use of τοῦ + infinitive here, see F. Blass and A. Debrunner, *Grammatik des neutestamentlichen Griechisch* (ed. F. Rehkopf; Göttingen: Vandenhoeck & Ruprecht, 15th edn, 1979), §400.8; also K. Beyer, 'Althebräische Syntax in Prosa und Poesie', in G. Jeremias *et al.* (eds.), *Tradition und Glaube: Das frühe Christentum in seiner Umwelt. Festgabe für Karl Georg Kuhn zum 65. Geburtstag* (Göttingen: Vandenhoeck & Ruprecht, 1971), pp. 76-96 (here p. 91 n. 74).

us from the curse of the law by becoming a curse [κατάρα] for us...'
Evidently, Paul assumes that 'we' have fallen under the curse
(κατάρα) of the law in Deut. 27.26 and therefore need redemption
through Christ. What exactly Paul means by this citation of Deut.
27.26 continues to be highly controversial. A few representative
examples will suffice to show the differences of opinion in the
ongoing debate.

1. *The Scholarly Debate on the Use of Deuteronomy 27.26* *in Galatians 3.10*

First of all, most scholars assume that Paul cites Deuteronomy in
order to show the impossibility of fulfilling the whole Torah (cf. Gal.
5.3; 6.13).[3] In support of this view, it must be acknowledged that Paul
cites the Septuagintal version of the text, which, unlike the underlying
Hebrew *Vorlage*, has the word 'all' twice (πᾶς ὅς οὐκ ἐμμένει
πᾶσιν τοῖς γεγραμμένοις). Yet Paul does not thereby explicitly state
that keeping the law is impossible. In fact, not only does Paul claim to
have been 'blameless' with regard to the law as a Pharisee (Phil. 3.6),
but Deuteronomy itself seems to assume that obedience to the law and
its attendant blessings were humanly possible (cf. Deut. 30.11-14).
How, then, can Paul assume that Deut. 27.26 makes the point that
keeping the whole law is impossible? Are we 'missing something that
Paul took for granted'?[4] This problem is particularly baffling if

---

3.   Cf., e.g., H. Räisänen, *Paul and the Law* (WUNT, 29; Tübingen: Mohr
[Paul Siebeck], 2nd edn, 1987), p. 94, with many other proponents listed in n. 2.
Also holding this position, H. Hübner ('Gal. 3,10 und die Herkunft des Paulus',
KD 19 [1973], pp. 215-31 [here pp. 222-26]) argues that Paul's use of Deut. 27.26
reveals the apostle's Pharisaic background in the school of Shammai (not the school
of Hillel, as Joachim Jeremias suggested); for the school of Shammai held that
proselytes must obey the whole law *without exception* or not be accepted. From this
position, says Hübner, it was only a small step to Paul's (post-conversion?) view,
based on Deut. 27.26, that one is cursed if the Torah is violated in even one point
(Gal. 5.3; cf. 3.10, 22).

4.   Cf. A.F. Segal, *Paul the Convert: The Apostolate and Apostasy of Saul the
Pharisee* (New Haven and London: Yale University Press, 1990), p. 119: 'Not
content with vituperation, Paul demonstrates his point exegetically with the deftness
of one who trained as a Pharisee—a *tour de force* based on Deut. 27.26, which states
that those who do not live by the law are under a curse. The puzzling part of this
quotation from Deuteronomy for any Jew [cf. *Paul the Convert*, p. 281] is that it

E.P. Sanders is correct that the Judaism of Paul's day believed in a system of covenantal nomism,[5] which did not require perfect obedience in order to avoid the curse of the law. According to Sanders, all that was required of the people was repentance, and God in his grace would provide atonement for transgression and forgiveness of sins.[6] In this way, the righteous status of the people—and thus their covenantal relationship with God—could be maintained uninterrupted despite disobedience.[7] If this description of Judaism is correct, then Paul's hard-line interpretation of Deut. 27.26 as requiring perfect obedience would seem to be a distortion.[8]

Secondly, C.K. Barrett suggests that Judaizers originally used Deut. 27.26 against Hellenistic Jewish Christians (including Paul) who held a reductionistic view of the law. From the perspective of the Judaizers, such Christians are under a curse per Deut. 27.26 because they do not fulfill the whole law. Barrett argues that Paul then turned the opponents' scriptural argument against them: 'By an exegetical *tour de force* Paul not only rebuts but reverses this argument. It is not the Christians who know themselves to be free from the law who are accursed, but their opponents', because the latter do not trust in God as constituting their righteousness (Lev. 18.5; Hab. 2.4).[9] According

also proves the converse of Paul's claims: those who live by Torah are blessed. The lack of exegesis of the full and plain meaning of the passage sounds like a non sequitur. We are likely missing something that Paul took for granted.' Segal goes on to suggest several possible assumptions which Paul may have held.

5.   For Sanders's definition of 'Covenantal Nomism', see his *Paul and Palestinian Judaism: A Comparison of Patterns of Religion* (Minneapolis: Fortress Press, 1977), pp. 75, 420, 544: 'Briefly put, covenantal nomism is the view that one's place in God's plan is established on the basis of the covenant and that the covenant requires as the proper response of man his obedience to its commandments, while providing means of atonement for transgression... *Obedience maintains one's position in the covenant, but it does not earn God's grace as such*... Righteousness in Judaism is a term which implies the *maintenance of status* among the group of the elect' (Sanders's emphasis).

6.   Cf. Sanders, *Paul and Palestinian Judaism*, pp. 158-59, 174-80, 182, 235-36.

7.   *Paul and Palestinian Judaism*, pp. 236, 546.

8.   So Räisänen, *Paul and the Law*, pp. 120-21, 188, 258-63.

9.   C.K. Barrett, *Freedom and Obligation: A Study of the Epistle to the Galatians* (Philadelphia: Westminster Press, 1985), pp. 23-24, 25-26 (here p. 26). Similarly, F. Watson, *Paul, Judaism and the Gentiles: A Sociological Approach* (Cambridge: Cambridge University Press, 1986), p. 71.

to Martin Hengel, however, it was Paul himself who, in his days as persecutor of the church, had used Deut. 27.26 against the Hellenistic Jewish Christians. Paul the Pharisee wanted to show that these Christians fell under the curse of the law because they did not do *all* that the law commanded.[10] If that is correct, however, it seems strange that Paul the apostle would cite Deut. 27.26 in Gal. 3.10 in order to show that all are under a curse, while himself subscribing to a reductionistic view of the law. Nevertheless, the suggestion is well taken that Paul may be employing a use of the Old Testament passage which he knew as a Pharisee, for this may point to a traditional Jewish use of the text.

Thirdly, there are other scholars who suppose that the citation of Deut. 27.26 proves that doing the law is wrongly motivated because it relies on works of the law to earn one's righteous status before God (legalism) rather than on believing in God's gracious provision.[11] Against this view, however, it must be pointed out that Paul speaks in Gal. 3.10 of a curse upon those who fail to do the law, not particularly upon those who (misguidedly) try to do it! Furthermore, there is no evidence that ὅσοι ἐξ ἔργων νόμου means 'those who rely on works of the law'. The expression ἔργα νόμου seems to correspond to the Hebrew מעשי תורה (4QMMT 3.29; 4QFlor. 1.7; cf. *2 Bar.* 57.2), and in Paul it refers to 'deeds of the law' in the comprehensive sense of Torah observance (cf. Rom. 3.20, 28; Gal. 2.16; 3.2, 5, 10). The expression ὅσοι ἐκ denotes origin (cf. Lam. 1.7; Sir. 41.10; Acts 4.6). Hence, the phrase 'as many as are of works of the law' conveys nothing pejorative per se and should not be overinterpreted.

Fourthly, according to Sanders's own view of Gal. 3.10, the citation of Deut. 27.26 should not be interpreted in light of its Old Testament context but in terms of what Paul says in his own words:

10. M. Hengel, 'Der vorchristliche Paulus', *Theologische Beiträge* 21 (1990), pp. 174-95 (here p. 195).

11. Cf., e.g., D.P. Fuller, 'Paul and "the Works of the Law"', *WTJ* 38 (1975), pp. 28-42, who assumes that this represents the view of 'all exegetes' (p. 31); F.F. Bruce, *The Epistle to the Galatians: A Commentary on the Greek Text* (NIGTC; Grand Rapids, MI: Eerdmans, 1982), p. 157 (on p. 159, however, he seems to hold the majority view); also *idem*, 'The Curse of the Law', in M.D. Hooker and S.G. Wilson (eds.), *Paul and Paulinism: Essays in Honour of C.K. Barret* (London: SPCK, 1982), pp. 27-36 (here p. 29).

It is a fairly common view that one should interpret what the proof-texts
[in Gal. 3.10-12] say in order to discover what Paul means. I think that
what Paul says in his own words is the clue to what he took the proof-
texts to mean. Thus in [Gal.] 3.10 Paul means that those who accept the
law are cursed.[12]

According to this interpretation, Paul incorporates the citation into his
argument because 'Deuteronomy 27.26 is the only passage in the LXX
in which *nomos* is connected with "curse"'.[13] Paul's point is that those
who continue in covenantal nomism are under a curse, because that
system of exclusively Jewish privilege does not provide for God's
ultimate purpose, that of saving the entire world by faith in Christ.[14]
We must ask, however, whether Paul's citation of Deut. 27.26 is
really meant to deny the particularism of Judaism in favor of the
universality of the gospel. The plain wording of the text would seem
to indicate that the curse comes on those who do not perform the
whole law (cf. 1QS 2),[15] not merely on those who continue in a
system. There is a 'plight' (the curse of the law) for which Paul sees a
'solution' (redemption through Christ). Furthermore, although there
can be no doubt that Paul does at times employ a *Stichwort* approach
in adducing Old Testament citations (e.g. *gezerah shavah*),[16] it is
always wise to consult the original Old Testament context of citations
and the subsequent Jewish tradition[17] based on them before we
conclude that Paul is engaging in an unmediated 'private reading' of
Scripture.[18]

12. E.P. Sanders, *Paul, the Law, and the Jewish People* (Philadelphia: Fortress
Press, 1983), pp. 21-22.

13. *Paul, the Law*, p. 21.

14. *Paul, the Law*, pp. 46-47. This position represents a shift from Sanders's
earlier opinion in *Paul and Palestinian Judaism*, that Paul was inveighing here against
a Judaism of works-righteousness which never existed in his day, and that Paul
arbitrarily broke with the law because it did not result in his being 'in Christ'.

15. See further below. Cf. also the critique of Sanders at this point in
R.Y.K. Fung, *The Epistle to the Galatians* (NICNT; Grand Rapids, MI: Eerdmans,
1988), p. 142 n. 28.

16. Examples of this hermeneutical principle from Galatians 3–4 will be
discussed below.

17. Sanders (*Paul and Palestinian Judaism*, p. 137) does this to some extent
but does not go far enough.

18. This is the chief disadvantage of R.B. Hays's approach in *Echoes of
Scripture in the Letters of Paul* (New Haven and London: Yale University Press,

Fifthly, according to James D.G. Dunn, Paul cites Deut. 27.26, not merely, as Sanders suggested, to show that those who continue in covenantal nomism are under the 'curse of the law,' but rather to stress that those who insist on 'works of the law' (i.e., circumcision, food laws, and Sabbath observance) as signs of Jewish prerogative and national monopoly are under 'the curse which falls on all who restrict the grace and promise of God in nationalistic terms, who treat the law as a boundary to mark the people of God off from the Gentiles, who give a false priority to ritual matters'.[19] In other words, this is 'the curse of a wrong understanding of the law'.[20] However, this interpretation of 'works of the law' ignores the fact that Deut. 27.26 refers to 'all' the commandments of the law, not just to certain 'badges' of Jewish nationalism. Furthermore, in picking up the idea of a curse from v. 10, Gal. 3.13 cannot mean to say that Christ delivers Jews from a mistaken view of the law!

Sixthly, several scholars interpret the citation of Deut. 27.26 to mean that the law itself is a curse. For example, Hans Dieter Betz quotes Heinrich Schlier approvingly to argue that those who are of the law are under a curse because the law itself is a curse.[21] It is difficult,

1989). For Hays, Paul engages in a private reading of Scripture, a spontaneous and intuitive reflection on the Old Testament text which is largely unaffected by intervening Jewish tradition because his reading occurs in the isolated 'cave of resonant signification'. To be sure, Hays acknowledges some influence of tradition in Paul's use of Scripture (cf. *Echoes of Scripture*, pp. 13, 39-40, 55, 80, 87), but he concludes that *Traditionsgeschichte* is an approach to Paul's use of the Old Testament which has been 'either answered in full or played out to a dead end' (*Echoes of Scripture*, p. 9). According to Hays, Paul is basically an idiosyncratic reader of the Old Testament with some Christian presuppositions and a few hermeneutical constraints (*Echoes of Scripture*, pp. 10, 160-64).

19. J.D.G. Dunn, 'Works of the Law and the Curse of the Law (Galatians 3.10-14)', in *Jesus, Paul, and the Law: Studies in Mark and Galatians* (Louisville, KY: Westminster Press/John Knox, 1990), pp. 215-36 (here p. 229).

20. Dunn, 'Works of the Law', p. 229.

21. H.D. Betz, *Galatians: A Commentary on Paul's Letter to the Churches in Galatia* (Hermeneia; Philadelphia: Fortress Press, 1979), p. 149 (cf. p. 146). Cf. O. Hofius, 'Das Gesetz des Mose und das Gesetz Christi', *ZTK* 80 (1983), pp. 262-86 (here p. 272): 'When in Gal. 3.10 Paul cites the threat of a curse from Deut. 27.26... he understands this passage—differently from Deuteronomy itself—not as a warning which presupposes the fundamental ability to do the commandment and threatens only the trespasser with the curse, but rather as the binding proclamation of the curse which already rests on all people.' R.P. Martin (*Reconciliation: A*

however, to see how Paul could be so positive about the law (Rom. 7.7-12), especially as a privilege of the Israelites (Rom. 9.4; cf. *m. Ab.* 3.14), if its original function was to condemn the people. We may also question whether such interpretations do justice to the Old Testament/Jewish tradition based on Deut. 27.26.

Seventhly, Christopher D. Stanley has recently suggested that Gal. 3.10 be seen not exclusively from the perspective of its abstract theological *content* but also, and especially, from the perspective of its rhetorical *function* within an ongoing argument to persuade the Galatians in a concrete historical situation. 'At bottom,' says Stanley, 'v. 10 can be said to function as a kind of "threat", intended to induce the Galatians to reconsider their contemplated course of action by pointing out its possible negative consequences and so inducing a sense of fear regarding its outcome.'[22] The citation of Deut. 27.26 is meant 'to define the circumstances under which its "curse" comes to be actualized',[23] and thus 'to *deter* the type of behavior that might lead to its actualization'.[24] Although Stanley is correct about the occasional nature of Paul's letter and about the need to keep the Galatian situation in view, such considerations cannot be used to contradict the fact that Gal. 3.13 clearly presupposes that the curse of the law in v. 10 has indeed come upon 'us'. To say that Gal. 3.13 describes 'how God in the death of Jesus Christ has opened up a way of escape for *Gentiles* from the "negative potentiality" associated with Torah-observance'[25] violates the plain meaning of the text. Christ redeemed 'us' from the curse of the law, not from a 'negative potentiality'.

Finally, in one of the few interpretations which tries to respect the original context of Deut. 27.26, Martin Noth argues that Paul takes the perspective of the Deuteronomist, that in hindsight disobedience and curse are already reality for the Israelites.[26] Whether or not Noth

---

Study of Paul's Theology [Grand Rapids, MI: Zondervan, rev. edn, 1989], p. 62) also views Deut. 27.26 as Paul's way of saying that the law is a curse (for believers!), but the argument seems confused.

22. C.D. Stanley, '"Under a Curse": A Fresh Reading of Galatians 3. 10-14', *NTS* 36 (1990), pp. 481-511 (here p. 501).

23. '"Under a Curse"', p. 499.

24. '"Under a Curse"', p. 500 (author's emphasis).

25. So Stanley ('"Under a Curse"', p. 506 [author's emphasis]).

26. M. Noth, 'For All who Rely on Works of the Law are under a Curse', in *The Laws in the Pentateuch and Other Studies* (Edinburgh: T. & T. Clark, 1966), p. 131, followed, for example, by G. Eichholz, *Die Theologie des Paulus im Umriß*

has captured the original sense of Deuteronomy with this interpretaton (cf. Deut. 30.11-14),[27] there is no doubt something historically correct about it: *from the perspective of the Old Testament, the curses of Deuteronomy had befallen the people of Israel in the past.*[28] Of course, it would be a quantum leap from recognizing this basic fact to saying, as Gal. 3.10 does, that the curse of Deuteronomy applied to the people in Paul's day.[29]

We have seen that although many attempts have been made to understand Gal. 3.10, none of them seems to be completely satisfactory. By the same token, none of these views has considered how Deut. 27.26 was taken up in Old Testament/Jewish tradition. As we shall see, the traditional background provides the key to the interpretation, as it so often does in Paul.

2. Deuteronomy 27.26 in Old Testament/Jewish Tradition

Paul combines Deut. 27.26 with Deut. 29.19b (or 28.58),[30] which shows that he reads Deuteronomy 27–32 as a unit and does not consider Deut. 27.26 as one verse in isolation.[31] In fact, the formulaic

---

(Neukirchen–Vluyn: Neukirchener Verlag, 4th edn, 1983), p. 247.

27. Cf. Räisänen, *Paul and the Law*, pp. 125-26.

28. So also F. Thielman, *From Plight to Solution: A Jewish Framework for Understanding Paul's View of the Law in Galatians and Romans* (NovTSup, 61; Leiden: Brill, 1989), p. 68.

29. Thielman argues, in essence, from the historical example of Israel that 'relying on works of the Law leads to disobedience and curse' (*From Plight to Solution*, p. 72); for in trying to keep the law, Israel had continually failed, with the result that the nation had been in a state of curse during her entire history up to Paul's day (cf. *From Plight to Solution*, pp. 69, 71, 86). This is actually a variation on the first argument discussed above, that fulfilling the whole law is impossible.

30. Cf. D.-A. Koch, *Die Schrift als Zeuge des Evangeliums: Untersuchungen zur Verwendung und zum Verständnis der Schrift bei Paulus* (BHT, 69; Tübingen: Mohr [Paul Siebeck], 1986), pp. 163-65. It is interesting to note that 1QS 2.4-19 combines the curse formulae of Deut. 27.15-26 with Deut. 29.17-20 in its rite for entrance into the covenant (cf. Jer. 11.3, 8 MT). In the same context, 'all people of the lot of God who walk perfectly according to all his ways' are to be blessed by the priests (1QS 2.1-2), whereas 'all people of the lot of Belial' are to be cursed (ll. 4-5). See further H. Lichtenberger, *Studien zum Menschenbild in Texten der Qumrangemeinde* (SUNT, 15; Göttingen: Vandenhoeck & Ruprecht, 1980), pp. 106-13.

31. Hays (*Echoes of Scripture*, p. 43) makes a similar point but restricts the unit to Deuteronomy 27–28.

expression γεγραμμένα ἐν τῷ βιβλίῳ τοῦ νόμου τούτου which Paul cites in Gal. 3.10 runs through Deuteronomy 27–32 like a leitmotif (cf. Deut. 28.58, 61; 29.19, 20, 26; 30.10). Paul is citing from Deuteronomy 27–32 (33), the section on Blessings and Curses which comes after the exposition of 'the statutes and the ordinances' in Deuteronomy 12–26. Paul's own argument in Gal. 3.10-14 is bound together by the contrast between 'curse' (vv. 10a, 13a) and 'blessing' (v. 14a; cf. v. 9). Therefore, it is necessary to begin with a survey of Deuteronomy 27–32 before turning to subsequent tradition.

Deuteronomy 27–32 in its Old Testament Context
Deuteronomy 27–32 repeatedly emphasizes that the sin of the nation would cause the 'curses' of the law—ultimately exile—to fall upon the people, but that, if they repented, God would eventually restore them to covenant relationship and to the land. Each chapter of this section contributes to this perspective.

First of all, Deuteronomy 27 prescribes a ceremony to be conducted on Mount Gerizim and Mount Ebal, in which the whole people are involved in the acceptance of the Deuteronomic laws. The chapter concludes with a series of twelve curses which the Levites are to recite to all the people of Israel from Mount Ebal and which the people are to affirm with 'Amen!' The twelfth and final curse, which Paul cites in Gal. 3.10, is the most comprehensive, especially in the Septuagintal wording which amplifies it with a twofold πᾶς and thus makes the curse apply to 'everyone' who does not keep 'all things' that are written in the book of the law.

Deuteronomy 28 pronounces a series of blessings that will follow obedience (vv. 1-14) and a series of curses that will be brought on by disobedience (vv. 15-68). Obviously, the emphasis is here put on the curses and especially on the curse of exile (cf. vv. 32, 36, 37, 41, 48, 63, 64, 68).

Deuteronomy 29 seems to suggest a covenant made in the plains of Moab as a supplement to that made at Horeb. Much of the chapter (vv. 19-28) describes the curses that will result from disobedience to the law, and again the ultimate curse which will befall the people is exile. The text is not necessarily calling for sinless perfection, but rather for covenant faithfulness to Yahweh as opposed to national apostasy:

> It is because they forsook the covenant of the Lord, the God of their fathers, which he made with them when he brought them out of the land of Egypt, and went and served other gods... therefore, the anger of the Lord was kindled against this land, bringing upon it all the curses written in this book; and the Lord uprooted them from their land in anger and fury and great wrath, and cast them into another land, as at this day (vv. 25-28).

Deuteronomy 30 is crucial to understanding the perspective on the curse of exile in Deuteronomy. For in vv. 1-8, the text completes the picture by including the hope of restoration:

> 1 And when all these things come upon you, the blessing and the curse, which I have set before you, and you call them to mind among all the nations where the Lord your God has driven you, 2 and return to the Lord your God, you and your children, and obey his voice in all that I command you this day, with all your heart and with all your soul; 3 then the Lord your God will restore your fortunes, and have compassion upon you, and he will gather you again from all the peoples where the Lord your God has scattered you. 4 If your outcasts are in the uttermost parts of heaven, from there the Lord your God will gather you, and from there he will fetch you; 5 and the Lord your God will bring you into the Land which your fathers possessed, that you may possess it; and he will make you more prosperous and numerous than your fathers. 6 And the Lord your God will circumcise your heart and the heart of your offspring, so that you will love the Lord your God with all your heart and with all your soul, that you may live. [...] 8 And you shall again obey the voice of the Lord, and keep all his commandments which I command you this day.

Again in Deut. 30.11-12, the offer is made of life or death, of blessing or curse: 'But if your heart turns away, and you will not hear...you shall not live long in the land which you are going over the Jordan to enter and possess' (vv. 17-18).

Finally, in Deuteronomy 31–32, Israel's rebellion and exile are predicted, and Moses is instructed to write down a song to teach to the Israelites as a witness against them. The song is supposed to function as a warning to the people after they enter the land (32.47), but it clearly assumes that the Israelites would break the covenant and that the curses would come upon them, including their being driven into exile (32.26). Nevertheless, even in this calamity, God will have compassion on his people Israel and vindicate them (32.34-43).

We can say, therefore, that Deuteronomy 27–32 contains the sin–exile–restoration (SER) pattern which is so familiar in Old Testament/

Jewish tradition.[32] The emphasis in this section, however, is clearly on the curse of exile which would come upon Israel for gross disobedience to the law in the form of national apostasy and fundamental covenant violation. Thus the perspective is predominantly national rather than individual, and that is precisely how Deuteronomy 27–32 was understood in much of Old Testament/ Jewish tradition.

Deuteronomy 27–32 in Old Testament/Jewish Tradition

In 587 BCE a new era of Israel's history was inaugurated. The curses of the law for disobedience had come upon the nation in a definitive way; Jerusalem lay in ruins; the exile had begun. The prophets envisioned that the period of wrath would someday end, that the twelve tribes of Israel would be regathered from the dispersion, and that the people (or at least a remnant) would be restored to a new covenantal relationship with God in the land. In that day, God would dwell in a new and glorified temple in Zion, a Davidic heir would rule the reunited nation, and the Gentiles would submit to God and his people. Yet despite some disappointing attempts at return and restoration after the edict of Cyrus, these hopes were never realized. As Ezra and Nehemiah acknowledged in their confessions on behalf of the people, the condition of sin and guilt which had precipitated the exile persisted even after the partial return to the land (cf. Ezra 9.6-15; Neh. 9.5-37).[33] Thus the hopes of final restoration continued to be postponed

---

32. J. Klausner (*The Messianic Idea in Israel from its Beginning to the Completion of the Mishnah* (trans. W.F. Stinespring; London: George Allen & Unwin, 3rd edn, 1956]) refers to this traditional pattern as the 'messianic chain' consisting of sin–punishment–repentance–redemption. However, SER is preferred here, firstly, because many Old Testament/Jewish texts which have these three elements in common do not explicitly mention repentance, redemption, or the messiah, and secondly, because under restoration we may subsume repentance, redemption and its aftermath (e.g., return of reunited Israel to the land, covenant renewal, glorified Temple). SER is also preferred to E.P. Sanders's description (*Jesus and Judaism* [Philadelphia: Fortress Press, 1985], pp. 78-90) which views the unified 'Old Testament/Jewish complex of themes' on the restoration without regard to the original causes of exile.

33. On Nehemiah 9, see H.G.M. Williamson, *Ezra, Nehemiah* (WBC, 16; Waco, TX: Word Books, 1985), pp. 316-17: 'Not considering that restoration from that severe judgment was yet complete, our author could not record the historical fulfillment of the final cycle [i.e., the threefold cycle in Neh. 9.26-27, 28, 29-31 of handing over to a foreign power, cry for help, and response by God in mercy and

throughout the Second Temple period and beyond. George W.E. Nickelsburg summarizes the situation this way: 'Much of post-biblical Jewish theology and literature was influenced and sometimes governed by a hope for such a restoration...'[34] In the meantime, Israel was to remain under the curse of the law which had sent her into exile in the first place. This is brought out by the well-known apocalyptic text of Daniel 9.

Daniel 9 and Deuteronomy 27–32. In Dan. 9.2, Daniel ponders the meaning of Jeremiah's prophecy that Jerusalem would remain desolate for 70 years as punishment for Judah's sin (Jer. 25.11-12; 29.10; cf. Zech. 1.12; 2 Chron. 36.20-21). From the chronology given in v. 1, Daniel's interest in Jeremiah comes before Jeremiah's prophecy of restoration should have found its realization. In this situation, Daniel offers, first, a prayer of confession for the sins of Israel (vv. 4-14), and secondly, a prayer of supplication (vv. 15-19). First, Daniel confesses the sins of Israel which had brought about the exile of the people and the desolation of the Temple. There is nothing strange about a prayer of confession at this point (rather than, say, a prayer for illumination), for, according to Deut. 30.1-8, national repentance was to be the prerequisite for Restoration (cf. also 1 Kgs 8.46-53). In the process of confessing the people's sin, Dan. 9.11 explicitly refers to the 'curse' of Deuteronomy 27–32: 'All Israel has transgressed your law and turned aside, refusing to obey your voice. And the curse [κατάρα] and oath which are written in the law of Moses [Deuteronomy 27–32!] the servant of God have been poured out upon

deliverance], but rather includes himself and his contemporaries within it as he actualizes the cry for help in words of confession, petition, and lament which arise from his present situation...'

34. G.W.E. Nickelsburg, *Jewish Literature between the Bible and the Mishnah: A Historical and Literary Introduction* (Philadelphia: Fortress Press, 1981), p. 18 (cf. pp. 9-18). In his book *Self-Fulfilling Prophecy: Exile and Return in the History of Judaism* (Boston: Beacon Press, 1987), Jacob Neusner argues that because the restoration did not happen in the sixth century as expected on the basis of the Torah framed in that period, all Judaic systems continued to push the expectation of return and restoration into the future and viewed themselves as living in an exile situation. See further A.M. Eisen, *Galut: Modern Jewish Reflection on Homelessness and Homecoming* (The Modern Jewish Experience; Bloomington: Indiana University Press, 1986).

us, because we have sinned against him.'[35] Having thus met the precondition of deliverance, Daniel's prayer continues, secondly, with a petition that God now turn away his 'wrath' (ὀργή)[36] and restore the Temple and the people (vv. 15-19). This clearly assumes that the nation continues to stand under the curse of the law mentioned in v. 11. The petition is dominated by motive clauses and phrases that indicate reasons why God should forgive and restore, one of which, incidentally, sounds quite Pauline: not 'on the basis of our right-eousness, but on the basis of your great mercy' (v. 18). The petition also argues on the basis of God's having rescued his people in the past from oppression in Egypt (vv. 15-16).[37]

Daniel's prayer is answered by the angel Gabriel in vv. 21-27.[38]

35. As is well recognized and often noted, the prayer of Dan. 9.4-19 is satu-rated with the Deuteronomic covenantal tradition, including the SER pattern (cf., e.g., A. Lacocque, 'The Liturgical Prayer in Daniel 9', *HUCA* 47 [1976], pp. 119-42). Again in v. 13, the text stresses that all the curses of the law came upon the people 'as it is written in the law of Moses'. In fact, the Deuteronomic perspective in the prayer has often been contrasted to the deterministic view of history in Dan. 9.24-27 (cf., e.g., Lacocque, 'Daniel 9', p. 123; J.J. Collins, *Daniel with an Introduction to Apocalyptic Literature* [FOTL, 20; Grand Rapids, MI: Eerdmans, 1984], pp. 93-96), even though Jewish tradition based on Daniel 9 (see further below) never felt the tension. Furthermore, the influence of Deuteronomy in Daniel comes by way of Jeremiah's prophecy, which is being contemplated in Dan. 9.2. There, too, the covenant has been broken (cf. Jer. 11.10; 31[38].32); the curses of the law have come upon Israel in accordance with Deut. 27.26; 29.19 (cf. Jer. 11.3, 8 MT); and a predetermined period of time has been set for the exile (cf. Jer. 25.11-12; 29.10). Hence, just as there is no real conflict between the Deuteronomic elements of Jeremiah and its 70 weeks of Babylonian exile, so also there is no fundamental contradiction between the Deuteronomic influence in Daniel's prayer and the 70 weeks of years in Dan. 9.24. In fact, O.H. Steck ('Weltgeschehen und Gottesvolk im Buche Daniel', in D. Lührmann and G. Strecker [eds.], *Kirche: Festschrift für Günther Bornkamm zum 75. Geburtstag* [Tübingen: Mohr (Paul Siebeck), 1980], pp. 53-78 [here pp. 71-74]) argues that Dan. 9.24-27 exhibits the same Deuteronomic influence as is found in Daniel's prayer.

36. Cf. Deut. 29.20, 23-24, 28 LXX.

37. Cf. Isa. 63.7–64.12; Jer. 32.16-25; Psalms 80; 106; Nehemiah 9.

38. Many scholars have argued that Daniel's prayer is a later interpolation that has been made to fit the context by the addition of v. 20, which duplicates v. 21, expanding it to fit the contents of the prayer (cf. P.R. Davies, *Daniel* [OTG; Sheffield: JSOT Press, 1985], pp. 60-62). In its present context, however, the prayer fits the typical literary pattern of prayer followed by epiphany (cf. Nickelsburg, *Jewish Literature*, p. 86, citing *1 En.* 12–16; *3 Bar.* 1; Tobit 3;

Daniel is told that the 70 weeks of Jeremiah's prophecy are actually to be interpreted as 70 weeks of years, that is, 490 years.[39] Whereas Jeremiah had spoken of 70 years of desolation for Jerusalem as the punishment due for Israel's sin, Daniel is told in essence that the chastisement is being exacted sevenfold (cf. Lev. 26.18, 21, 24, 28). In other words, the exile would persist centuries longer than originally anticipated! Peter R. Ackroyd aptly remarks,

> It is in effect an exile lasting 490 years, and with this we reach an understanding of exile and restoration which takes us well beyond the consideration of the sixth century. Here the exile is no longer an historic event to be dated to one period; it is much nearer to being a condition from which only the final age will bring release. Though bound to the historical reality of an exile which actually took place in the sixth century, the experience of exile *as such* had become a symbol of a period, viewed in terms of punishment but also in terms of promise...[40]

Lk. 3.21-22; 9.29), and it has many stylistic links with vv. 2, 21-27 (cf. M. Fishbane, *Biblical Interpretation in Ancient Israel* [Oxford: Clarendon Press, 1985], pp. 487-88; Collins, *Daniel*, pp. 90-91). In any case, the prayer of Dan. 9.4-19 is integral at least to the final form of the text as Paul would have known it.

39. On the *Wirkungsgeschichte* of Daniel's 70 weeks, see B.Z. Wacholder, 'Chronomessianism: The Timing of Messianic Movements and the Calendar of Sabbatical Cycles', *HUCA* 46 (1975), pp. 201-18; L.L. Grabbe, 'Chronography in Hellenistic Jewish Historiography', in P.J. Achtemeier (ed.), *SBL 1979 Seminar Papers*, II (2 vols.; SBLSP, 17; Missoula, MT: Scholars Press, 1979), pp. 43-68 (here pp. 55-58); R.T. Beckwith, 'Daniel 9 and the Date of Messiah's Coming in Essene, Hellenistic, Pharisaic, Zealot and Early Christian Computation', *RevQ* 40 (1981), pp. 521-42; K. Koch, *Das Buch Daniel* (Erträge der Forschung, 144; Darmstadt: Wissenschaftliche Buchgesellschaft, 1980), pp. 149-54; A.Y. Collins, 'Numerical Symbolism in Jewish and Early Christian Apocalyptic Literature', in *ANRW* II.21.2, pp. 1227-29; S. Bacchiocchi, 'Sabbatical Typologies of Messianic Redemption', *JSJ* 17 (1986), pp. 153-76.

40. P.R. Ackroyd, *Exile and Restoration: A Study of Hebrew Thought of the Sixth Century BC* (OTL; Philadelphia: Westminster Press, 1968), p. 242. *Pace* L.L. Grabbe, ' "The End of the Desolations of Jerusalem": From Jeremiah's 70 Years to Daniel's 70 Weeks of Years', in C.A. Evans and W.F. Stinespring (eds.), *Early Jewish and Christian Exegesis: Studies in Memory of William Hugh Brownlee* (Scholars Press Homage Series, 10; Atlanta: Scholars Press, 1987), pp. 67-72 (here p. 68).

The reason for this extended exile is given in v. 24:[41] 'Seventy weeks of years are decreed concerning your people and your holy city, to finish[42] the transgression, to put an end to sin, to atone for iniquity, to bring everlasting righteousness...' That is, Israel is still under the curse of the law which brought the exile in the first place (cf. v. 11); the period of wrath has not yet ended (cf. v. 16).[43] In fact, the people will remain under the curse for some time to come. Daniel 9 understands the exile as a state of judgment that is to be ended only by the intervention of God and the inauguration of the eschatological era, a point which is now widely recognized.[44]

Daniel 9 and Deuteronomy 27–32 in the Jewish penitential prayer tradition. It is unfortunate that Sanders's notion of covenantal nomism has so stressed continuity in the covenantal relationship between God and his people, and readily available atonement for sin by means of repentance, that texts on the exile which, like Daniel 9, emphasize prolonged discontinuity as punishment for sin,[45] have gone practically

41. Cf. Steck, 'Weltgeschehen', pp. 69ff. For an opposing view, see Collins, *Daniel*, pp. 94-95.

42. There is a textual question here whether to read כלא ('confine') as in the MT or rather כלה ('finish').

43. On Daniel's concept of the wrath of God continuing from 587 BCE to the end of time, see esp. Steck, 'Weltgeschehen', pp. 65-74. For example, Steck ('Weltgeschehen', p. 70 [emphasis mine]) writes: 'Was Daniel hier [v. 24] lernt, ist dies, daß es vom Fall Jerusalems unter Nebukadnezar... nicht einen kurzen Zeitraum von 70 Jahren, sondern einen langfristigen (vgl. 8,27!) von 70 Jahrwochen währen wird, der durch Sünde in Israel (vgl. 8,23) und *Zorn Gottes* (vgl. 8,19) qualifiziert ist, bis die Heilswende für Israel kommt, bezeichnenderweise gipfelnd in der Tempelweihe'.

44. Cf. Steck, 'Weltgeschehen', p. 74 n. 93; M.A. Knibb, 'The Exile in the Literature of the Intertestamental Period', *HeyJ* 17 (1976), pp. 253-72 (here p. 255); D.E. Gowan, 'The Exile in Jewish Apocalyptic', in A.L. Merrill and T.W. Overholt (eds.), *Scripture in History and Theology: Essays in Honor of J. Coert Rylaarsdam* (PTMS, 17; Pittsburgh: Pickwick Press, 1977), pp. 205-23; J.E. Goldingay, *Daniel* (WBC, 30; Dallas, TX: Word Books, 1989), pp. 238, 251; *idem, Daniel* (Word Biblical Themes; Dallas: Word Publishing, 1989), pp. 73-75; M. Hengel, *Judentum und Hellenismus. Studien zu ihrer Begegnung unter besonderer Berücksichtigung Palästinas bis zur Mitte des 2 Jh.s v.Chr.* (WUNT, 10; Tübingen: Mohr [Paul Siebeck], 2nd edn, 1973), pp. 328 (with n. 470), 334-35.

45. According to the clear witness of classical prophecy, the reason for this punishment was Israel's continual disregard for the commandments of Yahweh; in other words, an unrepentant attitude.

unnoticed[46] or have been labelled aberrant.[47] There are in fact a number of other Old Testament and Jewish texts which tend to call into question Sanders's business-as-usual concept of covenantal nomism.[48] The extensive penitential prayer tradition based on Dan. 9.4-19 and Deuteronomy 27–32 shows that the state of curse and exile was felt to continue throughout the Second Temple period and beyond.[49] For example, the second-century BCE text of Bar. 1.15–3.8

46. Sanders (*Jesus and Judaism*, p. 96 n. 19) makes only passing reference to Daniel 9 in this regard, without drawing out the consequences of this observation for his view of covenantal nomism. This is surprising in that Sanders stresses Old Testament/Jewish 'Restoration Eschatology' as the background for John the Baptist, Jesus, and the early church, including Paul (cf. *Jesus and Judaism*, pp. 77-119)! Sanders fails to observe that texts like Daniel 9 envision a prolonged disruption in the covenantal relationship (plight)—a protracted exile—before the inauguration of the restoration (solution).

47. By the standard of supposedly normative covenantal nomism, Sanders (*Paul and Palestinian Judaism*, p. 409) views *4 Ezra* as an idiosyncratic example of 'legalistic perfectionism' in which 'covenantal nomism has collapsed'. Similarly on p. 418: 'One has here [in *4 Ezra*] the closest approach to legalistic work-righteousness which can be found in the Jewish literature of the period; for only here are the traditional characteristics of God—he freely forgives and restores sinners and maintains the covenant promises despite transgression—denied.' The fact is, however, that *4 Ezra* must be understood as an SER text which depends heavily on the book of Daniel (e.g., Dan. 11.1–12.39), particularly in the assumption that Israel is in a state of protracted exile as the punishment for sin (cf. Knibb, 'The Exile', p. 269).

48. As O.H. Steck ('Das Problem theologischer Strömungen in nachexilischer Zeit', *EvT* 28 [1968], pp. 445-58 [here pp. 451-56]) has shown, there are two great theological mainstreams in the postexilic period: (1) a theocratic stream oriented exclusively on the Temple and the cult as re-establishing divine salvation for Israel and a means of maintaining that status before God (cf. Sanders's concept of covenantal nomism), and (2) an eschatological stream which sees the present status of Israel as still in exile, still accursed and under divine judgment until the eschatological intervention of God ('Ganz Israel ist nach wie vor im Exil...' [p. 454]).

49. Cf. G. von Rad, 'Gerichtsdoxologie', in R. Smend (ed.), *Gesammelte Studien zum Alten Testament*, II (TBü: Altes Testament, 48; Munich: Chr. Kaiser Verlag, 1973), pp. 245-54 (here pp. 246-47). Von Rad argues that the 'doxologies of judgment' in Daniel 9, Ezra 9, Nehemiah 9, and Bar. 1.15–3.8, containing unmistakable Deuteronomistic language, reflect groups who felt the catastrophe of 587 BCE as an undiminished reality, for, although 587 was long past, they considered themselves still under the judgment of Yahweh.

is composed of a corporate confession of sins and a petition that God withdraw his wrath[50] and return the exiles to their homeland. The logic of the prayer follows the SER scheme of Deuteronomy 27–32, with verbal parallels to Dan. 9.4-19 which indicate a very close relationship also to that prayer.[51] Thus in the section on the sin of Israel (Bar. 1.15-21), we read:

> From the day when the Lord brought our fathers out of the land of Egypt until today, we have been disobedient to the Lord our God, and we have been negligent, in not heeding his voice. So to this day there have clung to us the calamities and the curse (ἀρά) which the Lord declared through Moses his servant...' (vv. 19-20).

Thereupon, the exile is acknowledged as the result of the nation's sin (2.1-5), and the the Lord is petitioned to bring in the restoration of Israel (2.11-35). There is no hint here of a normal covenantal relationship along the lines which Sanders sets forth as covenantal nomism.[52] Instead, we find that the chief concern is the continuance of the curse of exile and the disgrace of Jerusalem.[53] This is all the more significant insofar as Baruch was regularly read as part of the liturgy of the synagogue.[54] The perspective of Baruch is summed up in the closing words of the prayer of repentance: 'Behold, we are today in our exile where you have scattered us, to be reproached and cursed and punished for all the iniquities of our fathers[55] who forsook the Lord our God' (3.8).[56]

---

50. As the narrative introduction to Baruch shows (1.1-14), the prayer in Bar. 1.15–3.8 was to be prayed on behalf of Jerusalem, because 'to this day the anger of the Lord and his wrath have not turned away from us' (Bar. 1.13).

51. There is much discussion about the relationship between Bar. 1.15–3.8 and Dan. 9.4-19, whether one of dependence either way or mutual dependence on a common source.

52. Characteristically, Sanders does not discuss Bar. 1.15–3.8 in *Paul and Palestinian Judaism*.

53. Cf. Gowan, 'Exile', p. 208.

54. Cf. H.-P. Rüger, 'Apokryphen I', *TRE*, III, p. 307: '...das Buch ist bestimmt zur Verlesung "am Feiertag und an anderen Festtagen" (1,14; vgl. damit die Nachricht von A[postolischen] Konst[itutionen] V,20, wonach Baruch am 10. Gorpiaios [September] im Synagogengottesdienst verlesen wurde)'.

55. According to Exod. 20.5; 34.7; Num. 14.18; Deut. 5.9; Jer. 32.18, God punishes the children for the sin of the fathers to the third and fourth generation.

56. In Bar. 4.5–5.9, the SER pattern occurs again: sin (4.5-8); exile (4.9-20); restoration (4.21–5.9). Here Mother Zion counsels her children to 'endure with

Another example of this penitential prayer tradition is found in the Prayer of Azariah, an addition to Greek Daniel (Dan. 3.26-45 LXX). In vv. 26-33, the author opens with a benediction which acknowledges that God's judgments are righteous and that Israel deserved to be delivered into the hands of lawless enemies.[57] Nevertheless, in vv. 34-36, the author appeals to God's covenantal mercy and to the promise made to the patriarchs, although he realizes that because of the nation's sin the promise of proliferation of Abraham's seed in Gen. 15.5 has actually been reversed in accordance with Deut. 28.62.[58] Moreover, the people are now without political leadership and prophetic voice,[59] and they lack the sacrificial means to make things right with God: 'And at this time there is no prince, or prophet, or leader, no burnt offering, or sacrifice, or oblation, or incense, or place to make an offering before you or to find mercy' (v. 38). The misfortunes brought on by the destruction of Jerusalem and the exile are still felt to prevail at the time of the writing. Hence, following David's precedent, the author asks that their humbled and crushed spirits be accepted in lieu of sacrifice (vv. 39-40; cf. Ps. 51.16-17). This is the repentance which Deuteronomy requires in order to initiate the restoration of the covenantal relationship (cf. vv. 29-31, 41; Deut. 30.1-3). Finally, in vv. 42-43, the author appeals, as typically in this penitential prayer tradition, to the mercy of God to deliver his people (cf. Dan. 9.18).

Sir. 36.1-17 provides yet another example of this penitential prayer tradition. This prayer for the deliverance and restoration of Israel pleads for God to 'hasten the day and remember the appointed time' (v. 8) when he would restore his people and defeat their enemies. The basis of the appeal is, again, the mercy of God (cf. Dan. 9.18) and the

---

patience the wrath (ὀργή) that has come upon you from God' (4.25).

57. God's righteous judgment is a characteristic of Jewish writings of the Second Temple period which are wrestling with the disparity between Israel's covenant status and her present misfortune (cf. Dan. 9.7; Bar. 1.15; 2.6; *Pss. Sol.* 2.16-18; 8.30-40).

58. Cf. Bar. 2.29 for an explicit citation of Deut. 28.62.

59. There is a widespread tradition in early Judaism that prophecy ceased with the death of the last writing prophets (Haggai, Zechariah, and Malachi), not to return again until the time of the restoration. Cf. J. Jeremias, *New Testament Theology: The Proclamation of Jesus* (New York: Charles Scribner's Sons, 1971), pp. 80-82. But see also D.E. Aune, *Prophecy in Early Christianity and the Ancient Mediterranean World* (Grand Rapids, MI: Eerdmans, 1983).

election of Israel: 'Have mercy, O Lord, upon the people called by
your name [Dan. 9.19], upon Israel, whom you have likened to a first-
born son' (v. 12; cf. Exod. 4.22; 4QDibHam 3). The hope is for the
regathering of 'all the tribes of Jacob' (v. 11), for pity on the city of
Jerusalem (v. 13), and for the filling of the Temple with the glory of
the Lord (v. 14). Here, as in the Prayer of Azariah (Dan. 3.38 LXX)
and often in this tradition,[60] the Second Temple (and its priesthood) is
seen to be deficient in the protracted period of exile before the final
restoration.[61]

Although there are many other prayers like Dan. 9.4-19 in the
Second Temple period which could be adduced here,[62] the foregoing
examples suffice to make the point. There is a widespread penitential
prayer tradition based on Daniel 9 which recognizes that the curse of
exile warned about in Deuteronomy 27–32 for violating the covenant

60. Cf. 2 Macc. 2.8; *1 En.* 89.73; 90.28-33; Tob. 14.5; *T. Levi* 16.1-5; 17.10-
11; *2 Bar.* 68.5-7; *T. Mos.* 4.8.

61. In his testamentary forecast (Tob. 14.4-7), Tobit makes perhaps one of the
strongest statements in this period that the Second Temple and the return at the end of
the sixth century were only provisional: 'But God will again have mercy on them,
and bring them back into their land; and they will rebuild the house of God, though it
will not be like the former one until the times of the age are completed. After this they
will return from the places of their captivity, and will rebuild Jerusalem in splendor'
(v. 5). For further discussion on these texts which are critical of the Second Temple,
see especially K. Koch, 'Sabbatstruktur der Geschichte: Die sogenannte Zehn-
Wochen-Apokalypse (1 Hen 93, 1-10; 91, 11-17) und das Ringen um die
alttestamentlichen Chronologien im späten Israelitentum', *ZAW* 95 (1983), pp. 403-
30 (here pp. 418-19); C.A. Evans, 'Jesus' Action in the Temple: Cleansing or
Portent of Destruction?', *CBQ* 51 (1989), pp. 237-70 (here pp. 252-56).

62. Cf. 2 Macc. 1.10–2.18; 4QDibHam. (esp. cols. 5 and 6); 1QS 1.24b–2.1
(on the influence of the prayer in Daniel 9 here, see Lichtenberger, *Menschenbild*,
pp. 93ff.; P. Stuhlmacher, *Gerechtigkeit Gottes bei Paulus* [FRLANT, 87;
Göttingen: Vandenhoeck & Ruprecht, 2nd edn, 1966], p. 160); CD 20.28-30; *Pss.
Sol.* 2; 8.23-32; 9; 11; 17; *Shemoneh Esreh*; also Ps. 78 (79); 105 (106); Esth. 4.17
(l-z) LXX; Ezra 9; Neh. 1.5-11; 9.5-37; Isa. 63.7–64.12. *T. Mos.* contains the SER
scheme (sin [2.7-9]; exile [3.1–4.4]; restoration [4.5-9]) and is heavily dependent on
Dan. 9.4-19 (cf. *T. Mos.* 4.1-4) and Dan. 9.24 (cf. *T. Mos.* 3.14 [the southern tribes
would be in bondage for 'about seventy and seven years'!]). Clearly, the exile is here
seen as an ongoing period of distress which will be brought to an end only when
God's kingdom appears (*T. Mos.* 10.1-10). G.W.E. Nickelsburg and M.E. Stone
(*Faith and Piety in Early Judaism: Texts and Documents* [Philadelphia: Fortress
Press, 1983], p. 127) call *T. Mos.* 'a paraphrase of the last chapters of
Deuteronomy', i.e., the SER scheme.

has indeed come upon Israel as of 587 BCE, and that the condition of exile would persist until God, in accordance with his own mercy and timetable, would listen to Israel's confession of sin and bring in the restoration as Deuteronomy 27–32 had promised.[63]

Daniel 9 and Deuteronomy 27–32 in other Second Temple literature. This concept is not limited to the penitential prayer tradition; it pervades Second Temple literature. In 2 Macc. 7, for example, the story of the martyrdom of seven brothers and their mother during the persecution of Antiochus Epiphanes illustrates the hope of the fulfillment of Deut. 32.36-43 in light of Daniel 9. The seventh brother acknowledges, as did the sixth (2 Macc. 7.18), that the Hebrew people are suffering persecution because of their own sins against God (v. 32; cf. Dan. 9.4-14). He goes on to say, 'I, like my brothers, give up body and life for the laws of our fathers, appealing to God to show mercy soon to our nation [cf. Dan. 9.15-19]…and through me and my brothers to bring to an end the wrath (cf. Dan. 9.16) of the Almighty which has justly fallen on our whole nation' (2 Macc. 7.37-38). This period of wrath is expected to last 'for a little while' in order to rebuke and discipline the nation (2 Macc. 7.33; cf. Dan. 9.24); then, God will have compassion on Israel, 'as Moses declared in his song which bore witness against the people to their faces [Deut. 32.1-43], when he said, "And he will have compassion on his servants" [Deut. 32.36]' (2 Macc. 7.6; cf. v. 33). These references to Deuteronomy 32 and Daniel 9[64] show that the seventh brother hopes for final restoration of Israel after the period of exile, which, from his perspective, climaxes in the crisis under Antiochus Epiphanes (cf. Dan. 9.25-27).

The Animal Apocalypse in *1 En.* 85–90 contains the traditional SER scheme and a clear dependence on the 70 years of Jeremiah's prophecy. After recounting the history of how the 'white sheep' (Jacob/Israel) descended from the line of 'white bulls' (Shem, Abraham, and Isaac) to become a nation distinct from other nations, the text goes on to describe how Israel's mounting apostasy led to a new period in the nation's history, the exile, beginning with the Assyrian or the Babylonian conquest (*1 En.* 89.59-67). During the

63. Cf. Gowan, 'Exile', pp. 219-20.
64. The influence of Daniel is seen also in the expectation of the resurrection of the righteous in 2 Macc. 7.9, 14, 23 (cf. Dan. 12.2).

exile, the Lord of the sheep summons 70 angelic shepherds, one for each of 70 periods of time, to pasture the flock successively until the Kingdom of God comes.[65] Thus the 70 years of Jer. 25.11-12 and 29.10 are interpreted here to refer to 70 periods of time along the lines of Daniel 9.[66] This whole protracted period of exile is seen as an evil time in which the Temple is polluted (*1 En.* 89.73) and Israel's eyes are blinded (v. 74). The perspective is much the same in the Apocalypse of Weeks in *1 En.* 93.1-10; 91.11-17, where the seventh week of ten in world history begins with the exile (93.8) and is characterized as a period of apostasy (93.9) which continues until the 'the chosen righteous from the eternal plant of righteousness will be chosen, to whom will be given sevenfold teaching concerning his whole creation' (93.10).[67] No mention is made of the return to the land in the sixth century. Evidently, the whole period from 587 BCE to the emergence of this reform movement is seen as exile.

In *Testament of Levi*, the patriarch tells his children:

> Now I have come to know that for seventy weeks you shall wander astray and profane the priesthood and defile the sacrificial altars. You shall set aside the law and nullify the words of the prophets by your wicked perversity. [...] You shall have no place that is clean, but you will be as a curse and a dispersion among the nations until he will again have regard for you, and will take you back in compassion (*T. Levi* 16.1-2, 5).

Since this prediction stands within the exile section of the SER scheme in *T. Levi* 14–18, the 70 weeks evidently refers to the same negative 70 weeks of years found in Dan. 9.24.[68]

The concept of a protracted exile in related Old Testament/Jewish tradition. It has been suggested that the 490 years of exile expected in

---

65. Cf. Knibb, 'The Exile', p. 258.

66. Knibb, 'The Exile', p. 256. The Epistle of Jeremiah defines the length of the exile as 'seven generations' (v. 2), which, assuming a generation of 40 years, would be 280 years.

67. Cf. Hengel, *Judentum und Hellenismus*, p. 329; Koch, 'Sabbatstruktur der Geschichte', pp. 418: 'Es (sc. das siebte שבוע) hebt mit dem Exil an, übergeht auffälligerweise den Neubeginn, sowohl den zweiten Tempel wie die Zeit Esras, und reiht alles, was seither in Israel geschah, unter der Überschrift "Abirrung" ein. Das trifft offenkundig die gesamte Geschichte der nachexilischen Kultgemeinde und ihre Organisation. Ein Umschlag wird erst für das Ende vorausgesetzt.'

68. Cf. Koch, 'Sabbatstruktur der Geschichte', p. 419.

Daniel 9 is either a recalculation of the 430 years of exile expected in Ezek. 4.4-8[69] or an adaptation of the rationale for the length of judgment given there.[70] In any case, Ezek. 4.4-8 provides an early example of a prophetic text which expects a protracted period of exile. During a symbolic seige of Jerusalem, the prophet is told to lie on his left side for 390 days and bear the punishment of the house of Israel (vv. 4-5), and then to lie on his right side for 40 days and bear the punishment of the house of Judah (v. 6). The days that the prophet is to lie on his sides (390 + 40 = 430) represent the total years of punishment for sin due the northern and southern kingdoms. This recalls the 430 years which Israel spent in Egyptian bondage (Exod. 12.40; cf. Gen. 15.13); for, as Ezek. 20.33-38 (cf. 1QM 1.2-3) shows, Ezekiel expects a new exodus at the conclusion of the period of punishment in exile.[71] This is in accordance with much Old Testament/Jewish tradition (e.g., Dan. 9.15-19) which views the deliverance from exile as a 'redemption' of Israel from bondage and as a new exodus.[72]

This tradition of the 430 years of exile is picked up at the beginning of the Damascus Document in the familiar passage about the origins of the Qumran community:

> For when they were unfaithful in that they forsook him, he hid his face from Israel and his sanctuary and gave them to the sword. But when he remembered the covenant with the men of former times, he left a remnant

69. So W.H. Brownlee, *Ezekiel 1–19* (WBC, 28; Waco, TX: Word Books, 1986), p. 71. On a possible connection between the 490 years of Daniel 9 and the 430 years of Exod. 12.40, see S. Kreuzer, '430 Jahre, 400 Jahre oder 4 Generationen: Zu den Zeitangaben über den Ägyptenaufenthalt der "Israeliten"', *ZAW* 98 (1986), pp. 199-210 (here p. 209 n. 41).

70. Cf. H. Bluhm, 'Daniel 9 und die chronistische Geschichtsdarstellung', *TG* 72 (1982), pp. 450-60 (here p. 454), '[Die Gerichtsursache war] nach dem eindeutigen Zeugnis der Prophetie die ständige Mißachtung der Gebote Jahwes, d.h. die mangelnde Bußgesinnung. Nach dem Vorbild Ezechiels (Ez 4,5.9) muß deshalb die gesamte Zeit als Gerichtszeit nachgeholt werden. Darauf weisen auch Bemerkungen in V. 24b, die von der Zeit des Zornes (über Israel) und von der noch zu sühnenden Schuld bis zum Termin des Eschatons sprechen, deutlich hin.'

71. Cf. W. Zimmerli, *Ezekiel*, I (2 vols.; BKAT, 13; Neukirchen–Vluyn: Neukirchener Verlag, 2nd edn, 1979), p. 121; Brownlee, *Ezekiel 1–19*, p. 71.

72. Cf. W. Haubeck, *Loskauf durch Christus: Herkunft, Gestaltung und Bedeutung des paulinischen Loskaufmotivs* (Gießen: Brunnen; Witten: Bundes-Verlag, 1985), pp. 7-135 *passim*.

to Israel and did not give them to destruction. And in the time of wrath, three hundred and ninety years after he had given them into the hand of Nebuchadnezzar king of Babylon, he visited them and caused a root of planting [cf. *1 En.* 93.10] to spring from Israel and Aaron, to inherit his land and to prosper on the good things of his earth. And they considered their iniquity and knew that they were guilty men; yet for twenty years they were like blind men who grope for the way. And God considered their deeds, for they sought him with a whole heart [cf. Deut. 30.2]; and he raised up for them a Teacher of Righteousness to lead them in the way of his heart (CD 1.3-11a).

The beginnings of the movement are attributed to divine intervention 390 years after the people went into exile in the time of Nebuchadnezzar (587 BCE). The reference to 390 + 20 years is based on Ezek. 4.4-8[73] and evidently leaves 20 more years before the end of the exile,[74] which is here described as the 'time of wrath' (cf. Dan. 9.16).[75] As Michael A. Knibb has observed,

73. Note, however, that some scholars view CD 1.3-11 against the background of the 490 years of Daniel 9 (cf., e.g., Grabbe, 'Chronography in Hellenistic Jewish Historiography', II, p. 57; H. Burgmann, 'Wer war der "Lehrer der Gerechtigkeit"?', *RevQ* 10 [1981], pp. 557-61). On this view, see the critique of B.Z. Wacholder, *The Dawn of Qumran: The Sectarian Torah and the Teacher of Righteousness* (Monographs of the Hebrew Union College, 8; Cincinnati: Hebrew Union College Press, 1983), pp. 178-81.

74. Cf. S. Talmon, 'Waiting for the Messiah: The Spiritual Universe of the Qumran Covenanters', in J. Neusner *et al.* (eds.), *Judaisms and their Messiahs at the Turn of the Christian Era* (Cambridge: Cambridge University Press, 1987), pp. 111-37 (here pp. 118-19); M.A. Knibb, 'Exile in the Damascus Document', *JSOT* 25 (1983), pp. 99-117 (here p. 113).

75. Some scholars interpret the 'time of wrath' in CD 1.5 to mean just the time of persecution under Antiochus Ephiphanes or merely the period in which the author was living (cf. Knibb, 'Exile in the Damascus Document', p. 113). In light, however, of Ezek. 4.4-8, on which the Damascus Document is based here, and of the use of 'wrath' elsewhere (cf. Dan. 8.19; 9.16 [see further above]; Bar. 1.13; 2.20; 2 Macc. 7.32-33, 37-38; Ps. 78[79].5), it seems best to interpret the expression as a reference to the whole 430-year period (cf. K. Koch, 'Die Bedeutung der Apokalyptik für die Interpretation der Schrift', in M. Klopfenstein *et al.* (eds.), *Mitte der Schrift? Ein jüdisch-christliches Gespräch: Texte des Berner Symposions vom 6.-12. Januar 1985* [Bern: Peter Lang, 1987], pp. 185-215 [here pp. 211-12]; P.R. Davies, 'Eschatology at Qumran', *JBL* 104 [1985], pp. 39-55 [here pp. 49, 52]). In the SER scheme of *Apoc. Abr.* 25–29, the exile is described as a period of 'four ascents' of 100 years each (= 400 years), during which God would pour out his 'anger' on the people and require 'retribution for their works' (28.4). Since

the implication of the passage... would seem to be that for the author the
Jews remained in a state of exile until the events in the second century
which led to the foundation of the Qumran community; this, in turn, was
to be the immediate prelude to the final judgement and the beginning of the
Messianic era.[76]

The author of the Damascus Document was saying in effect that 'the
events to which he was referring marked the end of the period of
Israel's punishment, i.e. the end of exile'.[77] Knibb goes on to state:

> Underlying this passage, as well as the other passages in the Damascus
> Document dealing with the origins of the Essene movement (III.9b-17a;
> V.20–VI.5) is a distinct theological pattern that is known to us from other
> literature of the period. According to this pattern Israel remained in a state
> of exile long after the return in the last decades of the sixth century, until
> the exile was brought to an end in the events of a much later period; see

Apoc. Abr. 15–29 is a midrash on Genesis 15, the 400 years here probably allude to
Gen. 15.13, the period of slavery in Egypt before the exodus (so L. Hartman, 'The
Function of Some So-called Apocalyptic Timetables', *NTS* 22 [1976], pp. 10),
which would put *Apoc. Abr.* 28.4 within the same tradition as the 430 years of exile
in Ezek. 4.4-8. For a different interpretation of *Apoc. Abr.* 28.4, see Knibb, 'The
Exile', p. 272; B. Philonenko-Sayar and M. Philonenko, *Die Apokalypse Abrahams*
(JSHRZ, 5.5; Gütersloh: Gerd Mohn, 1982), p. 449 n. 2.

76. Knibb, 'The Exile', p. 263; also Davies, 'Eschatology at Qumran',
pp. 49, 52-53 (on which see J.J. Collins, 'Was the Dead Sea Sect an Apocalyptic
Movement?', in L.H. Schiffman (ed.), *Archaeology and History in the Dead Sea
Scrolls: The New York University Conference in Memory of Yigael Yadin* [JSPSup,
8; JSOT/ASOR Monographs, 2; Sheffield, JSOT Press, 1990], pp. 25-51 [here
pp. 41-44]). Here it is interesting to note that this kind of expectation evidently
continued into the Tannaitic period, when calculations of the end time based on the
prototype of 400 years of exile in Egypt (Gen. 15.13) were condemned (cf. P.
Schäfer, 'Die messianischen Hoffnungen des rabbinischen Judentums zwischen
Naherwartung und religiösem Pragmatismus', in *Studien zur Geschichte und
Theologie des rabbinischen Judentums* [AGJU, 15; Leiden: Brill, 1978], p. 228 [cf.
pp. 230, 240 n. 29]). For other evidence of the 400 years of Gen. 15.13 being used
in rabbinic chronological speculation on the time of the messianic redemption, see
W.G. Braude, *Pesikta Rabbati: Discourses for Feasts, Fasts and Special Sabbaths* (2
vols.; Yale Judaica Series, 18; New Haven: Yale University Press, 1968), I, p. 46 n.
51 (on *Pes. R.* 1.7).

77. M.A. Knibb, *The Qumran Community* (Cambridge Commentaries on
Writings of the Jewish and Christian World 200 BC to AD 200, 2; Cambridge:
Cambridge University Press, 1987), p. 20.

for example Dan. 9.24-27; *1 En.* 93.9-10... The intention of the author
was thus... to make a theological point linking the beginning of the
movement with the ending of Israel's state of exile.[78]

From the perspective of the Damascus Document, this was the time
when a righteous remnant from Israel repented, and God 'made
atonement' (כפר)[79] for their sin and forgave them (cf. CD 2.5; 3.18;
4.6, 9b-10a; 20.34).[80]

The *Testaments of the Twelve Patriarchs* contain many SER
passages cast in the form of prophecies.[81] Typically, the patriarch
predicts that in the last days his descendants will fall into sin, that they
will be led therefore into captivity among the Gentiles, but also that
they will one day be restored to the land. For the *Testaments*, the
restoration to the land does not refer to the incomplete return from
Babylon at the end of the sixth century BCE, but rather, in keeping
with the contemporary expectation,[82] to an eschatological event which

78. Knibb, *The Qumran Community*, p. 20 (cf. pp. 21, 27, 33, 45-46, 47,
61). Cf. Nickelsburg and Stone, *Faith and Piety in Early Judaism*, p. 39. CD 1.3-11
should be compared with the concept of SER in the still unpublished manuscript of
4QMMT 3, which also explains the origins of the Qumran community. There the
authors acknowledge that 'some of the blessings and curses which are written in the
bo[ok of Mo]ses came about' (cf. Deut. 27–32), but go on to affirm that they are
living in the 'latter days when (some) in Israel will return to the To[rah], and they
will not turn ba[ck...]' (ll. 3-5), with a clear allusion to the hope of restoration in
Deut. 30.1-8 (ll. 21-24).

79. Cf. Dan. 9.24.

80. On God's work of atonement according to the Qumran literature, see
further B. Janowski and H. Lichtenberger, 'Enderwartung und Reinheitsidee: Zur
eschatologischen Deutung von Reinheit und Sühne in der Qumrangemeinde', *JJS* 34
(1983), pp. 31-62 (here pp. 44-48).

81. Cf. H.W. Hollander and M. de Jonge, *The Testaments of the Twelve
Patriarchs: A Commentary* (SVTP, 8; Leiden: Brill, 1985), pp. 53-56, 227 and *passim*.

82. Cf. E. Schürer, *The History of the Jewish People in the Age of Jesus
Christ (175 BC–AD 135)* (ed. G. Vermes, *et al.*; Edinburgh: T. & T. Clark, 1973–
87), II, pp. 530-31: 'That the dispersed of Israel would participate in the messianic
kingdom and return for this purpose to the Holy Land was so self-evident that this
hope would have been cherished even without the Old Testament prophecies...
Indeed, given the universality of this hope for the gathering of the dispersed, it is
remarkable that the return of the ten tribes was questioned at all by individuals [i.e.,
by Akiba, who argues on the basis of Deut. 29.28 (*m. Sanh.* 10.3 fin.)]'. See also
W.D. Davies, *Paul and Rabbinic Judaism* (Philadelphia: Fortress Press, 4th edn,
1980), pp. 79-82.

still lay in the future and would involve all twelve tribes of Israel.[83] In view of the pervasive SER pattern in the *Test. XII Patr.*, the integrity and Jewishness of even a passage like *T. Jud.* 24.1-3 seems probable. For although it has often been suspected of Christian influence, *T. Jud.* 24.1-3 is clearly part of the traditional restoration element of the broader context. Thus when v. 3 expects the people of God to be adopted in accordance with 2 Sam. 7.14 and endowed with the Spirit in the time of messianic restoration, this is comparable first and foremost to the expectation in *Jub.* 1.24, another SER text which looks forward to the divine adoption of Israel in accordance with 2 Sam. 7.14 and the endowment of the Spirit after the protracted exile.[84]

Tobit is presented as a member of the tribe of Naphtali (Tob. 1.1), one of the ten lost tribes of Israel. In ch. 13, Tobit praises God in the form of a benediction which anticipates the benediction to be sung in the ideal Jerusalem of the restoration (cf. v. 18). Tobit acknowledges that although captivity and dispersion are God's present punishment for Israel's sin (vv. 1-5a; cf. also Tob. 3.3-5), God will show mercy, gather his people from all the nations, and return them to Jerusalem rebuilt with gold and precious stones according to the promises of Isa. 54.11-12 and 60.17-18 (Tob. 13.5b-18; cf. also Tob. 14.4-7). In common with considerable Old Testament/ Jewish tradition,[85] Tobit also expects that the Gentiles will participate in the restoration: 'Many nations will come from afar to the name of the Lord God, bearing gifts in their hands...' (v. 11 [13]). And again in Tob. 14.6-7: 'Then

---

82. Cf. Knibb, 'The Exile', pp. 265-66.

83. Cf. Knibb, 'The Exile', pp. 265-66.

84. On the integrity and Jewishness of *T. Jud.* 24.1-3 and its connection to *Jub.* 1.24, see my *Adoption as Sons of God: An Exegetical Investigation into the Background of YIOΘEΣIA in the Pauline Corpus* (WUNT, 2.48; Tübingen: Mohr [Paul Siebeck], 1992), pp. 109-17.

85. Cf. Sanders, *Jesus and Judaism*, pp. 79-82, 85-86, 106-108, 117, 213-18; J. Jeremias, *Jesus' Promise to the Nations* (trans. S.H. Hooke; Philadelphia: Fortress Press, 1982), pp. 55-73. *Pace* Jeremias (*Jesus' Promise*, p. 14 with n. 17), however, Tob. 13.3-6 does not show that 'the term Diaspora lost its ill-omened connotation' or that 'Israel's dispersion among the Gentiles was no longer regarded as God's judgement, but came to be seen as a divinely-given opportunity to glorify him among the Gentiles'. For the idea of the inclusion of the Gentiles in the restoration (in some cases even before Israel!), see, e.g., Isa. 45.14-17, 20-25; 59.19-20; Amos 9.11-12; Mic. 4.1-8; *T. Zeb.* 9.8-9 (cf. the jealousy motif in Romans 9–11); *T. Ben.* 9.2; 11.2-3; *Targ. Onk.* Gen. 49.10.

all the Gentiles will turn to fear the Lord God in truth, and will bury their idols. All the Gentiles will praise the Lord, and...the Lord will exalt his people.'

Conclusion

I concur with the conclusion of Michael A. Knibb as representative of a growing consensus on the concept of the exile in many Jewish writings of the Second Temple period: 'Despite many differences in presentation, the writings...seem to share the view that *Israel remains in a state of exile long after the sixth century, and that the exile would only be brought to an end when God intervened in this world order to establish his rule.*'[86] This literature continues to understand the original reason for the exile to be national apostasy which, in accordance with Deuteronomy 27–32, brought a curse upon Israel. According to Ezek. 4.4-8 and the tradition dependent on it, the exile would last some 430 years until a new exodus liberated the people from captivity. According to Daniel 9 and the tradition dependent on it, the exile would last some 490 years, 'to finish [confine] the transgression, to put an end to sin, and to atone for iniquity...' (v. 24).

3. *The Use of Deuteronomy 27.26 in Galatians 3.10 in Light of the Old Testament/Jewish Background*

In light of the confession of national sin in Daniel 9 (and related traditon), we see that in citing Deut. 27.26 (+ 29.19b) in Gal. 3.10,[87] Paul argues not just on the basis of either a 'private reading' of the Old Testament or an eccentric 'retrospective judgment on the law', but rather on the basis of the Deuteronomy 27–32 tradition.[88] For just

86. Knibb, 'The Exile', pp. 271-72 (emphasis mine). Cf. Gowan, 'Exile', p. 216; *idem, Eschatology in the Old Testament* (Philadelphia: Fortress Press, 1986), p. 28.

87. Cf. 1QS 2.4-19, which combines the curse formulae of Deut. 27.15-26 with Deut. 29.17-20, after a communal confession of sin which is oriented on Dan. 9.4-19 (cf. 1QS 1.24–2.1). See further nn. 30, 62 above and 4QDibHam 3.9b-16 (on which see O.H. Steck, *Israel und das gewaltsame Geschick der Propheten: Untersuchungen zur Überlieferung des deuteronomistischen Geschichtsbildes im Alten Testament, Spätjudentum und Urchristentum* [WMANT, 23; Neukirchen–Vluyn: Neukirchener Verlag, 1967], pp. 118-19).

88. We may note here that Paul picks up this tradition again in a similar way in Rom. 2.1-29: cf. vv. 5 (Deut. 31.27), 8 (Deut. 29.27), 9 (Deut. 28.53, 55, 57), 29

as in Dan. 9.11 (καὶ ἐπῆλθεν ἐφ᾽ ἡμᾶς ἡ κατάρα καὶ ὁ ὅρκος ὁ γεγραμμένος ἐν τῷ νόμῳ Μωσῆ παιδὸς τοῦ θεοῦ, ὅτι ἡμάρτομεν αὐτῷ), Paul assumes here that the 'curse' (κατάρα) 'written' in Deuteronomy has come upon Israel because of the nation's sin,[89] and that the curse remains upon the people for a specific period of time until atonement for iniquity is accomplished (Gal. 3.10, 13; 4.4-5; cf. Dan. 9.24). In fact, the likeliest explanation as to why Paul considers Israel to be 'under' a curse (ὑπὸ κατάραν) is that the Deuteronomic 'curse' to which Dan. 9.11 refers came 'upon' the people (ἐφ᾽ ἡμᾶς).[90] Otto Betz has shown Paul's dependence on the Son of Man expectation in Dan. 7.13-14;[91] now we see that Paul's dependence on Daniel is even greater. With Daniel, Paul had at his disposal a tremendous scriptural advantage when he appealed to his Gentile addressees in Galatia to consider the means by which they received the Spirit (Gal. 3.1-5). He could evidently assume that his addressees knew and accepted Daniel 9 and the related Old Testament/Jewish traditions.[92] He could therefore confidently posit in Gal. 3.10 that the threatened curse of Deut. 27.26 had not only come upon Israel historically but also that it continued to abide on the people to his

(Deut. 30.6; *Jub.* 1.23). Hays (*Echoes of Scripture*, pp. 163-64) has recently emphasized the importance of Deuteronomy (esp. the latter chapters) for Paul.

89. This contrasts with much Pauline scholarship on Gal. 3.10 which emphasizes an individualistic interpretation of Deut. 27.26, either in terms of wrong motivation or the impossibility of perfect obedience. Paul himself, however, sees the national scope of Deuteronomy 27–32 from the historical perspective of Old Testament/Jewish tradition. The curse of Deuteronomy 27–32 applies to the nation as a whole. The fact that an individual like Paul the Pharisee can claim to be 'blameless' as to the law (Phil. 3.6) affects neither the cursed status of the nation, which lasts for a specified period of time, nor the individual's need to participate in the restoration (cf. Phil. 3.7-11). Even a man like Daniel, whose righteousness seems to have been renowned (cf. Ezek. 14.14-20?), identified with the sin of his people and confessed his own sin (Dan. 9.5 ['we have sinned'], 20).

90. There is no intended material difference between ὑπὸ κατάραν in Gal. 3.10a and ἐπικατάρατος in the citation (*contra* Stanley, '"Under a Curse"', p. 499); the former is used for the sake of the allusion to Dan. 9.11, which, in turn, also takes up Deuteronomy 27–32.

91. O. Betz, *Jesus und das Danielbuch. II. Die Menschensohnworte Jesu und die Zukunftserwartung des Paulus (Daniel 7,13-14)* (ANTJ, 6.2; Frankfurt a. M.: Peter Lang, 1985).

92. In view of the fact that in Gal. 3.10 Paul refracts Deut. 27.26 through the confession of national sin in Daniel 9.

day.[93] To the question, 'Did you receive the Spirit by works of the law, or by the hearing of faith?' (Gal. 3.2; cf. v. 5), Paul was answering in effect that the former possibility is completely ruled out on the basis of Old Testament/Jewish tradition: the law did not bring the Spirit, but rather a long-term curse on Israel.

That leaves, then, the second alternative as the only viable option: the Galatians received the Spirit by the hearing of faith. Indeed, that is the point toward which Paul's argument moves in Gal. 3.6-14 (cf. v. 14b). Here it is important to realize the traditional framework within which Paul's argument unfolds. In common with Old Testament/Jewish tradition, Paul believes that until the time when God restores them, those who are of works of the law are under a curse due to sin. The fact that the text moves from 'curse' (Gal. 3.10) to 'redemption'[94] from the curse through 'Christ' (v. 13)[95] and from there to the integrally related reception of the 'Spirit' (v. 14; cf. 4.5-6) shows unequivocally that Paul partakes here of restoration tradition.[96] For Deut. 30.1-8 (cf. 32.36-43) promised that if the people fell under the curse of the law, they would be regathered from exile and be restored.[97] The Old Testament prophets call this 'redemption,' comparing the event typologically to the exodus from Egypt.[98] Daniel 9 itself, to give a basis for the plea of deliverance

93. In view of this, Hays's observation that Paul adopts an exilic perspective in describing Israel's plight becomes particularly important (cf. *Echoes of Scripture*, pp. 37, 45-46, 47, 57, 61, 63, 119, 158). Against the Old Testament/ Jewish background, however, we see that this perspective is not a metaphor or a new symbolic world that Paul creates by a private reading of Scripture.

94. On ἐξαγοράζειν in the sense of 'redeem', see Haubeck, *Loskauf*, p. 153.

95. By this point at the latest, it is clear that in Gal. 3.13 the genitive in ἡ κατάρα τοῦ νόμου is not to be construed, with Betz (*Galatians*, p. 149) and others, as a genitive of explanation (the curse which the law itself is), but rather as a subjective genitive (the curse which the law pronounces). This accords with the Septuagintal use of κατάρα with the genitive (cf. Judg. 9.57; Prov. 3.33; Sir. 3.9).

96. For the Old Testament background of τὸ πνεῦμα as εὐλογία see Isa. 44.3 in the context of restoration.

97. Despite the fact that Deuteronomy itself balances the threat of curse by the promise of Restoration, Hays (*Echoes of Scripture*, p. 163) has difficulty reconciling Paul's use of Deuteronomy 27–32 to emphasize both the curse and the promise. The difficulty arises from Hays's mistaken assumption that Gal. 3.10 disparages Deuteronomy as 'a retrograde voice of legalism' (*Echoes of Scripture*, p. 163).

98. Cf. Haubeck, *Loskauf* (n. 72 above). See also, for example, 1 Macc. 4.9-11; Bar. 2.11-18.

from exile, addresses God as the one 'who brought your people out of the land of Egypt...' (v. 15). There is much Old Testament/ Jewish tradition which associates the messiah (Χριστός)[99] with this Second Exodus redemption, even to the extent of typologically comparing the messiah's work with that of Moses. In *Frag. Targ.* Exod. 12.42, for example, the significance of the Passover night is expressed as follows:

> The fourth night: when the world will reach its fixed time to be redeemed; the evil-doers will be destroyed, and the iron yokes will be broken; and Moses will go forth from the midst of the wilderness and the king Messiah, from the midst of Rome: this one will lead at the head of the flock, and that one will lead at the head of the flock; and the *memra* of the Lord will be between both of them; and I and they will proceed together. This is the Passover night before the Lord...[100]

At the time of the messianic redemption, furthermore, Old Testament/ Jewish tradition looked forward to God's bestowing the 'Spirit' on both the messiah and the people of Israel (cf. *T. Jud.* 24.3; *Jub.* 1.23-24). Thus all four elements of Gal. 3.10, 13-14—curse, Christ, redemption, and Spirit—are determined by the traditional expectation.[101] Gal. 3.10 should not be taken in isolation as a reaction against exclusivistic Jewish nationalism (*pace* Dunn); it should be seen together with vv. 13-14 as the negative side of the traditional hope

99. On Paul's use of 'Christ', see esp. M. Hengel, 'Erwägungen zum Sprachgebrauch von Χριστός bei Paulus und in der "vorpaulinischen" Überlieferung', in M.D. Hooker and S.G. Wilson (eds.), *Paul and Paulinism: Essays in Honour of C.K. Barrett* (London: SPCK, 1982), pp. 135-58 (here p. 143): 'When Paul speaks of "Christ", "Jesus Christ", or "Christ Jesus", he is using neither simply the traditional "messianic title", but also not simply a new, arbitrary additional name for Jesus from Nazareth; rather, he indicates... that *alone* this Jesus... is the Redeemer promised by the prophets of the Old Testament.' In Gal. 3.13, the forward thrusting of the anarthrous Χριστός in the asyndetic clause puts special stress on 'Christ'. In view of the possible connection of Gal. 3.13 to Dan. 9.24, does the mention of Χριστός here recall Dan. 9.25-26, which expects a Χριστός to be cut off after 62 (+ 7?) weeks (= 434 [or 483] years)? In both cases, the death of an anointed one is in view.

100. M.L. Klein, *The Fragment-Targums of the Pentateuch according to their Extant Sources* (2 vols.; AnBib, 76; Rome: Biblical Institute Press, 1980), I, p. 167; II, p. 126. On the rabbinic expectation of the future redemption on a Passover, see further Wacholder, 'Chronomessianism', pp. 212-13; A. Strobel, 'Die Passa-Erwartung als urchristliches Problem in Lc 17, 20f', *ZNW* 49 (1958), pp. 157-96; F. Dexinger, 'Exodusmotiv II', *TRE*, X, pp. 739-40.

101. Contrast Sanders, *Paul and Palestinian Judaism*, pp. 511-13.

which looks forward to the inclusion of the Gentiles in the restoration
of Israel (see further below).

4. *Implications of this Traditional Framework*
for the Rest of Galatians 3–4

To recognize the Old Testament/Jewish tradition behind Gal. 3.10, 13-
14 has far-reaching consequences for the interpretation of the rest of
Galatians 3–4, for we begin to see that Paul's thinking in these
chapters is unified by the traditional SER framework. For Paul, the
condition of being 'under the law' (i.e., under the curse of the law)[102]
is limited to the time until Christ, the messianic 'seed' of Abraham,[103]
came (cf. 3.19, 23-25). Gal. 4.4 calls this 'the fulness of time' (τὸ
πλήρωμα τοῦ χρόνου), the time which in *2 Bar.* 29.8 (cf. 29.3; 30.1)
coincides with the appearance with the messiah, and which is used
elsewhere of the end of the exile and/or the beginning of the
restoration.[104] In other words, Paul's view of an extended period of
the curse until the advent of Christ seems to match the protracted exile
before the restoration expected in much Old Testament/Jewish
tradition. Gal. 4.4-5 goes on to state, 'But when the fulness of time

102. For evidence of this metonymy, see immediately below.

103. According to a growing consensus of scholars, Paul's identification of
Christ as the seed of Abraham in Gal. 3.16 is based on the association of the
Abrahamic promise, e.g., in Gen. 17.7 (τὸ σπέρμα σου μετὰ σέ) and the Davidic
promise in 2 Sam. 7.12 (τὸ σπέρμα σου μετὰ σέ): cf. O. Betz, 'Die
heilsgeschichtliche Rolle Israels bei Paulus', *Theologische Beiträge* 9 (1978), pp. 1-
21 (here p. 12); N.A. Dahl, 'Promise and Fulfillment', in *Studies in Paul: Theology
for the Early Christian Mission* (Minneapolis: Augsburg, 1977), pp. 121-36 (here
pp. 130-31); W.A. Meeks, 'Social Functions of Apocalyptic Language in Pauline
Christianity', in D. Hellholm (ed.), *Apocalypticism in the Mediterranean World and
the Near East* (Tübingen: Mohr [Paul Siebeck], 1983), p. 696; D. Juel, *Messianic
Exegesis: Christological Interpretation of the Old Testament in the Early Church*
(Philadelphia: Fortress Press, 1988), pp. 85-88; Hays, *Echoes of Scripture*, p. 85.
The connection with 2 Sam. 7.12 has often been noted by Old Testament scholars:
cf., e.g., R.P. Gordon, *1 and 2 Samuel* (OTG; Sheffield: JSOT Press, 1984),
pp. 238-39; C. Levin, *Die Verheißung des neuen Bundes in ihrem theologischen
Zusammenhang ausgelegt* (FRLANT, 137; Göttingen: Vandenhoeck & Ruprecht,
1985), p. 253; M. Weinfeld, *Deuteronomy and the Deuteronomic School* (Oxford:
Clarendon Press, 1972), pp. 80-81.

104. Cf. Tob. 14.5; 1QpHab. 7.2; *4 Ezra* 4.35-37; 11.44; Mk 1.15. Compare
also Jer. 36(29).10 LXX.

came, God sent his Son...in order that he might redeem those under the law, that we might receive the adoption as sons.' Here the grammatical construction (double purpose clauses with ἵνα) and the vocabulary (ἐξαγοράζειν, [ἀπο]λαμβάνειν) recall Gal. 3.13-14; hence, for God to redeem 'those under the law' (4.5) means that Christ redeemed those who were 'under a curse' (3.10) 'from the curse of the law' by becoming a curse for them (3.13). Once again, we see that the messianic redemption brings deliverance from the curse of the law at the time of the second exodus. That being the case, we may ask whether 'the fulness of time' in Gal. 4.4 presupposes an Old Testament/ Jewish tradition of a predetermined period of time of punishment and curse before the redemption of the new exodus, such as the 490 years of Dan. 9.24 (cf. the exodus typology in v. 15) or the 430 years of Ezek. 4.4-8, which hearkens back to the 430 years of bondage in Egypt before the exodus (Exod. 12.40; cf. Gal. 3.17!)[105]

Gal. 4.4-5 goes beyond 3.13-14 in stating that the purpose for which God sent the messianic Son of God was in order that 'we' might receive the adoption (υἱοθεσία) as sons of God. Isa. 43.1-7 looks forward to the redemption of Israel as sons and daughters of God in a second exodus from the Egypt-like experience of exile (v. 6). This expectation becomes decidedly messianic in *T. Jud.* 24.3 and *Jub.* 1.23, where the divine adoptive sonship of 2 Sam. 7.14 (applied to the messiah in 4QFlor. 1.11) is applied to the eschatological people of God (with the messiah) at the time of the restoration (cf. 2 Cor. 6.18). As in Gal. 4.4-6, furthermore, these SER texts also connect divine adoption with the reception of the Spirit. In fact, the whole train of thought in Galatians 3–4 leads to the conclusion that τὴν υἱοθεσίαν in Gal. 4.5 refers to the divine adoption as sons expected on the basis of the 2 Sam. 7.14 tradition in the time of the restoration of Israel.

---

105. See also on CD 1.3-11a above. On the exegesis of Gal. 4.1-7 as a whole, see my *Adoption as Sons*, pp. 121-86, where many of the following points are elaborated. I argue there that the heir's being no different from a slave ἄχρι τῆς προθεσμίας τοῦ πατρός (Gal. 4.1-2) refers not to a hypothetical illustration from Greco-Roman law, but to Israel's experience of bondage in Egypt (Gen. 15.13). If that is correct, 'the time set by (God) the Father' recalls the 430 years of bondage in Egypt set by God (Exod. 12.40) and prophesied beforehand to Abraham and his seed (Gen. 15.13), to which Paul refers in Gal. 3.17. In that case, 'the fulness of time' (v. 4) in the second half of the comparision of Gal. 4.1-7 corresponds typologically to the time of the exodus from Egypt and inaugurates the second exodus redemption (cf. v. 5).

Paul's argument runs like this. (1) The divine sonship established by υἰοθεσία (Gal. 4.5) makes believers heirs to the Abrahamic promise: εἰ δὲ υἰός, καὶ κληρονόμος (4.7; cf. 3.29). (2) This is because divine sonship and Abrahamic heirship come by participation in Christ, the Son of God: divine sonship is established by faith in Christ Jesus and by being baptized into Christ (3.26-27), and this participation in Christ makes believers the 'seed' of Abraham and 'heirs' to the Abrahamic promise (3.29), since Christ is the 'seed' of Abraham *sensu stricto* (3.16). (3) But Christ is the 'seed' of Abraham (3.16) in that he is the messiah from David's 'seed' (2 Sam. 7.12; cf. Rom. 1.3) and thus fulfills the promise about Abraham's 'seed' (Gen. 15.18).[106] (4) As the seed of David, Christ also fulfills the promise about the messianic 'Son' of God in 2 Sam. 7.14 (cf. Rom. 1.4). (5) Therefore, believers are sons of God by υἰοθεσία and heirs to the Abrahamic promise, in that they participate in the messianic Son of God and heir to Abraham *sensu stricto* who fulfills the promises in 2 Sam. 7.12 and 14. That implies, of course, that the Spirit-impelled cry of 'Abba! Father!' in Gal. 4.6 (cf. Rom. 8.15) represents the impartation of Jesus' own self-understanding as Son to believers (cf. Mk 14.36; Lk. 11.1-4 par.). Thus we begin to see the link between Paul's concept of restoration and Jesus' own.

All of this emphasis on the messianic restoration in Galatians 3–4 is directed to Gentile Christians in Galatia, because according to the traditional expectation,[107] the Gentiles would be included in the restoration of Israel. Paul may handle this issue more definitively in Romans 9–11 and 15, but already here we see the traditional framework of his thinking.[108] Sanders has observed that Paul's Gentile mission is driven by the expectation of the restoration of Israel.[109]

---

106. See n. 103 above.

107. See n. 85.

108. Cf. also T.L. Donaldson, 'The "Curse of the Law" and the Inclusion of the Gentiles: Galatians 3. 13-14', *NTS* 32 (1986), pp. 94-112 (esp. pp. 98-100, 106-107).

109. Cf. Sanders, *Jesus and Judaism*, pp. 93-95; *idem, Paul, the Law, and the Jewish People*, pp. 171-72. Cf. also Hays, *Echoes of Scripture*, p. 162: 'Isaiah offers the clearest expression in the Old Testament of a universalistic, eschatological vision in which the restoration of Israel in Zion is accompanied by an ingathering of Gentiles to worship the Lord; that is why this book is both statistically [28 citations] and substantively the most important scriptural source for Paul.' Hays (*Echoes of Scripture*, pp. 163-64) sees the same framework in Deuteronomy (esp.

Paul takes up this traditional expectation when he states in Gal. 3.13-
14 that the purpose of Christ's redemption was 'in order that in Christ
Jesus the blessing (εὐλογία) of Abraham might come to the Gentiles'.
This recalls the citation of Gen. 12.3 (+ 18.18b)[110] in Gal. 3.8, which
is identified as the gospel promised beforehand to Abraham: 'In you
shall all nations/Gentiles be blessed (ἐνευλογηθήσονται ἐν σοὶ
πάντα τὰ ἔθνη)'. How can Paul say that the Abrahamic blessing of
Gen. 12.3 comes to the Gentiles in Christ the messiah? By *gezerah
shawah*, Paul associates the Abrahamic blessing in Gen. 12.3 (καὶ
ἐνευλογηθήσονται ἐν σοὶ πᾶσαι αἱ φυλαὶ τῆς γῆς) with the
messianic blessing in Ps. 72 (71).17 (καὶ εὐλογηθήσονται ἐν αὐτῷ
πᾶσαι αἱ φυλαὶ τῆς γῆς).[111] Yet this is more than a clever
association of words: the fact that Sir. 44.21 also associates Gen. 12.3
with Ps. 72.17 (and Ps. 72.8 = Zech. 9.10) shows Paul's dependence
on Jewish tradition here. According to Paul, Christ became a servant
to the Jews both in order to fulfill the promises to the patriarchs and
in order that the Gentiles might rejoice with his people Israel (Rom.
15.8-11, citing Deut. 32.43). The messiah is the hope also of the
Gentiles (Rom. 15.12, citing Isa. 11.10).

   The traditional framework of Paul's argument is evident also in the
concluding argument of Galatians 3–4, the provocative allegory in
4.21-31. In v. 21, Paul poses a rhetorical question to the Galatian
Gentile Christians, 'Tell me, you who want to be under the law, do
you not hear the law?' The apostle then proceeds to explain what the
Scriptures say by means of a symbolic representation which
superficially follows the Genesis account of Abraham and his family
in order to drive home his point (vv. 22-31). In view of the fact that
the previous context repeatedly contrasts the negative results of the
law (curse) with the positive results of redemption through Christ
(blessing), and all within the traditional SER framework, we are not
surprised to find a parting shot. The choice of Abraham and his
family as a vehicle of the allegory also stems from the previous
context, where the connection between Abraham and his seed was
made. Yet the way Paul addresses the Galatians ('you who want to be

Deuteronomy 32), another book which Paul uses frequently (15 citations). For Hays
(*Echoes of Scripture*, p. 164), 'Deuteronomy 32 contains Romans *in nuce*'.
   110. Cf. Koch, *Die Schrift als Zeuge*, pp. 124, 162-63.
   111. Note the use of *gezerah shawah* to combine the Abrahamic and Davidic
promises in Gal. 3.16 (see further above) and Rom. 4.3-9.

under the law') shows that his approach in this closing argument is satirical; for, as we have seen above, to be 'under the law' means to be 'under the curse of the law'. Nevertheless, the satirical nature of the passage, identifying as it does unbelieving Israelites and present Jerusalem with slavery, Hagar and Ishmael, must not obscure the fact that the basic point of orientation in the allegory is exactly the same as in the previous context. For Paul's whole allegorical argument unfolds around the concept of restoration in the citation of Isa. 54.1 (v. 27), which, with reference to Isa. 51.1-3 (Abraham, Sarah, and Zion), Paul embellishes in terms of the Genesis story.

Conclusion

In answer to the questions in Gal. 3.1-5, Paul argues in 3.6-29 against the notion that the Galatians received the Spirit by means of works of the law and in favor of the fact that they received it by means of the hearing of faith. As part of his argument, Paul confidently states in Gal. 3.10 that, 'As many as are of works of the law are under a curse', and cites Deut. 27.26 (+ 29.19b) in support of this assertion. Of course, Deut. 27.26 does not expressly state that ὅσοι ἐξ ἔργων νόμου are under a curse, and this has led many scholars to speculate about what kind of assumptions Paul brings to the text. Strangely enough, however, none of these speculations takes into account the Old Testament/Jewish background of Paul's citation. We have seen in light of extensive Old Testament/ Jewish tradition that Paul was making an assumption here that was fairly common in Jewish sources of the Second Temple period: the curses of Deuteronomy 27–32 had indeed fallen upon Israel in (722 and) 587 BCE, and would remain upon the nation until the time of the messianic redemption and the restoration. From Paul's perspective, however, ἦλθεν τὸ πλήρωμα τοῦ χρόνου. The time of the Restoration has come.

More work is needed on the theme of exile and restoration which was so influential in Old Testament and Jewish tradition. This theme may prove to be a key not only to understanding Paul's view of the law, as we have seen here, but also to constructing a comprehensive theology of the New Testament.

Abraham and Idolatry: Paul's Comparison of Obedience to the Law with Idolatry in Galatians 4.1-10

Nancy L. Calvert

From the second century BCE until the mid-second century CE Jewish authors portrayed Abraham as the Jew to be emulated above all others. Because the authors of these accounts of Abraham imported so much into their respective texts, a picture emerges not only of what the pious Jew was indeed to be like, but also of contemporary traditions about Abraham. As is often noted, Paul refers to Abraham in his letter to the churches in Galatia. Paul's Abraham is also to be emulated, albeit by those are 'in Christ'.

This investigation will proceed along the lines of a historical mode of research rather than along the lines of 'intertextual echo'.[1] In keeping with historical methodology,[2] I shall investigate the Abraham tradition at the time of Paul and the situation in which he uses the tradition. Although an investigation of Abraham in Gal. 4.1-10 may seem odd, since he is not explicitly mentioned in the text, my purpose is to show how the understanding of the traditions of Abraham contemporary to Paul lead to the conclusion that the figure of Abraham is indeed implicit in and necessary for a full understanding of Gal. 4.1-10.[3]

---

1. R.B. Hays, *Echoes of Scripture in the Letters of Paul* (New Haven and London: Yale University Press, 1989), pp. 15-21.

2. Hays mentions that one way to understand poetry is from a historical standpoint. This entails understanding the tradition to which the poet's allusion points, specifically, 'the way in which that tradition was understood in the poet's time and the contemporary historical experience or situation with which the poet links the tradition' (*Echoes of Scripture*, p. 18).

3. I am grateful to A.T. Lincoln for his valuable assistance in bringing together my intertestamental studies of Abraham with the Pauline texts and to J. McRay and J.J. Scott for their helpful insights.

1. *The Text: Galatians 4.1-10*

In the section preceding Gal. 4.1-10, Paul has provided his major scriptural argumentation using Abraham as his Old Testament example. He has concluded that all of those who are 'in Christ', Jews and Gentiles, are children of Abraham (3.29). 21 verses later, Paul resumes his use of the Genesis account of Abraham in his allegory built around Sarah and Hagar in 4.1–5.1.

In the text at hand, Paul is describing the former lives of the Jews and Gentiles in the context of the larger questions concerning the purpose of the law (3.12) and sonship (3.26).

In 4.1-2, he uses the imagery of an heir, who, as a child, is under 'guardians and trustees' until the date set by the father. Paul is probably referring to practices in Roman law in which guardians were appointed over a minor by the father either in a will or a court of law. The father could also stipulate the age at which the child would no longer be under such guardians. By using the terms ἐπίτροπος and οἰκονόμος Paul is referring to those who had 'effective control of the person, property, and finances of a minor'.[4] The temporary nature of the law is then asserted. It is in effect until the date set by the father. Meanwhile, the child's affairs are controlled not by himself but by his guardians. In this sense, the heir is no better than the slave.

In 4.3, Paul begins his comparison of the slave/heir with the situation in which believers presently find themselves. Considering Paul's recent discussion of the law as 'confining' (3.23), as a παιδαγωγός (3.25) and as acting as a guardian/trustee (4.1-2), it seems best to understand Paul as meaning Jews when he refers to the minor in 4.3.[5] Additionally, it is these minors who were enslaved to the στοιχεῖα τοῦ κόσμου. Scholars have debated about the meaning of this phrase. A.J. Bandstra maintains that it may be derived from στοῖχος, which was originally a military term meaning 'row'.[6]

---

4.   L.L. Belleville, '"Under Law" in Galatians 3.21–4.11', *JSNT* 26 (1986), p. 63.

5.   See also R.N. Longenecker (*Galatians* [WBC, 41; Dallas: Word Books, 1990], p. 165) who states: 'Paul's application repeats the basic components... God's people in their minority ("minors") being kept under supervisory custody ("enslaved")'.

6.   A.J. Bandstra, *The Law and the Elements of the World: An Exegetical Study*

Bandstra further maintains that the word derives its meaning from the context in which it is used[7] and that 'it seems entirely correct' to understand στοιχεῖα here as the 'fundamental, inherent component forces of the cosmos'.[8] G.B. Caird understands the term to mean 'the demonic forces of legalism...both Jewish and Gentile...'[9] Reicke identifies them with the angels of Gal. 3.19.[10] G. Howard sees the Galatian Gentiles who have accepted circumcision as enslaved once again to the στοιχεῖα τοῦ κόσμου because they are returning to their concept of local deities by losing the distinguishing mark of Christianity, which is 'belief in one God who is the Father of all men'.[11] Although the meaning of the phrase στοιχεῖα τοῦ κόσμου is by no means certain, its function is sure. The στοιχεῖα τοῦ κόσμου functioned to enslave those who turned to them.

In 4.4, Paul reasserts the concept that the previous age of slavery is over. The 'fulness of time' has come, which is parallel to the 'date set by the Father' in v. 2. When the fulness of time had come, God sent his son who was 'born of a woman' and 'born under law'. In v. 5, we are told that the son was sent 'in order that' he might redeem those under the law, presumably meaning Jews. Because the believers at Galatia are sons, God sent them the Spirit of his Son, through which they can experience an intimate relationship with God like that of a son to a father (4.6). If they are sons, they are no longer slaves but heirs (4.7). In 4.7, Paul again refers to the example of the child heir under guardians and stewards in vv. 1-2. The Galatians, presumably both Jews and Gentiles[12], are no longer slaves but true sons. The age of enslavement to the στοιχεῖα τοῦ κόσμου, which functioned as

in Aspects of Paul's Teaching (Kampen: Kok, 1964), p. 31.

7.   *The Law and the Elements of the World*, p. 33.

8.   *The Law and the Elements of the World*, p. 57.

9.   G.B. Caird, *Principalities and Powers* (Oxford: Oxford University Press, 1956), p. 51.

10.   B. Reicke, 'The Law and this World according to Paul: Some Thoughts concerning Gal. 4:1-11', *JBL* 70 (1951), pp. 261-63.

11.   G. Howard, *Paul: Crisis in Galatia* (SNTSMS, 35; Cambridge: Cambridge University Press, 2nd edn, 1991), p. 78.

12.   In 4.6-7 it seems best to assume that Paul is speaking of both Gentiles and Jews at Galatia. In 3.1-5, his proof that the Gentile Galatian Christians are the people of God is the Spirit. In 4.6-7, the Spirit is again proof of their being sons of God. Additionally, he continues his argument in 4.8 by referring to Gentiles who were formerly idolaters.

beliefs and customs which controlled the Jews and Gentiles in their experience previous to being 'in Christ', is over. The age of sonship for both Jews and Gentiles, under the control of the Spirit and evidenced by the Spirit, has begun.

Paul addresses the Gentiles alone in v. 8. In the previous age, they neither knew God, nor were they known by God. They were enslaved by things which by nature 'were not gods'. This phrase (μὴ οὖσιν θεοῖς) is a familiar one in LXX literature, where it refers to idols[13]. The Gentiles were formerly idolaters. Paul is accusing them of returning to their idols. What are the Galatian Gentile Christians actually doing which would cause Paul to make such an accusation?

From the letter itself, we find that Paul contends with persons who are being persuaded by certain 'agitators' to turn to a 'different gospel' (1.6-9). This different gospel is characterized primarily by circumcision (5.2-3; 6.12-13; 2.3-5) and may include other aspects of law, such as the calendrical observances noted in 4.10. The Galatian Gentiles are being persuaded to obey Jewish law. Paul compares their obedience to law to idolatry (4.8) and to enslavement under the στοιχεῖα τοῦ κόσμου (4.9). Thus, both obedience to law and idolatry are forms of enslavement under the στοιχεῖα τοῦ κόσμου (cf. 4.3-5a). Obedience to law is not only a denial that the Gentile Christians are already true children of Abraham; from the perspective of being 'in Christ' their obedience to law is tantamount to worshipping idols.

2. *The Jewish Understanding of Abraham Contemporary to Paul*

Between 200 BCE and 200 CE, Jewish authors were fond of re-interpreting the Genesis accounts of Abraham. Within this diverse literature, Abraham functions in two major ways. Foundationally, he is the first man who believes in the one God. This belief plays itself out in his deeds and speeches, the importance of which revolves around anti-idolatry. The only Old Testament text which alludes to Abraham leaving behind idolatry is Josh. 24.2-3.[14] Since this is the

---

13. For example, see 2 Chron. 13.9b-10; Isa. 37.18-19; Jer. 2.11-28.

14. Josh. 24.2-3 reads: 'And Joshua said to all the people, "Thus says the Lord, the God of Israel: long ago your ancestors—Terah and his sons Abraham and Nahor—lived beyond the Euphrates and served other gods. Then I took your father Abraham from beyond the River and led him through all the land of Canaan and made his offspring many. I gave him Isaac"' (NRSV).

case, the connection between Abraham and idolatry is imported into the text containing 'rewritten Bible'[15] by the early Jewish author in order to speak to the Jews and prospective Jewish proselytes of his day.

The second way that Abraham functions in these texts is that he is obedient to the law even before the law is given to Moses. It should be noted that in the Old Testament this also is mentioned only in passing when Abraham is said to have been obedient to the law in Gen. 26.5.[16] These additions to Jewish texts about Abraham's anti-idolatrous stance and obedience to the law probably mean that they were the concerns of the day. In that case, Abraham functions as a vehicle through which the authors can instruct the reader. It also means that the authors of these texts can instruct us not only about the concerns among Jews of the day, but also in regard to the important characteristics for which Abraham was known.

The tendency to portray Abraham as the archetypal Jewish anti-idolater and monotheist is found in literature spanning three centuries and a variety of geographical areas. This depiction of Abraham is found in Palestinian Jewish texts such as *Jubilees* (c. 168 BCE), Pseudo-Philo's *Liber Antiquitatum Biblicarum* (first century CE), and the *Apocalypse of Abraham* (70–150 CE). The same depiction is found in Hellenistic Jewish texts such as Josephus's *Antiquities*[17] and in the works of Philo.[18] The tendency to portray Abraham as obedient to law is also found in a few of these texts, although this portrayal of Abraham is not as pronounced as the first portrayal. The *Genesis Apocryphon* (first century BCE) and the *Testament of Abraham* (first to second century CE) do not portray Abraham in these ways; they will be noted in the following, however, in order that all the accounts of Abraham may be considered.

Each of the Palestinian Jewish texts seems to have been written with

15. In referring to 'rewritten Bible' I mean both Palestinian and Hellenistic Jewish texts near the turn of the era 'which take as their literary framework the flow of the biblical text itself and apparently have as their major purpose the clarification and actualization of the biblical story' (D.J. Harrington, 'Palestinian Adaptations of Biblical Narratives and Prophecies', in R.A. Kraft and G.W.E. Nickelsburg [eds.], *Early Judaism and its Modern Interpreters* [Atlanta: Scholars Press, 1986], p. 239).

16. Gen. 26.5 reads: '...because Abraham obeyed my voice and kept my charge, my commandments, my statutes, and my laws'.

17. For example, see *Ant.* 1.154-157.

18. For example, see *Virt.* 212-216; *Abr.* 68-71.

the purpose of encouraging Jews to maintain their beliefs and practices while living in the midst of Hellenistic culture. In *Jubilees*, Abraham leaves behind his idol-worshipping country and family in order to follow the true God.[19] He even tries to persuade his father, Terah, that idol worship is vanity. The speech that Abraham gives is meant not only for Terah, but for the readers of *Jubilees* as well:

> What help or advantage do we have from these idols before which you
>   worship and bow down?
> Because there is not any spirit in them, for... they are the misleading of
>   the heart.
> Do not worship them.
> Worship the God of heaven,
> who sends down rain and dew upon the earth,
> and who makes everything... by his word,
> and all life is in his presence.
> Why do you worship those who have no spirit in them?
> Because they are works of the hands,
> and you are carrying them upon your shoulders,
> and there is no help from them for you,
> except great shame for those who made them
> and the misleading of the heart for those who worship them.
> Do not worship them (*Jub.* 12.2b-5).[20]

Abraham's speech functions on two levels: the level of the story, in which Abraham is warning Terah not to worship idols, and at the level of the contemporary reader who is being told of the futility of idol-worship. This is important not only for Jewish readers of the text, but also for potential proselytes. Abraham provides an example for proselytes of one who leaves his religion and family behind and follows the true God.

Later in *Jubilees*, Abraham announces the importance of being separate from the Gentiles since the Gentiles are idolaters and as such are without law:

> Separate yourself from the gentiles,
> and do not eat with them,
> and do not perform deeds like theirs.
> And do not become associates of theirs.

---

19. *Jub.* 11.16-17; 12.2-8, 16-24; cf. Josh. 24.2-3, n. 14.

20. All quotations from Palestinian Jewish literature are taken from J.H. Charlesworth (ed.), *The Old Testament Pseudepigrapha* (2 vols.; Garden City, NY: Doubleday, 1983–85). Hereafter *OTP*.

> Because their deeds are defiled,
> and all of their ways are contaminated and despicable, and abominable.
> ... they have no heart to perceive,
> and they have no eyes to see what their deeds are,
> and where they wander astray,
> saying to the tree, 'you are my god';
> and to a stone, 'you are my lord, and you are my savior'
> and they have no heart.
> But (as for) you, my son, Jacob,
> may the God Most High... bless you.
> And may he turn you from their defilement
> and from all their errors (*Jub.* 22.16-19).

Again, this speech functions on two levels. Abraham is warning his grandson Jacob about the evil ways of the Gentiles based upon their idolatry. Because Jacob believes in the true God, he will follow the law, which in *Jubilees* is from before the time of Abraham.[21] Abraham himself observes aspects of the law.[22] In addition, the author of *Jubilees* capitalizes on the idea that not being circumcised is equal to being cast out of the covenant people, adding that those who are not circumcised not only have broken the covenant, but that they are 'destined to be destroyed and annihilated from the earth'.[23] The speech, Abraham's exemplary behavior, and the necessity of circumcision all serve to instruct the child of Abraham. He or she is to separate from Gentiles and their immoral practices. Faith in the one God and the observance of law are inseparable. They identify the children of Abraham.

In Pseudo-Philo, Abraham demonstrates his belief in God first by refusing to contribute to the building of the Tower of Babel. According to the author, contributing a brick to the tower was equal to participating in idolatry. When Abraham and the others were asked to contribute a brick, they answered, 'We are not casting bricks, nor are we joining in your scheme. We know the one Lord, and him we worship. Even if you throw us into the fire with the bricks, we will not join you' (*LAB* 6.4). Their request is answered; those building the

21. In *Jub.* 1.27-29, the angel of the presence dictates the law to Moses beginning with creation.

22. For example, see *Jub.* 15.1-2 where Abraham observes the Feast of the Firstfruits (cf. Lev. 23.15-20) and *Jub.* 16.20-21 where he observes the feast of Booths (cf. Lev. 23.34-43).

23. *Jub.* 15.26-27; cf. Gen. 17.9-14.

tower agree to throw the believers into the fire. All but Abraham find a way of escape. Abraham alone trusts in God enough to stay and face the consequences. Abraham is saved from the flames while 83,500 are burned. In Pseudo-Philo, Abraham functions as the first example of belief in God and rejection of idolatry.[24] Subsequent leaders of Israel who are idolaters perish.[25] Concerning the place of Abraham in Pseudo-Philo's *LAB*, Frederick J. Murphy states, 'Israel begins with Abraham's rejection of idolatry and the choice to serve God'.[26]

The structure of *LAB* itself is much like that of the book of Judges since it capitalizes upon the historic leaders of Israel. This may indicate that within his situation the author was interested in depicting leaders of old, since no good leaders currently existed. Whether a leader was good or bad depended to a large degree upon his or her fidelity to the true God. Abraham was the first example of such fidelity. Those leaders who maintained belief in the one God and avoided idolatry prospered; those who bowed down to foreign idols were destroyed. The function of *LAB* is to recall Israel to its true identity, which is founded upon 'its exclusive and uncompromising loyalty to God'.[27] For the Jews of the first century CE, the historic principles would still apply. Their loyalty to their one God distinguished them from the rest of the nations, and, as children of Abraham, they were constrained to remain faithful to that belief.

The *Apocalypse of Abraham* provides us with the most dramatic narrative depicting Abraham's rejection of idolatry. It is composed in two parts: chs. 1–8 contain narratives concerning Abraham, while the rest of the book gives the account of the revelation to Abraham. In true Hellenistic fashion, Abraham 'reasons' in chs. 1–7 that the gods of his father Terah, the idol-maker, cannot be the true God.

The culmination of his reasoning comes in ch. 7 when Abraham prays for God to reveal himself. It is a fitting preamble to the revelation which follows. Although ch. 7 may be an insertion,[28] the

---

24. 'And when all those inhabiting the land were being led astray after their own devices, Abraham believed in me and was not led astray with them' (*LAB* 23.5; *OTP*, II, pp. 332-33).

25. For example, see the stories of Aod (*LAB* 34) and Micah (*LAB* 44).

26. F.J. Murphy, 'Retelling the Bible: Idolatry in Pseudo-Philo', *JBL* 107 (1988), p. 276.

27. 'Retelling the Bible', p. 284.

28. R. Rubinkiewicz, 'Apocalypse of Abraham', in *OTP*, I, p. 684.

methods which Abraham uses to reason that there is one God are similar to those found in Philo and Josephus.[29]

In response to Abraham's reasoning, God reveals himself.

> ... the voice of the Mighty One came down from the heavens in a stream of fire, saying and calling, 'Abraham! Abraham!' And I said, 'Here I am.' And he said, 'You are searching for the God of gods, the Creator, in the understanding of your heart. I am he. Go out from Terah, your father...' (*Apoc. Abr.* 8.1-4).

At the conclusion of the apocalypse, Abraham is taken up into the heavens where he is shown the vindication of Israel (*Apoc. Abr.* 31.1, 4). This vindication is especially important since the *Apocalypse of Abraham* was written after the destruction of the Temple (*Apoc. Abr.* 27.1-7). According to the text, the Temple was destroyed because of the idolatry practiced by the seed of Abraham (*Apoc. Abr.* 25; 27.7). Those who are Abraham's true children will remain faithful to the one God (29.17). However, those who worship other gods will be destroyed along with the Gentiles:

> For the makers... who have chosen my desire and manifestly kept my commandments... will rejoice with merrymaking over the downfall of the men who remain and who followed after the idols and after their murders. For they shall putrefy in the belly of the crafty worm Azazel, and be burned by the fire of Azazel's tongue... and they glorified an alien (god). And they abandoned the Lord who gave them strength (*Apoc. Abr.* 31.4-8).

What is noticeable here is that besides their adhering to the worship of the one true God, those who are vindicated have also kept God's 'commandments'. Although Abraham is not depicted as obeying the law in the *Apocalypse of Abraham*, as he is in *Jubilees*, it is still important that the children of Abraham adhere to commandments of God.

In conclusion, these texts have provided us with a glimpse of how Abraham was portrayed in Palestinian Jewish literature. As noted, our first three texts re-interpreted the Genesis account whereby they

---

29. In *Apoc. Abr.* 7 Abraham reasons that idols are consumed by fire, which is overcome by water. Water, however, is subject to the earth, which in turn is subordinate to the sun. However, the sun is obscured at night by the moon and clouds, which also eventually dim. Thus, none of these things is God, but God directs them all. In the works of Philo and Josephus, Abraham also reasons that God exists by his observation of natural phenomena.

portrayed the figure of Abraham as the archetypal Jew. As such, he believed in God and rejected idolatry. To a lesser degree, he also obeyed the law. The re-interpretations provided an example for Jewish readers and potential proselyte Gentiles.

Two Palestinian Jewish texts which do not portray Abraham as the archetypal monotheist and anti-idolater are the *Genesis Apocryphon*[30] and the *Testament of Abraham*. In the *Genesis Apocryphon*, Abraham is portrayed as the wise man in the sense that he practices a form of eastern mantic wisdom. He dreams and interprets dreams (1QapGen 19.16-23), he dispenses wisdom (19.23-25), and he is a healer and exorcist (20.29). The Gentiles in the text benefit from his healing, and are unable to match his 'magic' (col. 20). The message of the text seems to be that the power of the Jewish God is greater than the power of the Gentile gods. Abraham beats the Gentiles at their own pagan 'games'. The text, then, does not portray Abraham as being against idolatry. However, it does portray him as a man of faith.

The *Testament of Abraham*, however, has an entirely different message. In this text, God tries repeatedly to bring about the death of Abraham through one of his mediators. Abraham repeatedly refuses, and is finally taken by surprise.[31] Between the various attempts to bring about Abraham's death, Abraham is taken to heaven. It is revealed that the twelve tribes will participate in the judgment process (13.6). The God of Israel reigns over heaven (cf. 8.1-2). However, judgment is not based upon Torah, but upon commonplace moral values. The soteriology of the text is universalistic—all are judged according to their deeds (11.9). It is Abraham's self-righteousness which gets him into trouble. He later repents of this self-righteousness (14.10-15). Abraham is portrayed as the father of the Jewish people in the *Testament of Abraham*, but not as having particularly great faith. The text does indicate the belief that it was the God of the Jews who

30. All references to the *Genesis Apocryphon* are found in J.A. Fitzmyer, *The Genesis Apocryphon of Qumran Cave I: A Commentary* (BibOr, 18A; Rome: Pontifical Biblical Institute, 2nd edn, 1971), pp. 49-75. References to the *Testament of Abraham* are found in E.P. Sanders, 'The Testament of Abraham', in *OTP*, I, pp. 882-95. All references are to recension A.

31. This would certainly explain why Abraham is not portrayed as giving a last testament in the Genesis account.

reigned over heaven, and consequently that their God was the true God.[32]

Before returning to Galatians, it is necessary also to inquire of Hellenistic Jewish texts which are contemporary to Paul. Philo (late first century BCE to first century CE) contains seemingly unending potrayals of Abraham. This entire chapter could be constructed around what Philo does with Genesis 12–15. However, for the purpose of further understanding Galatians, the texts in which Abraham is portrayed as believing in God and rejecting idolatry and as being obedient to law will be considered.

Philo's work is avowedly apologetic. He is interested in showing Gentiles that the Jewish faith is not only valid but, in many cases, superior to other beliefs. He is also interested in providing Jews who may be on the verge of apostasy with reasons not to turn from their religion. In support of his apologetic ends, Philo dresses Abraham in Hellenistic garb. Abraham possesses virtue, is endowed with excellent reason and rhetorical abilities (*Rer. Div. Her.* 26-30), has a good reputation, and is hospitable (*Abr.* 107-108). He possesses the four Greek cardinal virtues (*Migr. Abr.* 13): justice, wisdom (even beyond that provided by the Greek educational system, the *encyclia*; *Leg. All.* 3.244-245), self-control (Stoic reason over emotion; *Abr.* 242-244), and courage (he is honest with superiors, *Rer. Div. Her.* 5; he is a warrior, *Abr.* 225).

However, even though he is garbed in Hellenism, one is also able to see clearly that Abraham is a Jew. According to Philo, Abraham is the first to turn from polytheism to belief in the one true God. This change entailed not only the rejection of idolatry, but the ability to reason that one God indeed did exist. Philo maintains that Abraham was the son of an astrologer, one of those who

> think that the stars and the whole heaven and universe are gods, the authors... of the events which befall each man for good or for ill and hold that there is no originating cause outside the things which were perceived by our senses. What could be more grievous or more capable of proving the total absence of nobility in the soul than this, that its knowledge of the many, the secondary, the created, only leads it to ignore the One, the Primal, the Uncreated and Maker of all... Perception of these truths and divine inspiration induced him [Abraham] to leave his native country, his

32. As in many Jewish texts of the time, Abraham is said to be the 'friend of God'; cf. *T. Abr.* 4.7; 8.1-2; 20.14; and also Jas 2.23.

race, and paternal home, knowing that if he stayed the delusions of the polytheistic creed would stay within him and render it impossible for him to discover the One who alone is eternal and the father of all things... whereas if he removed, the delusions would also remove from his mind and its false creed be replaced by the truth... he is the first person spoken of as believing in God, since he first grasped a firm and unswerving conception of the truth that there is one Cause above all, and that it provided for the world and all there is therein (*Virt.* 212-216).[33]

In addition to the portrayal of Abraham leaving polytheism behind for monotheism, Philo's depiction of Abraham is similar to that found in *Jubilees* because he also maintains that Abraham obeyed the law before it was actually given to Moses. Philo introduces *De Abrahamo* by stating:

since it is necessary to carry out our examination of the law in regular sequence, let us postpone consideration of particular laws which are, so to speak, copies, and examine first those which are more general and may be called the originals of those copies. These are such men as lived good and blameless lives, whose virtues stand permanently recorded in the most holy scriptures, not merely to sound their praises but for the instruction of the reader and as an inducement to him to aspire to the same; for in these men we have laws endowed with life and reason, and Moses extolled them for two reasons. First, he wished to show that the enacted ordinances are not inconsistent with nature; and secondly, that those who wish to live in accordance with the laws as they stand have no difficult task, seeing that the first generations before any at all of the particular statutes was set in writing followed the unwritten law with perfect ease, so that one might properly say that the enacted laws are nothing else than memorials of the lives of the ancients, preserving to a later generation their actual words and deeds (*Abr.* 3-6).[34]

In Philo, the Torah is the revelation of the natural law to Moses. The natural law was the popular Hellenistic concept of law. By equating Torah with the natural law, Philo is making the concept of Jewish law attractive to his Hellenistic audience. At the same time, he is validating the law in the eyes of the Jewish reader who may be interested in attaining status within Philo's milieu, the Hellenistic world of Alexandria.

33. F.H. Colson, *Philo* (LCL, 8; Cambridge, MA: Harvard University Press, 1939), pp. 293-95. For similar statements about Abraham, see also *Abr.* 68-71; *Rer. Div. Her.* 97-99; *Mut. Nom.* 16-17.

34. Colson, *Philo*, pp. 5-7.

The figure of Abraham makes at least two things clear to the reader. In order to emulate Abraham, one should believe in the one God and obey the law. This belief in one God is made active in the avoidance of idolatry, particularly the idolatry of astrological speculation. The literal obedience to the law is also a mark of the child of Abraham.[35] According to the works of Philo, then, for one to be a true child of Abraham, one must believe in the one God and obey the law.

Josephus's *Antiquities of the Jews* (late first century CE) provides us with the last extensive portrayal of Abraham. Like Philo, Josephus is concerned to provide an apologetic for Judaism. With this in mind, he also portrays Abraham as a Hellenist. Abraham is hospitable and virtuous (*Ant.* 1.165, 256) and broad-minded. He is the perfect combination of philosopher (*Ant.* 1.161), rhetorician (*Ant.* 1.154-155), ambassador (*Ant.* 1.161), and military commander (*Ant.* 1.176-178). He is concurrently the father of culture (*Ant.* 1.166-167) who teaches arithmetic and astronomy to the Egyptians, who in turn instruct the Greeks in the same subjects.

One of the most noticeable themes in Josephus's portrayal of Abraham is Abraham proving monotheism through the use of reason (*Ant.* 1.154-157). It is actually because of this viewpoint that those in Chaldea 'rise against him', leading to his emigration (*Ant.* 1.157). According to Josephus, Abraham

> was...the first boldly to declare that God, the creator of the universe, is one, and that, if any other being contributed aught to man's welfare, each did so by his command and not in virtue of its own inherent power. This he inferred from the changes to which land and sea are subject, from the course of the sun and moon, and from all the celestial phenomena, for, he argued, were these bodies endowed with power, they would have provided for their own regularity, but since they lacked this last, it was manifest that...they render not in virtue of their own authority, but through the might of their commanding sovereign...it was in fact owing to these opinions that the Chaldeans and the other peoples of Mesopotamia rose against him... (*Ant.* 1.154-157).[36]

35. In *Migr. Abr.* 89-93 Philo argues that although the law has symbolic meanings, it is still to be practiced literally.

36. H.St.J. Thackeray, *Josephus: Jewish Antiquities Books I–IV* (LCL, 4; Cambridge, MA: Harvard University Press, 1930), pp. 77-79.

The proofs which Abraham uses in the above are similar to the form of the proofs for the existence of God promulgated by the Greek philosophic schools. The difference is that while the Greek philosophic schools used the regularity of the planets to prove the existence of God, Josephus maintains that Abraham proved the same through the irregularity of the planets.

Josephus does not depict Abraham as obeying the Mosaic law. However, Abraham is virtuous, which was an important Hellenistic concept related to natural law. Circumcision is mentioned in the Abraham story. When Isaac is eight days old, Abraham has him circumcised, 'to the intent that his posterity should be kept from mixing with others' (*Ant.* 1.192-193). Whether this is a prohibition against intermarriage is not clear. What is clear, however, is that circumcision signifies separation from the Gentiles.

Those Jews reading Josephus find their religion has been validated in the eyes of Hellenistic culture. Abraham is worthy of emulation from a Hellenistic viewpoint. However, he is still very much a Jew. He believes in one God. Because of this belief, he was forced to leave his homeland behind. The form of polytheism mentioned by Josephus is obviously related to astrology. Potential proselytes see in Abraham an example of one who leaves polytheism behind through reason. Abraham also had Isaac circumcised, which symbolised separation from the Gentiles. The children of Abraham, then, believe in one God and practice circumcision.

These Palestinian and Hellenistic Jewish texts have provided us with a glimpse of the important characteristics of Abraham for Jews roughly contemporary to Paul. Abraham is portrayed as one who rejects idolatry for belief in the one God, and to some degree as one who is obedient to the Jewish law. In conclusion, then, the way to be a child of Abraham was to remain faithful to the one true God by avoiding idolatry and to obey the law.

3. *Conclusion: Paul's Implied Reference to Abraham in Galatians 4.1-10*

A variety of scholars have noted the importance of Abraham in Paul's argumentation in his epistle to the Galatians.[37] Paul's use of Abraham

37. For example, see J.C. Beker, *Paul the Apostle: The Triumph of God in Life and Thought* (Philadelphia: Fortress Press, 1980), pp. 44-47; B.H. Brinsmead,

is usually attributed to Gal. 3.6-29 and 4.21–5.1. More often than not, it is also maintained that Paul's opponents used Abraham in their own argumentation. If the traditions about Abraham which we have discussed were popular, it may have been that these opponents were persuading the Gentile Galatian believers that now that they had rejected literal idolatry as Abraham had done, in order to be the true people of God they must now also obey the Jewish law.

In the epistle, Paul has consistently argued against the Galatians' being obedient to the law. The law is a curse (3.13), it produces transgressions and was mediated by angels rather than by the one God (3.19). The law is unable to impart salvation (3.21), and it is a form of enslavement (4.3-5) to the στοιχεῖα τοῦ κόσμου. Finally, Paul equates the law with idolatry (4.3, 8-10), since it also was a form of enslavement to the στοιχεῖα τοῦ κόσμου.

Both Jews and Gentiles are now true sons of Abraham (3.29; 4.6-7) which means that they are no longer slaves, but true sons and heirs. The outlined Jewish traditions about Abraham the anti-idolater and monotheist illuminate Gal. 4.1-10[38] because according to them the true children of Abraham are to avoid idolatry. Since Abraham was the archetypal anti-idolater, Paul makes the law the ultimate taboo for a child of Abraham by equating observance of law with idolatry.[39]

Galatians: Dialogical Response to Opponents (Chico, CA: Scholars Press, 1982), p. 114; J. Barclay, *Obeying the Truth: A Study of Paul's Ethics in Galatians* (Edinburgh: T. & T. Clark, 1988), p. 54. For a survey, see G.W. Hansen, *Abraham in Galatians: Epistolary and Rhetorical Contexts* (JSNTSup, 29; Sheffield: JSOT Press, 1989), p. 167.

38. If traditions about Abraham are implicit in Gal. 4.1-9, they may be implicit in 4.12-20 as well. In several early Jewish texts, Abraham is known for his hospitality (cf. *T. Abr.* 1.1; *Ant.* 1.196; *Abr.* 108-110). Paul mentions that the Galatians had received him like an 'angel of God' (Gal. 4.14). This may be an implicit parallel between their behavior and that of the hospitable behavior of Abraham to the messengers of God in Genesis 18–19, who are eventually referred to as 'angels' (Gen. 19.1; cf. the LXX). H.D. Betz (*Galatians: A Commentary on Paul's Letter to the Churches of Galatia* [Hermeneia; Philadelphia: Fortress Press, 1979], p. 226) notes the similarity between the Galatians' receiving Paul like an angel and the tradition in Genesis 18–19.

39. It may be feasible, since Paul makes implicit references to Abraham in Gal. 4.1-10, that his reference to the στοιχεῖα τοῦ κόσμου also contains another implied meaning. As we have seen from our survey of the Abraham material in early Jewish literature, Abraham was known particularly for his leaving behind idolatry in the form of astrology. Perhaps, then, the implied references to traditions about

The opponents of Paul, presumably Jewish Christians,[40] had been compelling the Gentile Christians in Galatia to live like Jews by adding the concept of law to the gospel. However, in his letter to the Galatians, Paul has used the Abraham traditions for his own purposes. Now that the Christians in Galatians are also children of Abraham by virtue of being 'in Christ', the idolatry which they are to avoid is obedience to the law.

Abraham also include an implied reference to astrology in Paul's use of the στοιχεῖα τοῦ κόσμου, which, like idolatry, formerly functioned to enslave the Gentile Christians in Galatia. See also Caird, *Principalities and Powers*, pp. 50-51.

40. J. Barclay, 'Mirror-Reading a Polemical Letter', *JSNT* 31 (1987), p. 88.

ASCENDING AND DESCENDING WITH A SHOUT:
PSALM 47.6 AND 1 THESSALONIANS 4.16

Craig A. Evans

The apostle Paul consoled Christians of the Thessalonian congregation, who had apparently experienced bereavement, with a fascinating apocalyptic description of Christ's return and the resurrection of believers:

> For this we say to you by the word of the Lord, that we who are alive and remain until the coming of the Lord will not precede those who sleep; because the Lord himself will descend from heaven with a shout, with the voice of the archangel, and with the trumpet of God, and the dead in Christ will rise first, then we who are alive and remain will be taken up together with them in the clouds to meet the Lord in the air (1 Thess. 4.15-17a).

It is obvious that many of these elements reflect well-known images in apocalyptic ideas and literatures current in Paul's time. Assessment of this background, however, has remained vague and imprecise, particularly with respect to v. 16. I believe that this is the case because an important background text and its exegesis in late antiquity have not been properly recognized and taken into account. This brief study, which limits itself to an analysis of 1 Thess. 4.16, will attempt to remedy this oversight.

Previous Discussion

Several passages have been suggested as the background against which Paul's apocalyptic picture of Jesus' return in 1 Thess. 4.16 may be viewed. In the New Testament the closest parallels are found in 1 Cor. 15.51-52 ('Behold, I tell you a mystery; all will not sleep, but all will be changed... for the trumpet will sound and the dead will be raised...'), in Mt. 24.31 ('and [the Son of Man] will send his angels with the great trumpet, and they will gather his elect...'), and in Rev. 11.12, 15

('They went up to heaven in a cloud...then the seventh angel blew his trumpet, and there were loud voices in heaven'). It is clear that the three passages are related. But what is less clear are the biblical antecedents. Among the most frequently suggested are Isa. 27.13 ('in that day they will sound a great trumpet'), Zech. 9.14 ('the Lord Almighty will sound the trumpet'), Joel 2.1 ('Sound the trumpet in Zion...for the Day of the Lord is present'), Zeph. 1.14-16 ('the great Day of the Lord is near...the day of the trumpet'), and *4 Ezra* 6.23 ('and the trumpet shall sound with a din, and when all hear it, they shall suddenly be terrified').[1] All of these texts contribute to the general idea of the eschatological trumpet, a trumpet that signals coming judgment and redemption. But none of these texts can be said to underlie 1 Thess. 4.16.

A Proposed Solution

There are two passages in the LXX that contain most of the vocabulary found in 1 Thess. 4.16. Curiously enough, these passages have not often been brought into the discussion. The first passage is Exod. 19.16-20, which describes Yahweh's descent upon Mount Sinai:

> When it was morning on the third day there were thunders and lightnings and a thick cloud upon Mount Sinai, and a loud sound of a trumpet... and Moses led the people out to meet God... and Mount Sinai was enveloped in smoke because God had descended upon it in fire and the smoke went up... as the sounds of the trumpet grew louder, Moses spoke and God answered him in a voice, and the Lord descended upon Mount Sinai... and Moses went up.

This passage contains most of the vocabulary found in 1 Thess. 4.16. There is the 'sound of the trumpet' (φωνὴ τῆς σάλπιγγος) and the descent of the Lord (κατέβη κύριος). Also, the references to the cloud in v. 16 and the meeting between God and Moses in v. 20 parallel items in 1 Thess. 4.17.

Early patristic interpretation, however, makes no connection between Exodus 19 and 1 Thessalonians 4. The Fathers tended to draw morals and spiritual lessons from Exodus 19 (e.g., abstaining from sensual pleasures and pursuits in order to hear the word of God).[2] No

---

1. All citations are according to the LXX, with the exception of *4 Ezra*, whose text is taken from the Vulgate.

2. See, e.g. Clement, *Stromateis* 3.11; Cyprian, *Treatises* §32.

examples of eschatological interpretation, at least not in the early Fathers, can be found. Even Cyprian's interpretation (*Treatises* §101), in which he links Exod. 19.18 ('and the whole of Mount Sinai smoked, because God had come down upon it in fire') with Acts 2.2-4 ('...and there appeared cloven tongues as if of fire...'), is not really eschatological. His point was simply to document his claim that the Holy Spirit frequently appeared in fire.

Rabbinic interpretation is more intriguing. Commenting on the first part of Exod. 19.3 ('And Moses went up to God') one midrash cites Ps. 68.19 (v. 18 in most translations: 'Thou didst ascend the high mount...') and says that Moses wrestled with angels 'on high' in order to receive Torah, a gift from heaven (cf. *Exod. R.* 28.1 [on 19.3]). It is interesting to observe that the New Testament interprets this verse against the ascension of Jesus and the descent of the Holy Spirit (cf. Eph. 4.8-10). The next section of the midrash adds: '[Moses] went up in a cloud and descended in a cloud, the merit of the fathers ascended and descended with him' (*Exod. R.* 28.2 [on 19.3]).[3]

The second passage, however, is more promising. Ps. 47.6 (46.6 in the LXX; 47.5 in most translations) contains most of the vocabulary found in 1 Thess. 4.16. Unlike the longer passage from Exodus 19, the linguistic parallels are found in a single verse made up of two synonymous lines:

Psalm 47	LXX Psalm 46	1 Thessalonians 4
עלה אלהים בתרועה	ἀνέβη ὁ θεὸς ἐν	αὐτὸς ὁ κύριος ἐν
יהוה בקול שופר	ἀλαλαγμῷ κύριος ἐν	κελεύσματι ἐν φωνῇ
	φωνῇ σάλπιγγος	ἀρχαγγέλου καὶ
		ἐν σάλπιγγι θεοῦ
		καταβήσεται ἀπ'
		οὐρανοῦ

Seven of the nine words of LXX Ps. 46.6 are found in 1 Thess. 4.16. The principal parallels are as follows. (1) The main verb is -βαίνω, ἀναβαίνω in the LXX, καταβαίνω in Paul's epistle. (2) The subject of both is θεός/κύριος. (3) Whereas in the LXX God ascends ἐν ἀλαλαγμῷ ('with a joyous shout'; that this shout is indeed joyful is confirmed by the parallel line in v. 2: ἀλαλάξατε τῷ θεῷ ἐν φωνῇ ἀγαλλιάσεως ['shout to God with a voice of rejoicing']), in Paul the

3. Translation based on S.M. Lehrman, 'Exodus', in H. Freedman and M. Simon (ed.), *Midrash Rabbah* (10 vols.; London and New York: Soncino), III, p. 332.

Lord descends ἐν κελεύσματι ('with a command'). This is the only important difference. The significance of this difference will be considered below. (4) Whereas the LXX reads ἐν φωνῇ σάλπιγγος ('with the sound of a trumpet'), the saying in 1 Thessalonians reads ἐν φωνῇ ἀρχαγγέλου ('with the sound [or voice] of the archangel') and ἐν σάλπιγγι θεοῦ ('with the trumpet of God'). (5) Although the LXX does not explicitly say that God ascended into heaven, which would correspond with Paul's explicit statement that the Lord will descend ἀπ' οὐρανοῦ ('from heaven'), the text could, and in fact was, so interpreted. The only truly unparalleled component is the appearance of ἀρχαγγέλου ('archangel'). Its appearance in a context such as this is, of course, not difficult to explain. Angels and archangels play prominent roles in the Jewish and Christian literatures of late antiquity, especially in apocalyptic (cf. Dan. 10.13, 21; 12.1; *4 Ezra* 4.36; Mk 13.27; Jude 9; Rev. 7.1; 8.2; 12.7 *passim*). Moreover, the appearance of an angel in this 'word of the Lord' is an important link with Mt. 24.31, which says that angels will be sent out with a loud trumpet call.

One obvious point that could tell against LXX Ps. 46.6 as the biblical text echoed in 1 Thess. 4.16 is that whereas the latter speaks of *descent*, the former speaks of *ascent*. Perhaps this explains why few commentators, despite such a high percentage of verbal agreement, have considered this verse from the Greek Psalter. One exception is C.F.D. Moule, who suggests, almost in passing, that the words of 1 Thess. 4.16 may possibly be a 'reminiscence' of Ps. 47.6.[4] Only a few others have cited the passage;[5] many have not.[6]

4. C.F.D. Moule, *The Origin of Christology* (Cambridge: Cambridge University Press, 1977), p. 42. F.F. Bruce (*1 & 2 Thessalonians* [WBC, 45; Waco, TX: Word Books, 1982], p. 101) notes Moule's comparison, but makes no comment.
5. E.g. E. von Dobschütz, *Die Thessalonicher-Briefe* (Göttingen: Vandenhoeck & Ruprecht, 1909), p. 196; A. Plummer, *A Commentary on St Paul's First Epistle to the Thessalonians* (London: Robert Scott, 1918), p. 76; W. de Boor, *Die Briefe des Paulus an die Thessalonicher* (Weppertal: Brockhaus, 1960), p. 82 n. 60.
6. E.g. J.E. Frame, *The Epistles of St Paul to the Thessalonians* (ICC; Edinburgh: T. & T. Clark, 1912), pp. 174-75; M. Dibelius, *An die Thessalonicher* (HNT, 11; Tübingen: Mohr [Paul Siebeck], 1937), p. 26; A.L. Moore, *1 and 2 Thessalonians* (The Century Bible; London: Nelson, 1969), p. 71; E. Best, *A Commentary on the First and Second Epistles to the Thessalonians* (BNTC; London: A. & C. Black, 1972), pp. 196-97; J.M. Reese, *1 and 2 Thessalonians* (Wilmington, DE: Michael Glazier, 1979), p. 53; I.H. Marshall, *1 and 2 Thessalonians* (NCB;

The *Nachleben* of Psalm 47 supports Moule's suggestion. In the following paragraphs I shall examine patristic and Jewish interpretations.

Patristic Exegesis

The possibility that the language and imagery of Ps. 47(46).6 do indeed lie behind 1 Thess. 4.16 is supported by patristic exegesis. Several Fathers interpret the verse from Psalm 47(46) as a prophecy of Christ's ascension. This approach is widely attested in the Greek Fathers:

1. Justin Martyr cites Ps. 47(46).6 as proof that the Old Testament predicted the ascension of Christ and his enthronement in heaven (cf. *Dialogus cum Tryphone* §37 and §38).

2. John Chrysostom repeatedly cites and interprets Ps. 47(46).6 with reference to the ascension: 'And with reference to the ascension [ἀνάληψις]: [Scripture says] "God went up with a shout"'.[7] In his *Expositions in the Psalms* Chrysostom links Hos. 13.14 (cf. 1 Cor. 15.55) and Ps. 68(67).18(19) (cf. Eph. 4.8-10) with Ps. 47(46).6. A few lines later he explicitly applies the Psalm to Christ's ascension:

> 'God went up with a shout': it did not say, 'he was dragged up' [ἀνεβιβάσθη], but, 'he went up' [ἀνέβη]. It shows that he did not ascend from the hand of another but he himself travels the road... the Only Begotten ascended with authority.[8]

In one of his homilies on 'the prophets of obscurity' Chrysostom cites several Psalms, including Ps. 47(46).6 and Ps. 110(109).1 ('The Lord said to my Lord, "Sit at my right hand..." '), interpreting these verses as 'concerning the ascension [ἀνάληψις], and concerning the seating at the right hand, and concerning his second coming'.[9] Similar exegeses appear elsewhere in the name of Chrysostom.[10]

London: Marshall, Morgan & Scott; Grand Rapids, MI: Eerdmans, 1983), p. 129; F. Laub, *1. und 2. Thessalonicher-Briefe* (Würzburg: Echter Verlag, 1985), p. 29; T. Holtz, *Der erste Brief an die Thessalonicher* (EKKNT, 13; Zürich: Benziger Verlag; Neukirchen–Vluyn: Neukirchener Verlag, 1986), pp. 198-204.

   7. *Pater, si possibile est* §2 (*PG* 51.33).

   8. *Expositiones in Psalmos* on Ps. 47(46).6 (*PG* 55.213).

   9. *De Prophetiarum Obscuritate* (Homily 2.2-3) (*PG* 56.178).

   10. *In Ascensionem* (Sermon 2) (*PG* 52.794); (Sermon 4) (*PG* 52.801); (Sermon 5) (*PG* 52.802); *In Psalmum 50* (*PG* 55.530); *In Sanctum Stephanum*

3. Eusebius quotes Psalm 47(46) and applies it to Christ:

> Therefore, he assigned this inheritance [words taken from vv. 4 and 5],
> which by the Father has been given to him, to his apostles and prophets
> ... having followed the oracles that have been set down. Having set all
> things right for his coming to humankind, the God-Word, concerning
> whom great things have been apportioned to us, 'went up with a shout'.
> Now the Apostle [Paul] interprets this, saying, 'what does "he went up"
> mean, except that first he descended into the bowels of the earth? He who
> himself descended [καταβάς] is the one who ascended [ἀναβάς] above
> the heavens' [Eph. 4.9-10a].[11]

Here Eusebius has interpreted Ps. 47(46).6 against the interpretation
of Ps. 68(67).18(19) in Ephesians. Finally, in his commentary on the
Psalms he quotes Ps. 47(46).6 and applies it to the 'ascent [ἀνάβασις]
of the Son of God to heaven'.[12]

4. Epiphanius cites Ps. 47(46).6 as one of the many scriptural
testimonia fulfilled in the life, death, resurrection, and ascension of
Christ: 'He will go into heaven: "God went up with a shout, the Lord
with the sound of the trumpet." '[13] After a description of the crucifixion and resurrection, Pseudo-Epiphanius says,

> But as I was thinking these things to myself, I saw him gloriously
> ascending into heaven, for which reason I fell away with shame.
> Therefore the Psalmist long ago cried out saying, 'All nations, clap your
> hands; make a joyful noise to God with the sound of rejoicing, because
> the Lord is exalted, the very fearful King, great upon all the earth' [Ps.
> 47(46).1-2(2-3)]; and again, 'God has gone up with a shout, the Lord
> with the sound of a trumpet' [Ps. 47(46).6].[14]

5. Athanasius twice cites the verse from the psalm, once in his
expositions, and again in his letter to Marcellinus:

> For this reason he also indicates beforehand his bodily way up to heaven;
> and he says in the twenty-third [Psalm]: 'Lift up your gates, O rulers, and
> be lifted up, eternal gates, and the king of glory will enter' [Ps. 24(23).9].
> And in the forty[-sixth Psalm]: 'God went up with a shout, the Lord with

---

Protomartyrem (*PG* 59.503); and *Memor fui Dei* (*PG* 61.692).

11. *Demonstratio Evangelica* (*GCS* 23.2).
12. *Commentaria in Psalmos* (*PG* 23.224).
13. *Testimonia ex Divinis et Sacris Scripturis* 86.1.
14. *Homilia in Assumptionem Christi* (*PG* 43.484).

the sound of the trumpet' [Ps. 47(46).6]. He announces the seating, and he says in [Psalm] 109: 'The Lord said to my Lord...' [Ps. 110 (109).1].[15]

> 'God went up with a shout': the way up to heaven is predicted of the Lord by these things. The Lord (went up) with the sound of a trumpet. The praises of those who ascend with him he has called 'the sound of a trumpet'. Sing praise to our God, sing; sing to our King, sing. Since the angels, he says, sing hymns to the one who ascends, even you, O nations, securing the same liturgy, sing psalms to the reigning God of the earth.[16]

Pseudo-Athanasius offers an interesting exegesis:

> Christ came visibly as God and was seen upon the earth, and he bowed heaven and descended. And again he mounted upon Cherubim, and he flew, and as God he ascended into heaven with a shout...

> Now concerning the ascension [ἀνάληψις] of Christ, it is written in Psalm 17: 'And he mounted upon the Cherubim, and he flew; he flew upon the wings of the wind' [Ps 18(17).10(11)]. And again in Psalm 46: 'God went up with a shout, the Lord with the sound of a trumpet'. And in Zechariah the prophet: 'And on that day the feet of the Lord will stand on the Mount of Olives, opposite Jerusalem from the east' [Zech. 14.4]. Now concerning the glorious second coming of the Son of God Daniel the prophet says: 'I was watching in the night vision, and behold, with the clouds of heaven one like a Son of Man was coming...' (Dan 7.13).[17]

6. Cyril of Jerusalem quotes Ps. 47(46).6, Ps. 68(67).18(19), and Amos 9.6 ('who builds his ascension [ἀνάβασις] into heaven') as the biblical background to Acts 1.9 and 12. He comments: 'From a cloud he descended to Bethlehem; from the Mount of Olives he ascends in a cloud.'[18]

Other Greek Fathers interpreted Ps. 150.4 ('with the sound of the trumpet') as either having to do with the resurrection[19] or with Christ's return.[20] A very important exegesis offered by Origen will be considered at the end of this section.

The Latin Fathers also interpreted Ps. 47(46).6 as fulfilled in the

---

15. *Epistula ad Marcellinum de Interpretatione Psalmorum* (*PG* 27.17).
16. *Expositiones in Psalmos* on Ps. 47(46).6 (*PG* 27.217).
17. *Quaestiones ad Antiochum Ducem* (*PG* 28.685, 697).
18. *De Christi Resurrectione* (*Catechesis* 14.24) (*PG* 33.856-57).
19. Clement of Alexandria, *Paedagogus* 2.4 (*PG* 8.441). See also *Did.* 16.6.
20. Origen, *Selecta in Psalmos* on Ps. 150.4 (*PG* 12.1684).

ascension of Christ. The following interpreted the verse in terms of the ascension described in Acts 1:

1. According to Jerome, Ps. 47(46).6 was fulfilled when Jesus ascended from the Mount of Olives (he cites Acts 1.11: 'Men of Galilee, why do you gaze into heaven? This Jesus, who was taken up from you into heaven, will come in the same way as you saw him go into heaven').[21]

2. Cassiodorus offers a similar exegesis, citing Ps. 47.6 as fulfilled in the ascension described in Acts 1.11.[22]

3. Augustine is quite explicit, interpreting the phrase, 'God is gone up with jubilation' as 'Our God, the Lord Christ, is gone up with jubilation'. Filled with joy, the disciples watched Jesus ascend into heaven (again Acts 1.11 is cited).[23]

For our purposes the most important exegesis comes from Origen, or at least from an early Greek Father whose selected comments on the Psalms came to be identified with the famous exegete and theologian:

> 'God went up with a shout, etc.' Even as the Lord will come 'with the voice of an angel, and with the trumpet of God he will descend from heaven,' so 'God went up with a shout.' But the Lord 'with the sound of a trumpet' (went up) meaning possibly with the shout of all the nations clapping their hands, shouting to God with the sound of rejoicing. To these ones I expect God to ascend. But if some one should praise him with the sound of a trumpet, even the one who ascends will himself ascend with the sound of a trumpet.[24]

Not only has Origen interpreted Ps. 47(46).6 in terms of the ascension of Christ, something that several Greek and Latin Fathers did, he explicitly relates the verse from the psalm to 1 Thess. 4.16: 'Even as the Lord..."will descend [καταβήσεται] from heaven", so "God went up [ἀνέβη] with a shout"'. Apparently what has drawn the two passages together is their common language, especially ἀναβαίνειν/καταβαίνειν.

The potential significance of these exegeses is apparent. Many of the church's earliest exegetes and theologians interpreted Ps. 47(46).6 in terms of Christ's ascension. At least one specifically links Ps. 47(46).6

21. *Breviarium in Psalmos* on Ps. 47(46).6 (*PL* 26.1020-21).
22. *Expositio in Psalterium* on Ps. 47(46).6 (*PL* 70.334).
23. *Enarratio in Psalmum* on Ps. 47(46).6 (*PL* 36.528).
24. *Selecta in Psalmos* on Ps. 47(46).6 (*PG* 12.1437). There is some doubt about the authorship of the *Selecta*.

with 1 Thess. 4.16. Why was the association of Ps. 47(46).6 with
Christ's ascension so widespread? Is it possible, even probable, that
the Fathers assumed that Psalm 47(46) had something to do with
Christ's ascension, because it had been observed, probably from a
very early period, that Christ's descending return had something to do
with this Old Testament passage? Perhaps they recognized that this
verse from the Psalms lay behind the 'word of the Lord' in
1 Thessalonians 4.[25] What we could have here is a chain of interpretation that had its origin in a prophetic utterance that Paul has paraphrased in his discussion of Christ's return and the resurrection and
gathering of the Lord's faithful.[26] While only part of the whole
exegesis is witnessed in 1 Thess. 4.16 (that of the descent of Christ),
the whole exegesis (ascent as well as descent) is witnessed in the
Fathers, particularly in Origen.

Jewish Exegesis

Jewish exegesis of the passage also coheres at important points with
Pauline usage. Although most of these writings are late, some of the
traditions found within them are early (i.e., Tannaitic) and may represent ideas that were in circulation in the first century. Commenting on
Exod. 19.19 ('as the sound of the trumpet grew louder and louder') a

25. It is interesting to note that the Fathers typically cite and apply verses to
Christ that had been cited and similarly applied in the New Testament. For example,
Chrysostom (*Pater, si possibile est* §2) speaks 'with reference to the resurrection'
and then cites Ps. 16(15).10 (cf. Acts 2.31; 13.35), speaks 'with reference to the
ascension' and then cites Ps. 47(46).6, and then speaks 'with reference to the seating
at the right hand' and then cites Ps. 110(109).1 (cf. Acts 2.34; *passim*). From this it
is possible to infer that Chrysostom assumed that his christological interpretation of
Psalm 47, like those of Psalm 16 and 110, was apostolic. Similarly, in *Expositiones
in Psalmos* he cites Hos. 13.14 (cf. 1 Cor. 15.55), Ps. 47(46).6, and Ps. 68(67).18
(19) (cf. Eph. 4.8-10). Should we assume that he regarded his citation of Psalm 47
as different, in that it lacked the authority that the New Testament had invested in the
other two citations? In all of these examples, Chrysostom cites the Old Testament
passages without reference to the New Testament passages that had cited them.
26. Best (*Thessalonians*, p. 194) rightly concludes that v. 15 is Paul's sum-
marizing introduction to the prophetic utterance that is preserved in vv. 16-17a. He
reconstructs the original 'word of the Lord' as follows: 'The Lord himself, accompanied by a command, the cry of an archangel and the trumpet of God, will descend
from heaven, and the dead (in Christ) will rise and the living will be snatched up
simultaneously with them in the clouds to a meeting with the Lord in the air'.

Tanna cites Ps. 47.6, along with Isa. 27.13 ('and in that day a great
trumpet will be blown, and those who were lost in the land of
Assyria...will come and worship the Lord') and Zech. 9.14 ('then the
Lord will appear...the Lord God will sound the trumpet'), and says,
'In the sacred writings wherever the horn is mentioned it augurs well
for Israel, as when it says: "God has gone up with a shout"' (*Mek.* on
Exod. 19.19 [*Bahodesh* 4.28]).[27]

Although judgment is not a major theme in Psalm 47 (v. 3 speaks of
having subdued the nations), the judgment theme is emphasized in
rabbinic exegesis of this text. Commenting on Ps. 47.6, Judah son of
Rabbi Nahman is reported to have said:

> When the Holy One, blessed be he, ascends and sits upon the throne of
> judgment, he ascends with the intention of passing [severe] judgment...
> But whenever Israel should take their horns and blow them in the
> presence of the Holy One, blessed be he, he rises from the throne of judg-
> ment and sits upon the throne of mercy—for it is written, 'The Lord
> amidst the sound of the horn' [Ps. 47.6b]—and he is filled with com-
> passion for them, taking pity upon them and changing for them the
> attribute of justice to one of mercy' (*Lev. R.* 29.3 [on 23.24]; the same
> exegesis is repeated in *Midr. Ps.* 47.2 [on 47.9]).[28]

Another relatively late exegesis believes that בתרועה hints at the terror
of the wicked that will immediately precede the passing of judgment
(*Pes. R.* 40.5). That is, the 'shout' of Ps. 47.6 will be the shouts and
screams of terror as the wicked face the day of judgment. An
abridgement of this interpretation is found in *Pes. K.* 1.4.

In at least one midrash the sounding of the horn carries with it a
messianic implication:

> As for the king, the Messiah, [God] will clothe him in his [God's] own
> robes; for it says: 'Honor and majesty[29] will you lay upon him' [Ps.
> 21.6]. What is written in Scripture? 'God has gone up amidst shouting,
> the Lord amidst the sound of the horn' [Ps. 47.6]. The Holy One, blessed
> be he, said to Moses: 'I have made you a king!' as it says: 'And there was

27. Translation based on J.Z. Lauterbach, *Mekilta De-Rabbi Ishmael* (3 vols.;
Philadelphia: Jewish Publication Society, 1933), II, pp. 222-23.

28. Translation based on J. Israelstam and J.J. Slotki, 'Leviticus', in Freedman
and Simon (eds.), *Midrash Rabbah*, IV, pp. 371-72.

29. Based on the similar language in Ps 104.1, 'honor and majesty' are understood as referring to apparel. See J.J. Slotki, 'Numbers', in Freedman and Simon
(eds.), *Midrash Rabbah*, VI, p. 654 n. 4.

a king in Jeshurun' [Deut. 33.5]. 'As in the case of a king, when he goes forth, the sound of the trumpets precedes him, so you also' (*Num. R.* 15.13 [on 10.1]).[30]

Although Ps 47.6 is cited here, it is one text of a series of quotations and brief comments assembled to expound upon the silver trumpets mentioned in Num. 10.1. Therefore, the citation of Ps. 47.6 may not bear any relation to the preceding reference to 'Messiah' or to the subsequent reference to the 'king in Jeshurun'.

Three important areas of thematic coherence emerge from this survey. First, most of the rabbinic exegeses understand Ps. 47.6 as having something to do with eschatology, something that is not at all obvious in the psalm itself. Similarly, the Pauline context (1 Thess. 4.13–5.11) is eschatological. Secondly, some of the exegeses view Ps. 47.6 as having to do with the judgment of the wicked. Paul also speaks of the judgment that is coming upon the world (1 Thess. 5.1-10). Thirdly, at least one rabbinic exegesis associates the trumpet with the appearance of king messiah. That is, of course, precisely Paul's understanding in 1 Thess. 4.16. This coherence provides a measure of support for the possibility that Ps. 47.6 lies behind the language and imagery of 1 Thess. 4.16. If this is correct, then we have evidence that Christian exegesis and Christology were informed to some extent by Jewish exegesis. In other words, the formulation found in 1 Thess. 4.16 was not entirely Christian; it was to some extent part of the wider Jewish interpretive tradition.

In Israel's early history the horn (or trumpet) was used primarily for military purposes, either to warn or summon Israelites (Num. 10.9; Judg. 3.27; 6.34; cf. 1 Macc. 3.54) or to frighten the enemy (Judg. 7.16-23). Later the horn came to have liturgical (2 Sam. 6.15; 1 Chron. 15.24; Neh. 12.41) and cultic (Lev. 23.23-25; 25.9) functions. Eventually it took on symbolic value, especially in eschatological contexts (Isa. 18.3; 27.13; Joel 2.1, 5; Zech. 9.14, 16).[31]

---

30. Translation based on Slotki, 'Numbers', in Freedman and Simon (eds.), *Midrash Rabbah*, VI, p. 655. For more Jewish parallels, most from even later periods, see J. Klausner, *From Jesus to Paul* (New York: Macmillan, 1943), pp. 537-47.

31. See the helpful essay by M.N.A. Bockmuehl, '"The Trumpet Shall Sound": *Shofar* Symbolism and its Reception in Early Christianity', in W. Horbury (ed.), *Templum Amicitiae: Essays on the Second Temple Presented to Ernst Bammel* (JSNTSup, 48; Sheffield: JSOT Press, 1991), pp. 199-225. I am indebted to this

In the intertestamental period (and later) the horn (or trumpet) plays a prominent role in eschatology. A trumpet will sound when Jerusalem's redemption is at hand (*Pss. Sol.* 11.1-2). The trumpet will sound and God's 'chosen one' will summon his people (*Apoc. Abr.* 31.1). Trumpets announce the final period of tribulation before the end (*4 Ezra* 6.23; *Sib. Or.* 4.174). Trumpets play an important role in the final battle between the sons of light and the sons of darkness (1QM 7.13–9.6). This could be the same idea in 11QMelchizedek 26, which quotes Lev. 25.9 ('and you shall sound the horn in the seventh month').[32] Trumpet blasts will announce several apocalyptic stages (*Apoc. Zeph.* 9.1; 10.1; 11.1; 12.1). Israel petitioned God to 'blow the great horn for our liberation and lift a banner to gather our exiles' (*Amida* §10 [both rescensions]).[33] At the sound of the trumpet, the dead will be brought back to life (*Targ. Ps.-J.* [Exod. 20.15]), a concept which parallels 1 Thess. 4.16.

Besides Mt. 24.31 and 1 Cor. 15.52, already mentioned, the closest New Testament parallels are those found in the Apocalypse (1.10; 4.1; 8.2, 6, 13; 9.14). There is an allusion to the Sinai theophany in Hebrews (12.18-19; cf. Exod. 19.12-22; 20.18-21). The reference in 1 Cor. 14.8 is irrelevant, but the references in Mt. 24.31 and 1 Cor. 15.52 are most germane.

But the suggestion that Ps. 47(46).6, which speaks of ascent, lies behind 1 Thess. 4.16, which speaks of descent, probably implies that ascent/descent Christology had come to expression in some early Christian circles. There is evidence of such thinking in the New Testament. The Fourth Gospel attributes such a saying to Jesus himself: 'No one has ascended [ἀναβέβηκα] to heaven except the one who descended [καταβάς] from heaven' (Jn 3.13; cf. 6.33, 38, 62; 20.17).

study at many points. See also G. Friedrich, 'σάλπιγξ κτλ', *TDNT*, VII (1971), pp. 71-88.

32. A.S. van der Woude ('Melchisedek als himmlische Erlösergestalt in den neugefundenen eschatologischen Midraschim aus Qumran Höhle XI', *OTS* 14 [1965], pp. 354-73) believes that the horn of Lev. 25.9 was understood as the last trumpet of the Day of Judgment, as in 1 Thess. 4.16. J.A. Fitzmyer ('Further Light on Melchizedek from Qumran Cave 11', *JBL* 86 [1967], pp. 25-41), however, cautions that the fragmentary condition of the ending of the text 'hinders any interpretation' (p. 41).

33. From W. Förster, *Palestinian Judaism in New Testament Times* (Edinburgh and London: Oliver and Boyd, 1964), p. 229. For the Hebrew text, see G. Dalman, *Die Worte Jesu* (Leipzig: Hinrichs, 1898), pp. 300, 302.

Paul and the Scriptures of Israel

As already noted, Eph. 4.8-10 quotes and interprets Ps. 68(67).18(19) in a christological sense. But these traditions may be late. Is there evidence of the antiquity of this tradition? There is. The appearance of the tradition in Rom 10.6-8 provides evidence of the tradition's antiquity, and of Paul's acquaintance with it: 'Do not say in your heart, "Who will ascend [ἀναβήσεται] into heaven?" that is, to bring Christ down; or, "Who will descend [καταβήσεται] into the abyss?" that is, to bring Christ up from the dead' (Rom. 10.6-8; cf. Deut. 30.12-14). Thus, christological employment of ἀναβαίνειν/ καταβαίνειν language was known to Paul.

The potential relevance of these Jewish and Christian traditions for the study of 1 Thess. 4.16 is obvious. The final part of this study will take a new look at this verse and its 'echo' of Scripture[34] in its immediate and wider contexts and consider its possible implications for a major New Testament and early church doctrine.

1 Thessalonians 4.16 in Context

Our passage is part of a larger eschatological section (1 Thess. 4.13–5.11). Several elements from dominical and LXX prophetic traditions give the section its character and substance. The most significant parallels are as follows:

> 1 Thess. 5.2: 'you know that the day of the Lord thus comes as a thief at night'
> Mt. 24.42-44: 'you do not know on what day your Lord comes... if the householder had known when the thief comes... you do not know at what hour the thief comes'
> Lk. 12.39-40: 'if the householder had known at what hour the thief was coming... You also must be ready; for the Son of Man is coming at an hour you do not suppose'
>
> 1 Thess. 5.3a: 'whenever they say, "peace and safety"'
> Jer. 6.14; 8.11; Ezek. 13.10: 'saying, "peace, peace", when there is no peace'
>
> 1 Thess. 5.3b: 'then sudden destruction will come upon them'
> Mk 13.36: 'lest coming suddenly he should find you sleeping'
> Lk. 21.34: 'But watch yourselves lest... that day come upon you suddenly like a snare'

---

34. I refer here, of course, to the work of R.B. Hays, *Echoes of Scripture in the Letters of Paul* (New Haven and London: Yale University Press, 1989). Hays does not treat 1 Thess. 4.16.

1 Thess. 5.8-9: 'let us put on the breastplate of faith and love and the helmet, the hope of salvation, because God has not destined us for wrath'
Isa. 59.17: 'He put on righteousness as a breastplate, and a helmet of salvation upon the head; he put on clothing of vengeance, even the mantle, the one who will pay back retribution, (and) reproach to those who oppose'
Wis. 5.15-20: 'But the righteous live forever, and their reward is with the Lord; the Most High takes care of them... The Lord... will put on right-eousness as a breastplate, and wear impartial justice as a helmet; he will take holiness as an invincible shield, and sharpen stern wrath for a sword'

Three aspects of these traditions call for comment. (1) The element of the suddenness and unexpectedness of the day of the Lord is derived from the dominical tradition. Paul's reference to the 'thief' likely echoes the eschatological saying found in Mt. 24.43-44 (cf. Lk. 12.39-40). The thief simile was apparently widespread (2 Pet. 3.10; Rev. 3.3; 16.15). In all of these passages the simile is intended as a warning of coming judgment. Because of the imminence of judgment, believers are to be prepared at all times. (2) Paul's description of the wicked who say 'peace and safety' is drawn from the prophetic tradition, while the prediction of sudden destruction is derived from the dominical tradition. (3) The command to don spiritual armor derives primarily from Isa. 59.17, though the more forceful and colorful version in Wis. 5.15-20 may have been in mind as well. The passage in the Wisdom of Solomon, of course, is based upon Isaiah. The context of Wisdom 5 is that of eschatological judgment. The wicked will be judged, the righteous will be vindicated. The judgment that will fall upon the earth will be terrific (vv. 21-23). In Isaiah and Wisdom it is God himself who puts on his armor to defend his faithful, but in 1 Thessalonians the faithful are to put on this armor in preparation for the trials of the day of the Lord. In a later epistle this armor is described in much greater detail (cf. Eph. 6.10-17).

It is clear that Paul has pulled together a variety of traditions in forming 1 Thess. 4.13–5.11. But I suspect that much of this material had taken shape before Paul's usage. It is not necessary, therefore, to suppose that Paul was conscious of the precise biblical origin of each tradition. The echo of Psalm 47 in 1 Thess. 4.16 is probably another instance of the same phenomenon. Imbedded within a tradition that Paul has inherited is biblical material of which the apostle may or may not have been conscious.

Psalm 47 is a psalm that calls for the celebration of God's

sovereignty. The Lord is to be feared, he is a great king over all the earth, he has subdued nations, and he has promised his people an inheritance. Having ascended, he now sits on his holy throne (at least, as later interpreters understood the passage). The rulers of his people have been gathered before him. The picture portrayed by this psalm coheres with Paul's apocalyptic portrait in 1 Thessalonians, and it coheres at specific points with the prophetic vision of God's judgment described in Isaiah 59 and Wisdom 5.

Paul, like other Jewish interpreters, evidently understood Ps. 47.6 in a judgmental way, as seen especially in 1 Thess. 5.1-10. The judgmental aspect could explain the usage of κέλευσμα in place of ἀλαλαγμός. Whereas the latter is a word of joy and celebration (hence the Fathers readily applied Ps. 47[46].6 to Christ's ascension, an event which gave the disciples joy, according to Augustine), the former is not. Rather, it is usually employed to express the command or order of a master or a military officer.[35] Christ, rejected, crucified, resurrected, and ascended, will return with authority, commanding the angels of heaven. Believers will be gathered before him for evaluation and reward (2 Cor. 5.10; cf. many of Jesus' parables). Knowing this, Christians have reason to celebrate their savior's return. Unbelievers, however, thinking that there is 'peace and safety' (1 Thess. 5.3), will be judged and condemned.

We may speculate whether the original 'word of the Lord', based upon the language of Ps. 47.6, also reflected the tone of this verse from the LXX. That is, the resurrection and ascension of Christ were a cause of rejoicing. But by transforming this echo of Scripture into an apocalyptic image of Christ's return, an element of judgment became necessary. Hence the inappropriateness of the word ἀλαλαγμός was sensed. Its replacement with κέλευσμα fits the new context much better. This may have been Paul's contribution. Christ descends and the archangel shouts commands (not cries of joy). Believers are raised; unbelievers are judged. Although not cited as a prooftext, or as a prophecy fulfilled, Ps. 47.6 has, nevertheless, made a significant contribution to the eschatological ideas of 1 Thessalonians.

Concluding Postscript

There is another aspect to the hearing of the echo of Ps. 47.6 that warrants comment. It is remarkable that the early church (evidently

---

35. See L. Schmid, 'κέλευσμα', *TDNT*, III (1965), pp. 656-59.

before Paul wrote 1 Thessalonians, one of his earliest epistles) applied to Jesus an Old Testament passage such as this. Applying to Jesus such a passage as this one suggests that 'high Christology' had come to expression at a very early time. (Recall that the Christ hymns of Phil. 2.5-11 and Col. 1.15-20 antedate the epistles in which they are now found.) It is likely that early Christians, most of whom were Jewish, knew what was meant when Ps. 47.6 was applied to Jesus. The potentially blasphemous nature of this exegesis could not have gone unnoticed.[36] Consider this very different interpretation of who ascends and who descends: '"Who has ascended into heaven (and descended?)" [Prov. 30.4] alludes to the Holy One, blessed be he, of whom it is [also] written, "God has gone up amidst shouting" [Ps. 47.6]' (*Num. R.* 12.11 [on 7.1]).[37] Psalm 47 speaks of *God* ascending, as this rabbinic interpretation understands. The early Christian interpretation of 1 Thessalonians applies the text to the risen and returning *Christ*.

36. According to L.W. Hurtado (*One God, One Lord: Early Christian Devotion and Ancient Jewish Monotheism* [Philadelphia: Fortress Press, 1988], pp. 93-128) it was this sort of devotion to and veneration of Jesus that guaranteed Judaism's repudiation of Christianity.

37. Translation based on Slotki, 'Numbers', in Freedman and Simon (eds.), *Midrash Rabbah*, V, p. 479.

THE INTERTEXTUALITY OF ISAIAH 66.17 AND 2 THESSALONIANS 2.7: A SOLUTION FOR THE 'RESTRAINER' PROBLEM

Stephen G. Brown

The interpretation of 2 Thessalonians 2 hinges on the identification of the so-called 'restrainer' in vv. 6-7. Depending on such identification, practically any eschatological bias can be supported. The complexity of the problem, plus the tendency toward eisegesis in solving it, is apparent from the diverse and varied proposals. Identifications include 'Rome/the emperor, civil government, God and His power, Michael the archangel, the preaching of the Gospel/Paul, Satan, general evil forces, a combination of benevolent forces, the Jewish state, and James, or a mythic symbol with no particular context' according to Douglas Moo.[1] Others see the Holy Spirit, the church, Gentile world dominion, Elijah, the apostles, the saints in Jerusalem before its destruction, the Mosaic law, or Seneca.[2]

I propose a solution for the identification of the restrainer based on the coordination of three methods more commonly associated with Old Testament scholarship: (1) rhetorical criticism, (2) mythopoetic imagery, and (3) inner biblical exegesis. Respectively, they deal with literary or rhetorical structure, traditional symbols and ideas, and earlier or original literary contexts. The value of combining these three approaches is illustrated by a comparison with the work of Bible translators, who have found that the fields of linguistics, anthropology, and study of the Bible itself must be thoroughly integrated in order to communicate effectively with other language groups. The failure to integrate these three methods helps to account for the inability of so many efforts to solve the 'restrainer' problem of 2 Thess. 2.6-7. This

---

1. R. Reiter et al., *The Rapture* (Grand Rapids, MI: Zondervan, 1984), p. 190.
2. R.L. Thomas, *The Expositor's Bible Commentary* (Grand Rapids, MI: Zondervan, 1978), II, p. 324. For a history of the views, see C.H. Giblin, *The Threat to Faith* (AnBib, 31; Rome: Pontifical Biblical Institute, 1967).

investigation shows that each method agrees with the other two to provide confirmation for a long-overdue solution to this biblical crux.

Before proceeding with the study, appreciation is due to Richard B. Hays for his provocative and articulate *tour de force* which appeals to these very same methods in matters of intertextual reflection and signification. His assertion provides an eloquent introduction to my investigation:

> Claims about intertextual meaning effects are strongest where it can credibly be demonstrated that they occur within the literary structure of the text and that they can plausibly be ascribed to the intention of the author and the competence of the original readers.[3]

Thus, the intertextuality and meaning of 2 Thessalonians 2 is demonstrated by relating its structure to its early literary source.

1. *A Rhetorical, Structural Analysis of 2 Thessalonians 2*

Structural Parallels and Correspondences
Our purpose of understanding 2 Thess. 2.6-7 will be adequately achieved by focusing upon vv. 3b-12 which answers the concern of vv. 1-3a with an exposition of the Day of the Lord. This paragraph is best understood as a bifid parallel structure separated by v. 5 into two halves with vv. 3b-4 matching vv. 6-12.[4] Since the use of the present tense in vv. 5-7 breaks the chronological sequencing of vv. 3-12, a conceptual rather than a sequential relationship between the two halves should be understood. The second half answers the rhetorical question of v. 5 and deals with the same material as the first, but amplifies or

---

3. R.B. Hays, *Echoes of Scripture in the Letters of Paul* (New Haven and London: Yale University Press, 1989), p. 28.

4. J. Callow, *A Semantic Structure Analysis of Second Thessalonians* (Dallas: Summer Institute of Linguistics, 1982), p. 55. Verses 3-12 are conducive to a rhetorical critical analysis sensitive to the structural parallelism so common in Old Testament studies. The unit is divided into six sentences which are terminated at vv. 4, 5, 6, 7, 8 and 12. Callow suggests that the linkage of these sentences through the use of an initial καί, 'and' (2.6, 8, 11), or γάρ, 'for' (2.7), shows that the progression in thought has no major change in topic. There is no change in the general topic until the δέ in v. 13. The only non-initial sentence without a formal link (i.e., not beginning with a conjunction) is the rhetorical question of v. 5 which grammatically and logically divides vv. 3-12 into two halves.

clarifies it in greater detail.[5] An ABA'B' pattern is evident with v. 3 (A) matching vv. 6-8 (A') and v. 4 (B) matching vv. 9-12 (B'). A and A' basically deal with the actuality or the *appearance* of rebellion and B and B' describe the *activity* of the rebels.[6]

The clear definition of B and B' helps to establish the parallelism of A and A' and deserves attention. The parallel between v. 4 and vv. 9-12 is evident in both content and structure. First of all, both B and B' begin as subordinate clauses qualifying a man of sin who has just been revealed, but who is explicitly described as suddenly destroyed in the preceding verses (v. 3d, v. 8).[7] Secondly, these initial verses in B and B' introduce the same sequence: (1) the forthright description of the open self-exaltation and defiance against God (v. 4a; vv. 9-10); and (2) the result or consequences of such blasphemy (v. 4b; vv. 11-12).[8]

Both A (v. 3) and A' (vv. 6-8) explain the nonappearance of the man of sin. Each begins with an initial or present manifestation of wickedness (vv. 3b, 6-7) and ends by referring to the final or future revelation and destruction of the man of sin (vv. 3c, 8).[9] The semantic unity of vv. 6-8 is apparent from the implicit nature of vv. 6-7, which requires the explicit statement of v. 8.[10] This connection of vv. 6-7 with v. 8 requires a common subject for the aorist passive form of ἀποκαλύπτω, 'to be revealed', used in vv. 3c, 6b, and 8a. Thus, the antecedent of the pronoun αὐτόν, 'he', in v. 6b finds its

5. For head–amplification and generic–specific relationships, see J. Beekman, J. Callow and M. Kopesec, *The Semantic Structure of Written Communication* (Dallas: Summer Institute of Linguistics, 1981), pp. 96-97.

6. See M. Barnouin, 'Les problèmes de traduction concernant II Thess. II. 6-7', *NTS* 23 (1977), p. 483.

7. Callow, *Semantic Structure*, p. 62.

8. The unity of vv. 9-12 is apparent from the obvious parallels between vv. 9-10 and vv. 11-12. Note the sequence of the words ἐνέργειαν...ψεύδους... ἀδικίας...ἀληθείας...εἰς τό in vv. 9-10 and their antiphonal recurrence in vv. 11-12. Note also the parallel use of tenses with vv. 9 and 11 in the present and vv. 10 and 12 in the aorist.

9. The equivalence of vv. 3 and 8 is commonly accepted. See Giblin, *The Threat to Faith*, p. 63; Barnouin, 'Les problèmes de traduction', pp. 483-84.

10. The τότε 'then' of v. 8 refers back to vv. 6-7 which are 'intended to explain more precisely when "then" is', according to Callow (*Semantic Structure*, pp. 64-65). See also Giblin, *The Threat to Faith*, p. 232; Barnouin, 'Les problèmes de traduction', p. 487; and P. Ellingworth and E. Nida, *A Translator's Handbook on Paul's Letters to the Thessalonians* (Stuttgart: United Bible Societies, 1975), p. 172.

antecedent in the man of sin of v. 3c. Any attempt to find another masculine antecedent, such as God in v. 4, certainly overlooks the grammatical and structural parallels, as well as any semblance of logical progression of thought.[11] As Ellingworth and Nida remark, 'the pronoun "he" almost certainly refers to "the man of lawlessness", that is, the Wicked One, who is Paul's main concern in this passage'.[12] To reiterate, vv. 3c and 8 refer to the explicit revelation of the man of sin, who is also the subject of v. 6b where the same form of the verb ('revealed') is used.

The parallel between the graphic, incarnate manifestation of wickedness in vv. 3c and 8 points to the preceding parallel between the spiritual, more intangible and nebulous manifestation of wickedness in vv. 3 and 7. In other words, the 'apostasy' of v. 3 can be identified with 'the mystery of wickedness' in v. 7. The temporal use of particles in A and A' supports this conclusion. The use of πρῶτον in v. 3 suggests the apostasy was already occuring (cf. 1 Tim. 4.1) and nicely parallels the particles νῦν, 'now' (v. 6a), ἤδη, 'already', and ἄρτι, 'just now' (v. 7).[13] These parallels indicate that the wickedness normally associated with the man of sin was affecting Paul's readers at that time and obviously accounted for their suffering (cf. 1 Thess. 4.4-5). Thus, the church at Thessalonica experienced or tasted the apostasy and its arch-agent.[14] Unlike the verses before and after,

---

11. See Barnouin, 'Les problèmes de traduction', p. 484.

12. Ellingworth and Nida, *Translator's Handbook*, p. 169.

13. Giblin notes that 'anti-God forces are verified in all periods of the earthly existence of the Church (cf. 1 John 2, 18.22; Matt 24, 4.5...)' (*The Threat to Faith*, p. 175). If the force of νῦν is resumptive, 'as it is', according to F.F. Bruce (*1 & 2 Thessalonians* [WBC; Waco, TX: Word Books, 1982], p. 170), the fact of a present manifestation of the apostasy does not change. With Thomas (*Expositor's Bible Commentary*, p. 325), and C.J. Ellicott (*Commentary on the Epistles of St Paul to the Thessalonians* [Grand Rapids, MI: Zondervan, 1957], p. 113), the νῦν is probably temporal in order to honor the outside edge of the chiastic pattern of v. 6 where 'now' is juxtapositioned with the temporal 'in his own time'. See Callow, *Semantic Structure*, p. 66; Giblin, *The Threat to Faith*, p. 206.

14. For Paul, Satan was alive and active on earth. While Satan was not yet completely 'self-evident,', his appearance was 'in the making' (v. 9). The personal experience of the saints is stressed by the use of οἶδα, 'to know', in v. 6, which is used to acknowledge experiential knowledge rather than speculative or conceptual knowledge. See Giblin, *The Threat to Faith*, pp. 159-161, 170; also Ellingworth and Nida, *Translator's Handbook*, pp. 168-69.

vv. 5-7 are in the present and reflect, as Giblin says, 'Paul's habit of seeing the present in the light of the future (i.e. in the light of absolute fulfillment)'.[15]

Once vv. 6-7 are explained as the present manifestation of v. 3, their relationship to each other is immediately raised. The occurrence of the same verb used as a present participle in the first halves of vv. 6 and 7 and the use of the aorist referring to some future change of status in the second half of each verse suggests that the two verses are, in fact, just one of the many smaller parallels throughout vv. 3-12.[16] As Barnouin asserts, vv. 6 and 7 consist of one and the same action.[17] The parallelism of vv. 6 and 7 is indicated by the explicative, emphatic, or confirmatory use of γάρ ('for/that is', 'indeed') which introduces v. 7.[18]

The Interpretation of κατέχω

Despite the shift from the neuter participle κατέχον (v. 6) to the masculine participle κατέχων (v. 7), Callow sees a clear correspondence between them. It is simply a shift in focus from an abstract or

---

15. Giblin, *The Threat to Faith*, p. 175. More specifically, E. Best sees the κατέχων as 'the force of rebellion at work in the world' who maintains the rebellion until the man of sin can appear (*The First and Second Epistles to the Thessalonians* [New York: Harper & Row, 1972], p. 301).

16. Besides the larger ABA´B´ structure, parallels occur on a smaller scale throughout vv. 3-12. Note the frequent use of the conjuction καί, 'and', joining parallel statements into couplets. Verses 3-12 is a series of tight-knit units of two halves with the second half restating, qualifying or amplifying the first. In v. 1, καί parallels the 'coming' and 'gathering'. In v. 3, καί joins 'the apostasy comes' with 'the man of rebellion is manifested'. In v. 4 καί joins the participles 'opposing' and 'exalting' to describe the man of sin. In v. 4b, 'sitting' and 'showing' oneself are juxtaposed, a fashion of parallelism in the sense of being coupled together. In vv. 8b and 8c, καί parallels 'the Lord Jesus slays...' with 'bring to an end'. Cf. Ellingworth and Nida, *Translator's Handbook*, p. 172. The same force of καί occurs in vv. 10a and 11a. The use of καί at the beginning of v. 11 seems to indicate the parallelism cited above between vv. 9-11 and vv. 11-12. Looking at vv. 9-10, there appears to be an *abb´a´* chiastic structure with *b* (v. 9b) and *b´* (v. 10a) being joined by καί in v. 10a to describe the manner of the man of sin's coming. Looking at the location of the καί in v. 11, the parallels cited earlier intend a correspondence between v. 9a and v. 11, and also between v. 10b and v. 12. Finally, the reference to disbelief in both v. 11 and v. 12 provides a parallel between those two verses.

17. Barnouin, 'Les problèmes de traduction', p. 487.

18. Giblin, *The Threat to Faith*, p. 219; also Ellicott, *Commentary*, p. 113.

impersonal power to a *personal* one.[19] As Giblin suggests, the neuter participle brings out the role (verbal aspect) of the participle while the masculine draws to mind the figure's face (nominal aspect). The neuter speaks of the situation, the motives of the individual, or his role and function. The masculine focuses on the fact and nature of the person himself. Simply put, the neuter 'concretizes' the Mystery and the masculine personalizes it.[20] Ernest Best concurs: 'we assume that both refer to the same reality under different aspects'.[21]

Comparisons have been made to Mk 13.14 (neuter 'abomination' with masculine participle 'standing'), Rom. 13.4 (abstract 'authority' commuted to the masculine noun 'servant'), and Lk. 43.5 (neuter 'spirit' is identified with a human being) to explain the use of the neuter for the masculine participle in 2 Thess. 2.6,[22] but a comparison with 2 Thess. 2.7 provides the answer. The explanation of the shift can be found in the accomodation of the neuter participle to the thought and parallel location of the neuter μυστήριον, 'mystery', in v. 7.[23] Parallel to the 'mystery of lawlessness', the neuter κατέχον represents an agent for the mystery itself or is so closely identified with it that its normal usage as a personal force in the masculine is temporarily altered.[24] The masculine κατέχων in v. 7 represents a return to normal usage. It refers to a person and is a point of clarification.

With the first halves of vv. 6 and 7 parallel, it is logical to assume that the last halves of each verse (vv. 6b, 7c) are also parallel. Since v. 6b clearly refers to the revelation of the man of sin, as seen above, it only remains to be determined whether v. 7c can support the same meaning. Since the κατέχον and the κατέχων are one and the same

19. Callow, *Semantic Structure*, p. 69; Ellingworth and Nida, *Translator's Handbook*, p. 170; Bruce, *1 & 2 Thessalonians*, p. 171; cf. R.D. Aus, 'God's Plan and God's Power: Isaiah 66 and the Restraining Factors of 2 Thess. 2.6-7', *JBL* 96 (1977), pp. 537-53.

20. Giblin, *The Threat to Faith*, pp. 218-19, 222.

21. Best, *Thessalonians*, p. 295.

22. Giblin, *The Threat to Faith*, pp. 217-18; Ellicott, *Commentary*, p. 114; Barnouin, 'Les problèmes de traduction', p. 485.

23. Giblin, *The Threat to Faith*, p. 219. A more remote possibility is the neuter πνεύματος 'spirit' in v. 2.

24. Giblin notes an obvious but worthy point, 'Underlying the function known by experience in v. 6a is some concrete, personal source' (*The Threat to Faith*, p. 223).

agent, then it stands to reason that this agent is working the mysterious rebellion in the present and must be one with the future man of sin in v. 6b.[25] The proposed parallel of v. 6b with v. 7c would make the κατέχων the subject of v. 7c. This is the natural reading. No other subject is available for v. 7c.[26]

The meanings of κατέχω and the phrase ἕως ἐκ μέσου γένηται represent the major stumbling blocks for interpreters. The interpretation of κατέχω falls into two basic camps: (1) a good force hostile to evil, perhaps God; or (2) an evil power, perhaps even Satan, as the subject. Based on the structure of the passage and the assumption that the text is highly integrated and self-contained, it is proposed that the only possible antecedent is an evil force.[27] There is no antecedent adequate to support the first view, while the second view can connect the use of κατέχω with the impersonal or personal manifestation of wickedness (the apostasy or man of sin in v. 3).[28] Despite this problem, the first view is accepted by most scholars who commonly supply for the participle κατέχον in v. 6a the direct object αὐτόν 'him', understood to be the man of rebellion.[29] The second view simply asserts that the subject of γένηται is found in the twice-mentioned participle which can be traced back through the personal pronouns in

25. To assume that a present, presumably historical, agent will be revealed at a later time simply requires that the chief antagonist to the Thessalonians was Satan (who can be charged, ultimately, with every historical instance of rebellion against God). Satan certainly bore this role in 1 Thess. 2.18 and 3.5. As Giblin notes, '...Satan is not bound in Paul's theology' (*The Threat to Faith*, p. 171). See also 2 Cor. 2.1; Eph. 2.2; 1 Tim. 5.5.

26. See Giblin who states that a subject other than κατέχων would have been expressed (*The Threat to Faith*, p. 210). Bruce concurs: 'The subject of γένηται cannot be other than κατέχων' (*1 & 2 Thessalonians*, p. 171). Cf. Barnouin, 'Les problèmes de traduction', p. 490.

27. On this point, Giblin agrees, citing N.F. Freese (*The Threat to Faith*, p. 177). I am indebted to Gordon Whitney for citing the applicability of Joos's Law, a recognized linguistic principle which says that the best interpretation makes the least changes in the total context. See M. Joos, 'Semantic Axiom Number One', *Language* 48 (1972), p. 257; also A.A. Hill, 'Laymen, Lexicographers, and Linguists', *Language* 40 (1970), p. 255. In other words, taking the context as it is, there would be no way for an unbiased reader to see a good force in vv. 6-7.

28. The first view sees the κατέχων, according to Giblin (*The Threat to Faith*, p. 167), as 'an element totally distant and different' from anything in the text, especially the man of sin.

29. See Aus, 'God's Plan', p. 549.

vv. 6b and 4b to the man of sin in v. 3. As Barnouin affirms, this second view is unpopular, but it conforms to the text.[30]

I conclude that the first view of a good force, restraining evil, puts an unneccesary and unbearable strain upon the passage, both grammatically and historically. Grammatically, it is better to see Paul using κατέχων to allude to the cause of the disturbance at Thessalonica. It is in no way a restrainer of the antichrist who delays the coming of the latter and thereby the coming of the Lord. Historically, we must remember that Paul is trying to account for the inordinate amount of suffering of 2 Thess. 1.1-5 and not for the wonderful blessing brought about from the effective restraining of evil.

Rejecting God or some good force as the subject of κατέχον, the sense of 'to delay, to retard' deduced by most commentators from the meaning 'to prevent, hinder, impede, obstruct' should probably be rejected.[31] The verb κατέχω basically means 'to hold fast' and, according to Giblin, is not used elsewhere in the New Testament in the · sense of 'restraining or detaining another'. Commonly used for Hebrew אחז, 'to grasp', Giblin sees a 'grabbing or seizing action of a hostile force or figure' which is a 'threat to faith'.[32] Similarly, E. Best suggests the more conventional idea of 'occupying' or 'possessing': 'That the force of evil "possesses" or "occupies" the present world fits suitably into apocalyptic thought'.[33]

The meaning of κατέχω has neither a positive nor a pejorative meaning by itself, but is determined by the context.[34] A pejorative or

---

30. Barnouin states, '...cette lecture conforme aux apparences doit, malgré son succès, être critiquée...' ('Les problèmes de traduction', p. 490). Similarly, E. Best concludes that the sense of a hostile evil force 'falls into line with the other forces referred to in the passage and its meaning does not have to be forced' (*Thessalonians*, p. 301).

31. *Thessalonians*, p. 491.

32. Giblin, *The Threat to Faith*, pp. 180-83, 192, 197-204, 230, 234, 243, 246. Used intransitively, Giblin suggests the connotation of 'a self-interested act'. Specifically, the κατέχον is not a power 'in possession', nor a 'spirit attempting to possess', but is a 'power grasping for control, a seizing power'. He appeals, particularly, to the use of κατέχω in Dionysiac, demonic rites involving pseudo-prophetic mania. Similarly, Barnouin interprets the participle intransitively in an attributive sense and suggests a meaning 'garder avec soi' or 'tenir garde' ('Les problèmes de traduction', p. 492).

33. Best, *Thessalonians*, p. 301.

34. Barnouin, 'Les problèmes de traduction', pp. 491-92. See various meanings

negative sense is required in vv. 6 and 7. Rom. 1.18 is a telling cross-reference, for it uses a negative sense for men who are 'keeping a lid' on the truth while being under the imminent judgement of God. The sense of 'suppress' or even just 'hold' is adequate for Rom. 1.18 and for vv. 6 and 7 as well. The negative connotation of κατεχόντων in Rom 1.18 is due more to the phrase 'in unrighteousness' than to the nature of the verb. Likewise, the perversity of the verb κατέχω in 2 Thess. 2.6-7 is due to its subject, who is the operating force of the 'mystery of wickedness'.[35] In other words, the semantics of κατέχω is not as important as its subject in this context. Even if the meaning of 'restrain' or 'hinder' is insisted upon here, it would fit well with the subject as an evil force who covertly and surreptitiously resists the servants of God.

The Interpretation of ἕως ἐκ μέσου γένηται
This phrase is the most crucial and perplexing phrase in all of 2 Thessalonians 2. The popular rendering is 'until he is taken out of the way' which gives a totally different meaning than the strictly literal rendering of 'until he appears out of the middle'. The popular view suggests the removal of a beneficent figure from the world to heaven; the latter connotes the manifestation or metamorphosis of an evil force from a private, hidden place to a public arena.

The parallels of vv. 6 and 7 noted above suggest that v. 7c speaks of the disclosure of the man of sin who terminates the covert activity of v. 7ab. Just as we find the antecedent of v. 6b in v. 6a, so we would expect to find the antecedent of v. 7c in v. 7ab. If this is true, v. 7c means that the κατέχων leaves the 'middle' where the 'mystery of lawlessness' operated.[36] Verse 7c appears to bridge the period between the mysterious operation of wickedness (vv. 6a, 7ab) and the full manifestation of the man of sin in v. 8a.[37] Verse 7c would thus parallel v. 6b and represent the inceptive act marking the man of sin's

in Ellingworth and Nida, *Translator's Handbook*, p. 168.

35. See Giblin, *The Threat to Faith*, p. 186.

36. The identity or meaning of μέσος, 'middle', is problematic, but Barnouin cites Plutarch where the phrase γένηται ἐκ μέσου signifies leaving a group of people ('Les problèmes de traduction', p. 493). Cf. Bruce, *1 & 2 Thessalonians*, p. 170; Callow, *Semantic Structure*, pp. 68-69.

37. Barnouin, 'Les problèmes de traduction', pp. 494-95; cf. Aus, 'God's Plan', p. 551.

full revelation in v. 8 along with the encumbant phenomena of vv. 9 and 10.

A final solution to the meaning of v. 7c does not depend upon the verb γένηται, which can be variously understood, but upon the meaning of μέσος, 'middle', in this context. Citing Plutarch, Barnouin suggests the meaning of an active political or religious group or a state of restriction, favoring the latter.[38] The idea of a holy community appeals to Giblin, while Barnouin compares the unholy communion of Ezek. 8.7-12.[39] Such disagreements cannot be fully resolved until the exact meaning of μέσος is determined in its proper historical context. Richard Hays stresses the need for just such a determination:

> to hear and understand the poet's allusions we need to know not only the tradition to which the allusion points but also the way in which that tradition was understood in the poet's time and the contemporary historical experience or situation with which the poet links the tradition.[40]

2. *The Mythopoetic Tradition of* μέσος, *'the Middle'*

The Concept of the Term 'Middle'
The term 'middle' has mystified many interpreters for lack of definition and association. Most understand some central place with attention focused upon some human context or involvement. It is proposed here that Paul did not use the term in random fashion, but was alluding to a concept commonly understood in the ancient Near East. Accepting Hays's general distinction between an allusion, used for obvious intertextual references, and an echo, for subtler ones, the term 'middle' should probably be viewed as an allusion.[41]

The term 'middle' or 'center', simply put, is mythic imagery, an archetypal symbol referring to a sacred center, a place where earth and heaven met and originally, where 'creation began and unfolded',

---

38. Barnouin, 'Les problèmes de traduction', pp. 492-96. See also Bruce, *1 & 2 Thessalonians*, p. 170.

39. Giblin, *The Threat to Faith*, pp. 179, 230; Barnouin, 'Les problèmes de traduction', p. 492 n. 2.

40. Hays, *Echoes of Scripture*, p. 18.

41. Hays, *Echoes of Scripture*, p. 29.

the primal place which was the 'paradigm of all origins'.[42] In short, 'the middle' or 'the center' is a synecdoche for the Garden of Eden which focuses on the middle of the Garden where the Tree of Life and the Tree of the Knowledge of Good and Evil were rooted in the ground and lifted their branches to heaven. The term is best understood in its original use in Gen. 2.9 and 3.3. The 'middle' is the place where God and human beings live. It is the 'Garden of God' (Ezek. 28.13) and the home of humanity. For Michael Fishbane, the paradise of Eden is an *axis mundi*, the navel or omphalos from which all life flows and is sustained.[43] This center is actually the 'mountain of God' (Ezek. 28.14) from which the four rivers flowed down and marked off the four quadrants of the world. It was a 'world mountain' symbolizing 'order, harmony, and beneficence'.[44] This Mountain-Garden complex, or sacred center, according to Fishbane, provides a symbolic structure of such magnitude that it is preserved and transformed as a paradigm throughout biblical history and the history of Israel.[45] Indeed, the concept of a middle or sacred center provides for Fishbane the unifying and all-pervasive foundation for his theological interpretation of the Old Testament canon.[46]

I would suggest that Paul's reference to a 'middle' was neither nebulous nor obscure, but was familiar to his audience, either by its widespread currency in the ancient world or by Paul's previous instruction. An investigation of secular and biblical references provides evidence for understanding Paul's reference to a 'middle' in terms of a mythopoetic background. The Bible naturally rejects the pagan version of a 'middle', which posed a constant threat to Israelite faith from the time of Solomon, but a study of various traditions helps to understand the meaning of this all-pervasive idea.[47]

---

42. M.A. Fishbane, *Text and Texture* (New York: Schocken Books, 1979), p. 111.

43. M.A. Fishbane, 'The Sacred Center: The Symbolic Structure of the Bible', in M.A. Fishbane and P.R. Flohr (eds.), *Texts and Responses* (Leiden: Brill, 1975), p. 9.

44. Fishbane, *Text and Texture*, p. 111.

45. Fishbane and Flohr (eds.), *Texts and Responses*, p. 26.

46. *Texts and Responses*, pp. 14, 19-21, 24-25; also Fishbane, *Text and Texture*, pp. 112-14, 118-19.

47. For a comprehensive introduction to the idea of a sacred center or 'middle', see M. Eliade, *The Sacred and the Profane* (New York: Harcourt Brace Jovanovich, 1959), *passim*.

The 'Middle' in World Traditions

To synthesize various pagan traditions of the primeval paradise, the World Tree and the Central Mountain were 'only more elaborate forms of the Cosmic Axis or Pillar of the World'.[48] The tree, the pillar, the mountain, and the omphalos (navel) all symbolized the same basic idea. They represented two channels, one going to the under-world where the soul dwelt and the other coming from the eternal light above. Associated with the two channels were two shamans, one chthonic and one celestial, who were hostile to each other. Sometimes this celestial shaman, sanctified person, or priest, symbolized by the omphalos and pillar, was portrayed as 'radiant or transfigured'.[49] Identified with this omphalos complex, the kings of Mesopotamia were actually considered the tree of life, the great binding-post connecting heaven and earth.[50]

The 'Middle' in Biblical Tradition

The utilization of such omphalic motifs in the practice of the Mother Earth cult in Israel's and Judah's apostasies is not completely known, but there is sufficient evidence to indicate its occurrence throughout the monarchic period, probably beginning with the reign of Solomon.[51] This omphalic myth of the 'middle' was a very real threat to Israel's faith because it represented pagan efforts to recapture the privileges and advantages enjoyed in the Garden of Eden. An affront

48. E.A.S. Butterworth, *The Tree at the Navel of the World* (Berlin: de Gruyter, 1970), p. 3, citing M. Eliade's *Le Chamanisme et les techniques archaïques de l'extase* (Paris: Payot, 1951), p. 244.

49. Butterworth, *The Tree*, pp. 51, 54, 65-66.

50. *The Tree*, p. 71. This is probably reflected in the fact that there was no image of a god on the top of the ziggurat (*The Tree*, p. 170). Upon ascending the ziggurat during the Babylonian *akitu* festival, the king himself was the link between heaven and earth, hoping to secure fertility for the year. See also P.W. Coxon, 'The Great Tree of Daniel 4', in J.D. Martin and P.R. Davies (eds.), *A Word in Season* (JSOTSup, 42; Sheffield: JSOT Press, 1986), p. 104.

51. S. Terrien, 'The Omphalos Myth and Hebrew Religion', *VT* 20 (1970), pp. 317-31; also M.C. Callaway, *Sing, O Barren One* (Atlantia: Scholars Press, 1986), p. 79. According to Terrien, the solar cult, snake worship, the ritual concern for the primeval abyss, chthonian forces and the primeval paradise are all traceable to the myth of the omphalos and the adoration of the *Terra Mater*. He also includes male prostitution and the worship of Ashera as products of the omphalos myths which were probably introduced through the cultic function of the Queen Mother.

to Israel's divinely sanctioned worship, the audacity of the myth was magnified by its threat to appropriate or contaminate Israel's own version of a 'middle' or sacred center for its own purposes.

Like Israel of old, churches at Thessalonica and elsewhere were confronted with similar encroachments that threatened their sanctity. Wherever and whenever people have gathered to worship or hear the word of God at some sacred center or 'middle', the church has had to contend with imposters who have pretended to be angels of light, apostles of Christ and servants of righteousness (2 Cor. 11.13-15).[52]

That 2 Thess. 2.6-7 refers to such a threat or individual is confirmed by the identification and utilization of Paul's source passage. Such an analysis takes on added significance in light of Richard Hays's assertion that Paul himself operated within the interpretive tradition of inner-biblical exegesis:

> To read Paul against this background of 'inner-biblical exegesis' is to understand his place in the stream of tradition in a new way. He saw himself as a prophetic figure, carrying forward the proclamation of God's word as Israel's prophets and sages had always done, in a way that reactivated past revelation under new conditions.[53]

I believe that Paul's treatment of 2 Thessalonians falls into this category, but that it is fundamentally different than what Hays envisages in his study of Romans. Whereas Hays discerns a poetic tone in Romans that is focused on a common idea (that is, 'the problem of God's saving righteousness in relation to Israel'),[54] my study of 2 Thessalonians suggests an expositional mode that is focused on a specific text.

---

52. The motif of a sacred center is particularly discernible in the New Testament in the writings of the apostle John, who portrays Jesus Christ as the ultimate fulfillment of certain aspects of the omphalos myth. Jesus is the great ladder or channel to heaven (Jn 1.51), the serpent on the tree lifted up vertically to heaven (3.14), the light of the world (8.10; cf. Rev. 21.22-23), the one promising the water of life from one's belly (7.37), and the gateway to heaven (10.1-9). Identified with the tree on which he died, Jesus becomes a veritable Tree of Life himself (over against the ancient Mesopotamian kings), as he is enthroned in a heavenly Eden near the Tree of Life (Rev. 22.1-2).

53. Hays, *Echoes of Scripture*, p. 14.

54. *Echoes of Scripture*, pp. 19, 34.

3. *Paul's Exposition of Isaiah 66*

2 Thessalonians 1–2 and Isaiah 66

Is there a literary source, a parent passage, that can determine the meaning of μέσου beyond any reasonable doubt? Interesting comparisons have been made with several biblical and extrabiblical sources, but none have supplied a direct reference.[55] Intertextual allusions are not understood apart from their original source and no source text has been located to fully resolve the perplexity of 2 Thess. 2.6-7.

In 1976 and 1977 Roger Aus demonstrated the many allusions and quotations in 2 Thessalonians 1 and 2 from Isaiah 66.[56] His findings suggest that 2 Thessalonians is virtually an exposition of Isaiah 66. This study hopes to go even further than Aus: first, by comparing the structure of Isaiah 66 and 2 Thessalonians 1 and 2; secondly, by showing how Paul's exposition honored the chiastic structure of Isaiah 66; and thirdly, by providing a conclusive answer for the source and meaning of 2 Thess. 2.6-7.

First, the dependence of Paul on Isaiah must be established by reviewing the parallels made by R. Aus. (1) The phrase in 2 Thess. 1.6, 'it is just before God to repay with affliction those who afflict you', utilizes the motif and phraseology of Isa. 66.6, 'the voice of the Lord rendering recompense to his enemies'.[57] (2) The judgment theophany of 2 Thess. 1.7-10 uses the judgment theophany of Isa. 66.15-16.[58] Specifically, 1.7 speaks of the 'revelation' of the Lord Jesus 'with his mighty angels in flaming fire' as does Isa. 66.15d where the Lord comes in fire with his chariots, rebuking 'with flames of fire'.[59]

---

55. Biblical passages include Isaiah 14; Ezekiel 28; Daniel 7, 11; Matthew 24; Mark 13; Revelation 12; see Reiter *et al.*, *The Rapture*, p. 188; Giblin, *The Threat to Faith*, p. 60. For extrabiblical sources, see Giblin, *The Threat to Faith*, pp. 168-76, 192-201; Bruce, *1 & 2 Thessalonians*, p. 170; Barnouin, 'Les problèmes de traduction', p. 492.

56. R.D. Aus, 'The Relevance of Isaiah 66.7 to Revelation 12 and 2 Thessalonians 1', *ZNW* 67 (1976), p. 76; Aus, 'God's Plan'.

57. Aus, 'The Relevance of Isaiah', p. 266.

58. Aus, 'God's Plan', p. 540.

59. Aus suggests that the term 'revelation' in 2 Thess. 1.7 may reflect the fact that the targum used the word 'reveal' for the appearance of the Lord or the messiah in 66.7, 14, and 15 ('The Relevance of Isaiah', p. 267). Similarly, the use of the motif 'might' in 2 Thess. 1.7 may reflect *Targ. Isa.* 66 where the motif is added to vv. 2, 14-15, and 19.

In addition, the words 'inflicting vengeance' in 1.8 follow the Septuagint's rendering of 'to return his anger' in Isa. 66.15c. The vengeance motif of 1.8 is possibly due to a conflation of Isa. 66.4 with 66.15.[60] Paul apparently continued by using Isa. 66.16 in 2 Thess. 1.9, since they are strikingly similar, both dealing with the destruction of the disobedient.[61] (3) The phrase in 2 Thess. 1.12 'so that the name of our Lord Jesus may be glorified in you' comes from the Septuagint of Isa. 66.5 'in order that the name of the Lord be glorified'.[62] The glory theme in 1.10 might have also been connected with Isa. 66.18 and 19, but it will be demonstrated that Paul was following an exegetical strategy which required that Isa. 66.5 be utilized.

The quotations and allusions from Isaiah 66 continue in 2 Thessalonians 2. There is no argument with Aus's views on 2 Thess. 2.4 and 8. (1) Verse 4 is a conflation of Ezek. 28.2 and Dan. 11.36 that is modified by Isa. 66.6, which probably supplied the apocalyptic motif of ναός, 'temple', and the singular participle ἀντικείμενος, 'opposing'.[63] (2) Verse 8 uses ὁ ἄνομος, 'the lawless one', from the Septuagint of Isa. 66.3 (where it is used for Hebrew 'one who kills a man').[64]

There is a problem with Aus's view on 2 Thess. 2.6 and 7. Aus thinks the neuter κατέχον is a translation of עצר, 'shut up, restrain', in

60. 'The Relevance of Isaiah', p. 267; cf. Giblin, *The Threat to Faith*, p. 229; also see n. 73 below.

61. The glory theme in 2 Thess. 1.10 might have also appealed to Isa. 66.18 and 19, but Paul, as we shall see below, was following an exegetical strategy which required that the glory theme of Isa. 66.5 be utilized instead. If the glory theme of Isa. 66.18-19 is referred to at all, it would be after the central discussion in 2 Thess. 2.14. The theme of glory and the kingdom could then correspond to Paul's prologue and serve to frame chs. 1–2. It is very possible that Paul's exegetical strategy, after utilizing Isa. 66.3-4 in 2 Thess. 2.8-12, required returning to Isa. 66.18b-19 to finish his discussion of Isa. 66.15-24.

62. Aus, 'The Relevance of Isaiah', p. 267; Giblin, *The Threat to Faith*, p. 7. The similar phrase in 2 Thess. 1.10 comes from the Septuagint of Ps. 89.8; see Aus, 'God's Plan', p. 538.

63. Aus, 'God's Plan', pp. 539-42. The plural participle ἀντικειμένοις is used to describe the 'enemies' of God in the Septuagint of Isa. 66.6.

64. Aus argues convincingly for this parallel from the fact that 'the lawless one' of Isa. 66.3 is surely one of the 'opposers' judged in Isa. 66.6 to whom Paul had just alluded in 2 Thess. 2.4 ('God's Plan', p. 541). In other words, the proximity of Isa. 66.3 and 66.6 supports them as the reason for their proximity in 2 Thess. 2.4 and 2.8.

Isa. 66.9 and refers to the mission to the Gentiles spoken of in Isa. 66.19.[65] This requires an explanation of why Isaiah uses the verb עצר to show that God *would not* 'prevent' or 'restrain' the womb (i.e., the coming of Zion's sons) while Paul uses the verb κατέχω to say that God *would* restrain Jesus' coming (in order to fulfill his mission to the nations). To resolve this problem, Aus states that Paul 'modified the context' to incorporate the messianic significance of Isa. 66.7 and that he 'intentionally modified the meaning of Isa. 66.9 to emphasize the delay needed for the spread of the gospel...'[66] Similarly, Aus chooses the 'mystery of wickedness' as the subject of γένηται in 2 Thess. 2.7c, attributing such poor grammar to carelessness due to Paul's excitement.[67] He finds a parallel for γένηται in the *hophal* perfect הוסר, 'taken away' or 'removed', in Dan. 12.11 (cf. Dan. 11.31), which denotes the removal of the regular sacrifice.[68]

Aus's thorough treatment represents a significant breakthrough to show Paul's use of Isaiah 66, but his views on 2 Thess. 2.6-7 are strained to conform to the popular view of κατέχων as 'restrainer' and γένηται as 'removed' or 'disappears'.[69] The appeal to Isa. 66.9 is unconvincing and the argument for Dan. 12.11 is questionable. There is a better solution which not only strengthens Aus's argument for Paul's dependence on Isaiah 66 but which perfectly fits Paul's exegetical strategy.

2 Thessalonians 2.7 and Isaiah 66.17

The best verse to account for 2 Thess. 2.6-7 is Isa. 66.17, which depicts false worshippers led by a shaman or wizard who fully conforms to our view of the κατέχον or κατέχων. The rites in v. 17 are sacrilegious and covert, a threat to true worship like the 'mystery of wickessness' in 2 Thess. 2.7.[70] The apostates are going, probably as a

65. Aus, 'God's Plan', pp. 540, 545-47. Since there is little or no evidence for a messianic tradition or delaying factor in Isa. 66.9, Aus proposes that Paul applied the messianic tradition of *Targ. Jonathan* about the 'son' of Isa. 66.7 to the verb עצר in Isa. 66.9. See also Aus, 'The Relevance of Isaiah', p. 258.
66. Aus, 'God's Plan', pp. 545, 547.
67. 'God's Plan', p. 551.
68. 'God's Plan', pp. 542-43, 550.
69. 'God's Plan', pp. 539 n. 13; p. 550.
70. The false 'sanctification' of the participants is obviously a mockery of worship which complements their hypocritical scorn in Isa. 66.5. Their true character is evident from their diet, representing the three forbidden classes of creatures in

procession, to the gardens אחר אחד בתוך, 'after one in the middle'.[71] The gardens appear to represent an omphalic center, a purported replica of Eden. The term 'one' is evidently some object of worship or shaman figure. The phrase 'in the middle' probably means 'in the crowd or procession of worshippers' (cf. Ps. 68.25). Most importantly, the reference to the 'middle' appears to be the source of ἐκ μέσου, 'out of the middle', in 2 Thess. 2.7. Virtually equivalent in meaning, both תוך and μέσος invariably precede a modifying genitive. The rare occurrence of either term without a modifying genitive makes it all the more remarkable that both terms occur as such in each passage. This occurrence is more than mere coincidence, but requires the acknowledgment of an intentional reference by Paul to Isa. 66.17 in 2 Thess. 2.7. These two anomalous references to the 'middle' have mystified Hebrew and Greek commentators alike. Separated, they are inscrutable. Together, they explain each other. Isa. 66.17 satisfies questions about the κατέχων, the mystery of wickedness, and 'the middle' in 2 Thess. 2.6-7, and appears to stands uncontested as Paul's source for 2 Thess. 2.6-7.

The use of Isa. 66.17 in 2 Thess. 2.7 is confirmed by showing how Paul adhered to the literary structure of Isaiah 66 when he aligned his quotations into two parallel sequences. Edwin C. Webster has shown that Isaiah 66 is made up of three chiastic structures, with the word 'enemies' marking the end of the first two chiasmi at vv. 6 and 14.[72] Paul does not quote from nor allude to the middle section (vv. 7-14) which contains a riddle (vv. 7-9) and an *abcb'a'* chiasm (vv. 10-14).

Leviticus 11: (1) the 'swine' speaks of the unclean animals of Lev. 11.4-8; (2) the 'detestable things' are grouped together in Lev. 11.10-23; and (3) the 'mice' represent all the unclean swarming things of Lev. 11.24-31. Such a diet has been mentioned before in Isa. 65.3-4 where other activities include offering sacrifices in gardens, burning incense on bricks, sitting among graves, spending the night in secret places, eating swine flesh, using unclean meat-pots, and bearing a condescending and arrogant spirit.

71. Most claim the meaning of this phrase cannot be determined. Cf. H.L. Ginsberg and H. Orlinsky (eds.), *The Prophets: Nevi'im* (Philadelphia: The Jewish Publication Society of America, 1978), p. 507. 'One' probably refers to a leader; on the 'middle'; see J. Calvin, *Commentary on the Book of the Prophet Isaiah* (Grand Rapids, MI: Eerdmans, 1948), pp. 430-31.

72. E.C. Webster, 'A Rhetorical Study of Isaiah 66', *JSOT* 34 (1986), p. 103. See also pp. 94-95, 100-102, for the *abcc'b'a'* chiasmus of vv. 1-6 and the *ABCcba* chiasmus of vv. 15-24.

Paul restricts his quotes to the first and third chiastic structures (66.1-6, 15-24).

By comparing the three quotes in 2 Thessalonians 1 with the three quotes in 2 Thessalonians 2, one is struck by the way in which corresponding quotes come from adjoining verses or phrases in either the first or the third chiastic structure. Paul does this as he carefully selects for ch. 1 the words or phrases that deal with the Lord's return and for ch. 2 those words or phrases that are appropriate to the apostasy and the man of sin. For both 2 Thess. 1.6-12 and 2.3-12, Paul selects his first quotes from the end of the first chiasmus, quoting from v. 6. He applies Isa. 66.6b to ch. 1 and 66.6a to ch. 2.

For his second quotations in 2 Thessalonians 1 and 2, Paul moves to Isa. 66.15-18, paragraph A of the third chiasmus. For 2 Thessalonians 1, Paul quotes from v. 15 and possibly v. 16. For 2 Thessalonians 2, Paul turns to the only verse left in vv. 15-18 that serves his purpose, v. 17. Paul completes his references to Isaiah 66 by returning to the first chiasm, appropriately choosing v. 5 for 2 Thessalonians 1 (to emphasize the triumph of the saints) and v. 3 for 2 Thessalonians 2 (to dwell on the downfall of the wicked).[73]

It is important to note that the sequence of verses quoted by Paul proceeds backwards when quoting from Isa. 66.1-6, but forwards when quoting or alluding to verses in 66.15-24. This is true for the sequence within each chapter (2 Thessalonians 1 quotes Isa. 66.6b before 66.5; 2 Thessalonians 2 quotes Isa. 66.6a before 66.3). It is also true of the sequence between chapters (66.6b is utilized before 66.6a, 66.5 is quoted before 66.3, and 66.15 is used before 66.17). In other words, Paul is working away from the middle of the chapter.

Since Isa. 66.3-6 and 66.15-18 seem to be Paul's source of quotations, it would be natural for him to quote from v. 17 when he did. The fact that Paul stopped short of v. 17 while drawing from vv. 15-16 in 2 Thessalonians 1 makes v. 17 the obvious choice as the missing verse behind the puzzle of 2 Thess. 2.7. Looking at the problem from another perspective, if 2 Thess. 1.6-12 and 2.4-8 begin and end with quotes from Isa. 66.3-6, then it is to be suspected that if the middle of one passage quotes from Isa. 66.15-18, then the middle of the other

---

73. Aus compares Isa. 66.4 with 2 Thess. 1.8 ('The Relevance of Isaiah', p. 267); more likely, the Septuagint ἐμπαίγματα, 'mockeries', of Isa. 66.4 is the great deception of 2 Thess. 2.11 since Paul had just referred to Isa. 66.3 in 2 Thess. 2.8.

passage would also. Stated simply, (1) Isa. 66.17 is the only verse left to quote; (2) 66.17 fits unerringly into the sequence of Paul's quotations; and (3) 66.17 fits exactly into the appropriate position and limited space of 2 Thess. 2.6-7.

Once accepted, further light is cast on ἐκ μέσου by Isa. 66.6a, which says, 'A voice of uproar from the city, a voice *from the temple* (ἐκ ναοῦ)'. Paul does not randomly choose to follow his reference to Isa. 66.6a by jumping to 66.17; rather, his exegesis apparently took into account their correspondence and merged the concept of the 'middle' in 66.17 with the Septuagint phrase ἐκ ναοῦ, 'out of the temple', to produce the phrase ἐκ μέσου in 2 Thess. 2.7. If this is correct, Paul follows Isaiah by using the term μεσος in 2.7 as an alias for the temple mentioned in 2.4. The conjunction of the terms 'middle' and 'temple' suggests that both Isaiah and Paul were alluding to traditions about a sacred center or omphalos which seriously threatened true worship during their respective ministries.

There is good reason for Paul's use of Isa. 66.17 in ch. 2. 2 Thessalonians 1 demanded the triumphant and positive tone of Isa. 66.15-16, but 2 Thessalonians 2 required the ominous and unholy sense of v. 17. The corresponding use of vv. 15 and 17 by Paul in chs. 1 and 2 to contrast the respective revelations of the Lord Jesus and the man of sin is logical and appropriate. Since Paul had parallel sequences of verses unwinding from the chiastic structures of Isaiah 66, there is no merit in or need for an appeal beyond those structures to solve the difficulties and explain the meaning of 2 Thess. 2.6-7.

Paul's Exegetical Method

Plotting the verses in the order they were quoted shows that Paul followed the same route through Isaiah 66 to set up a comparison between 2 Thessalonians 1 and 2. The corresponding quotations from 2 Thessalonians 1 and 2 always come from adjoining verses or phrases in the same chiasmus of Isaiah 66.

Paul's sequence of going backward in the first chiasmus and forward in the third chiasm, starting from the edge of the second and middle chiasmus, apparently indicates that he recognized and respected the three chiastic structures of Isaiah 66. Paul's movement away from the center of the chapter also suggests that the chapter contains one over-arching chiasmus. Following Paul's sequence, it is possible to match up vv. 6b and 15 (the Lord's attack), vv. 4-5a and 16 (the

Lord's vengeance), vv. 3 and 17 (the wicked idolaters), vv. 2b and 18-19 (the righteous participants), vv. 1-2a and 20-23 (the Lord's house, heaven and earth, rest/sabbath).

If this is the case, then it is unlikely that Paul overlooked the second and central section of Isa. 66.7-14, which serves as a fitting climax to Isaiah 40–66 by echoing 40.1-2 and comforting Jerusalem in her sorrow. As the center section of any ABA' structure usually has the dominant motifs and ideas, Aus is not amiss in appealing to the first verse of the middle section (v. 7) which 'was understood messianically precisely because of the "birth pangs" or "woes" associated with the Messiah's coming'.[74] Paul undoubtedly chose Isaiah 66 as his main text to help comfort the Thessalonians precisely because he did associate their intense suffering with the birth pangs of the messiah.[75] As Paul begins to quote from just outside the central section of Isa. 66.7-14 in 2 Thess. 1.6, it appears that his prologue of 2 Thess. 1.1-5 was based on the central section of comfort in Isa. 66.7-14. Common themes are: (1) the suffering of the saints (Isa. 66.7-9; 2 Thess. 1.4-5); (2) the positive expression of God's grace (Isa. 66.10 and 2 Thess. 1.3-4); and (3) the promise of great reward in the kingdom (Isa. 66.11-14; 2 Thess. 1.5). It is safe to say that these themes constitute the chief concerns in Paul's mind. As a result, the emphasis on comfort in Isa. 66.7-14 becomes the central thrust and purpose of 2 Thessalonians (cf. 2.13-17).

Assuming that Paul began his letter by focusing upon the center of Isaiah 66, 2 Thessalonians virtually becomes an exposition of a chiasmus. As such, 2 Thessalonians is also a hermeneutical model which carefully demonstrates how a chiasmus can be unravelled into another format. Paul does this by producing two parallel statements that juxtapose the manifestation of righteousness and wickedness in the latter days. More than likely, he would not appreciate efforts to explain 2 Thess. 2.6-7 apart from Isaiah 66. Furthermore, there is no need to look beyond Isa. 66.17 for the meaning of μέσου in 2 Thess. 2.7. The intertextual interlocking of the structures of Isaiah 66 and 2 Thessalonians 1 and 2 verify the intent, the meaning, and the usage of μέσος, the key word in understanding the passage.

Final observations on Richard Hays's thesis about intertextual allusions and echoes are now due. Hays appears to have overstated his case

---

74. Aus, 'The Relevance of Isaiah', p. 268; also p. 258.
75. 'The Relevance of Isaiah', pp. 264-65.

against Paul's ever using any formal or systematic exegetical method, even to the extent of claiming that Paul never sat down with the biblical text, looked up a passage, tried to work out what it meant by using a particular exegetical procedure, nor composed his argument by weaving together the various themes of the text. Instead, Hays says that Paul's mind apparently 'leaped—in moments of metaphorical insight—to intuitive apprehensions of the meaning of the texts', which accounts for Paul's arbitrary, 'helter-skelter intuitive readings, unpredictable, ungeneralizable'.[76] Granted, Paul may not have been guided by formal considerations in his exegesis, but he certainly demonstrated a masterful command of the text which he may have committed to memory through many hours of diligent study and meditation. If he intuitively leaped to his conclusions, it was only possible because he meditated on a text that had become second nature to him. In other words, rather than say that Paul leaped to apprehend new insight, it would be better to say that the insight leaped off the text to Paul's attentive mind and heart. Paul may not have been following formal criteria when composing 2 Thessalonians, but he apparently recognized how Isaiah 66 was woven and stitched together into a well-known and conventional literary pattern, that of a chiasmus. He was not following a formal exegetical method as much as he was honoring the literary or linguistic peculiarities of the Hebrew text itself. In this sense, Paul was a true translator, for he transposed a conventional structure of ancient Hebrew into a format intelligible and acceptable to another culture and language. To the extent that Paul followed the contours and configurations of Isaiah 66, one can say that he was observing a method, even if it was more informal than formal. Paul obviously understood Old Testament rhetorical conventions too well for us to attribute his discourse to naked intuition. If he intuitively or unconsciously interpreted the chiastic features of Isaiah 66, it was because its structure and meaning had previously become a conscious part of his knowledge.

Hays objects to formal methodological considerations and favors 'material (i.e. theological)' concerns as the basis of Paul's interpretation.[77] This is true of 2 Thessalonians 2 in the sense that Paul, while he transmuted Isaiah 66 into a new format, still preserved its contents. At the same time, it should be emphasized that material and method

76. Hays, *Echoes of Scripture*, pp. 43, 160-61.
77. Hays, *Echoes of Scripture*, p. 161.

are not incompatible. Inasmuch as the theology of Israel was codified in rhetorical patterns that were designed according to conventional literary standards, then some method is involved in both the original composition and the later interpretation. Material and methodological considerations do not necessarily have to be in conflict. They can be complementary.

In conclusion, it must be asserted that Paul did recognize and understand Old Testament literary genres, structures, and conventions. In addition, he knew how they should be interpreted and explained to foreign readers, even to the point of emulating their structural patterns in his own composition. To summarize, the basis of Paul's interpretation was the exercise of excellent literary sense and judgment, along with the judicious use of a somewhat informal method that recognized and respected the formal, structural peculiarities of his text.

As a postscript, several questions should be answered. Did Paul recognize the skeletal, literary structures of the Old Testament text in his interpretation? Did he understand how to give an exegesis of or transpose a chiasmus as he preached and taught in another language? And finally, did the Old Testament text control his creative impulses to reflect its structural patterns in his own composition? The answer to all of these questions is 'yea and amen'.

Appendix One: *Parallel Structures with Intertextual Correspondances*

2 Thessalonians 2: Man of Sin	Isaiah 66	2 Thessalonians 1
2.3 A APPEARANCE OF MAN OF SIN		
3b a Apostasy: 'unless the apostasy comes first'		
3c b Revealed: 'and the man of sin is revealed'		
3d c Future Destruction: 'the son of destruction'		
2.4 B ACTIVITY OF MAN OF SIN	6b Lord repays--------1.6	
4a d Rebellion: 'opposes and exalts himself'----------6b enemies (opposers)		
4b e Deception: 'so that αὐτόν in temple as God' --------6a voice from temple		
2.5--------------------------------Divider--------		
2.6-8 A´ APPEARANCE OF MAN OF SIN		
6 a Apostasy: 'now the κατέχον [neut.] you know'		
6b b Revealed: 'so that he (αὐτόν) is revealed'		
7a a Apostasy: 'μυστήριον [neut.] is already at work'		
7b 'κατέχων [masc.] now'		
7c b Revealed 'out of middle (ἐκ μέσου) he appears'------17 after one in middle		
8a 'lawless one is revealed'----------------3 lawless one slays man		
8bc c Future Destruction: 'Lord slays lawless'	15d flaming fire--------1.7	
'bring to an end'	15c, 4 retribution--------1.8	
2.9-12 B´ ACTIVITY OF MAN OF SIN		
9-10 d Rebellion: Present (9)/Aorist (10)	16.18-19 glory------1.9-10	
11-12 e Deception: Present (11)/Aorist (12)		
'God sends delusion'----------------4 God chooses delusions		
	5 name glorified------1.12	

Appendix Two: *Corresponding Verses*

2 Thessalonians	Isaiah	Isaiah	2 Thessalonians
1.6 For after all it is only *just for God to repay with affliction those who afflict you,* **7** and to give relief to you who are afflicted and to us as well when the LORD Jesus shall be *revealed from heaven with His mighty angels in flaming fire,* **8** *dealing out retribution* to those who do not know God and to those do not obey the gospel of our LORD Jesus. **9** And these will pay the penalty of eternal destruction, away from the presence of the LORD and from the glory of His power, **10** when He comes to be glorified in His saints on that day, and to be marveled at among all who have believed—for our testimony to you was believed. **11** To this end also we pray for you always that our God may count you worthy of your calling, and fulfill every desire for goodness and the work of faith with power; **12** *in order that the name of our* LORD *Jesus may be glorified in you,* and you in Him, according to the grace of our God and the LORD Jesus Christ.	**66.6b** the voice of the LORD *rendering recompense* to his enemies **66.15** For behold, the *LORD will come in fire And His chariots* like the whirlwind, To render His anger [*inflicting vengeance,* LXX] with fury, and His rebuke *with flames of fire.* **66.5** *in order that the name of the LORD be glorified* [LXX]	**66.6a** A voice of uproar from the city, a voice *from the temple* **66.6b** ... to His enemies [*those opposing,* LXX] **66.17** Those who sanctify and purify themselves [to go] to the gardens, after *one in the middle* . . . shall *come to an end* . . . **66.3** He who kills an ox is like one who slays a man [*the lawless one,* LXX]. . . **66.4** So I will choose their *delusions* [*mockeries,* LXX]. . . *they did not listen.* And they did evil. . .	**2.3** Let no one in any way deceive you, for [that day will not come] unless the apostasy comes first and the man of lawlessness is revealed, the son of destruction, **4** *who opposes* and exalts himself above every so-called god or object of worship, so that he takes his seat in the *temple* of God, displaying himself as being God. **5** Do you not remember that while I was still with you, I was telling you these things? **6** And you know what seizes now, so that in his time he may be revealed. **7** For the mystery of lawless is already at work; only he who now seizes [will do so] until he appears out of the *middle.* **8** And then that *lawless one* will be revealed whom the LORD will slay with the breath of His mouth and *bring to an end* by the appearance of His coming; **10** *they did not receive* **11** And for this reason *God will send upon them a strong delusion*

INDEXES

INDEX OF REFERENCES

OLD TESTAMENT

Genesis			
2.9	264		
3.3	264		
12–22	158		
12–15	232		
12	149, 153		
12.1	151		
12.2-3	151		
12.3	220		
12.4	151		
15	149, 153, 159-61, 210		
15.3	158, 210		
15.4-5	158		
15.5	204		
15.6	158		
15.7-18	159		
15.13	208, 210, 218		
15.18	219		
16	149		
17	153, 159-61		
17.1	159		
17.2-10	159		
17.7	217		
17.10-11	159		
17.14	159, 161		
18–19	150, 236		
18	150		
18.2	150		
18.9-10	150		
18.13	150		
18.18	220		

19	150		
19.1	236		
21	148, 153		
22	149, 153		
22.12	88		
22.16	88		
26.5	226		

Exodus			
3–4	147		
3	146		
3.1	175		
3.10-12	146		
3.14	146		
4	147		
4.10-12	147		
4.10	146, 147		
4.11-12	147		
4.22	99, 205		
12.40	208, 218		
16.18	44		
19	239, 240		
19.3	240		
19.5-6	175		
19.12-22	249		
19.16-20	239		
19.18	240		
19.19	246		
20.5	203		
20.17	88		
20.18-21	249		
24.16-17	175		
32.16	175		
34	16, 45, 144, 148, 159, 165, 168, 174, 175, 185		

34.1-4	155
34.4-7	175
34.7	203
34.27-28	155, 157
34.28-35	165, 166, 168, 185
34.28-34	173
34.29-35	148, 175
34.29-30	184
34.33ff.	180, 181
34.34	13

Leviticus	
11.4-8	270
11.10-23	270
11.24-31	270
18.5	67, 68, 92
23.15-20	228
23.23-25	248
23.34-43	228
25.9	248, 249
26.18	200
26.21	200
26.24	200
26.28	200

Numbers	
10.1	248
10.9	248
14.18	203
27.20	170

MIDRASHIM

PHILO

194, 214, 215, 217, 219, 220,
222, 250, 255, 260, 263, 273, 274
Hellholm, D. 217
Hengel, M. 22, 190, 201, 207, 216
Herbert, G. 44
Hill, A.A. 260
Hill, D. 7
Hofius, O. 15, 187, 192
Hollander, H.W. 211
Hollander, J. 43, 59, 72, 73, 80, 119
Holtz, T. 242
Hooke, S.H. 212
Hooker, M.D. 14, 140, 190, 216
Horbury, W. 248
Horgan, M.P. 100
Howard, G. 224
Hübner, H. 14, 188
Hütenmeister, F. 27
Hurtado, L. 253
Hvalvik, R. 120, 140, 141
Hyatt, J.P. 105, 111

Israelstam, J. 247

James, M.R. 173
Janowski, B. 211
Jastrow, M. 169, 170, 182
Jeremias, G. 187
Jeremias, J. 105, 112, 188, 212
Jewett, R. 153
Johnson, S.E. 110, 111
Jong, M. de 211
Joos, M. 260
Juel, D. 217

Kasher, M. 169
Kaufman, S.A. 169
Käsemann, E. 122
Kelber, W.H. 18, 19
Kittel, G. 10, 134
Klausner, J. 197, 248
Klein, M.L. 169, 216
Klopfenstein, M. 209
Knibb, M.A 201, 202, 207, 209-13
Knox, J. 71, 153, 192
Koch, D.-A. 119-21, 123-25, 194
Koch, K. 200, 205, 207, 209, 220
Kopesec, M. 256

Kraft, R.A. 226
Kreuzer, S. 208
Kristeva, J. 79
Kugel, J.L. 14, 48
Kuhn, K.G. 111, 187

Lacocque, A. 199
Lampe, G.W.H. 99
Laub, F. 242
Lauterbach, J.Z. 32, 247
Leaney, A.R.C. 176
Lehrman, S.M. 240
Levin, C. 217
Lichtenberger, H. 194, 205, 211
Lieberman, S. 19
Lincoln, A.T. 222
Lindars, B. 13, 58, 119
Longenecker, R.N. 13, 223
Lord, G. 45
Lührmann, D. 199
Luther, M. 68, 93
Lyons, G. 151

Macdonald, J. 177
Mann, J. 28
Manson, T.W. 109
Marks, H. 59, 61, 62, 80-82
Marshall, I.H. 14, 241, 242
Martin, D.B. 81
Martin, J.D. 265
Martin, R.P. 192, 193
Martyn, J.L. 79, 242
Mayer, B. 137
McKnight, S. 14
McNamara, M. 49, 166, 169, 170, 174
McRay, J. 222
Medico, H.E. del 100, 101
Meeks, W.A. 14, 50, 217
Merrill, A.L. 201
Meslin, M. 21
Meyers, R. 19
Michel, O. 14, 121
Migliore, D.L. 15
Miller, M.P. 165
Moore, A.L. 241
Moule, C.F.D. 71, 241, 242
Muilenburg, J. 116
Murphy, F.J. 229

JOURNAL FOR THE STUDY OF THE NEW TESTAMENT

Supplement Series